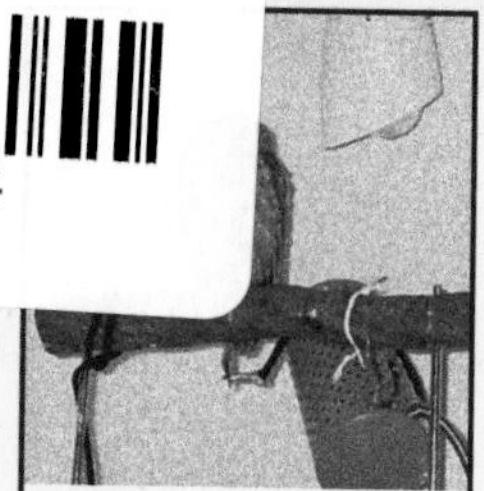

武井宏之

This is my pet owl. I named him Horokko (because his cry sounds like "hoorokkyo"). I'm not sure what species he is, but he looks like a tropical screech owl or a small fish owl (he's about six inches long). I actually don't even know whether he's a boy or a girl (you can only tell when they're babies), or how old he is (they can live up to 15 years). And he's not tame (they have to be hand-fed as owlets for that).

–Hiroyuki Takei

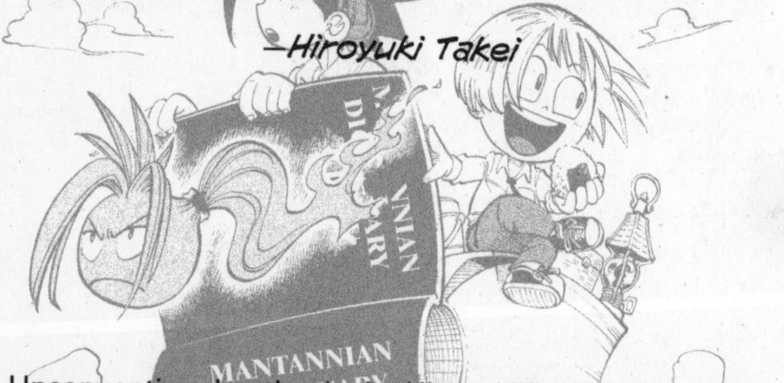
MANTANNIAN

Unconventional author/artist Hiroyuki Takei began his career by winning the coveted Hop Step Award (for new manga artists) and the Osamu Tezuka Award (named after the famous artist of the same name). After working as an assistant to famed artist Nobuhiro Watsuki, Takei debuted in **Weekly Shonen Jump** in 1997 with **Butsu Zone**, an action series based on Buddhist mythology. His multi-cultural adventure manga **Shaman King**, which debuted in 1998, became a hit and was adapted into an anime TV series. Takei lists Osamu Tezuka, American comics and robot anime among his many influences.

SHAMAN KING VOL. 21
The SHONEN JUMP Manga Edition

STORY AND ART BY
HIROYUKI TAKEI

English Adaptation/Lance Caselman
Translation/Lillian Olsen
Touch-up Art & Lettering/John Hunt
Design/Nozomi Akashi
Editor/Carol Fox

Editor in Chief, Books/Alvin Lu
Editor in Chief, Magazines/Marc Weidenbaum
VP, Publishing Licensing/Rika Inouye
VP, Sales & Product Marketing/Gonzalo Ferreyra
VP, Creative/Linda Espinosa
Publisher/Hyoe Narita

Printed in the U.S.A.

Published by VIZ Media, LLC
P.O. Box 77010
San Francisco, CA 94107

SHONEN JUMP Manga Edition
10 9 8 7 6 5 4 3 2 1
First printing, March 2009

viz media
www.viz.com

RATED T FOR TEEN
PARENTAL ADVISORY
SHAMAN KING is rated T for Teen and is recommended for ages 13 and up. This volume contains violence.
ratings.viz.com

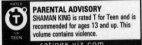

SHONEN JUMP MANGA

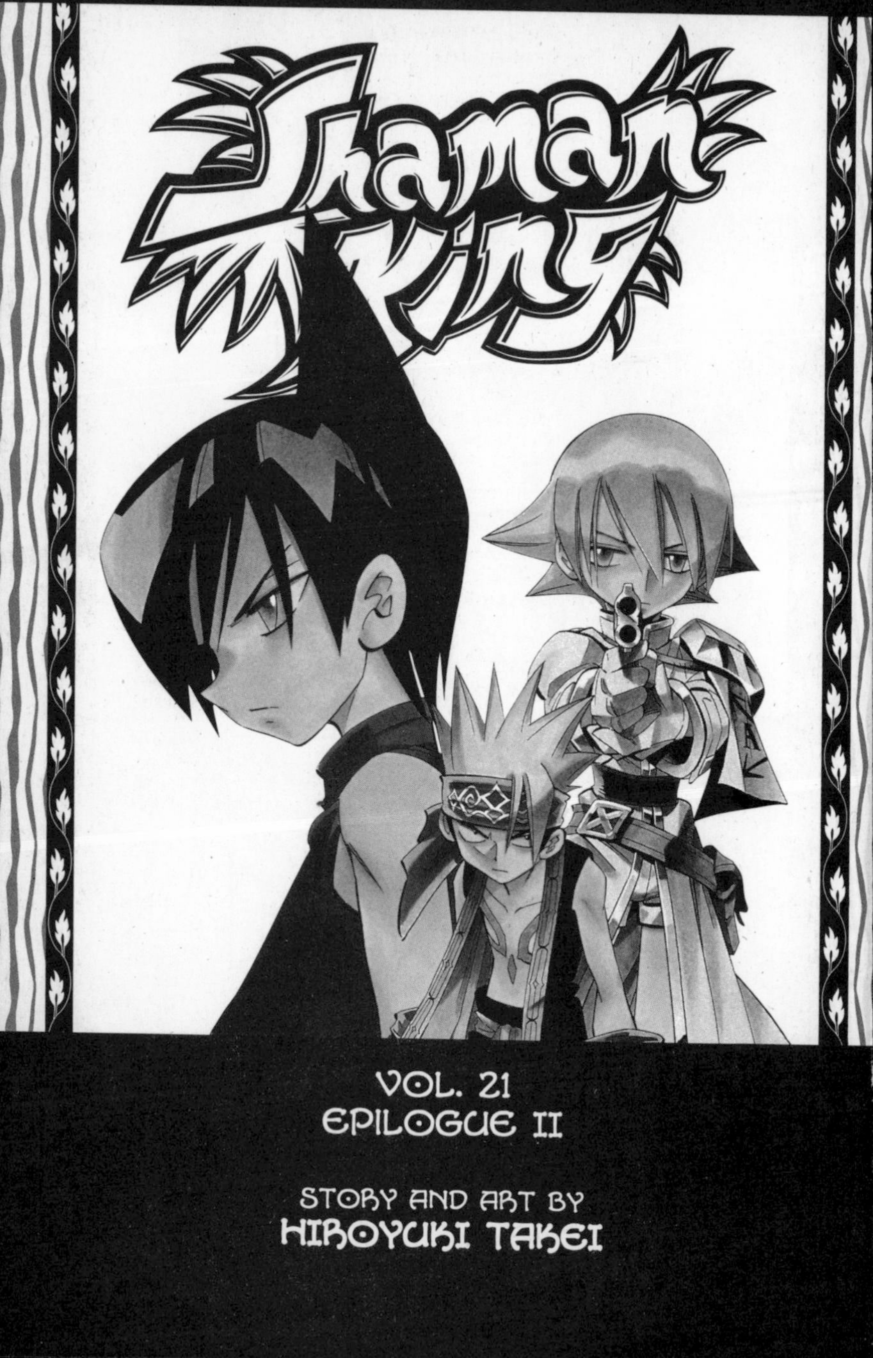
Shaman King

VOL. 21

EPILOGUE II

STORY AND ART BY

HIROYUKI TAKEI

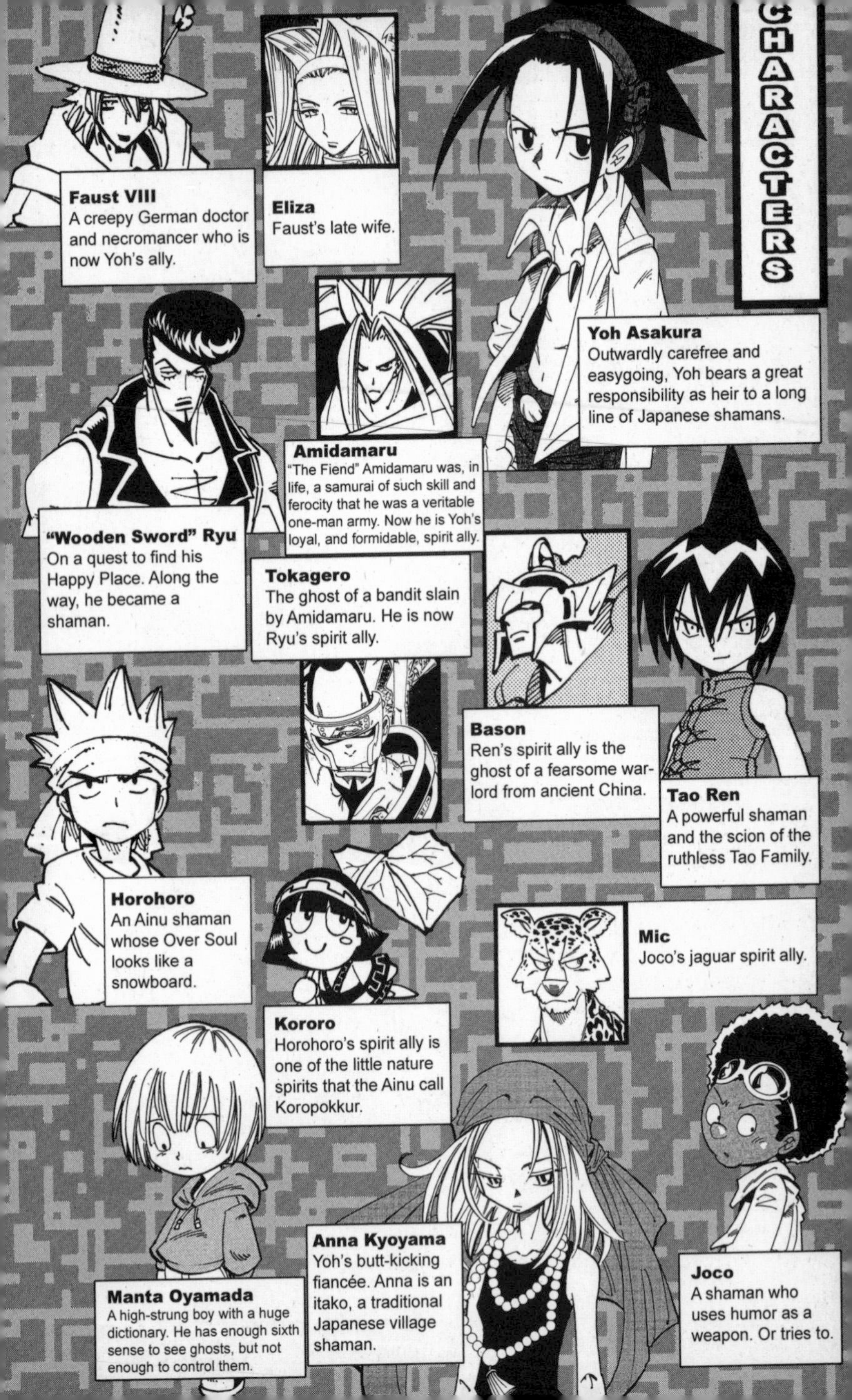
CHARACTERS
Yoh Asakura
Outwardly carefree and easygoing, Yoh bears a great responsibility as heir to a long line of Japanese shamans.
Eliza
Faust's late wife.
Faust VIII
A creepy German doctor and necromancer who is now Yoh's ally.
Amidamaru
"The Fiend" Amidamaru was, in life, a samurai of such skill and ferocity that he was a veritable one-man army. Now he is Yoh's loyal, and formidable, spirit ally.
"Wooden Sword" Ryu
On a quest to find his Happy Place. Along the way, he became a shaman.
Tokagero
The ghost of a bandit slain by Amidamaru. He is now Ryu's spirit ally.
Tao Ren
A powerful shaman and the scion of the ruthless Tao Family.
Bason
Ren's spirit ally is the ghost of a fearsome war-lord from ancient China.
Horohoro
An Ainu shaman whose Over Soul looks like a snowboard.
Mic
Joco's jaguar spirit ally.
Kororo
Horohoro's spirit ally is one of the little nature spirits that the Ainu call Koropokkur.
Joco
A shaman who uses humor as a weapon. Or tries to.
Anna Kyoyama
Yoh's butt-kicking fiancée. Anna is an itako, a traditional Japanese village shaman.
Manta Oyamada
A high-strung boy with a huge dictionary. He has enough sixth sense to see ghosts, but not enough to control them.

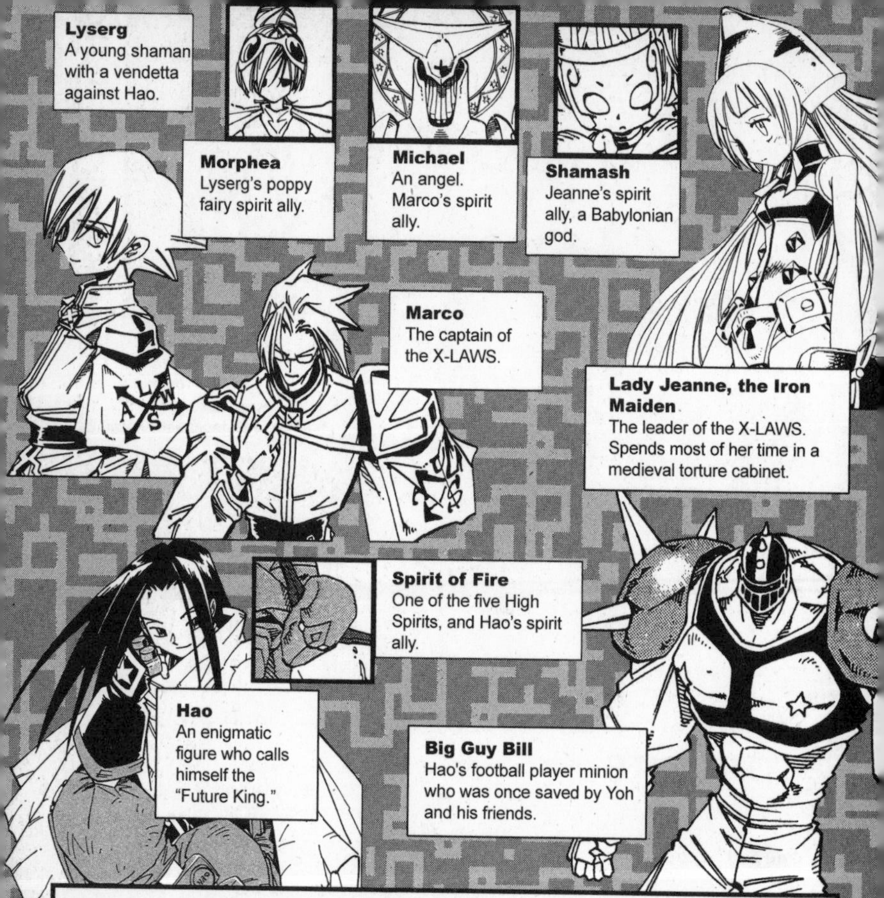
Lyserg
A young shaman with a vendetta against Hao.
Morphea
Lyserg's poppy fairy spirit ally.
Michael
An angel. Marco's spirit ally.
Shamash
Jeanne's spirit ally, a Babylonian god.
Marco
The captain of the X-LAWS.
Lady Jeanne, the Iron Maiden
The leader of the X-LAWS. Spends most of her time in a medieval torture cabinet.
Spirit of Fire
One of the five High Spirits, and Hao's spirit ally.
Hao
An enigmatic figure who calls himself the "Future King."
Big Guy Bill
Hao's football player minion who was once saved by Yoh and his friends.

THE STORY THUS FAR

Yoh Asakura not only sees dead people, he talks and fights with them too. That's because Yoh is a shaman, a traditional holy man able to interact with the spirit world. Yoh's abilities have brought him to the Shaman Fight, a tournament held every 500 years to decide who will become the Shaman King and shape humanity's future.

But when Ren is mortally wounded, Yoh is forced to drop out of the Shaman Fight so that Lady Jeanne will save Ren's life. Worried about how Anna will react to the news, Yoh tells Amidamaru how he and Anna first met and why he swore to become the Shaman King.

Meanwhile, Marco, unhappy with the idea of his mistress saving the life of a killer, plots to destroy Ren as soon as he is revived.

SHAMAN KING 21

エピローグII

目次

VOL. 21
EPILOGUE II

CONTENTS

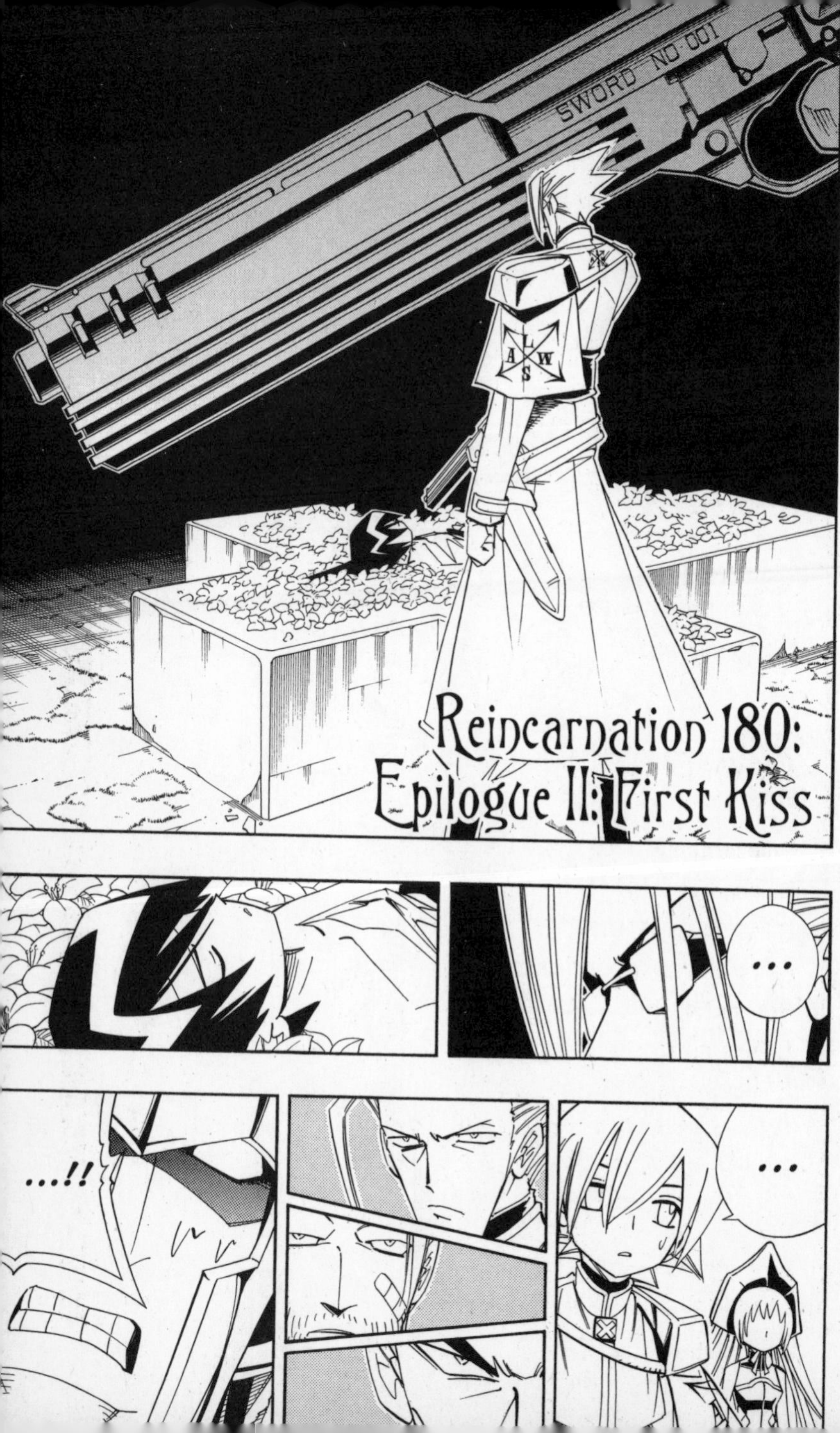
SWORD NO 001
Reincarnation 180:
Epilogue II: First Kiss
...
...
...!!

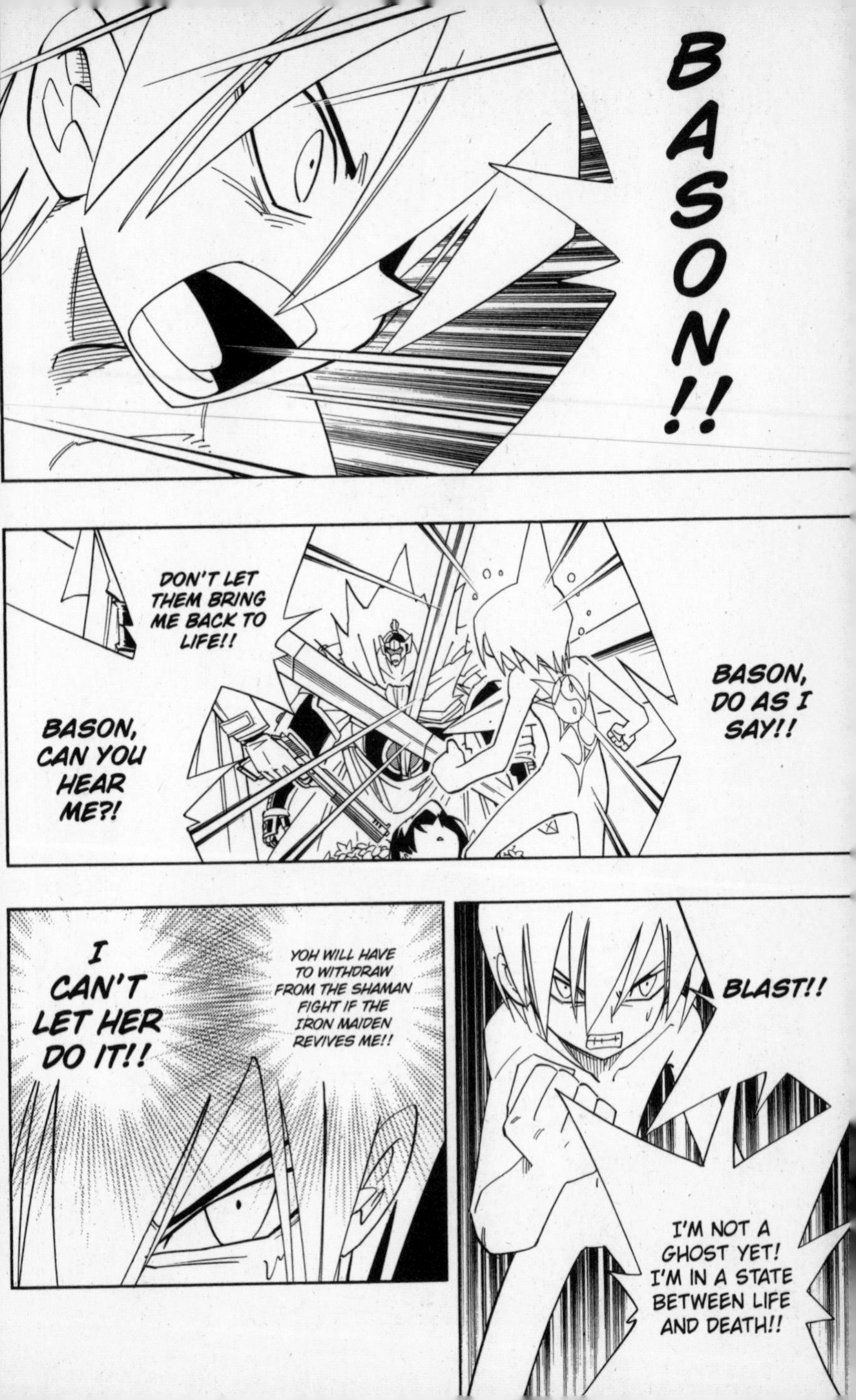
BASON!!
BASON, DO AS I SAY!!
DON'T LET THEM BRING ME BACK TO LIFE!!
BASON, CAN YOU HEAR ME?!
BLAST!!
I'M NOT A GHOST YET! I'M IN A STATE BETWEEN LIFE AND DEATH!!
YOH WILL HAVE TO WITHDRAW FROM THE SHAMAN FIGHT IF THE IRON MAIDEN REVIVES ME!!
I CAN'T LET HER DO IT!!

Reincarnation 180: Epilogue II: First Kiss

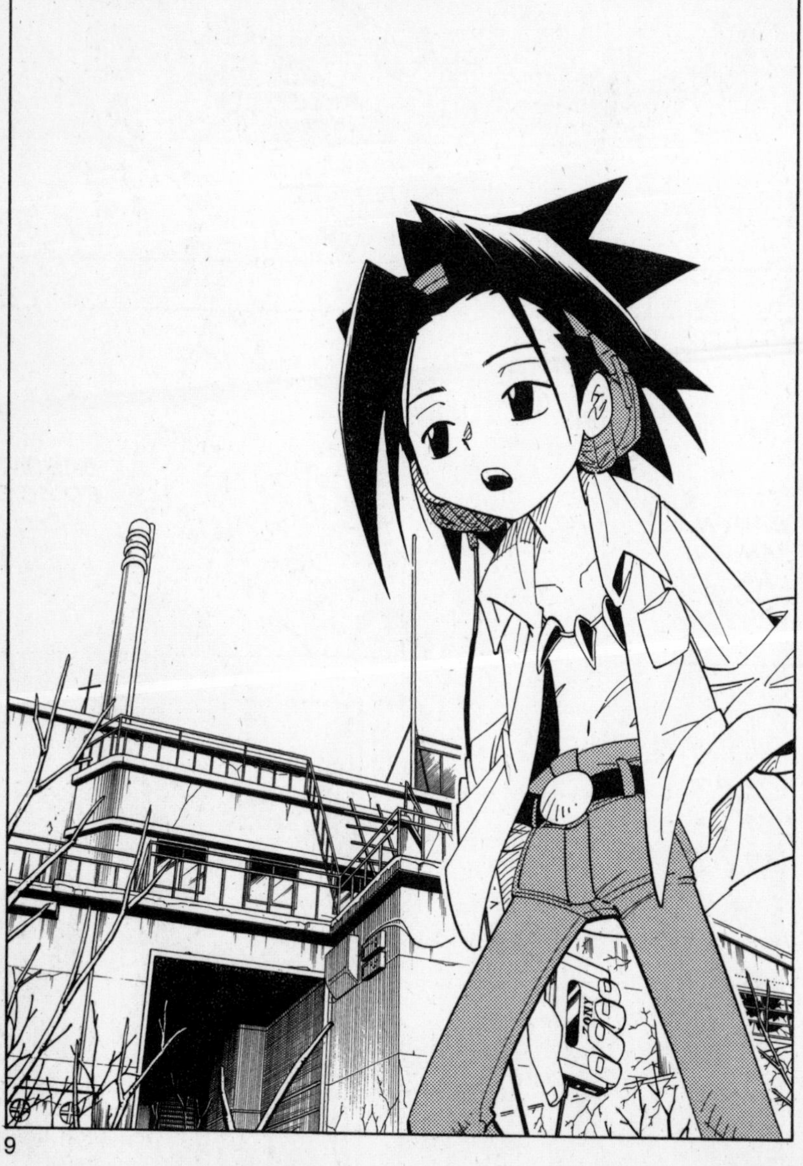
ZONY

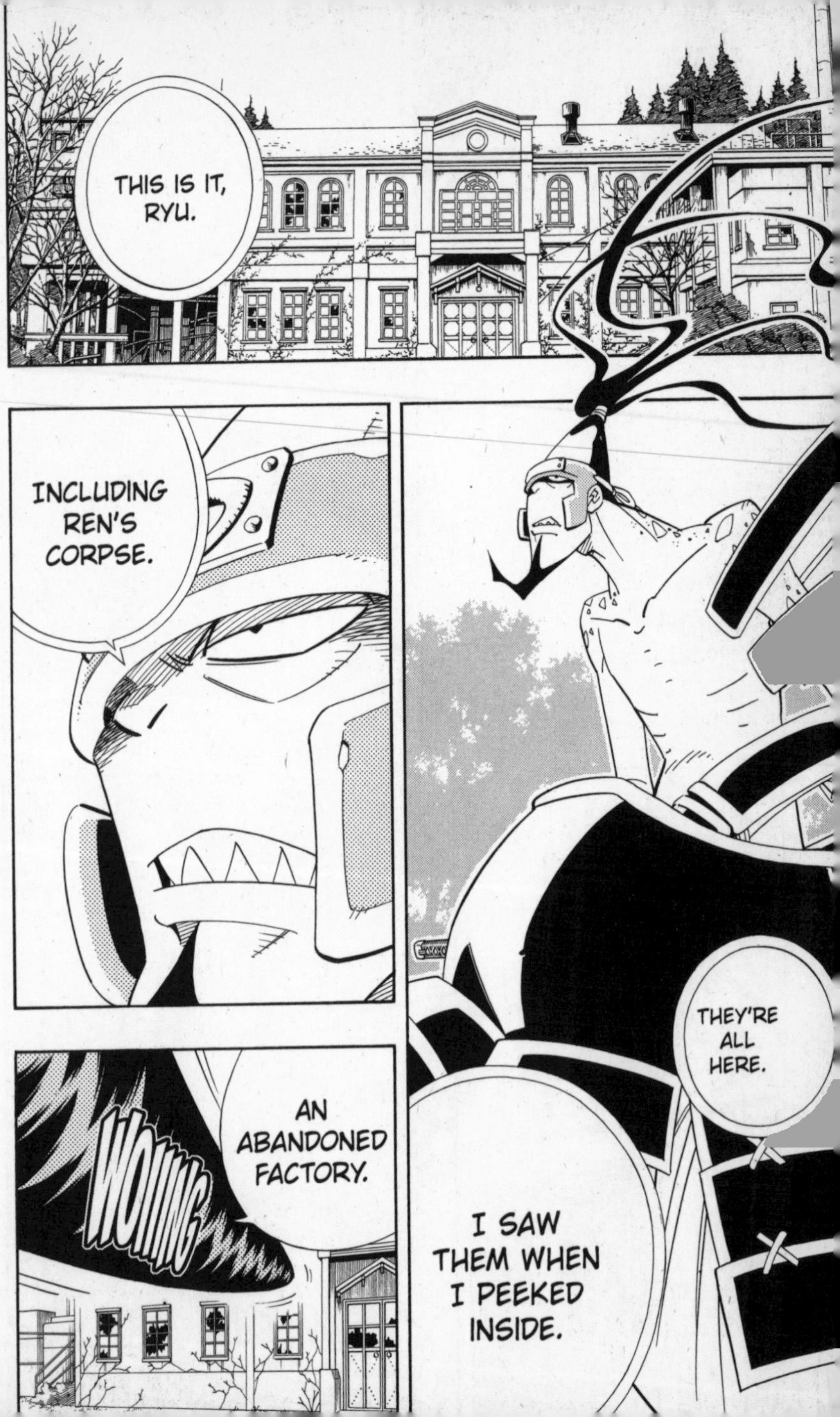
THIS IS IT, RYU.
THEY'RE ALL HERE.
I SAW THEM WHEN I PEEKED INSIDE.
INCLUDING REN'S CORPSE.
AN ABANDONED FACTORY.
WOING

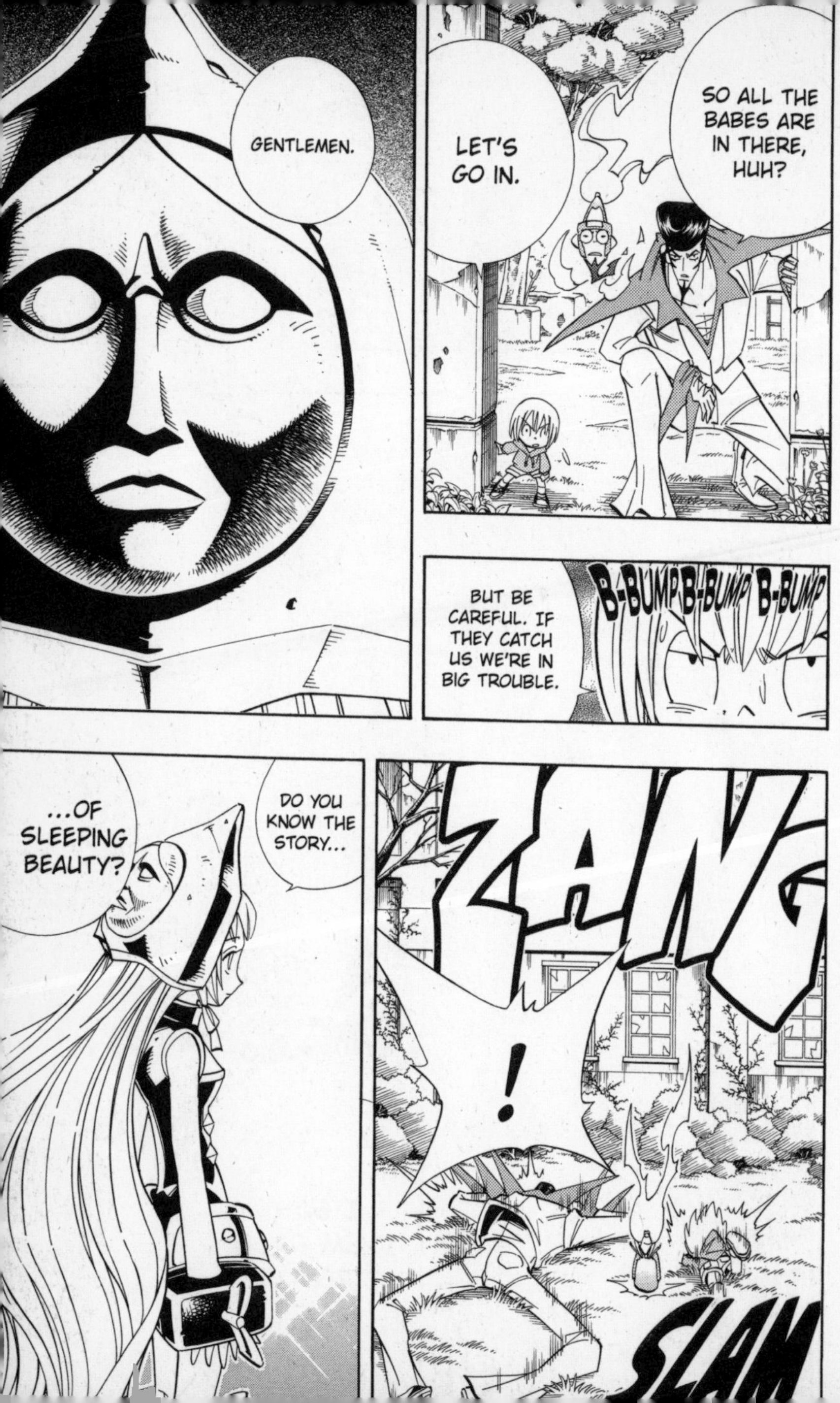
SO ALL THE BABES ARE IN THERE, HUH?
LET'S GO IN.
B-BUMP B-BUMP B-BUMP
BUT BE CAREFUL. IF THEY CATCH US WE'RE IN BIG TROUBLE.
GENTLEMEN.
ZANG
!
SLAM
DO YOU KNOW THE STORY...
...OF SLEEPING BEAUTY?

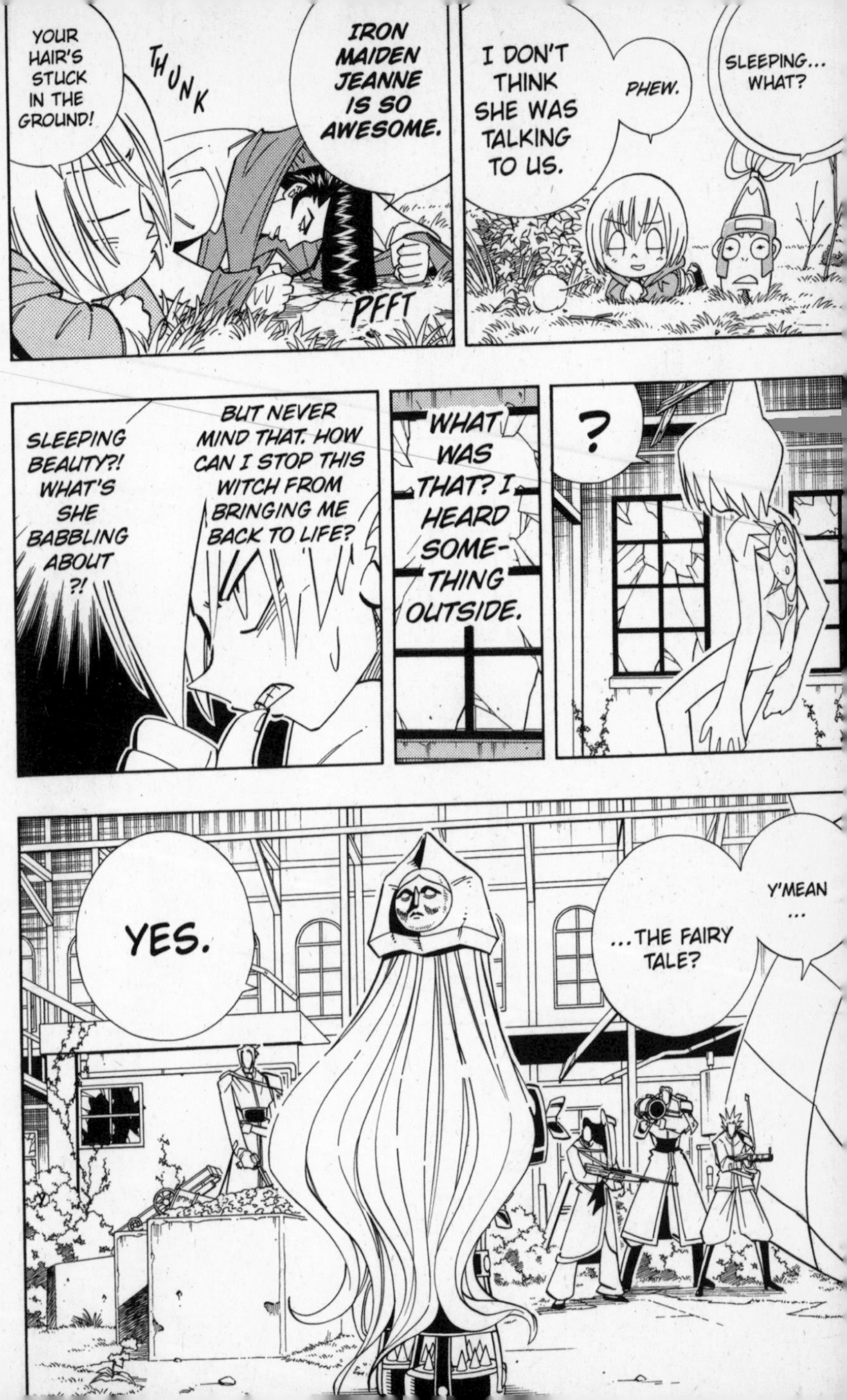
SLEEPING... WHAT?
PHEW.
I DON'T THINK SHE WAS TALKING TO US.
IRON MAIDEN JEANNE IS SO AWESOME.
THUNK
YOUR HAIR'S STUCK IN THE GROUND!
PFFT
?
WHAT WAS THAT? I HEARD SOME-THING OUTSIDE.
BUT NEVER MIND THAT. HOW CAN I STOP THIS WITCH FROM BRINGING ME BACK TO LIFE?
SLEEPING BEAUTY?! WHAT'S SHE BABBLING ABOUT?!
Y'MEAN ...
...THE FAIRY TALE?
YES.

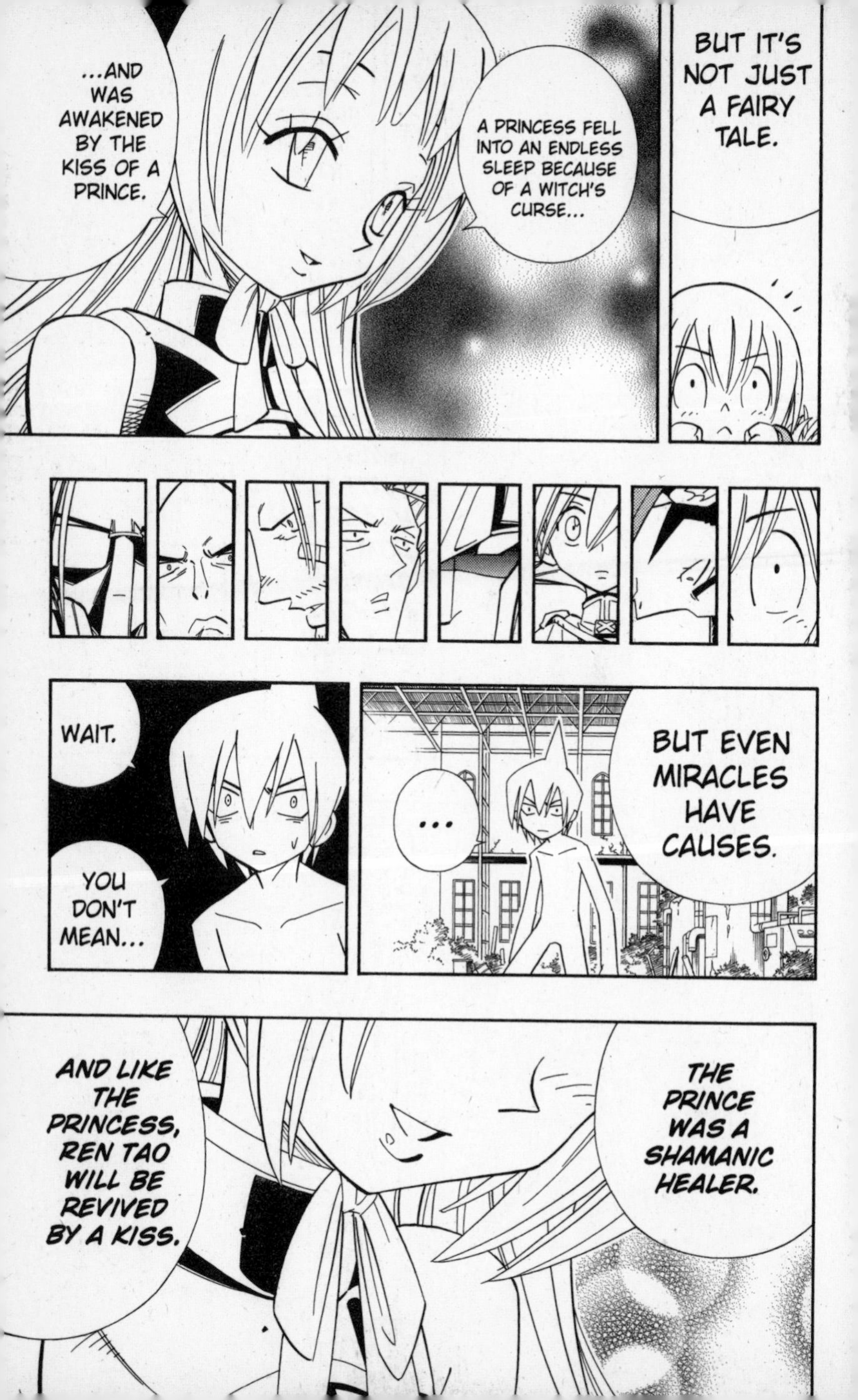
BUT IT'S NOT JUST A FAIRY TALE.
A PRINCESS FELL INTO AN ENDLESS SLEEP BECAUSE OF A WITCH'S CURSE...
...AND WAS AWAKENED BY THE KISS OF A PRINCE.
BUT EVEN MIRACLES HAVE CAUSES.
...
WAIT.
YOU DON'T MEAN...
THE PRINCE WAS A SHAMANIC HEALER.
AND LIKE THE PRINCESS, REN TAO WILL BE REVIVED BY A KISS.

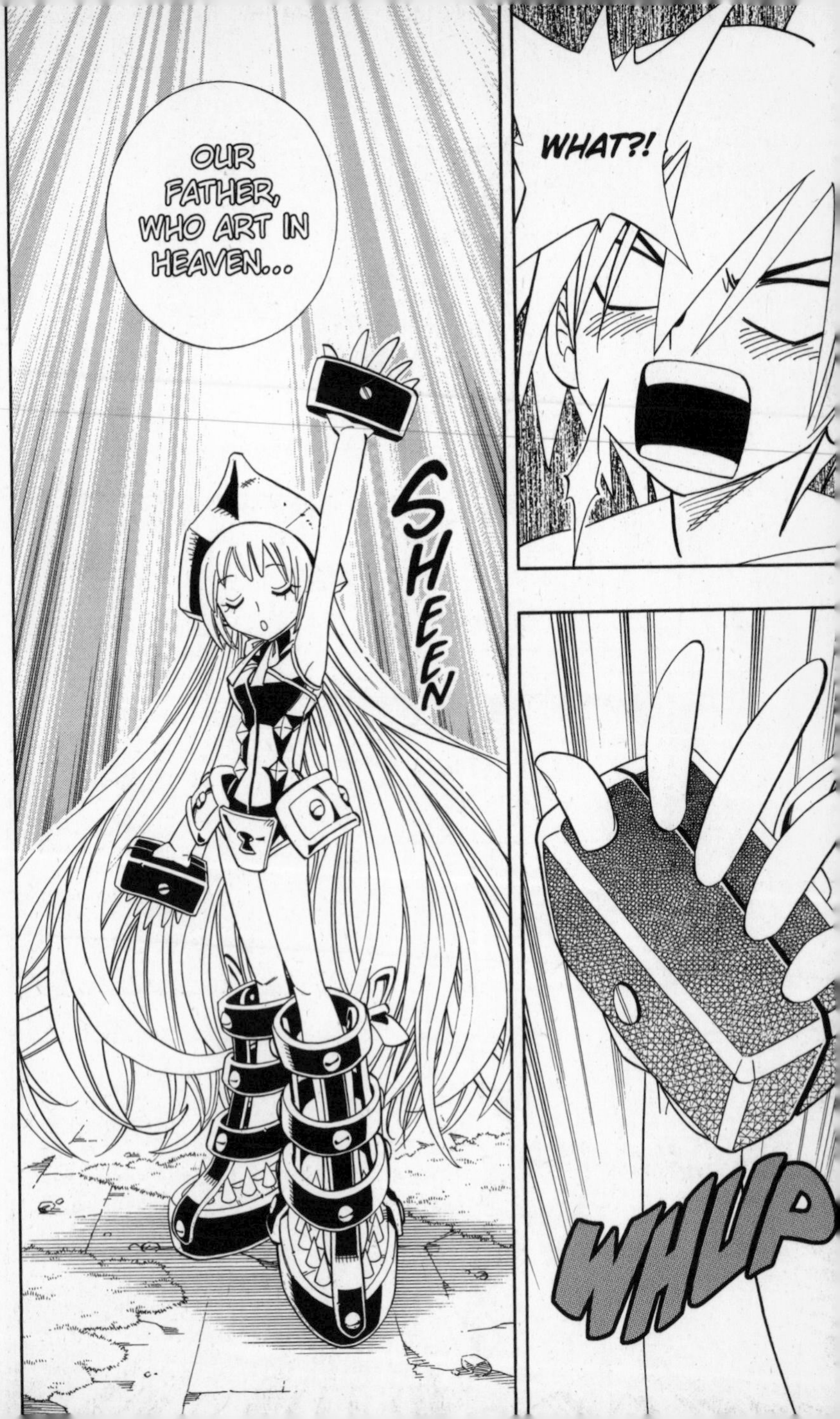
WHAT?!
WHUP
OUR FATHER, WHO ART IN HEAVEN...
SHEEN

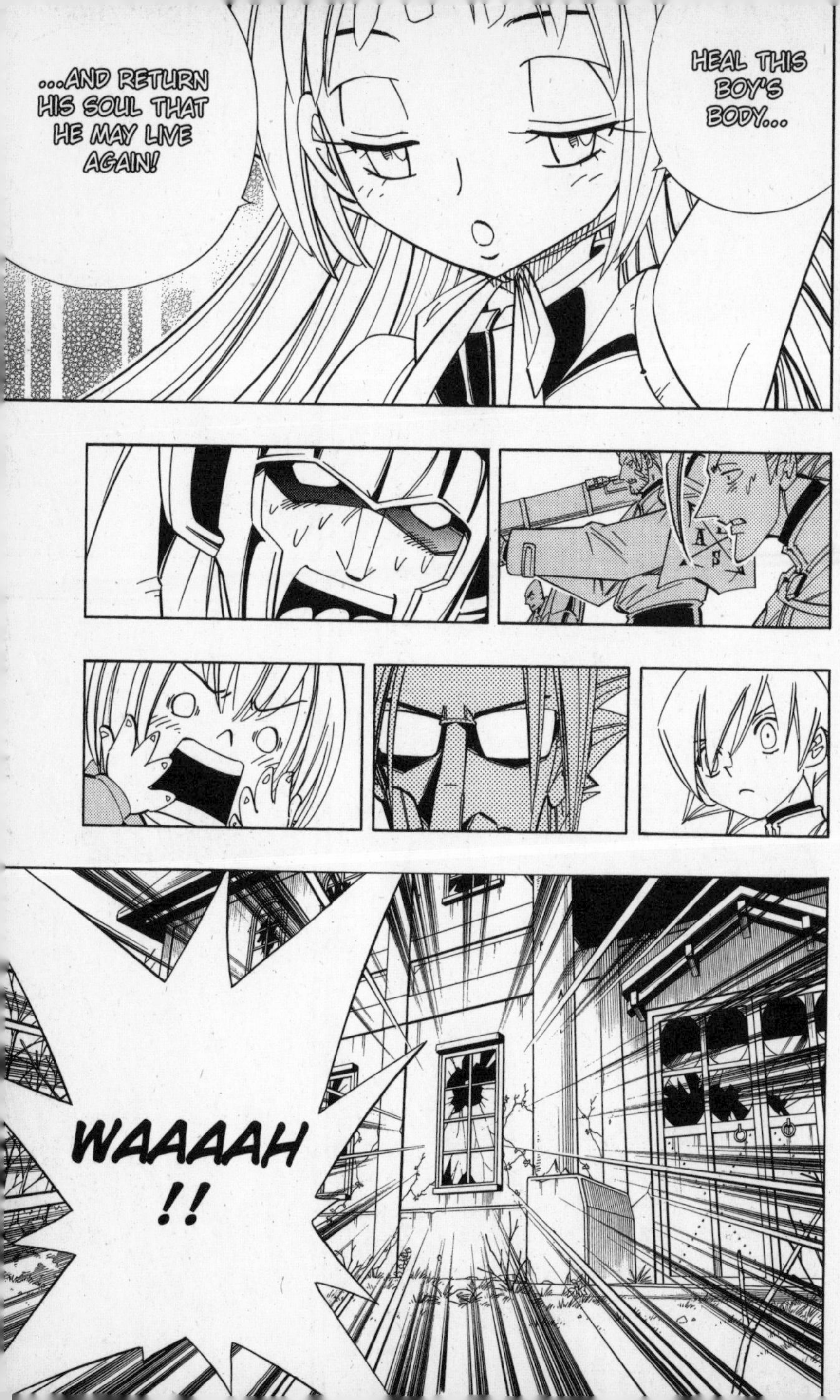
HEAL THIS BOY'S BODY...
...AND RETURN HIS SOUL THAT HE MAY LIVE AGAIN!
WAAAAH !!

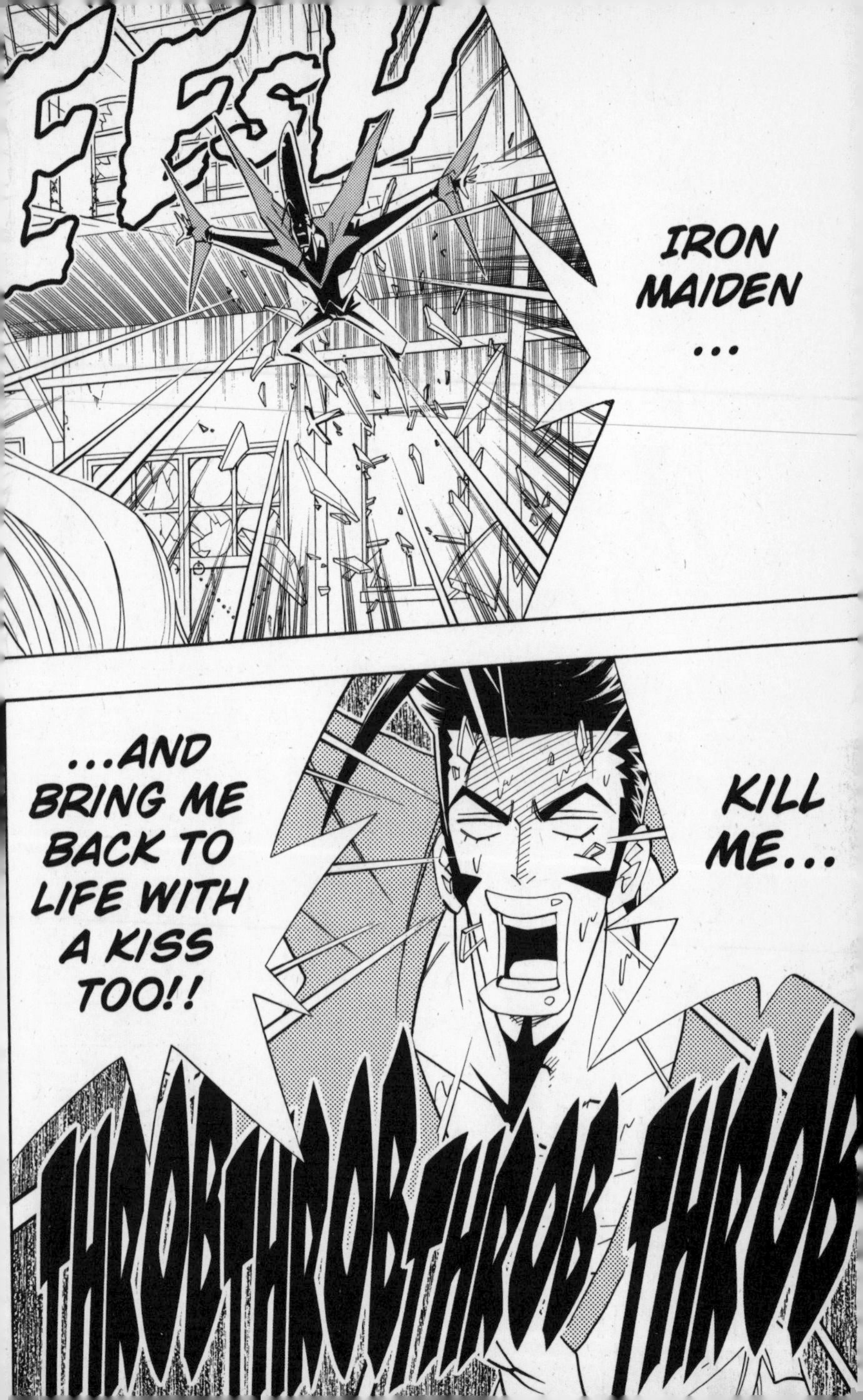
ZZSH
IRON MAIDEN ...
KILL ME...
...AND BRING ME BACK TO LIFE WITH A KISS TOO!!
THROB THROB THROB THROB

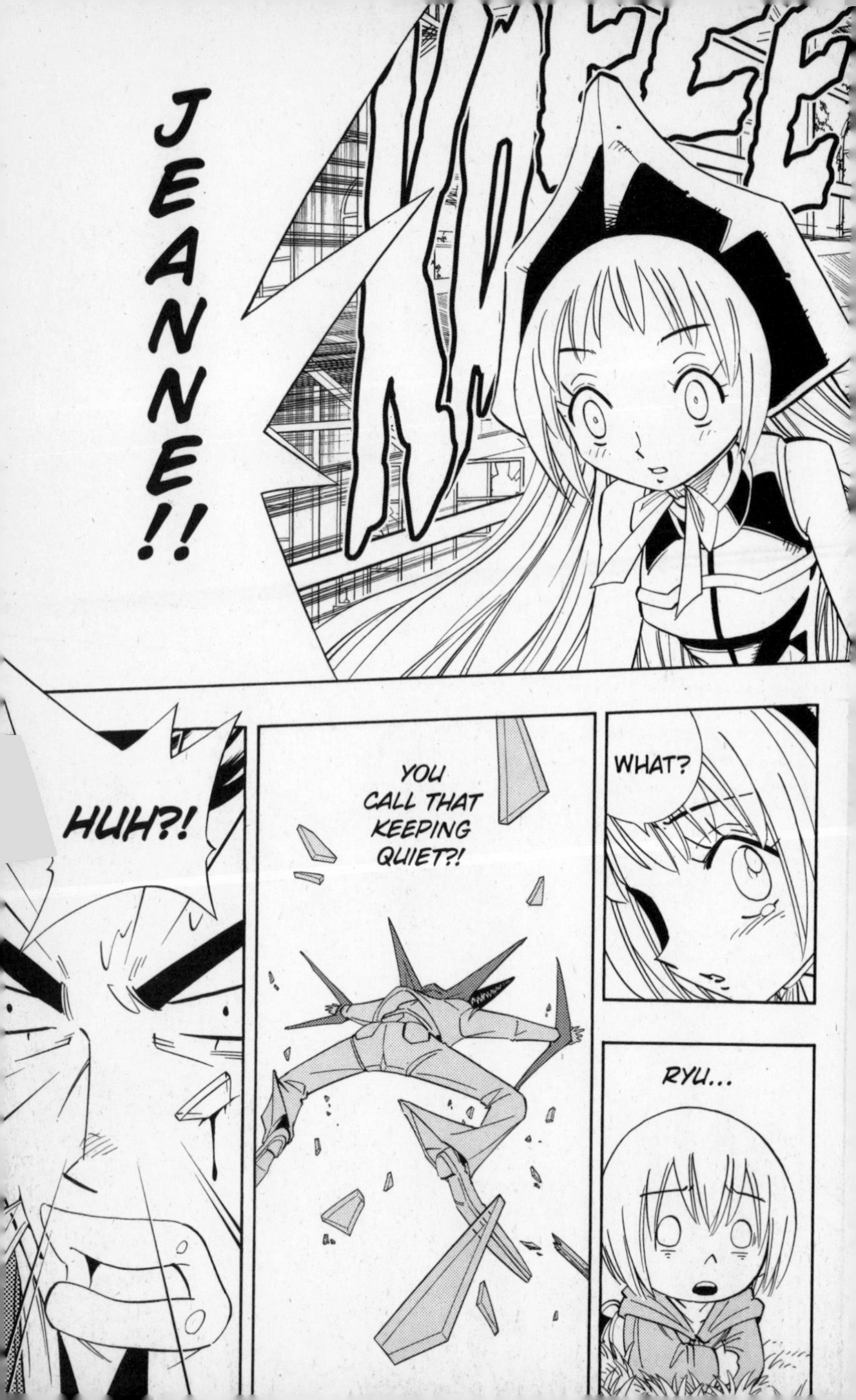
JEANNE!!
WHAT?
RYU...
YOU CALL THAT KEEPING QUIET?!
HUH?!

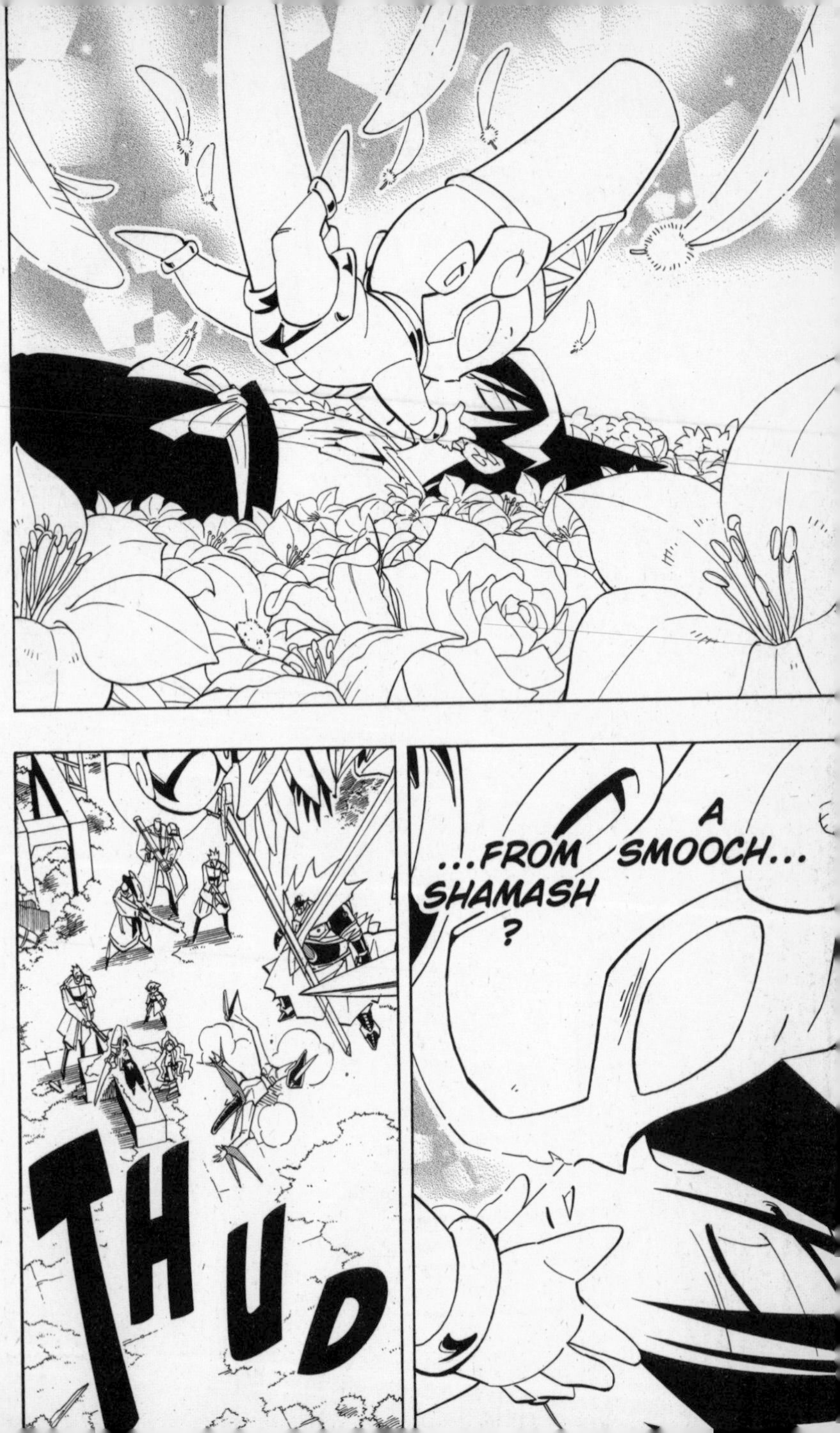
A SMOOCH...
...FROM SHAMASH?
THUD

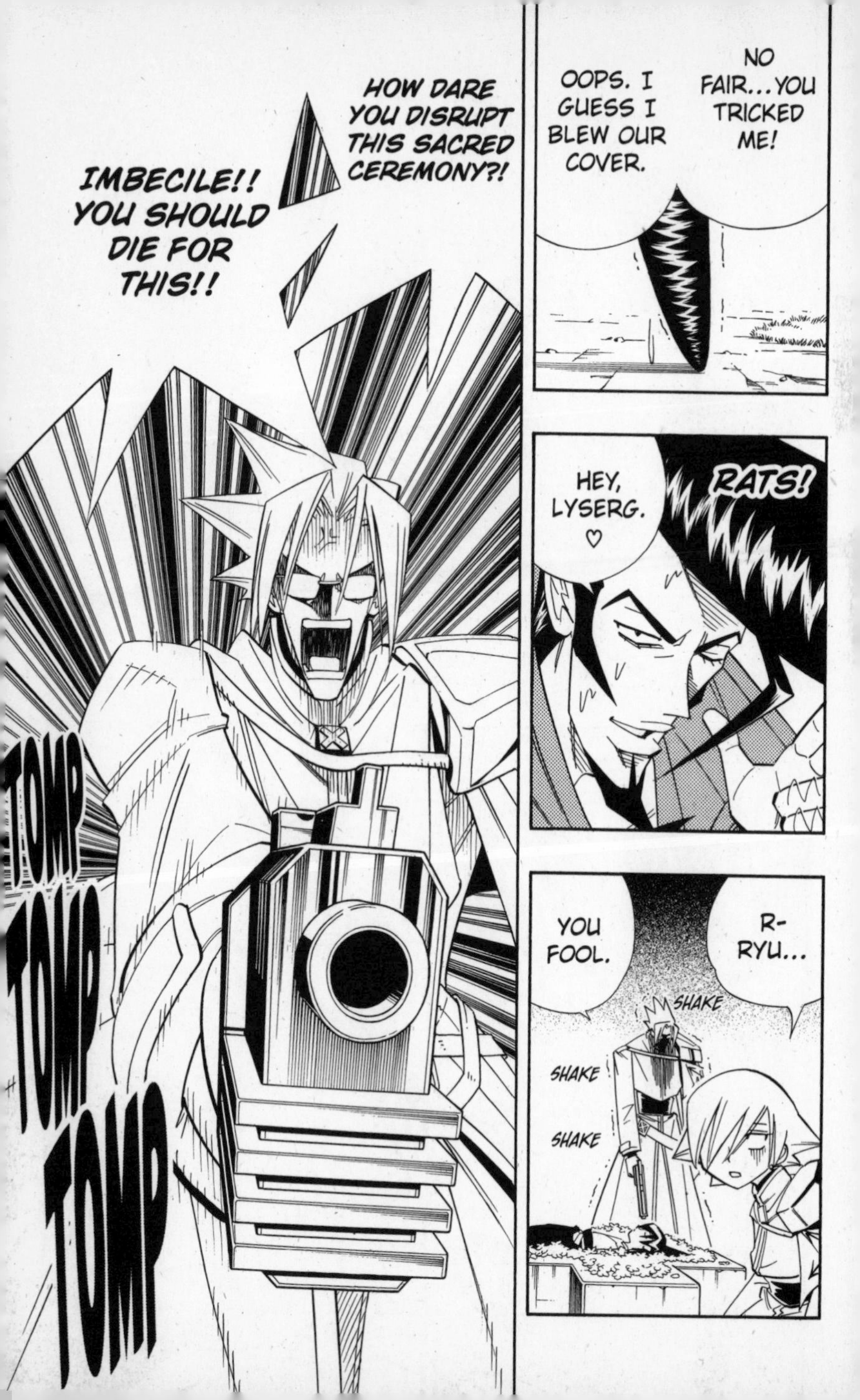
NO FAIR...YOU TRICKED ME!
OOPS. I GUESS I BLEW OUR COVER.
RATS!
HEY, LYSERG. ♡
R-RYU...
YOU FOOL.
SHAKE
SHAKE
SHAKE
HOW DARE YOU DISRUPT THIS SACRED CEREMONY?!
IMBECILE!! YOU SHOULD DIE FOR THIS!!
TOMP
TOMP
TOMP
TOMP

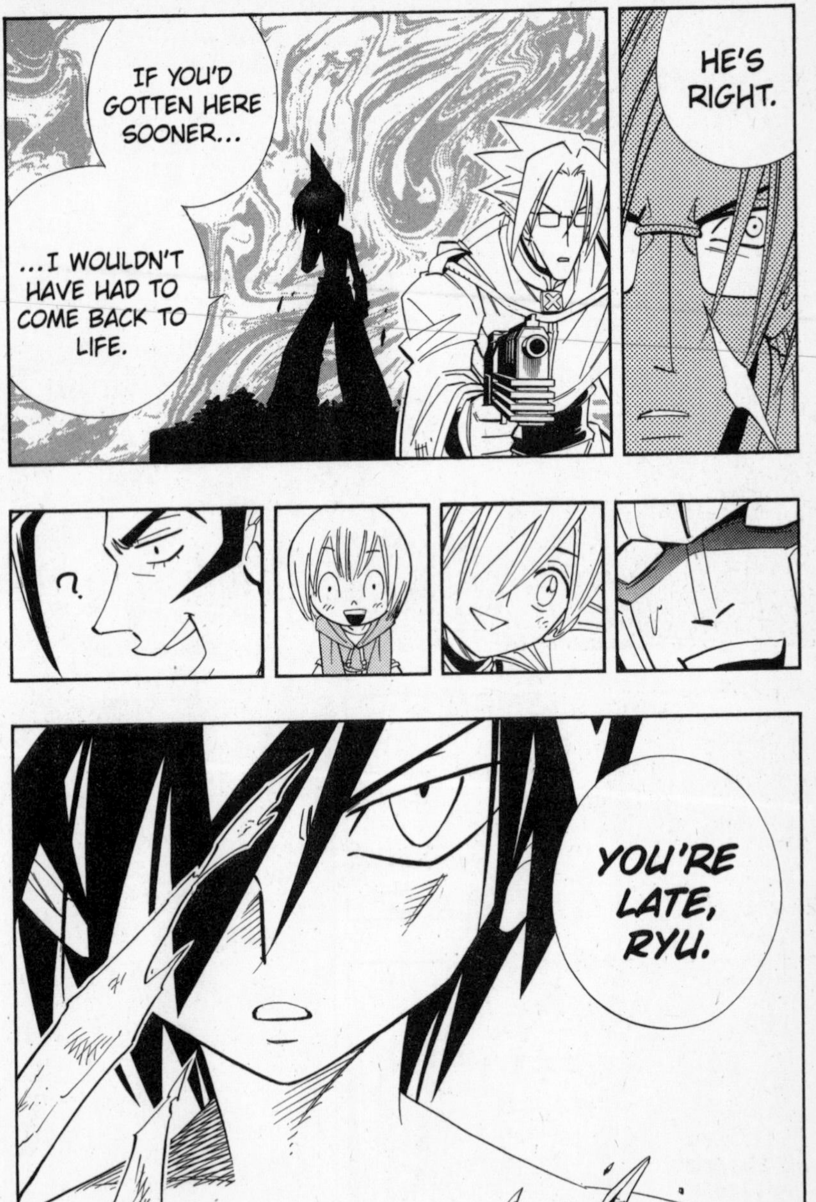
HE'S RIGHT.
IF YOU'D GOTTEN HERE SOONER...
...I WOULDN'T HAVE HAD TO COME BACK TO LIFE.
?
YOU'RE LATE, RYU.

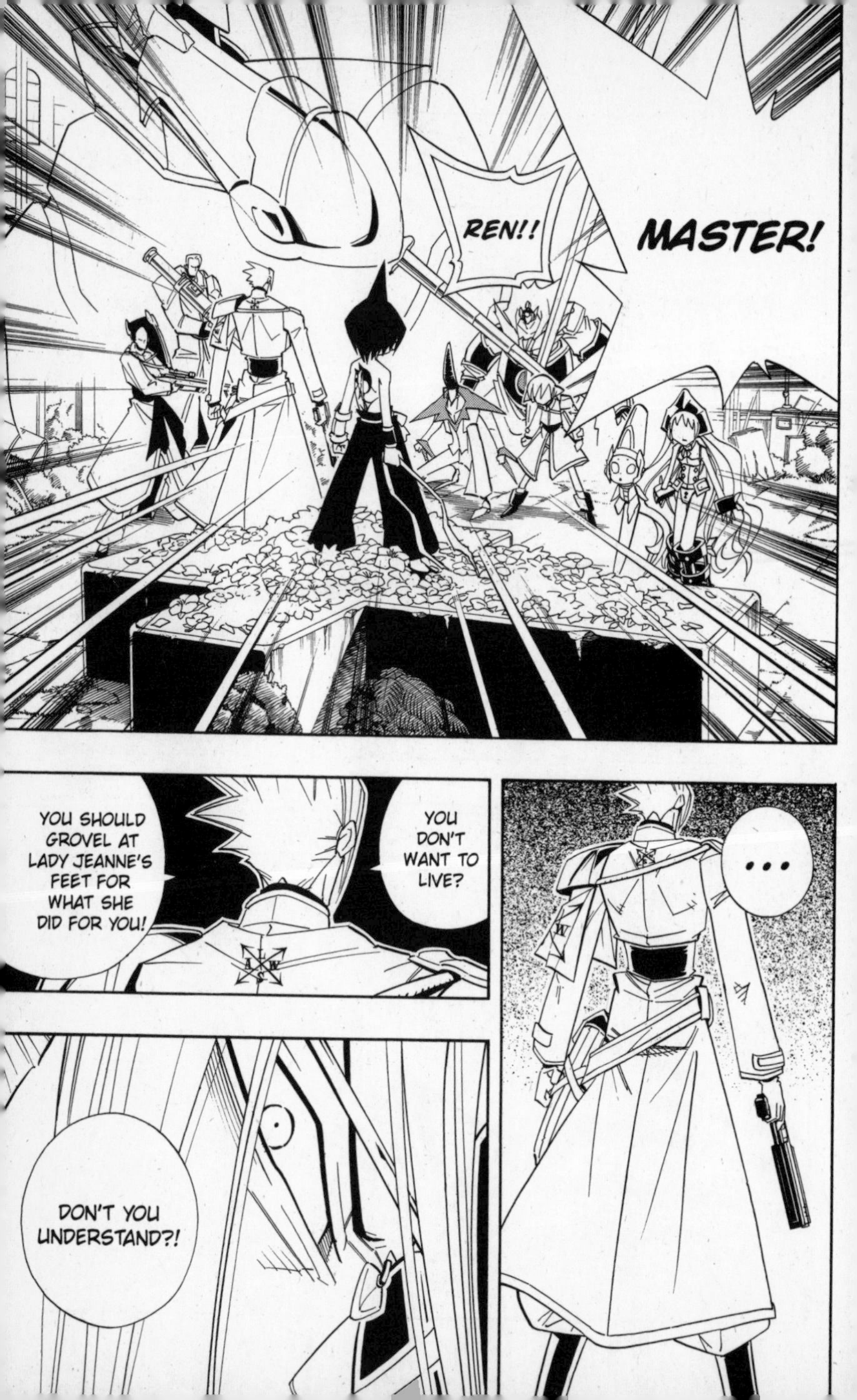
MASTER!
REN!!
...
YOU DON'T WANT TO LIVE?
YOU SHOULD GROVEL AT LADY JEANNE'S FEET FOR WHAT SHE DID FOR YOU!
DON'T YOU UNDERSTAND?!

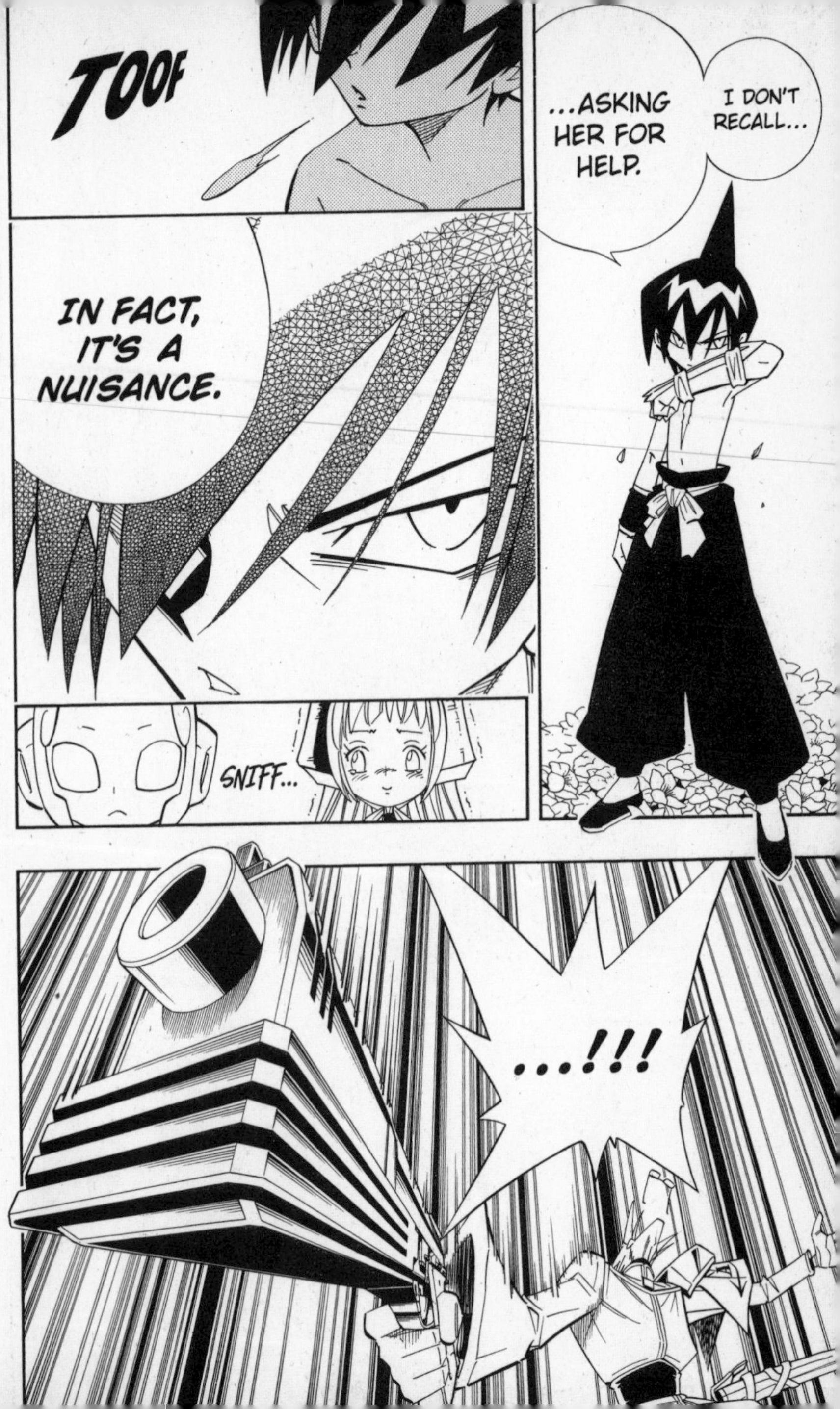
I DON'T RECALL...
...ASKING HER FOR HELP.
TOOF
IN FACT, IT'S A NUISANCE.
SNIFF...
...!!!

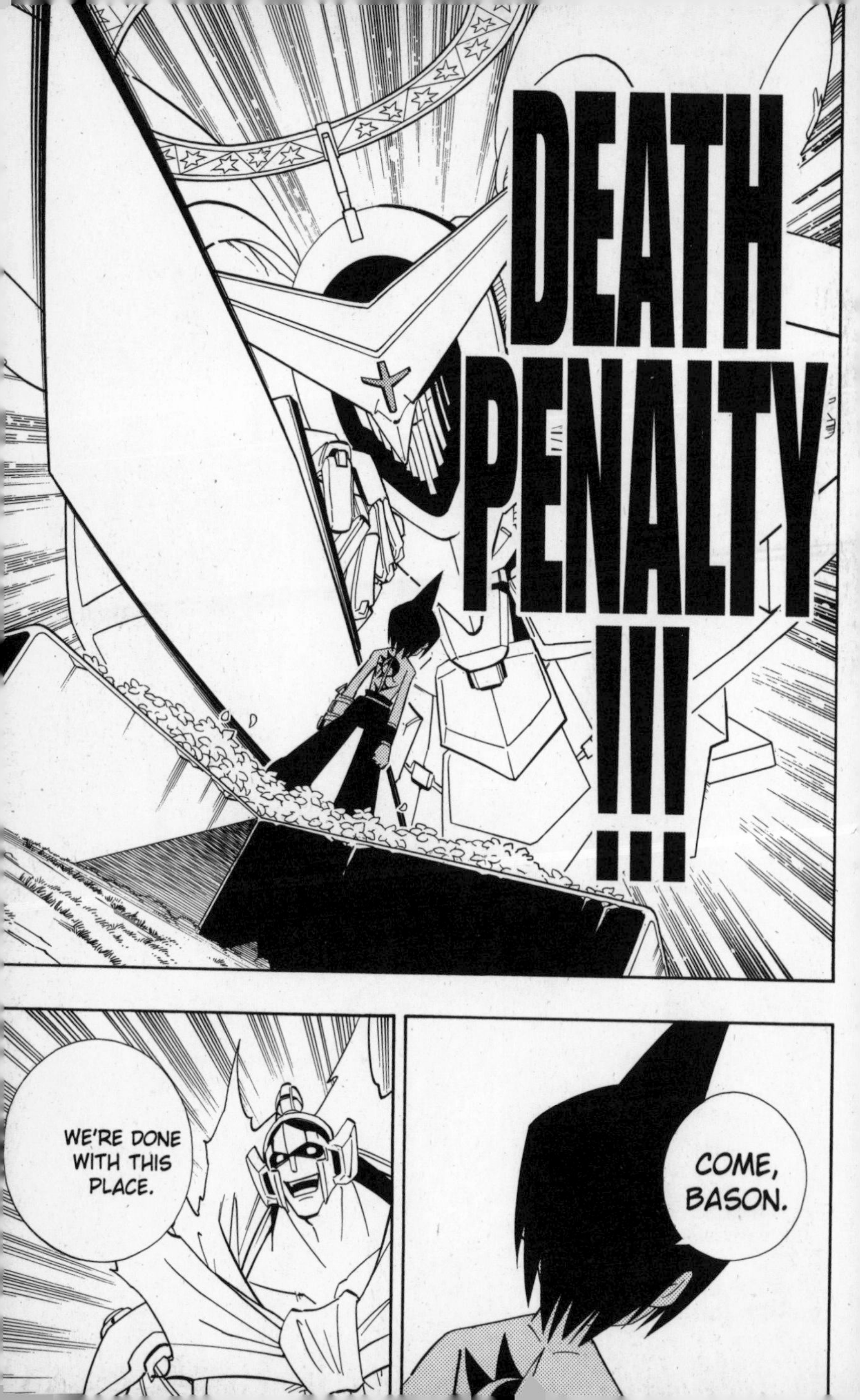
DEATH PENALTY!!!
COME, BASON.
WE'RE DONE WITH THIS PLACE.

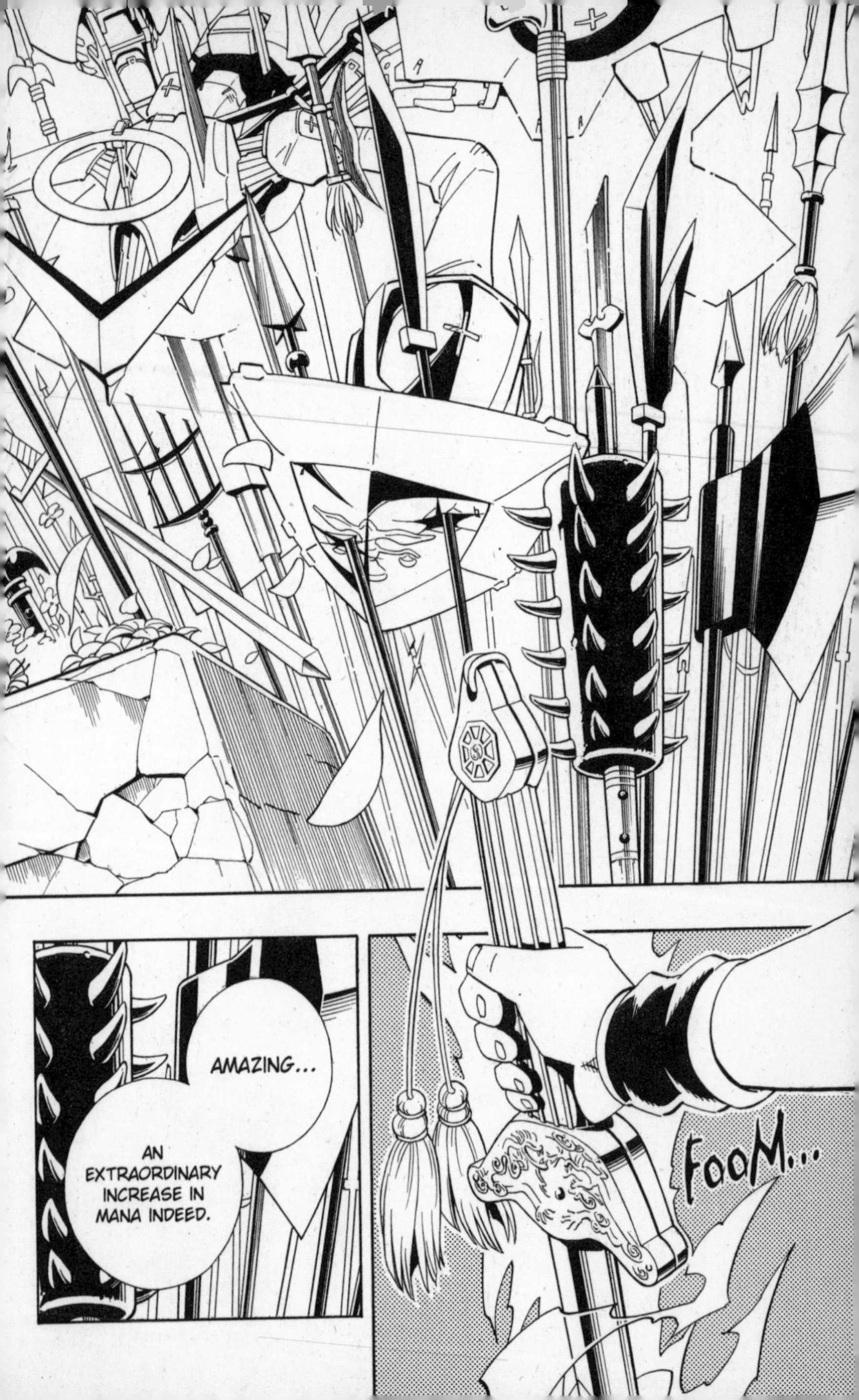
FOOM...
AMAZING...
AN EXTRAORDINARY INCREASE IN MANA INDEED.

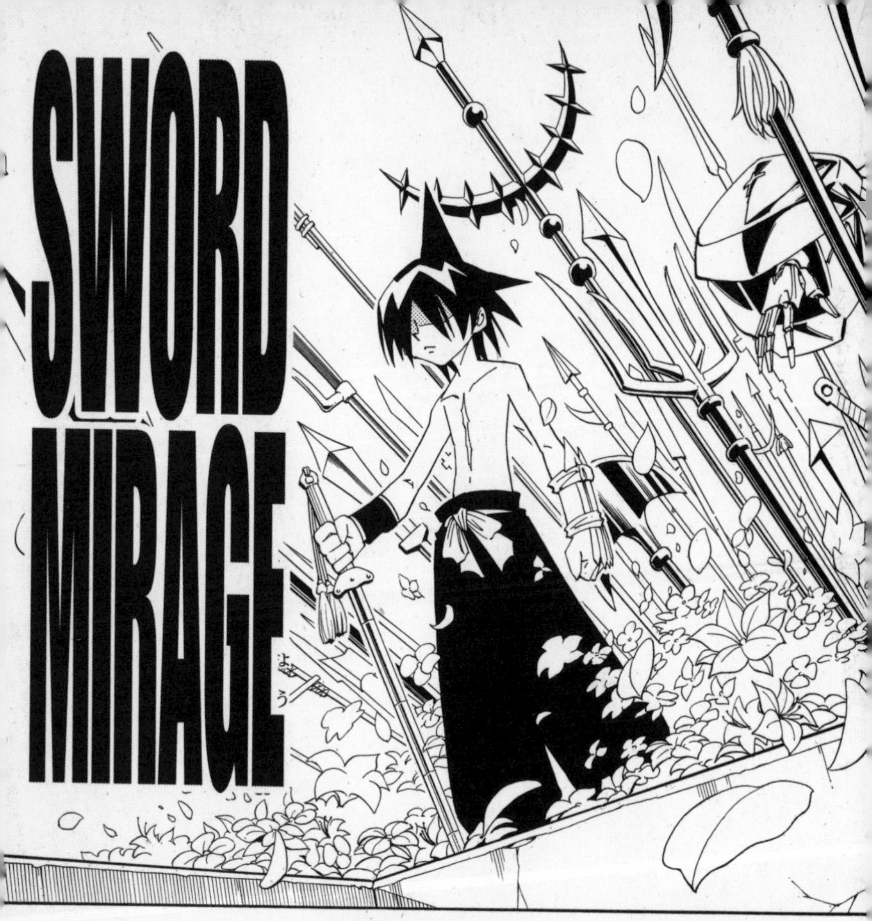
SWORD MIRAGE

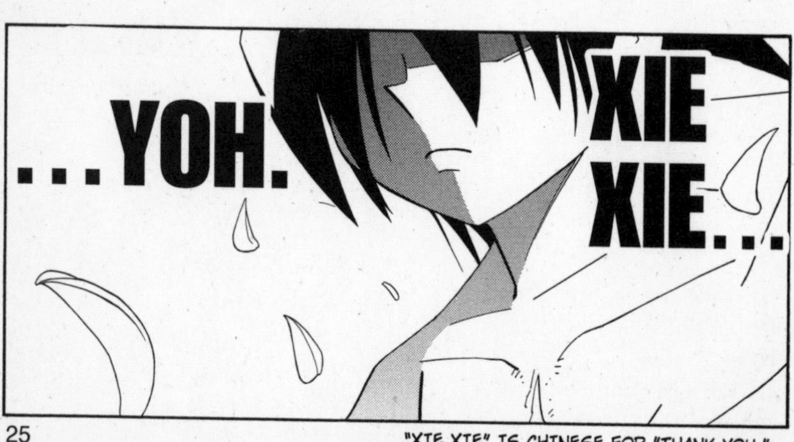
XIE XIE...
...YOH.

"XIE XIE" IS CHINESE FOR "THANK YOU."

ビッグガイ・ビル

BIG GUY BILL

2001
(JAN)

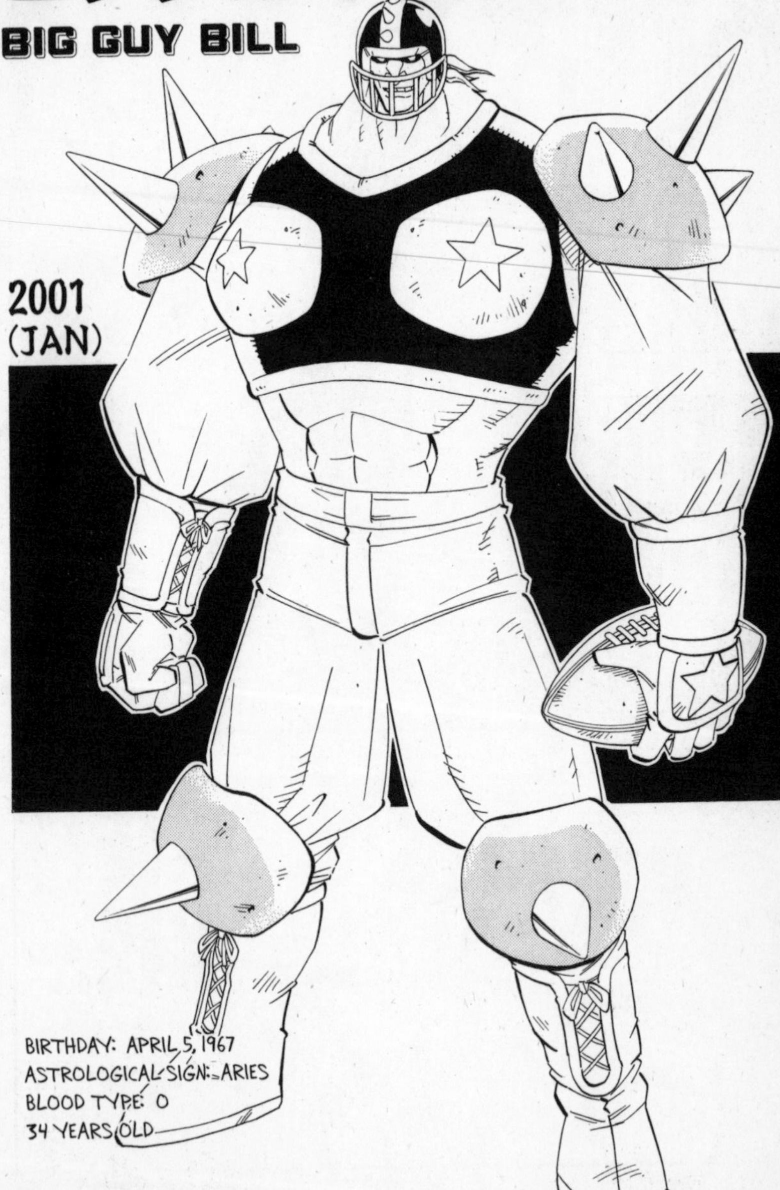

BIRTHDAY: APRIL 5, 1967
ASTROLOGICAL SIGN: ARIES
BLOOD TYPE: O
34 YEARS OLD

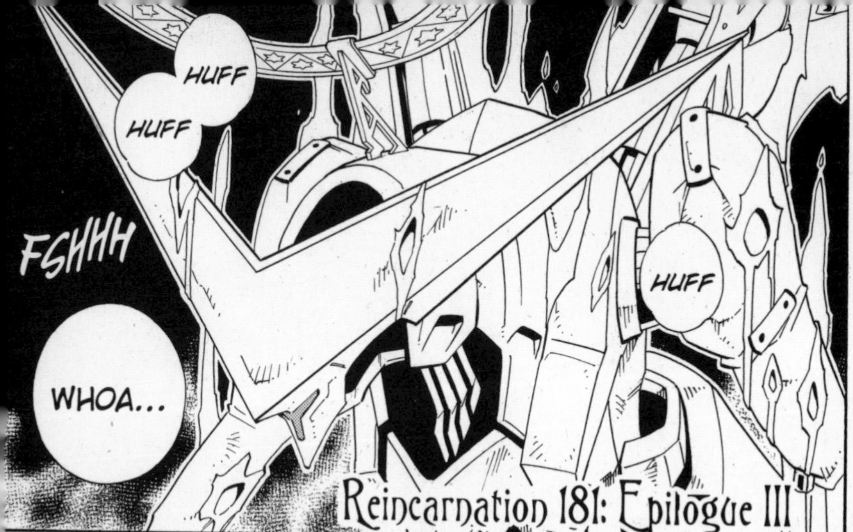
HUFF
HUFF
HUFF
FSHHH
WHOA...
Reincarnation 181: Epilogue III

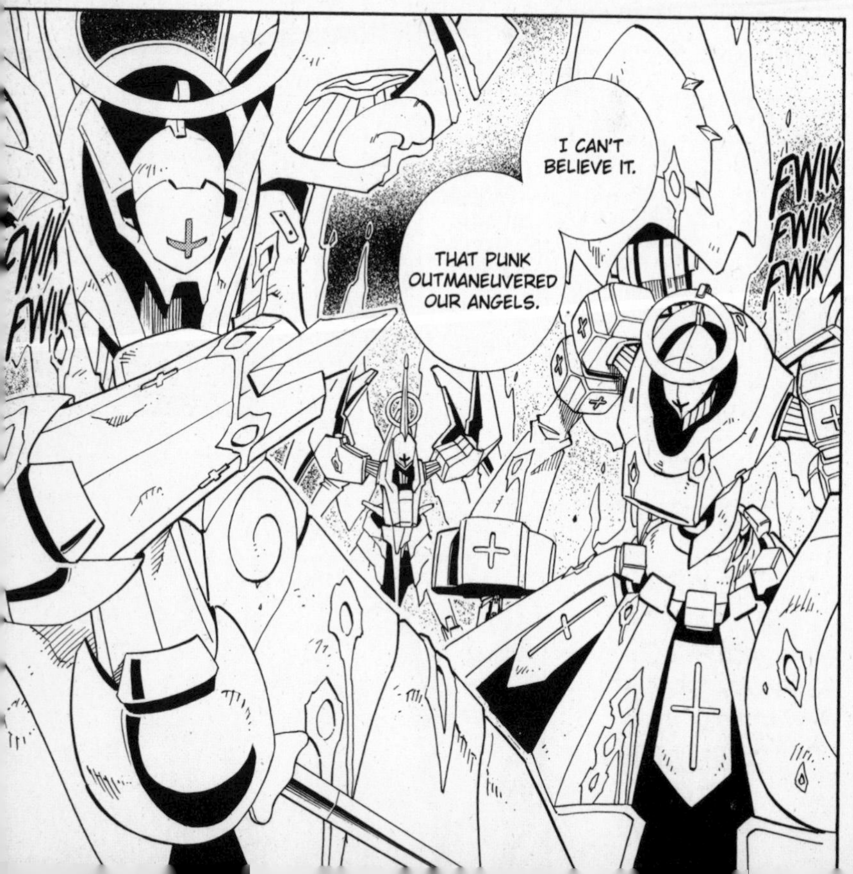
FWIK FWIK FWIK
I CAN'T BELIEVE IT.
THAT PUNK OUTMANEUVERED OUR ANGELS.
FWIK FWIK

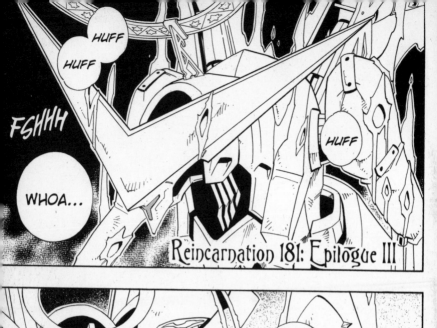

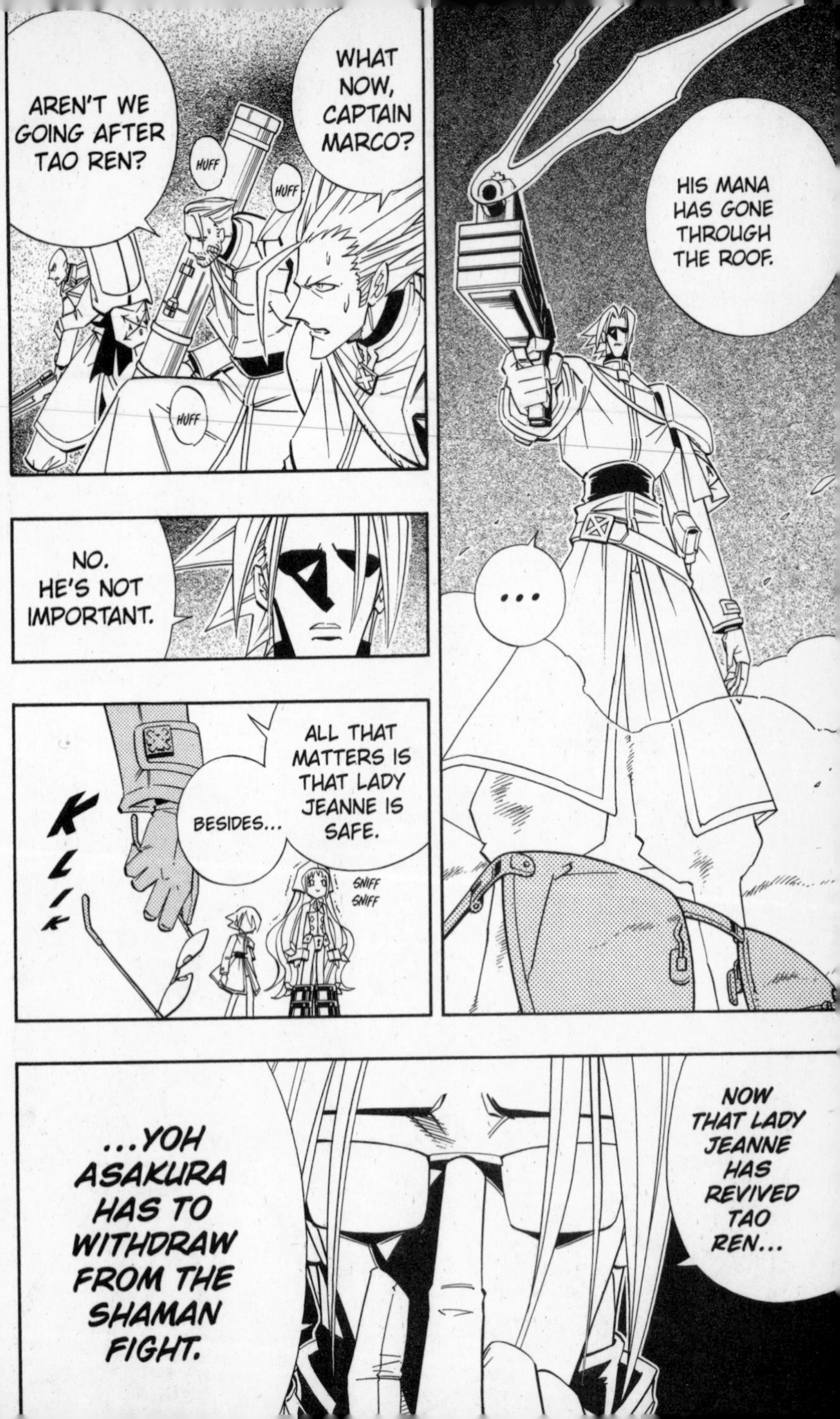
HIS MANA HAS GONE THROUGH THE ROOF.
...
WHAT NOW, CAPTAIN MARCO?
HUFF
HUFF
AREN'T WE GOING AFTER TAO REN?
HUFF
NO. HE'S NOT IMPORTANT.
ALL THAT MATTERS IS THAT LADY JEANNE IS SAFE.
BESIDES...
SNIFF SNIFF
KLIK
NOW THAT LADY JEANNE HAS REVIVED TAO REN...
...YOH ASAKURA HAS TO WITHDRAW FROM THE SHAMAN FIGHT.

Reincarnation 181: Epilogue III

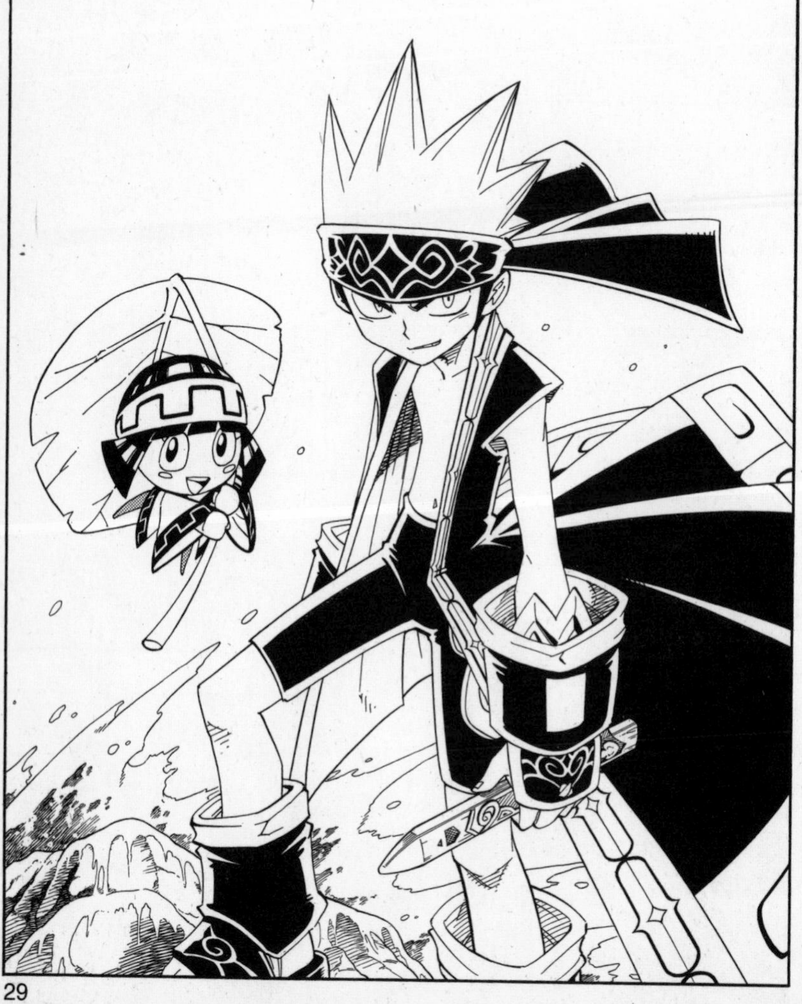

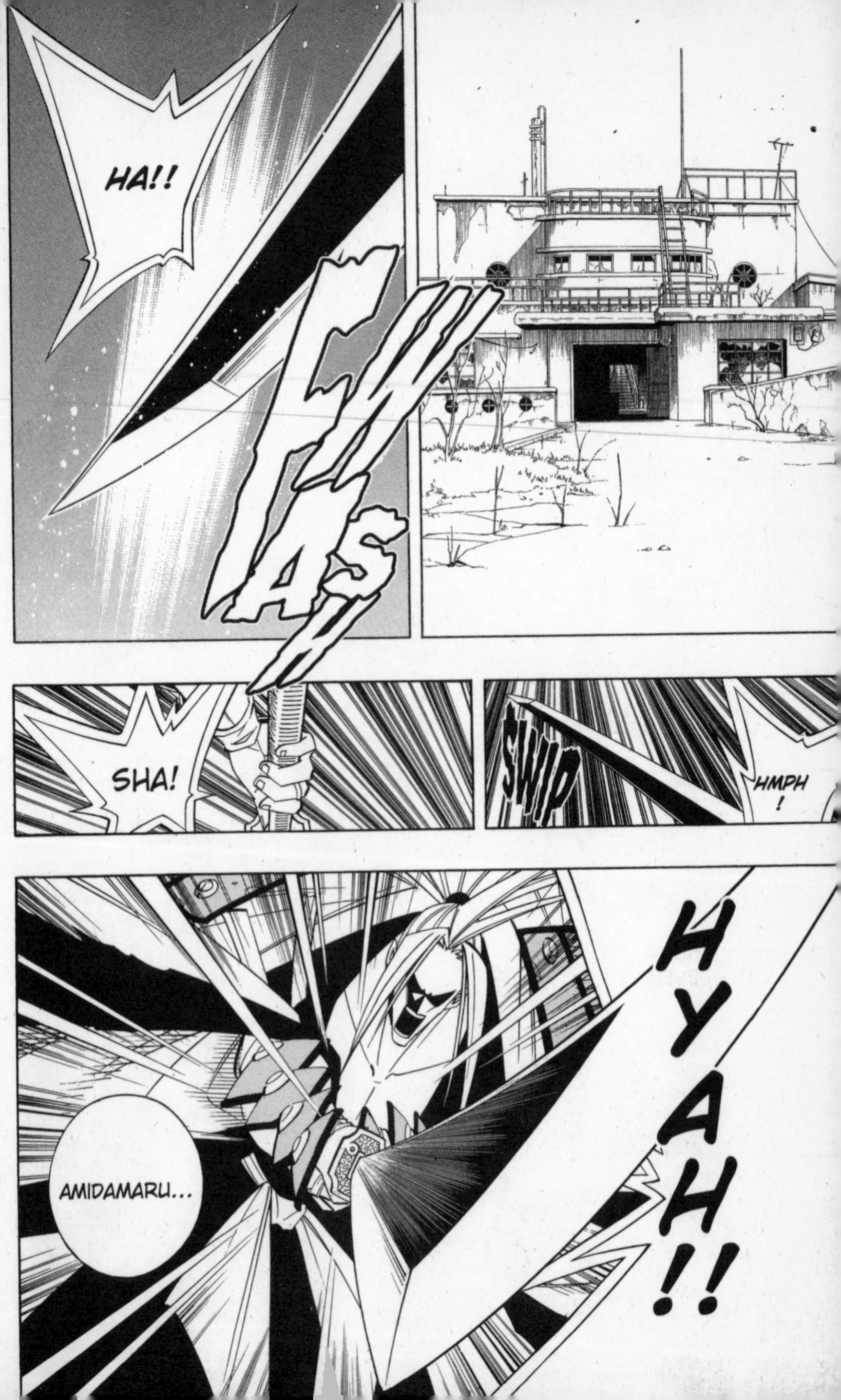
HA!!
FWASH
SWIP
HMPH !
SHA!
HYAH!!
AMIDAMARU...

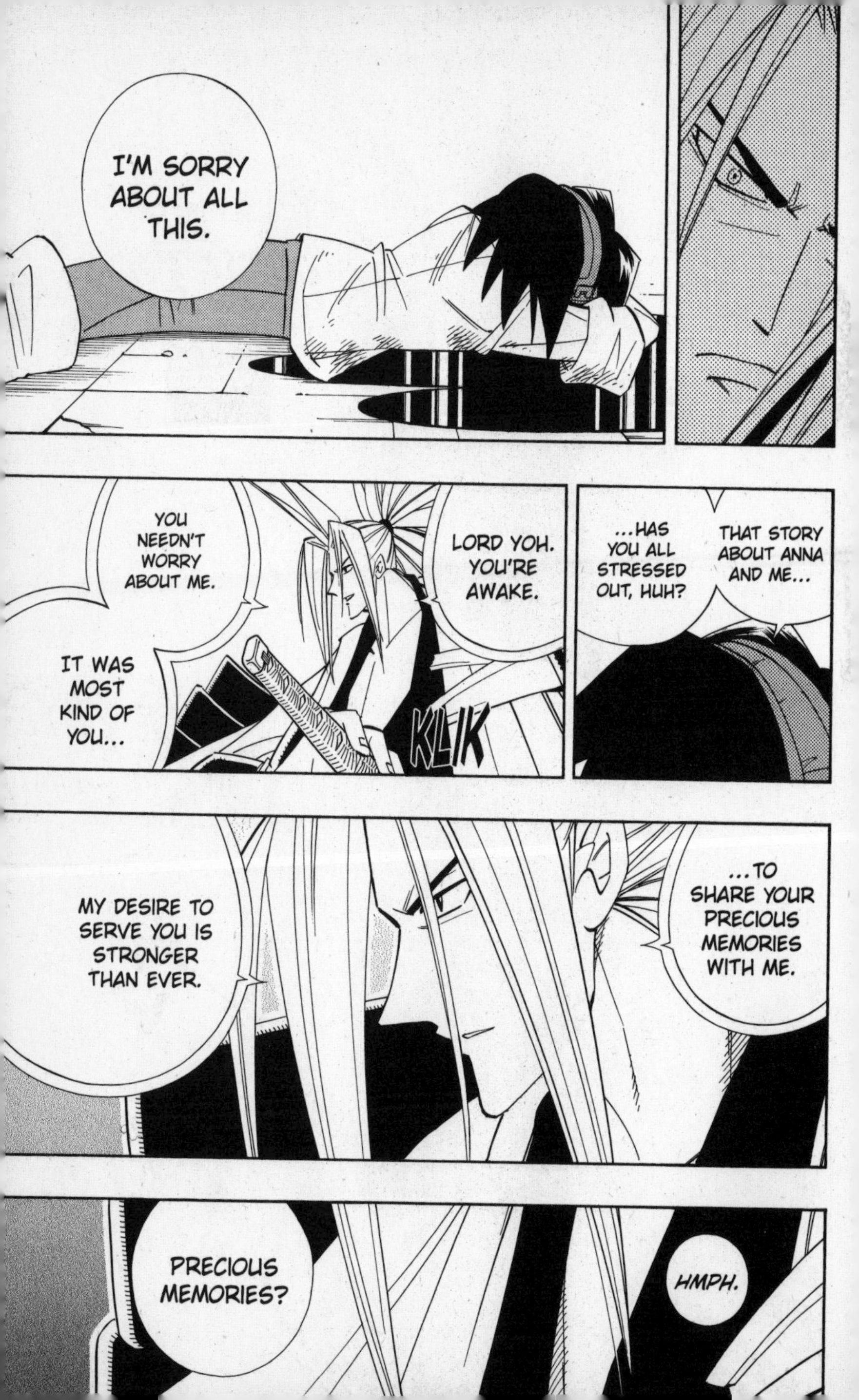

I'M SORRY ABOUT ALL THIS.
THAT STORY ABOUT ANNA AND ME...
...HAS YOU ALL STRESSED OUT, HUH?
LORD YOH. YOU'RE AWAKE.
KLIK
YOU NEEDN'T WORRY ABOUT ME.
IT WAS MOST KIND OF YOU...
...TO SHARE YOUR PRECIOUS MEMORIES WITH ME.
MY DESIRE TO SERVE YOU IS STRONGER THAN EVER.
HMPH.
PRECIOUS MEMORIES?

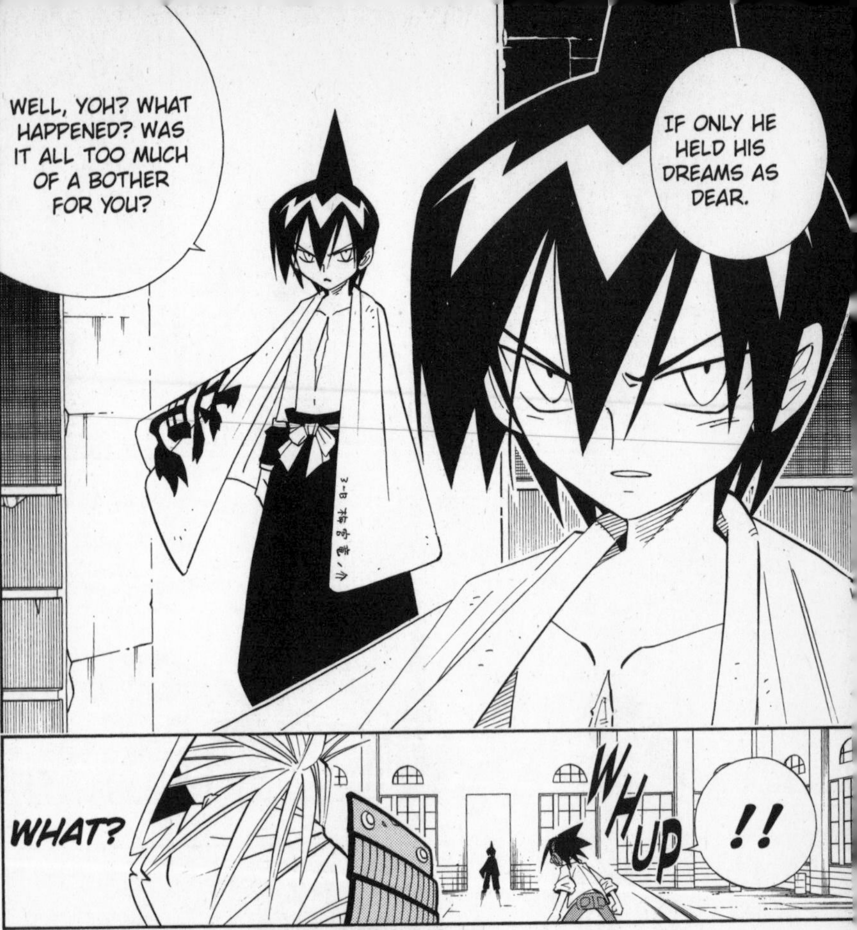
IF ONLY HE HELD HIS DREAMS AS DEAR.
WELL, YOH? WHAT HAPPENED? WAS IT ALL TOO MUCH OF A BOTHER FOR YOU?
!!
WHUP
WHAT?

TOWEL: RYUNOSUKE UMEMIYA, ROOM 3-B

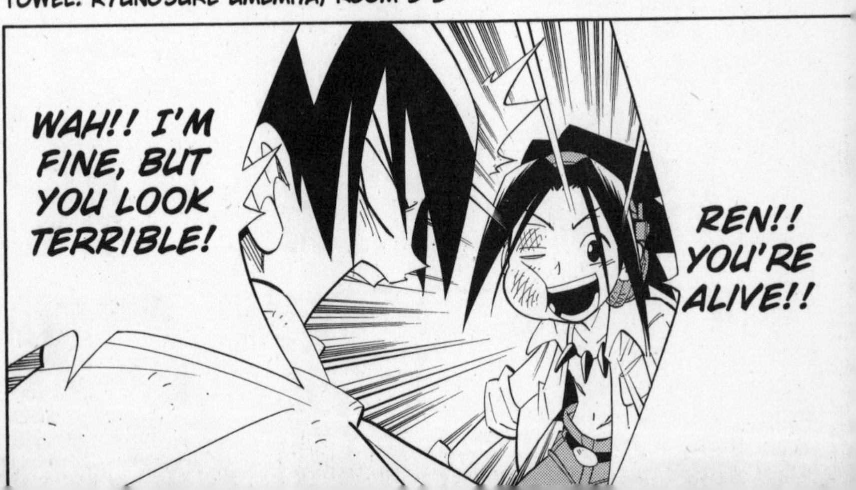
REN!! YOU'RE ALIVE!!
WAH!! I'M FINE, BUT YOU LOOK TERRIBLE!

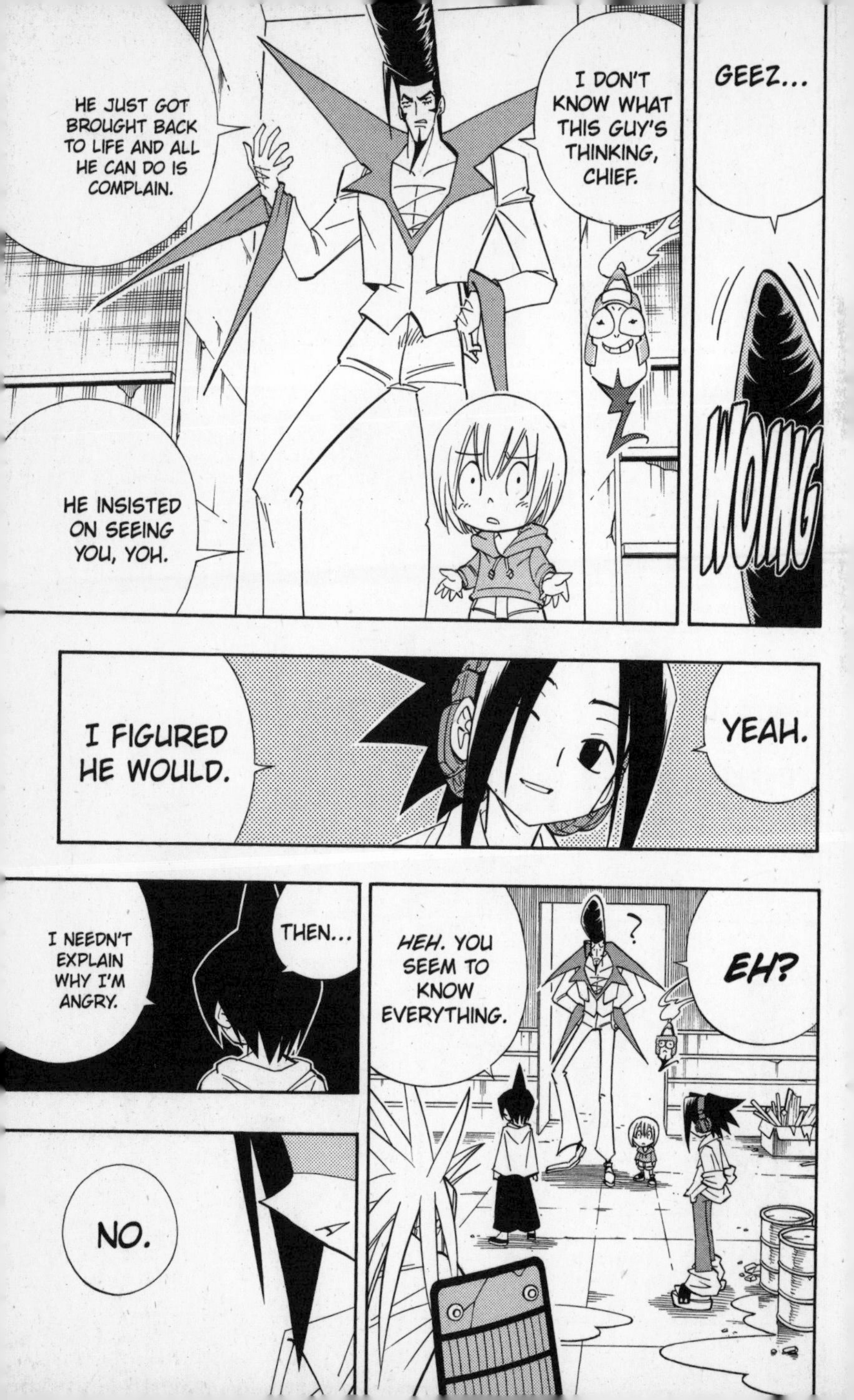
GEEZ...
WOING
I DON'T KNOW WHAT THIS GUY'S THINKING, CHIEF.
HE JUST GOT BROUGHT BACK TO LIFE AND ALL HE CAN DO IS COMPLAIN.
HE INSISTED ON SEEING YOU, YOH.
YEAH.
I FIGURED HE WOULD.
EH?
?
HEH. YOU SEEM TO KNOW EVERYTHING.
THEN...
I NEEDN'T EXPLAIN WHY I'M ANGRY.
NO.

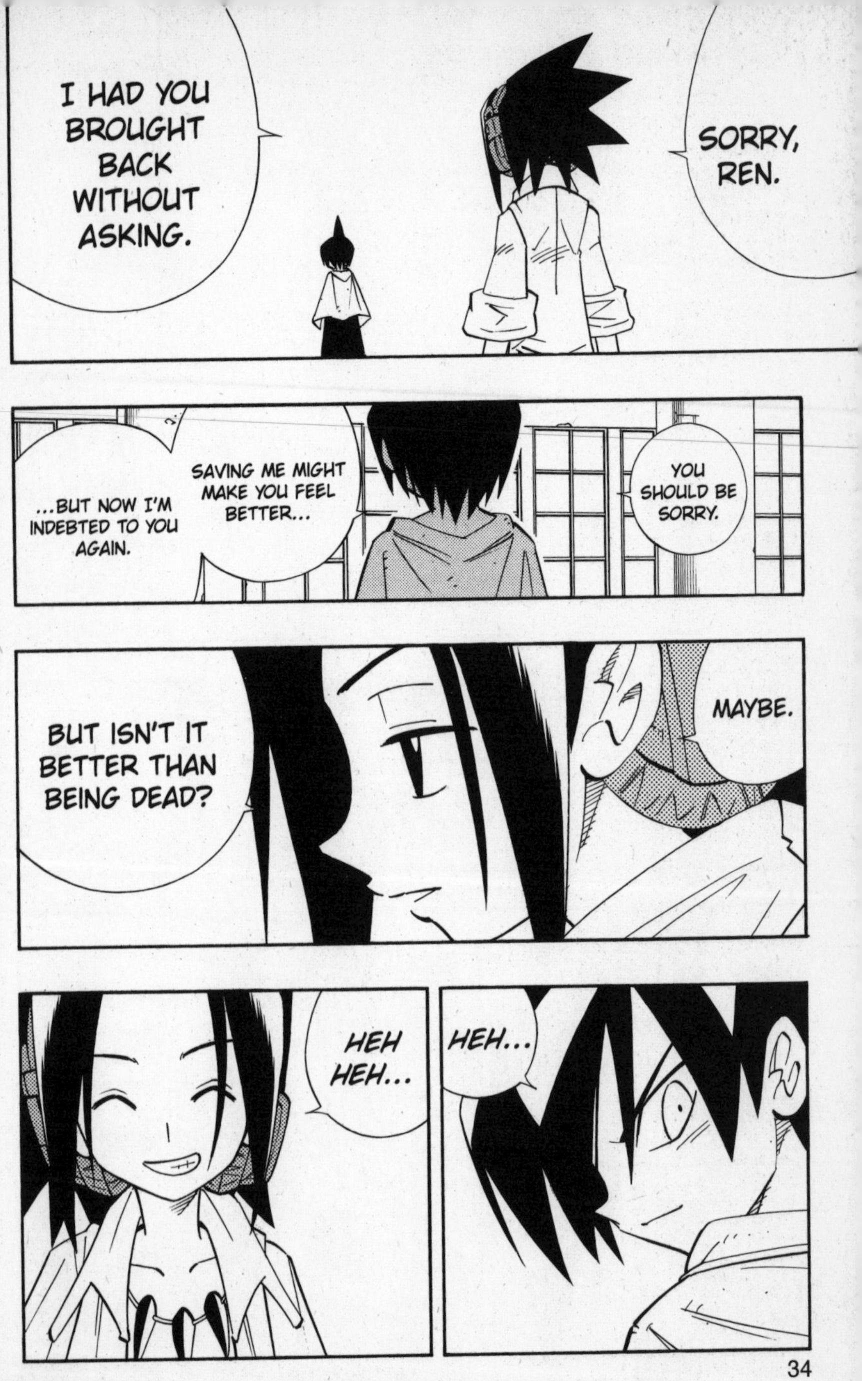
SORRY, REN.
I HAD YOU BROUGHT BACK WITHOUT ASKING.
YOU SHOULD BE SORRY.
SAVING ME MIGHT MAKE YOU FEEL BETTER...
...BUT NOW I'M INDEBTED TO YOU AGAIN.
MAYBE.
BUT ISN'T IT BETTER THAN BEING DEAD?
HEH...
HEH HEH...

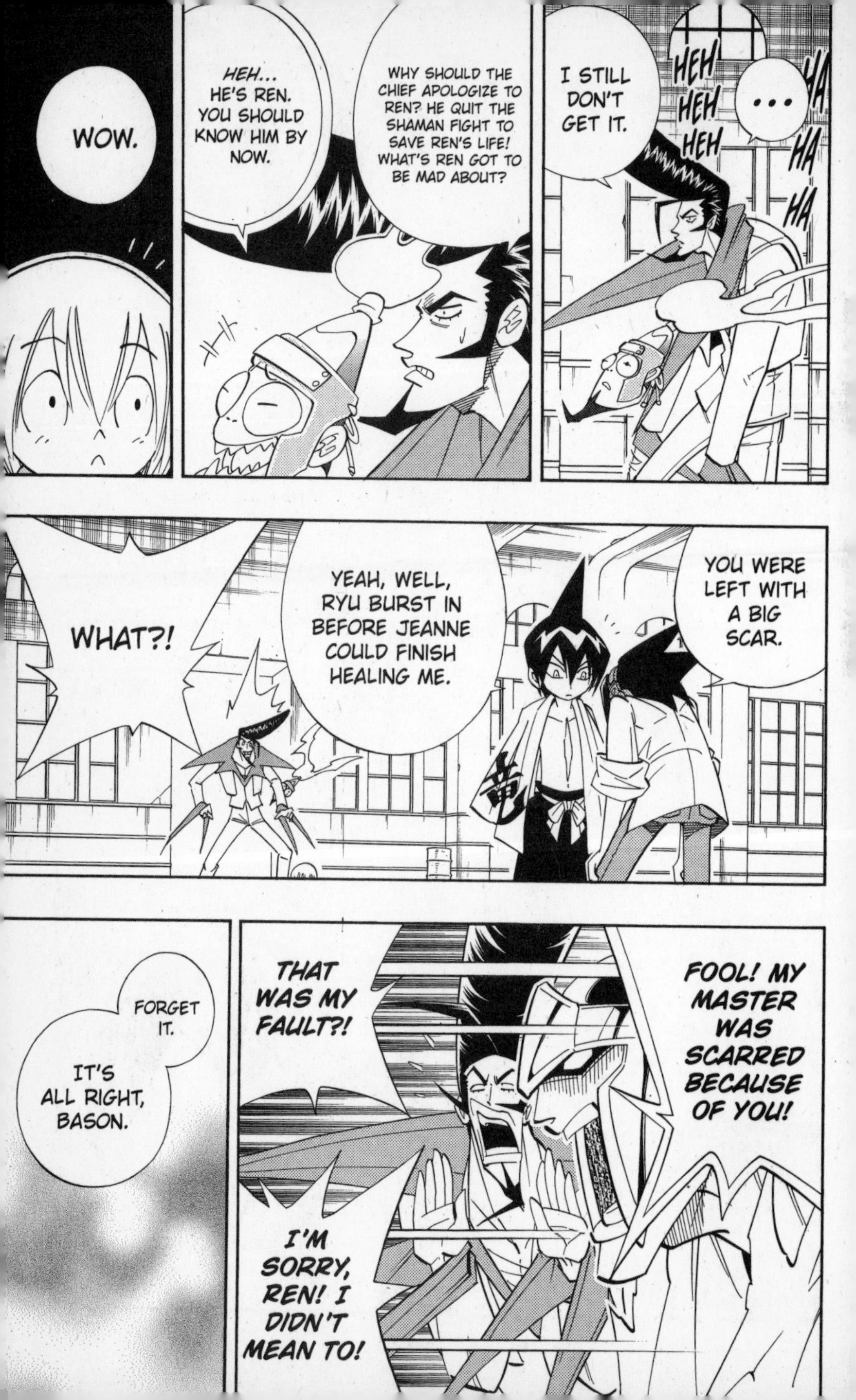
HA HA HA HA
...
HEH HEH HEH
I STILL DON'T GET IT.
WHY SHOULD THE CHIEF APOLOGIZE TO REN? HE QUIT THE SHAMAN FIGHT TO SAVE REN'S LIFE! WHAT'S REN GOT TO BE MAD ABOUT?
HEH... HE'S REN. YOU SHOULD KNOW HIM BY NOW.
WOW.
YOU WERE LEFT WITH A BIG SCAR.
YEAH, WELL, RYU BURST IN BEFORE JEANNE COULD FINISH HEALING ME.
WHAT?!
FOOL! MY MASTER WAS SCARRED BECAUSE OF YOU!
THAT WAS MY FAULT?!
I'M SORRY, REN! I DIDN'T MEAN TO!
FORGET IT.
IT'S ALL RIGHT, BASON.

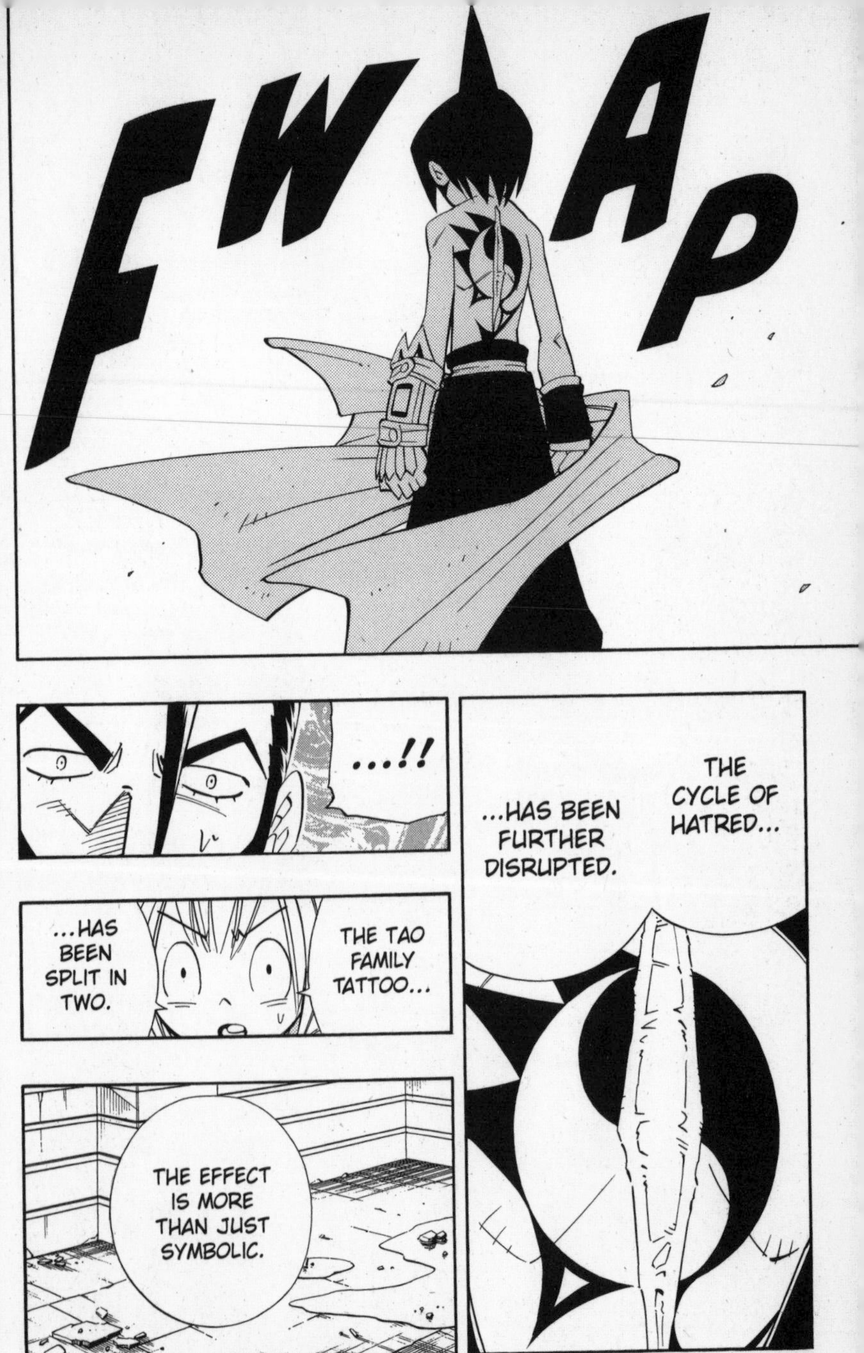
FWAP
THE CYCLE OF HATRED...
...HAS BEEN FURTHER DISRUPTED.
...!!
THE TAO FAMILY TATTOO...
...HAS BEEN SPLIT IN TWO.
THE EFFECT IS MORE THAN JUST SYMBOLIC.

READ THIS WAY

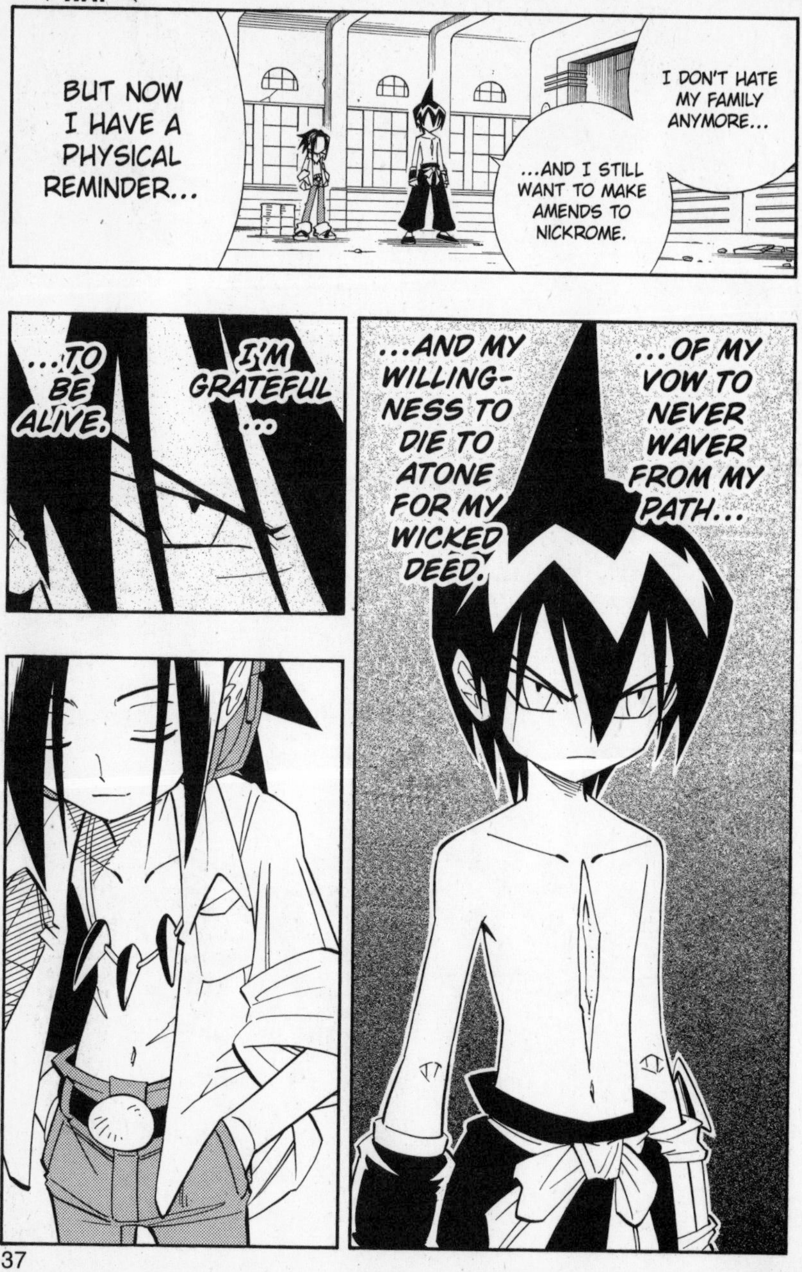

I DON'T HATE MY FAMILY ANYMORE...
...AND I STILL WANT TO MAKE AMENDS TO NICKROME.
BUT NOW I HAVE A PHYSICAL REMINDER...
...OF MY VOW TO NEVER WAVER FROM MY PATH...
...AND MY WILLING-NESS TO DIE TO ATONE FOR MY WICKED DEED.
I'M GRATEFUL...
...TO BE ALIVE.

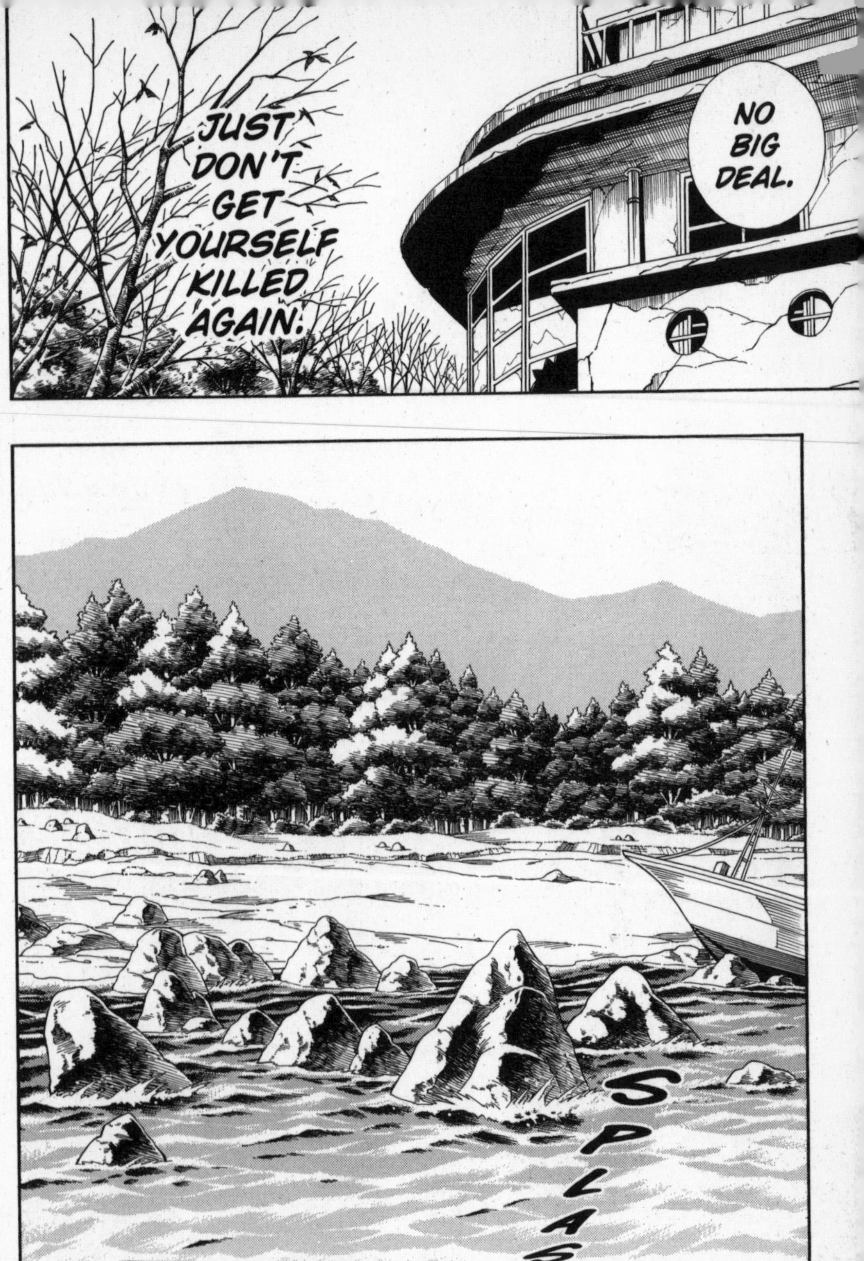
NO BIG DEAL.
JUST DON'T GET YOURSELF KILLED AGAIN.
SPLASH

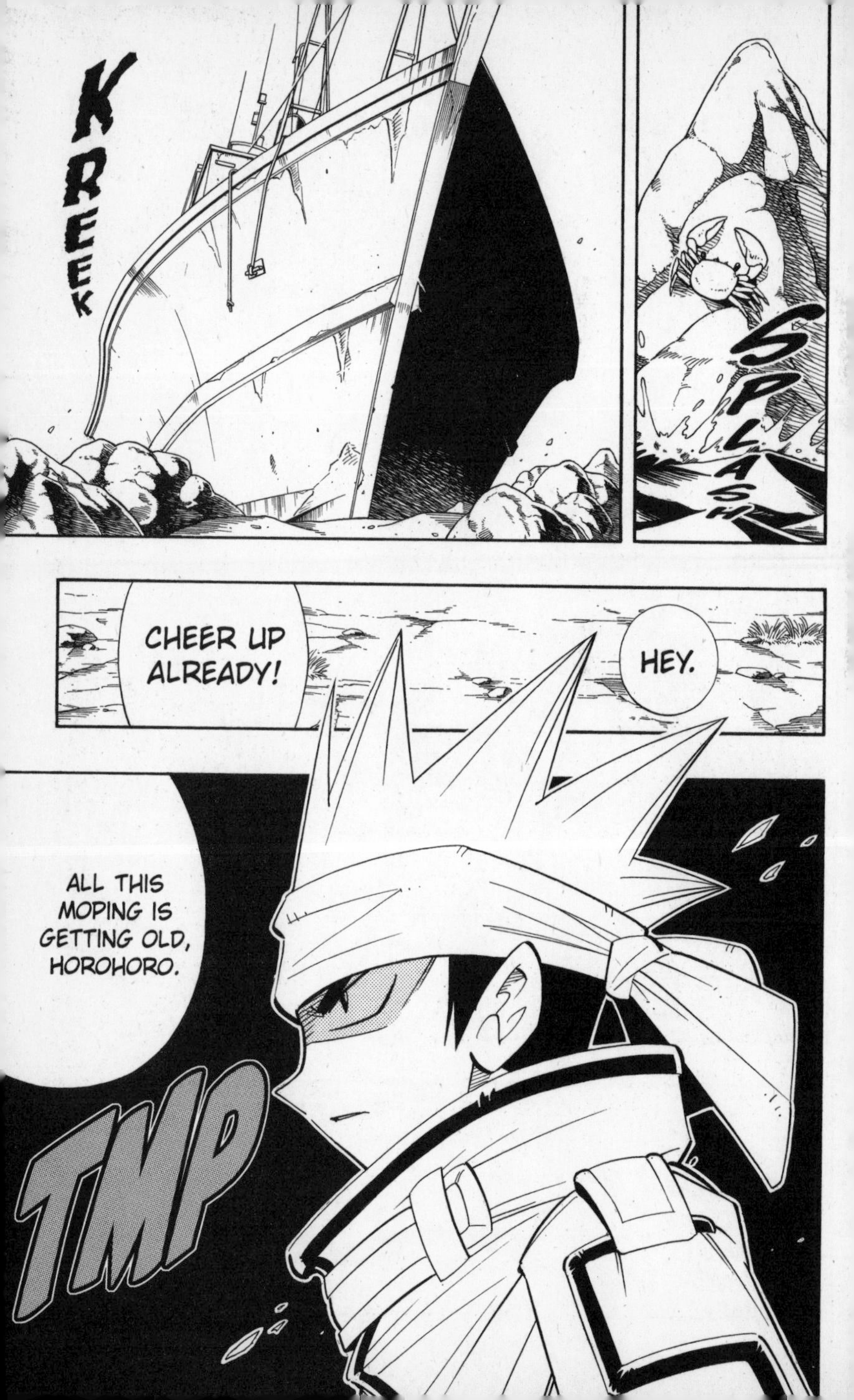
SPLASH
KREEK
HEY.
CHEER UP ALREADY!
ALL THIS MOPING IS GETTING OLD, HOROHORO.
TMP

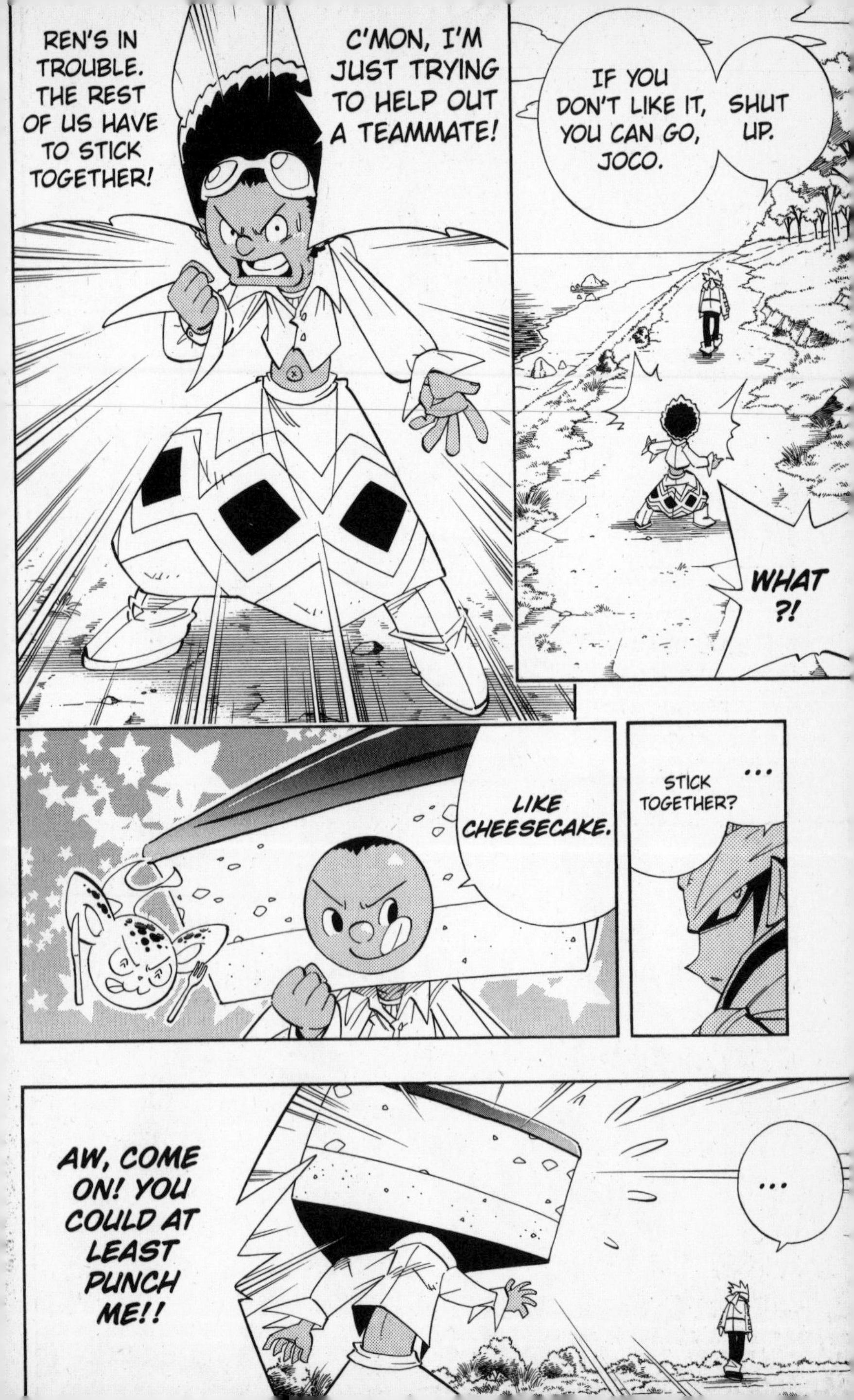
SHUT UP.
IF YOU DON'T LIKE IT, YOU CAN GO, JOCO.
WHAT?!
C'MON, I'M JUST TRYING TO HELP OUT A TEAMMATE!
REN'S IN TROUBLE. THE REST OF US HAVE TO STICK TOGETHER!
...
STICK TOGETHER?
LIKE CHEESECAKE.
...
AW, COME ON! YOU COULD AT LEAST PUNCH ME!!

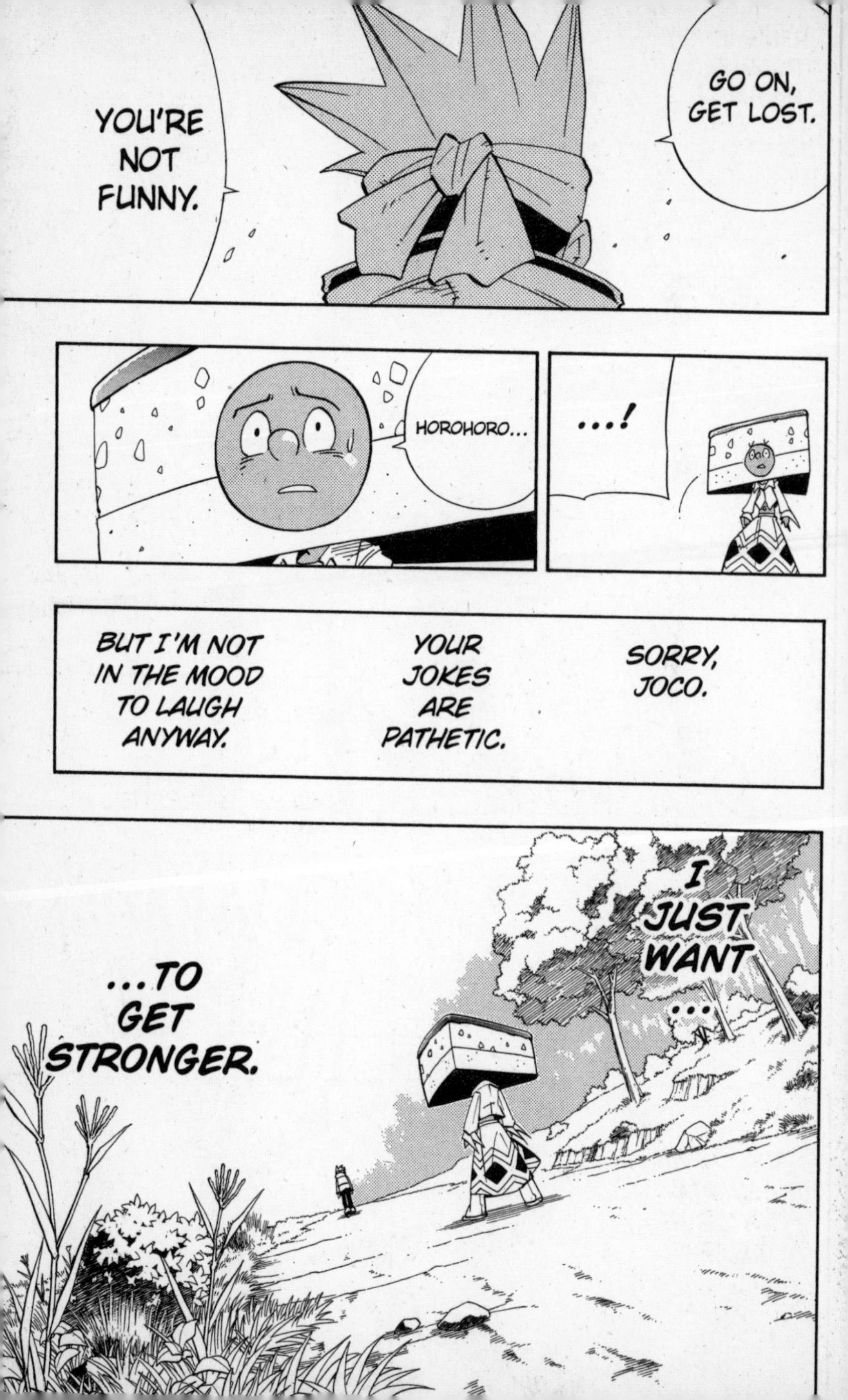
GO ON, GET LOST.
YOU'RE NOT FUNNY.
...!
HOROHORO...
SORRY, JOCO.
YOUR JOKES ARE PATHETIC.
BUT I'M NOT IN THE MOOD TO LAUGH ANYWAY.
I JUST WANT...
...TO GET STRONGER.

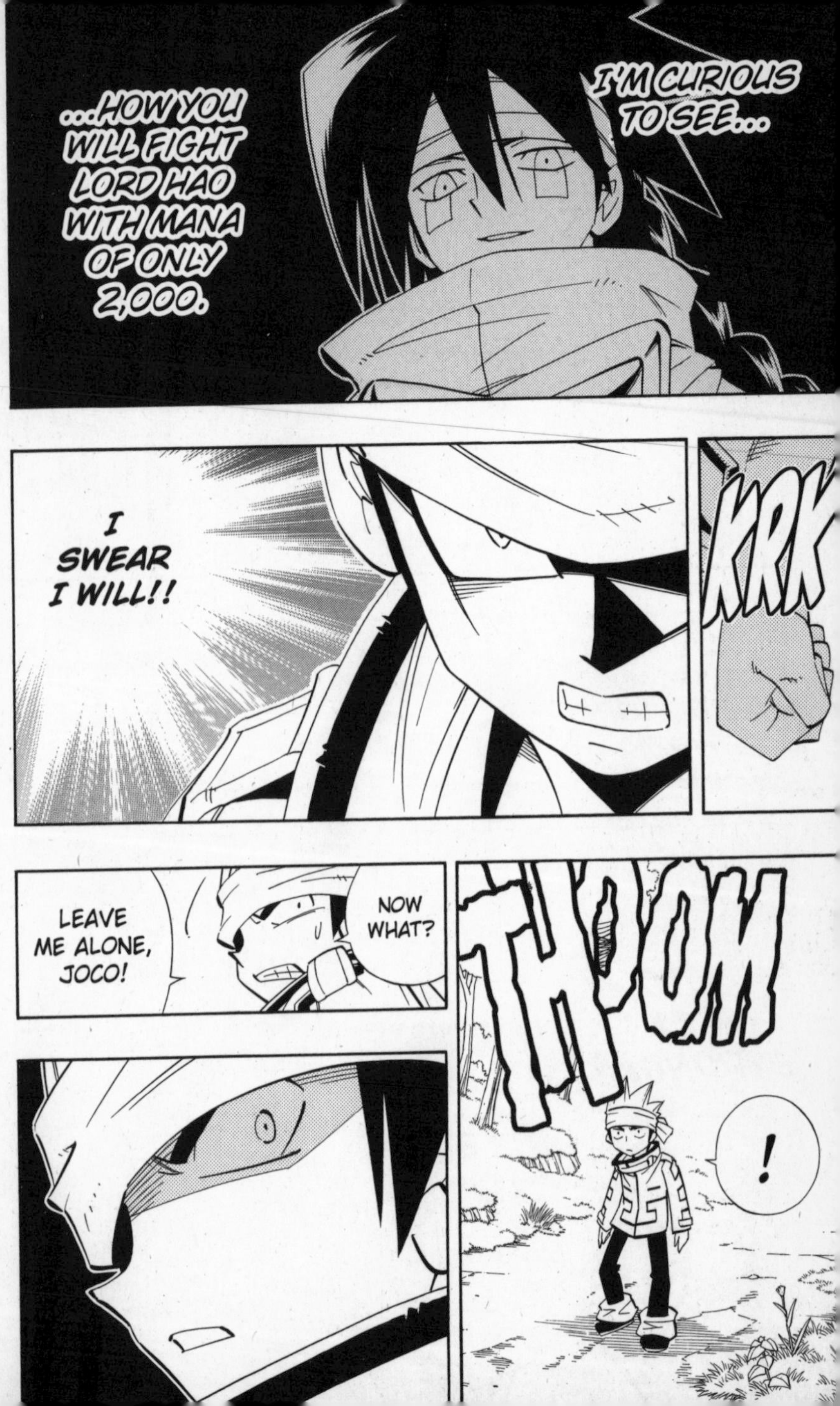
I'M CURIOUS TO SEE...
...HOW YOU WILL FIGHT LORD HAO WITH MANA OF ONLY 2,000.
KRK
I SWEAR I WILL!!
THPOM
!
NOW WHAT?
LEAVE ME ALONE, JOCO!

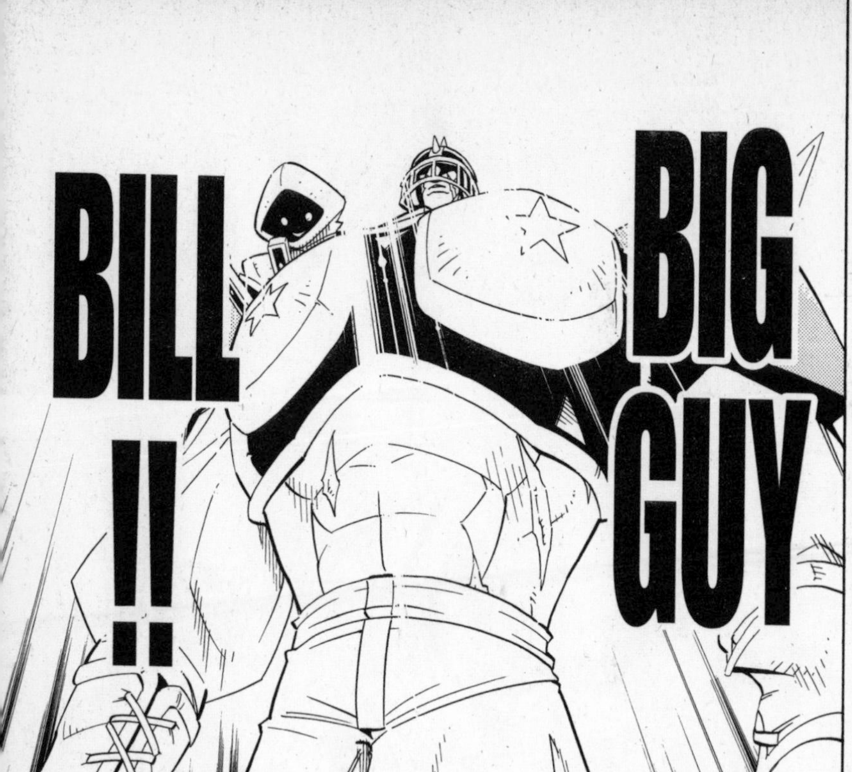
BIG GUY
BILL!!

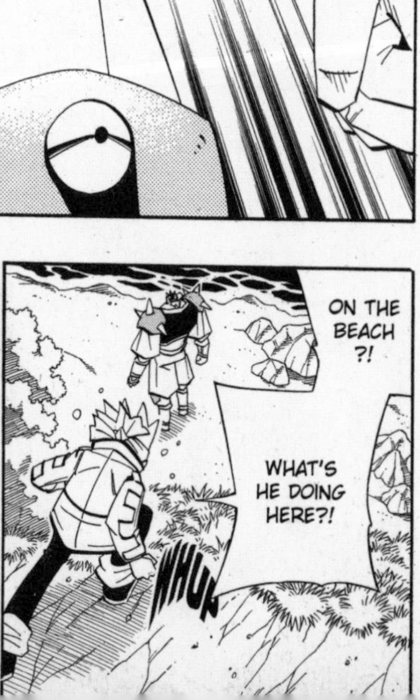
ON THE BEACH?!
WHAT'S HE DOING HERE?!
WHUP

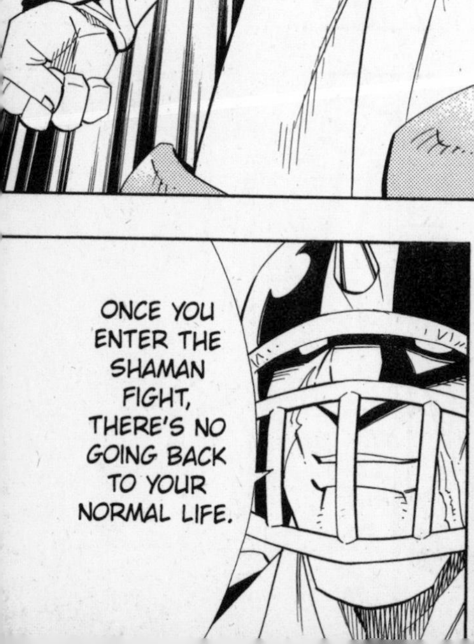
ONCE YOU ENTER THE SHAMAN FIGHT, THERE'S NO GOING BACK TO YOUR NORMAL LIFE.

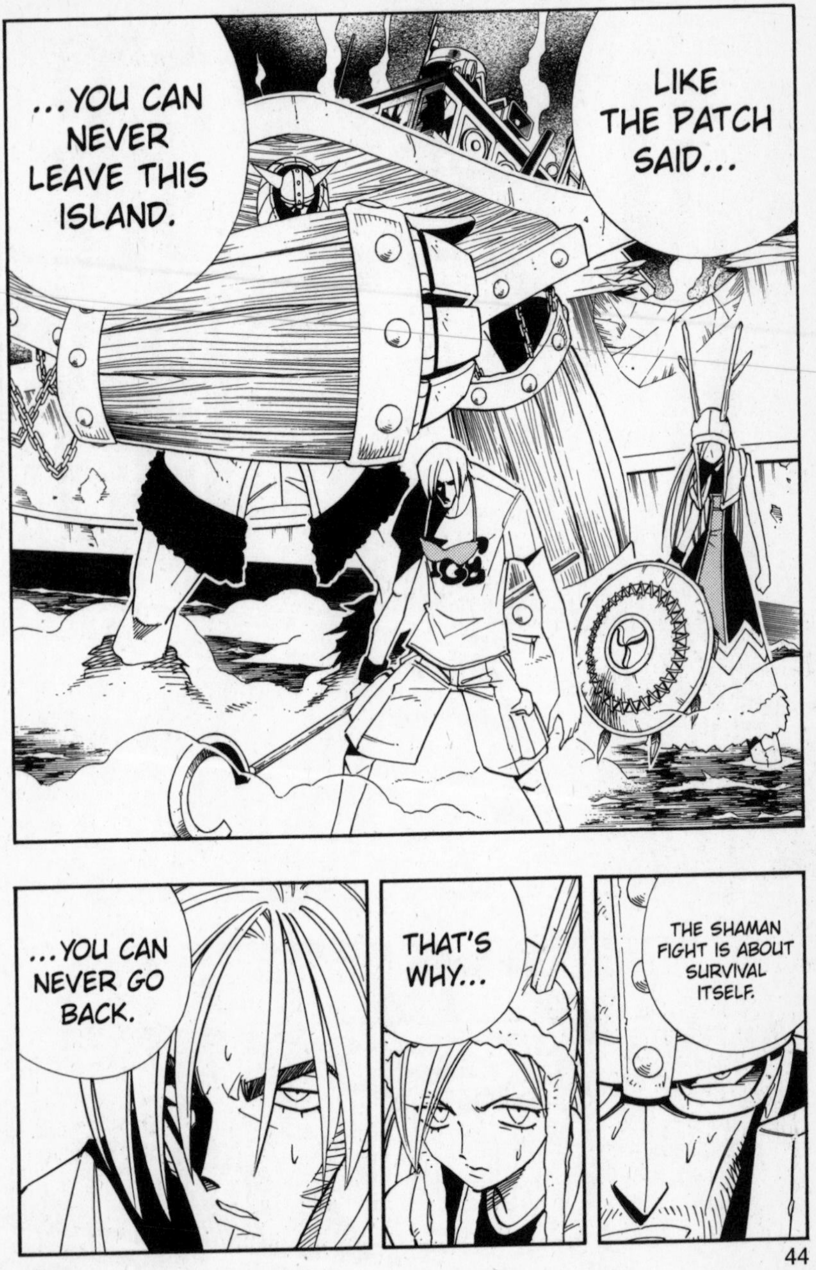
LIKE THE PATCH SAID...
...YOU CAN NEVER LEAVE THIS ISLAND.
THE SHAMAN FIGHT IS ABOUT SURVIVAL ITSELF.
THAT'S WHY...
...YOU CAN NEVER GO BACK.

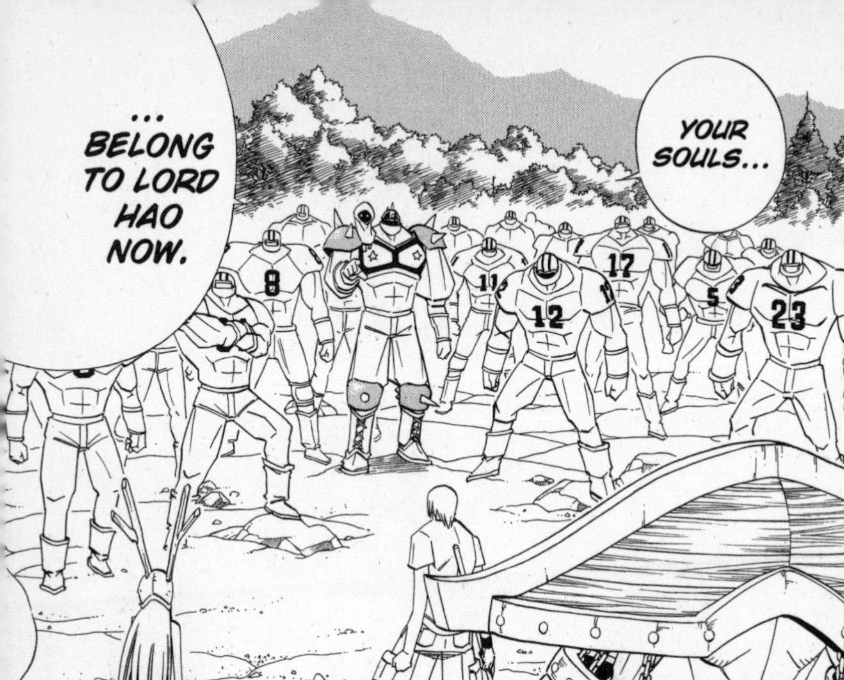
YOUR SOULS...
... BELONG TO LORD HAO NOW.

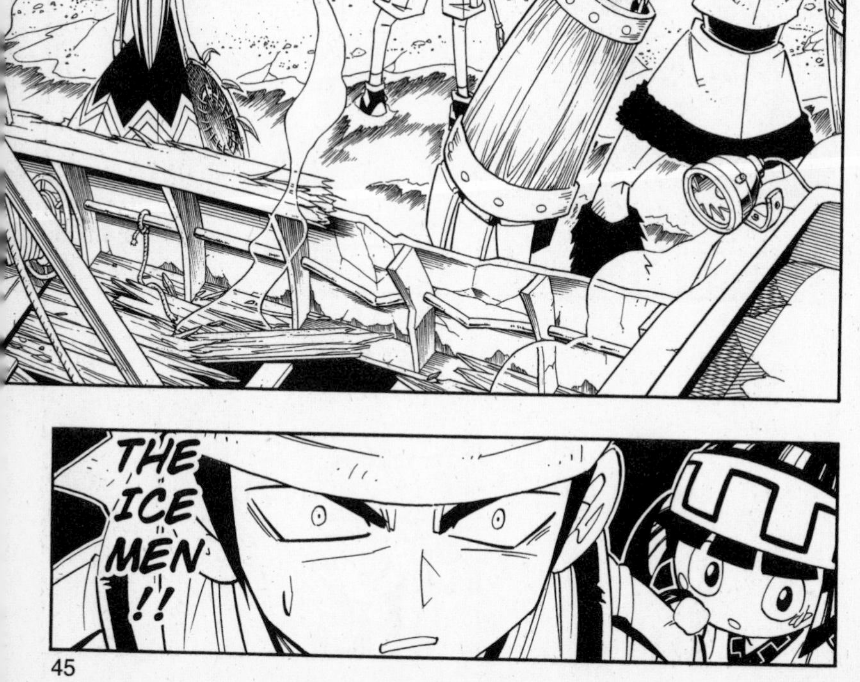
THE ICE MEN!!

SHAMAN KING CHARACTER FILE No.111

チームメイツ

TEAMMATE

2001
(JAN)

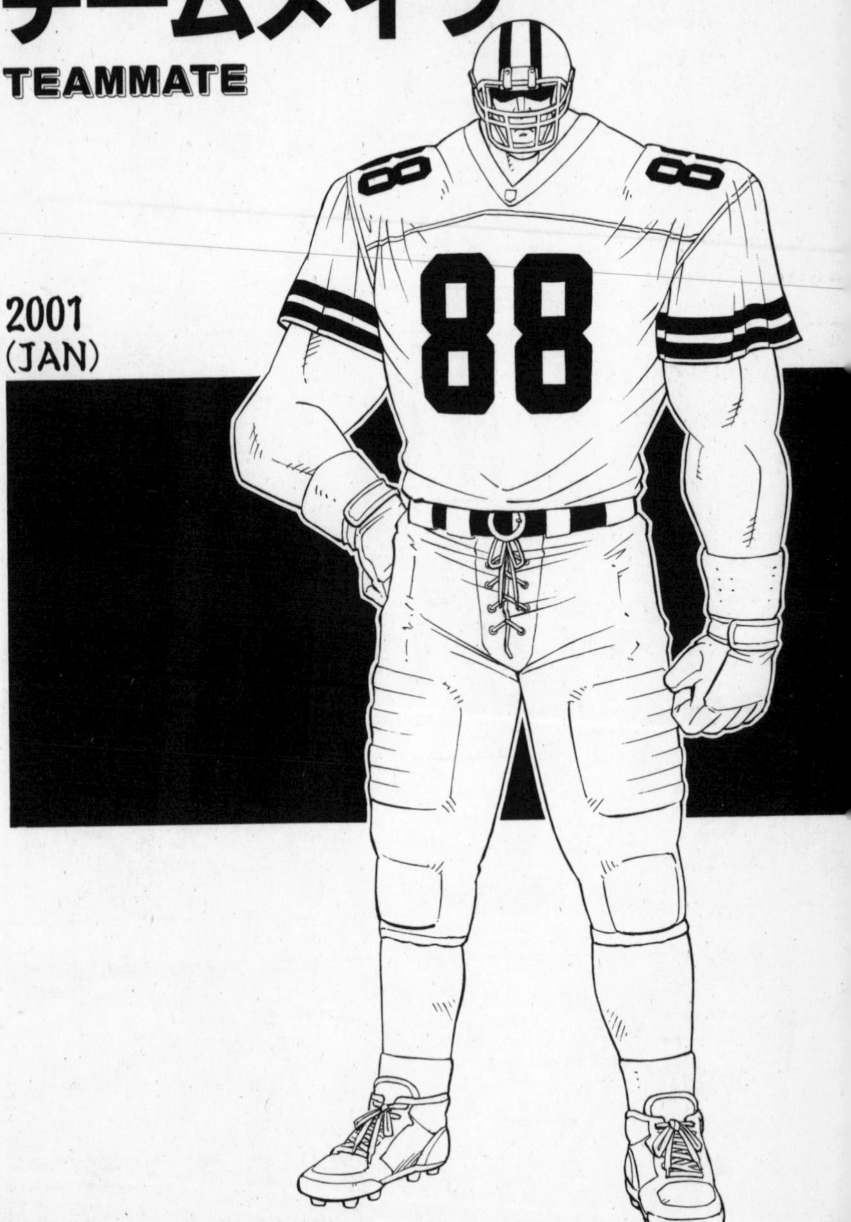

88
88
88

Reincarnation 182: Epilogue III: Fool

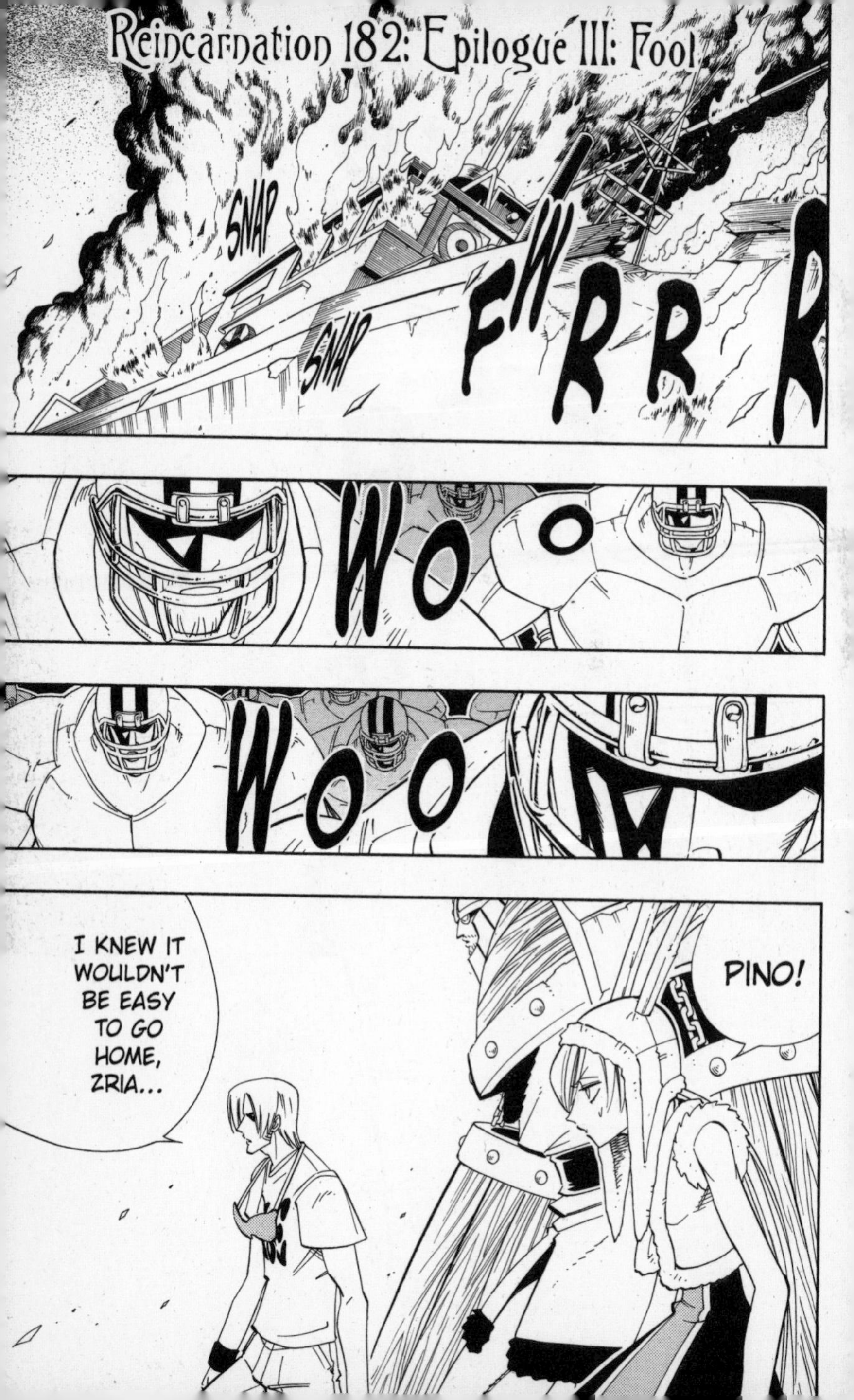
SNAP
SNAP
FWRRR
WOO
WOO
PINO!
I KNEW IT WOULDN'T BE EASY TO GO HOME, ZRIA...

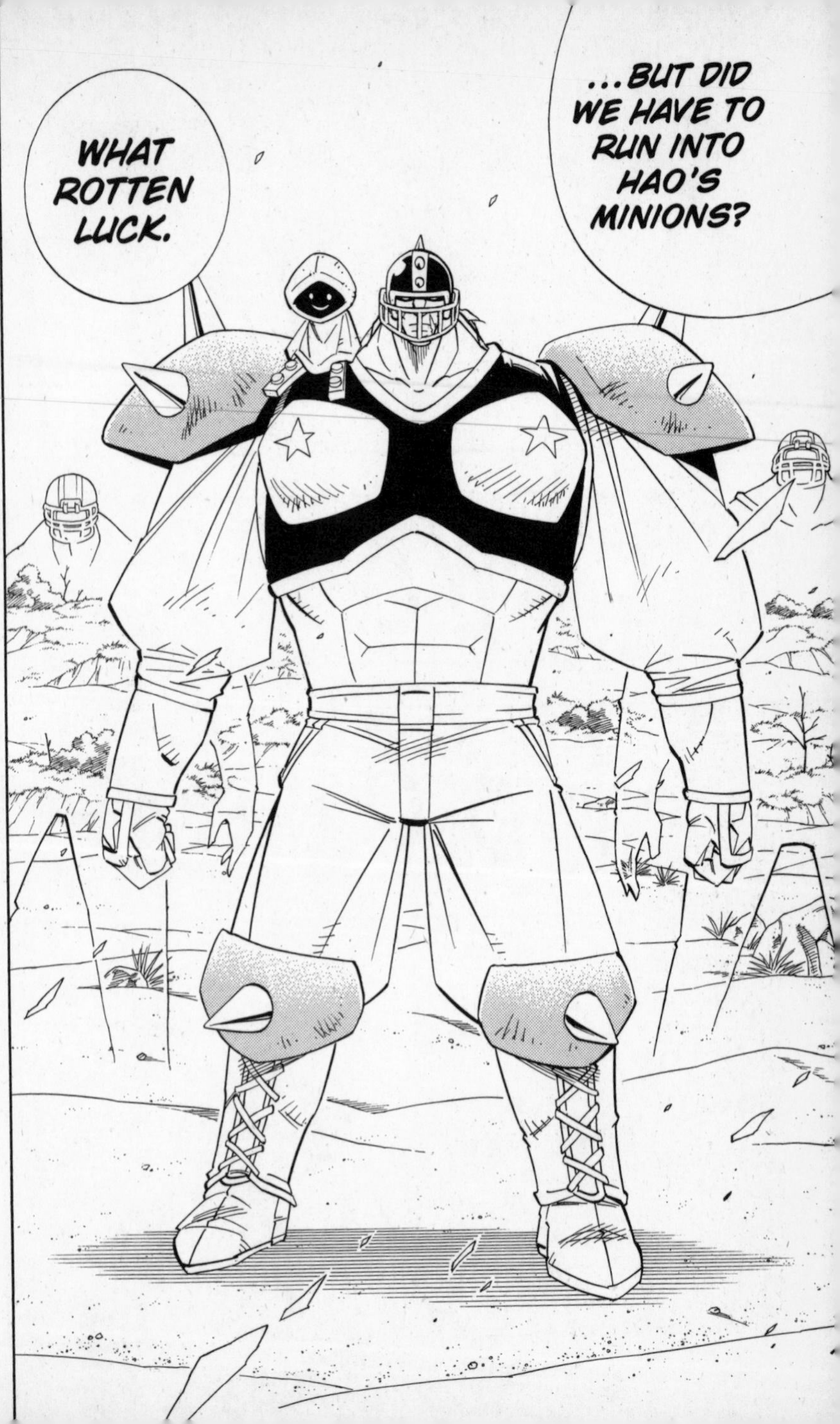
...BUT DID WE HAVE TO RUN INTO HAO'S MINIONS?
WHAT ROTTEN LUCK.

Reincarnation 182: Epilogue III: Fool

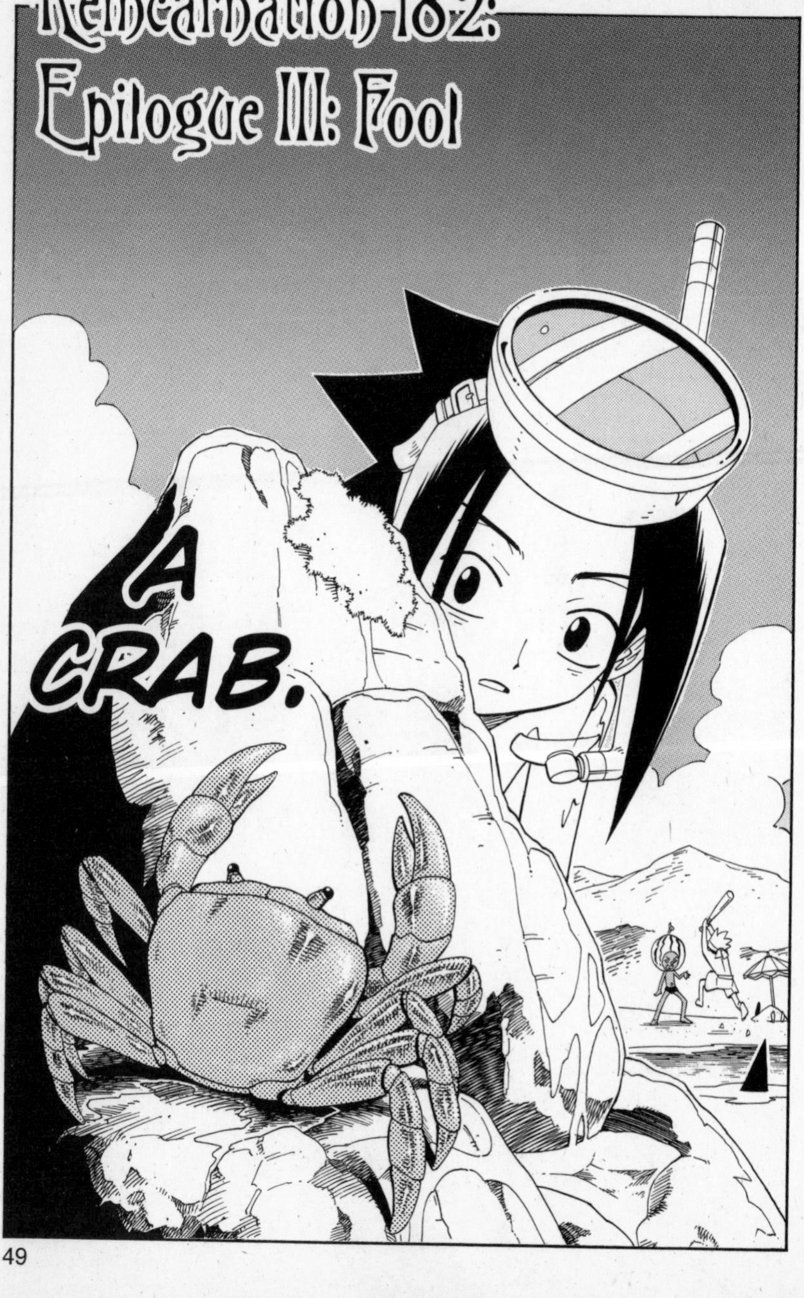

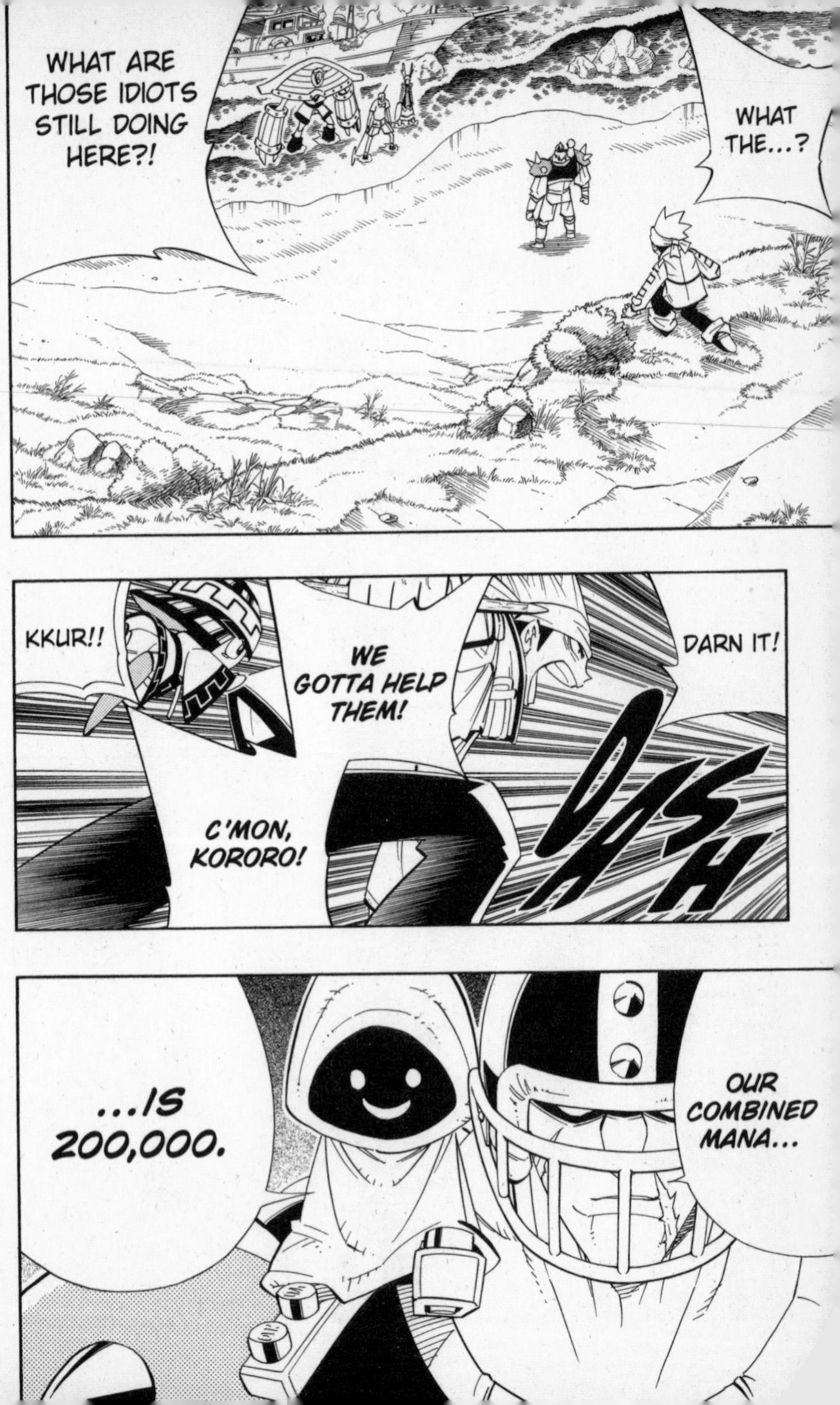
WHAT THE...?
WHAT ARE THOSE IDIOTS STILL DOING HERE?!
DARN IT!
WE GOTTA HELP THEM!
KKUR!!
DASH
C'MON, KORORO!
OUR COMBINED MANA...
...IS 200,000.

READ THIS WAY

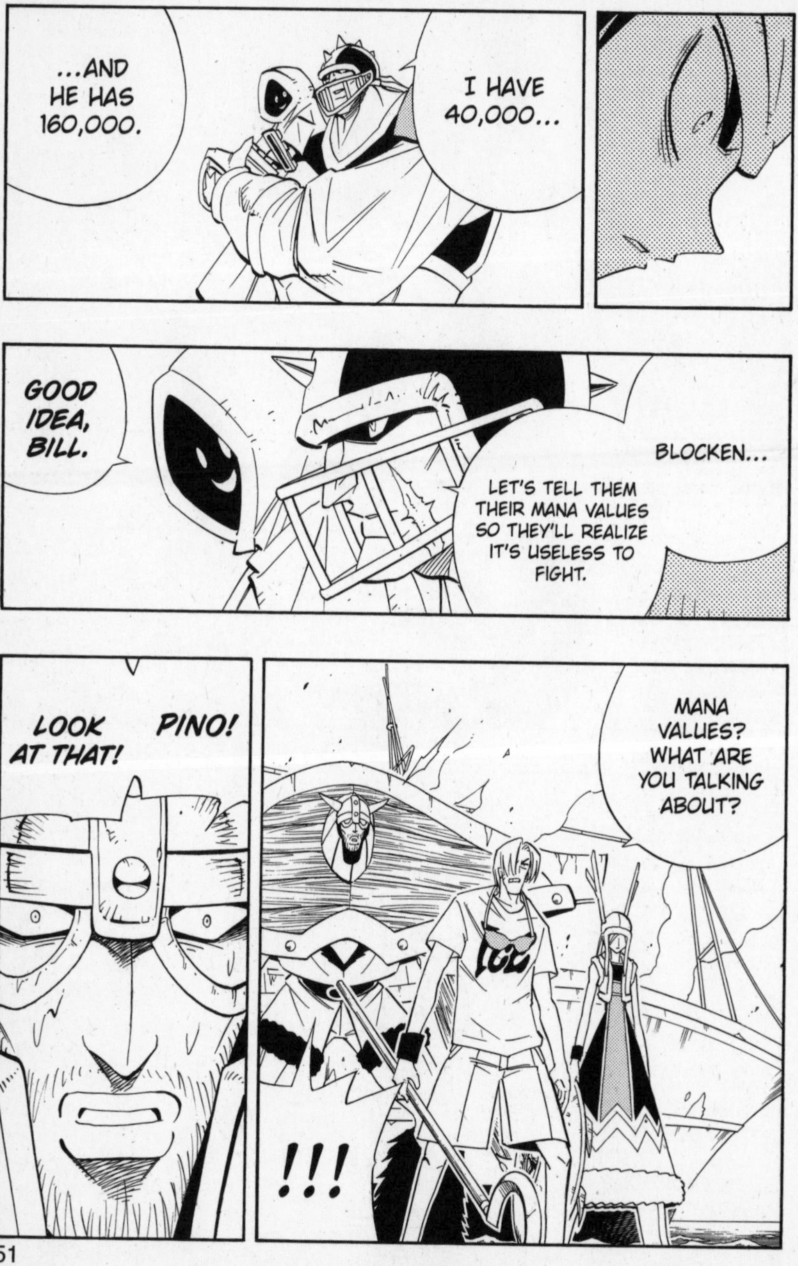
I HAVE 40,000...
...AND HE HAS 160,000.
BLOCKEN...
LET'S TELL THEM THEIR MANA VALUES SO THEY'LL REALIZE IT'S USELESS TO FIGHT.
GOOD IDEA, BILL.
MANA VALUES? WHAT ARE YOU TALKING ABOUT?
!!!
PINO!
LOOK AT THAT!

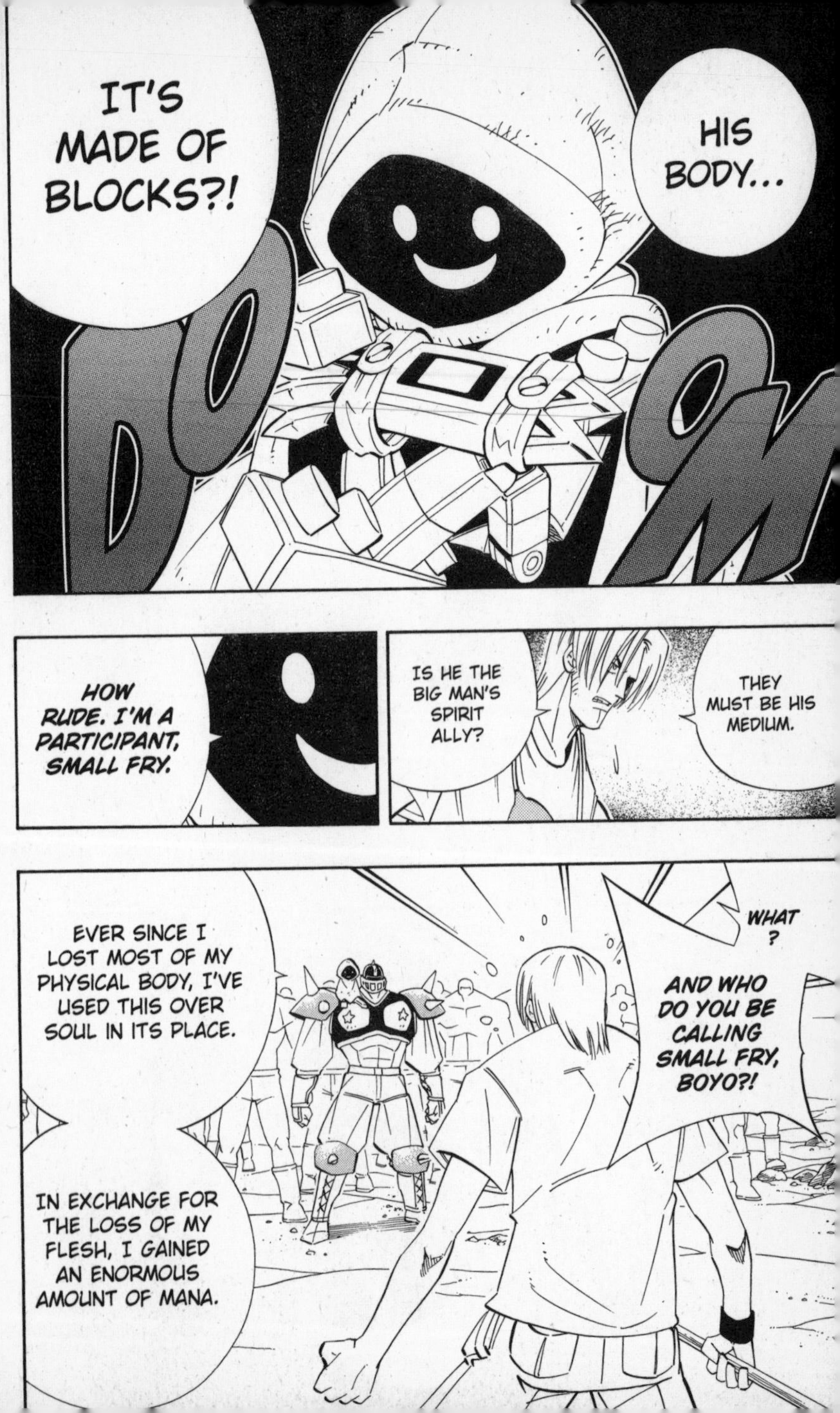
HIS BODY...
IT'S MADE OF BLOCKS?!
DOOM
IS HE THE BIG MAN'S SPIRIT ALLY?
THEY MUST BE HIS MEDIUM.
HOW RUDE. I'M A PARTICIPANT, SMALL FRY.
WHAT?
AND WHO DO YOU BE CALLING SMALL FRY, BOYO?!
EVER SINCE I LOST MOST OF MY PHYSICAL BODY, I'VE USED THIS OVER SOUL IN ITS PLACE.
IN EXCHANGE FOR THE LOSS OF MY FLESH, I GAINED AN ENORMOUS AMOUNT OF MANA.

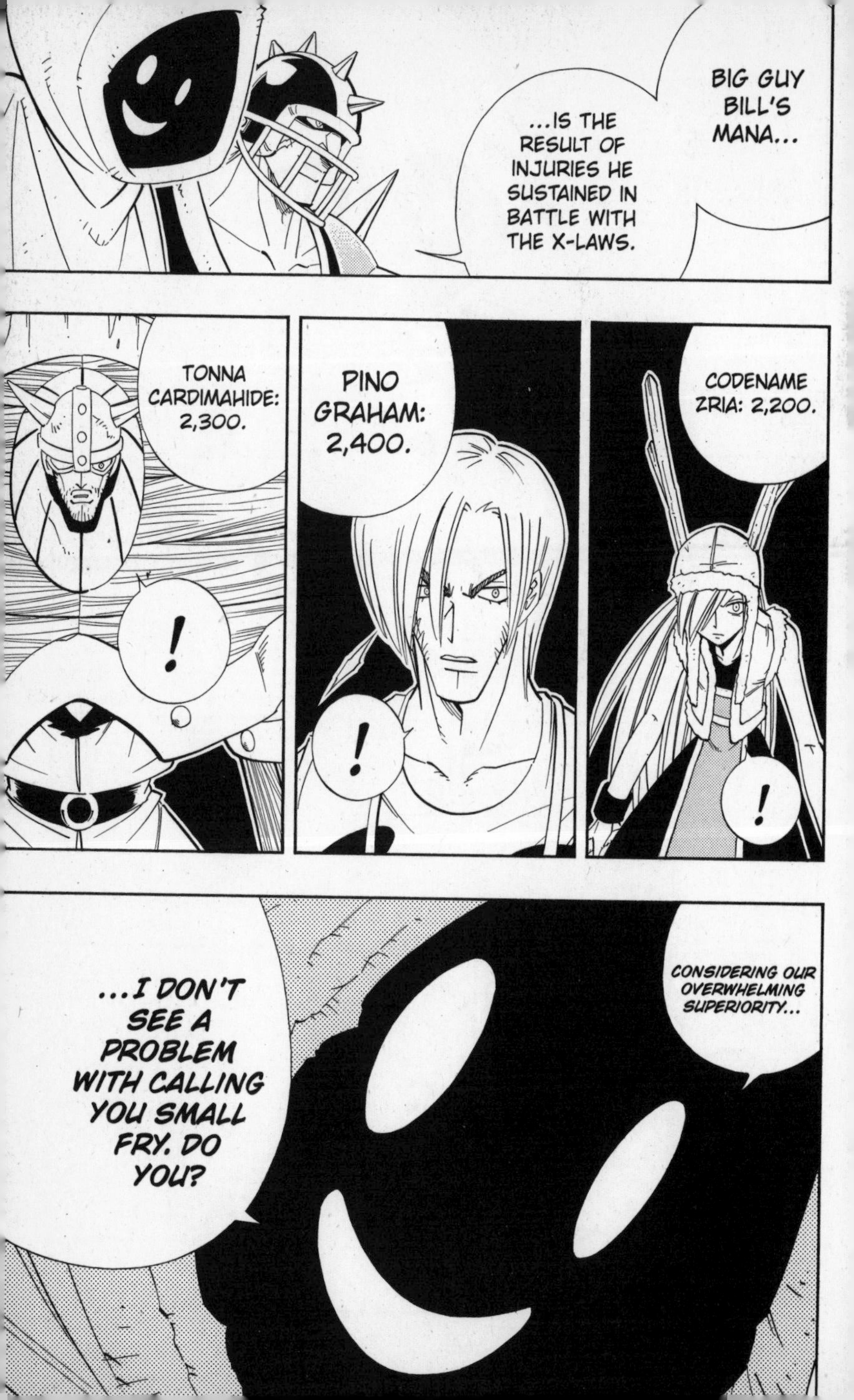
BIG GUY BILL'S MANA...
...IS THE RESULT OF INJURIES HE SUSTAINED IN BATTLE WITH THE X-LAWS.
CODENAME ZRIA: 2,200.
!
PINO GRAHAM: 2,400.
!
TONNA CARDIMAHIDE: 2,300.
!
CONSIDERING OUR OVERWHELMING SUPERIORITY...
...I DON'T SEE A PROBLEM WITH CALLING YOU SMALL FRY. DO YOU?

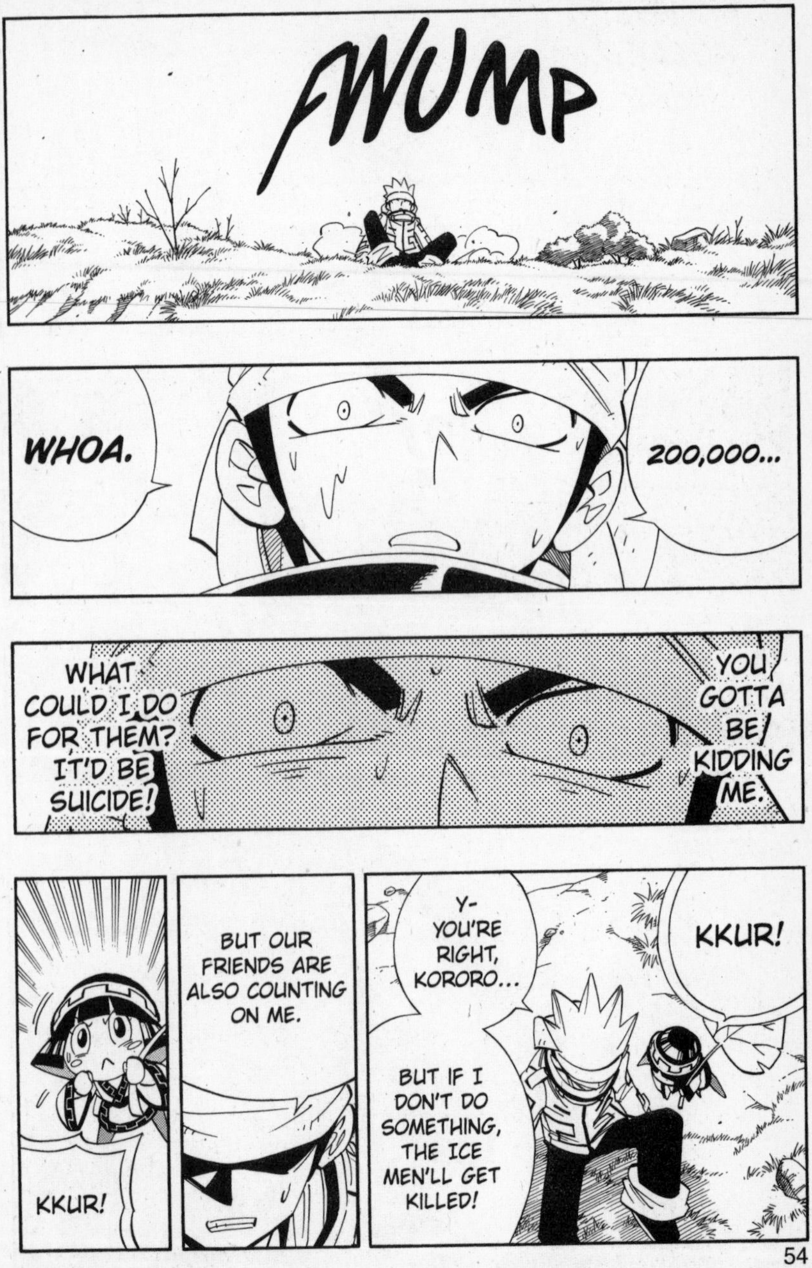
FWUMP
200,000...
WHOA.
YOU GOTTA BE KIDDING ME.
WHAT COULD I DO FOR THEM? IT'D BE SUICIDE!
KKUR!
Y- YOU'RE RIGHT, KORORO...
BUT IF I DON'T DO SOMETHING, THE ICE MEN'LL GET KILLED!
BUT OUR FRIENDS ARE ALSO COUNTING ON ME.
KKUR!

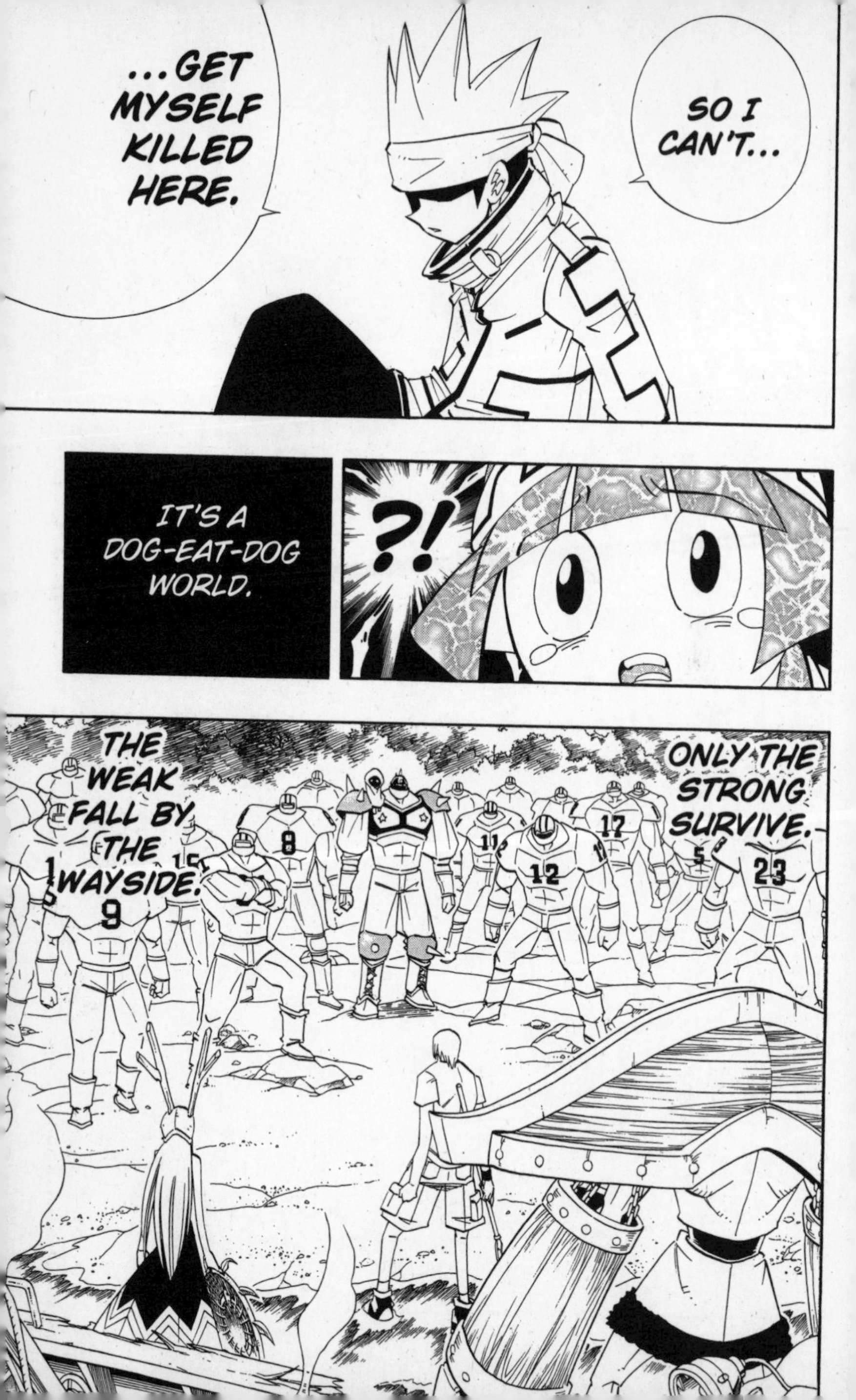
SO I CAN'T...
...GET MYSELF KILLED HERE.
?!
IT'S A DOG-EAT-DOG WORLD.
ONLY THE STRONG SURVIVE.
THE WEAK FALL BY THE WAYSIDE.

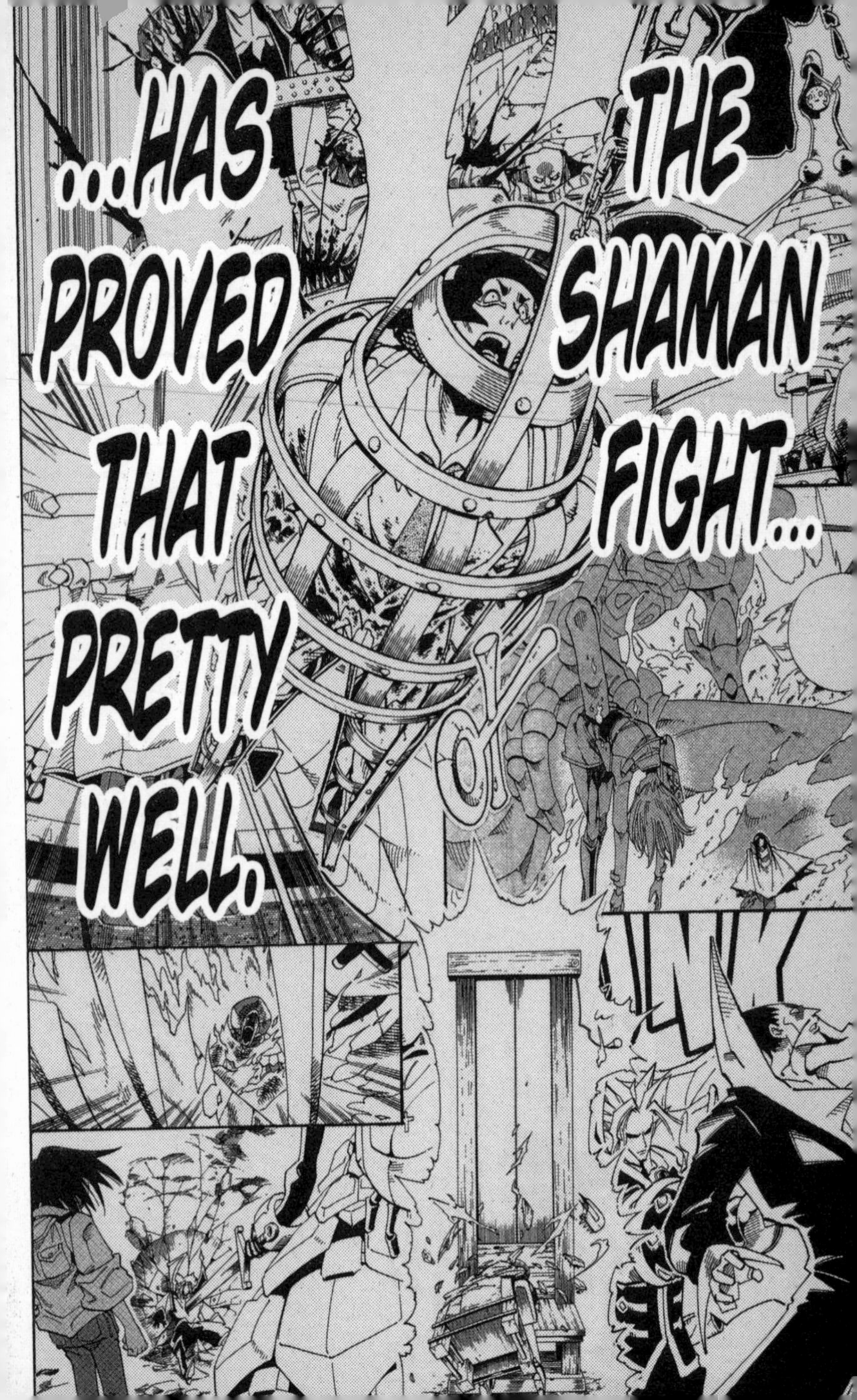
THE SHAMAN FIGHT...
...HAS PROVED THAT PRETTY WELL.

SORRY, GUYS.

NO WAY AM I GONNA...

...CHARGE IN AND GET KILLED FOR NOTHING. I'M NOT THAT STUPID.

WHUP

...ICE MEN.

SORRY...

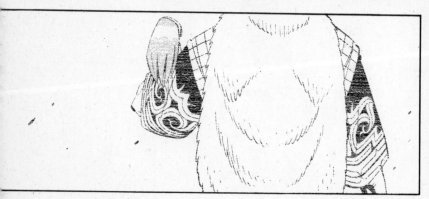

SORRY, DAD.

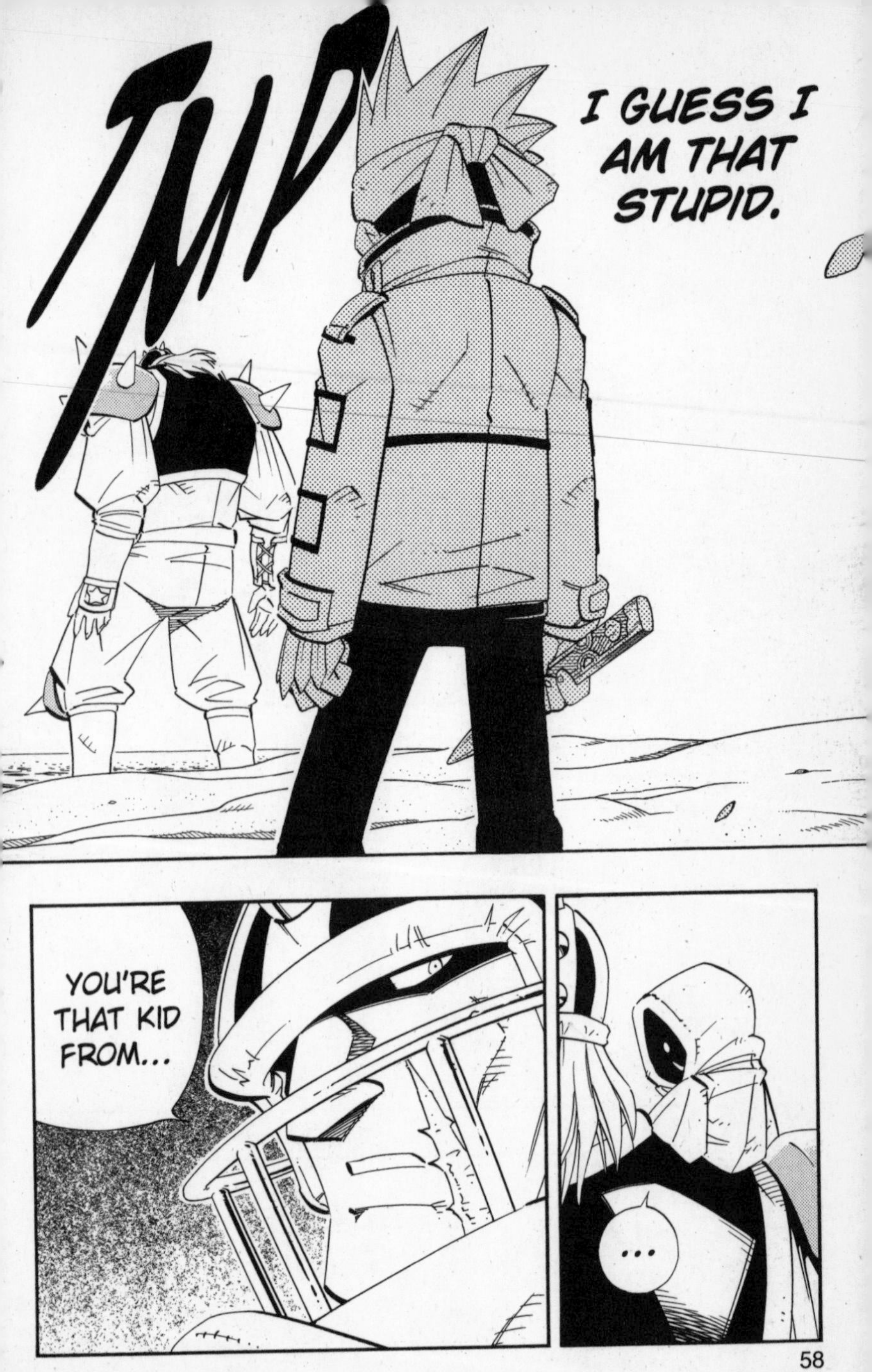
I GUESS I AM THAT STUPID.
TMP
...
YOU'RE THAT KID FROM...

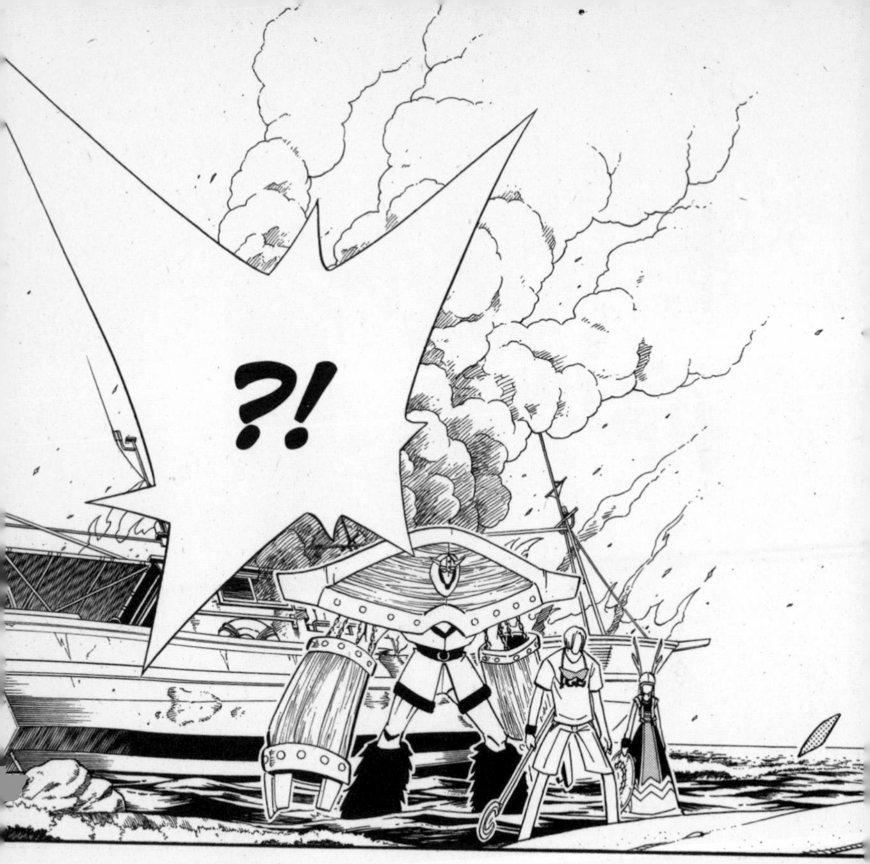
?!

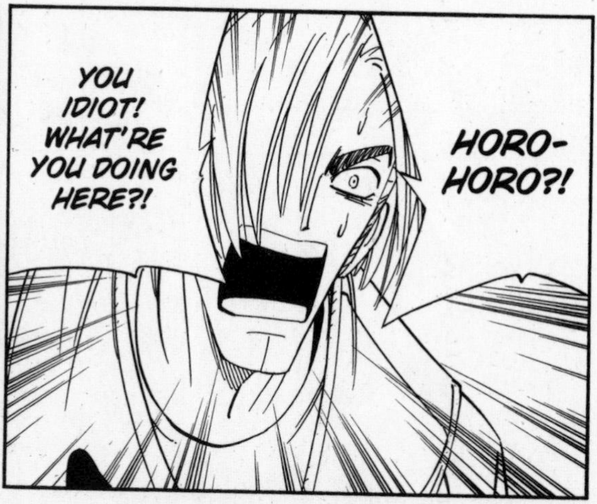
HORO-HORO?!
YOU IDIOT! WHAT'RE YOU DOING HERE?!

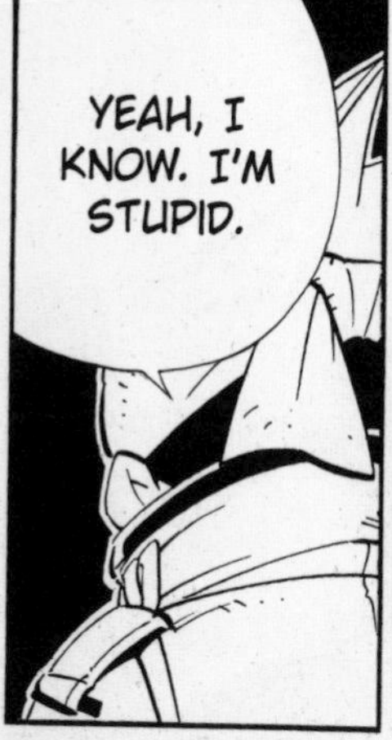
YEAH, I KNOW. I'M STUPID.

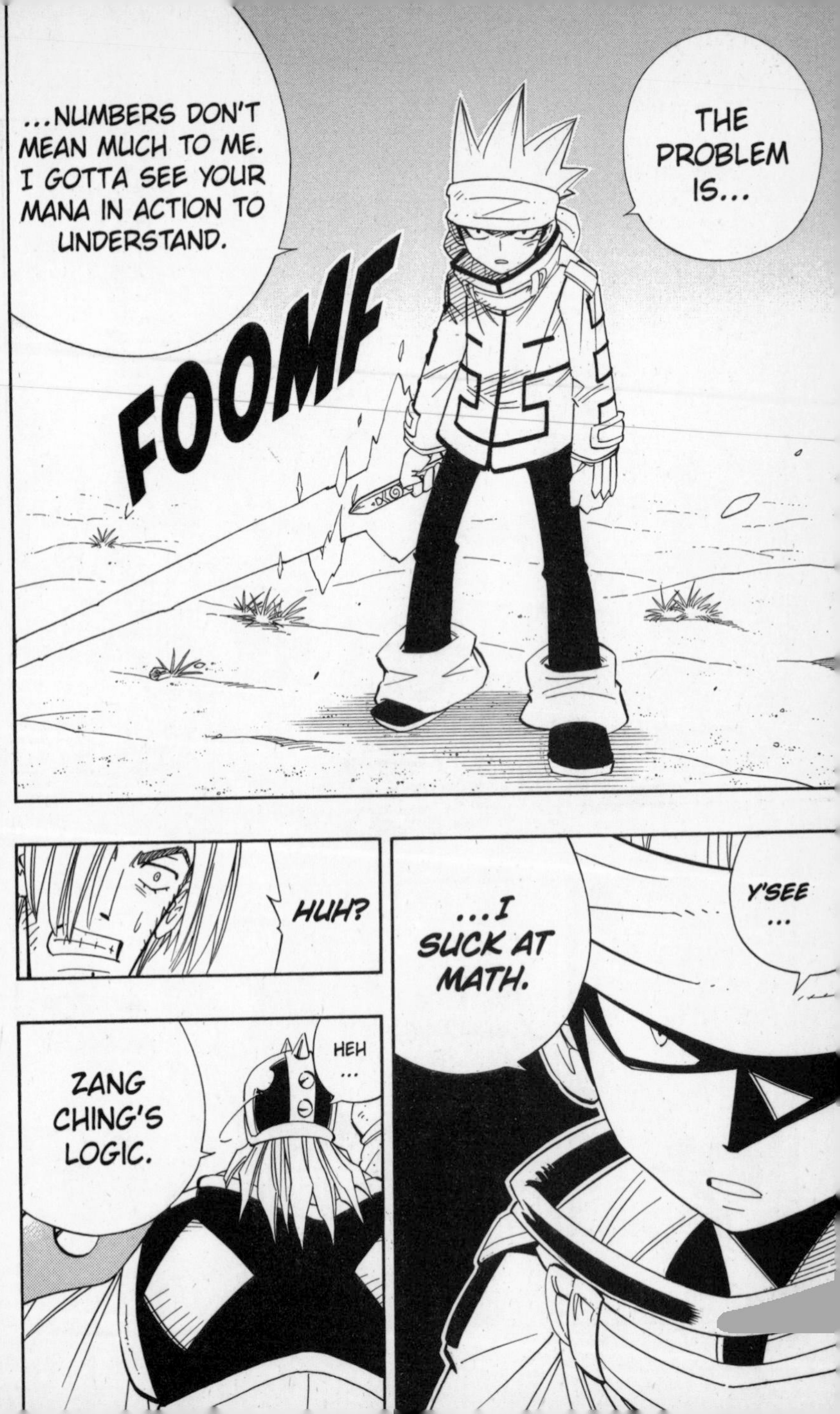
THE PROBLEM IS...
...NUMBERS DON'T MEAN MUCH TO ME. I GOTTA SEE YOUR MANA IN ACTION TO UNDERSTAND.
FOOMF
Y'SEE ...
...I SUCK AT MATH.
HUH?
HEH ...
ZANG CHING'S LOGIC.

READ THIS WAY

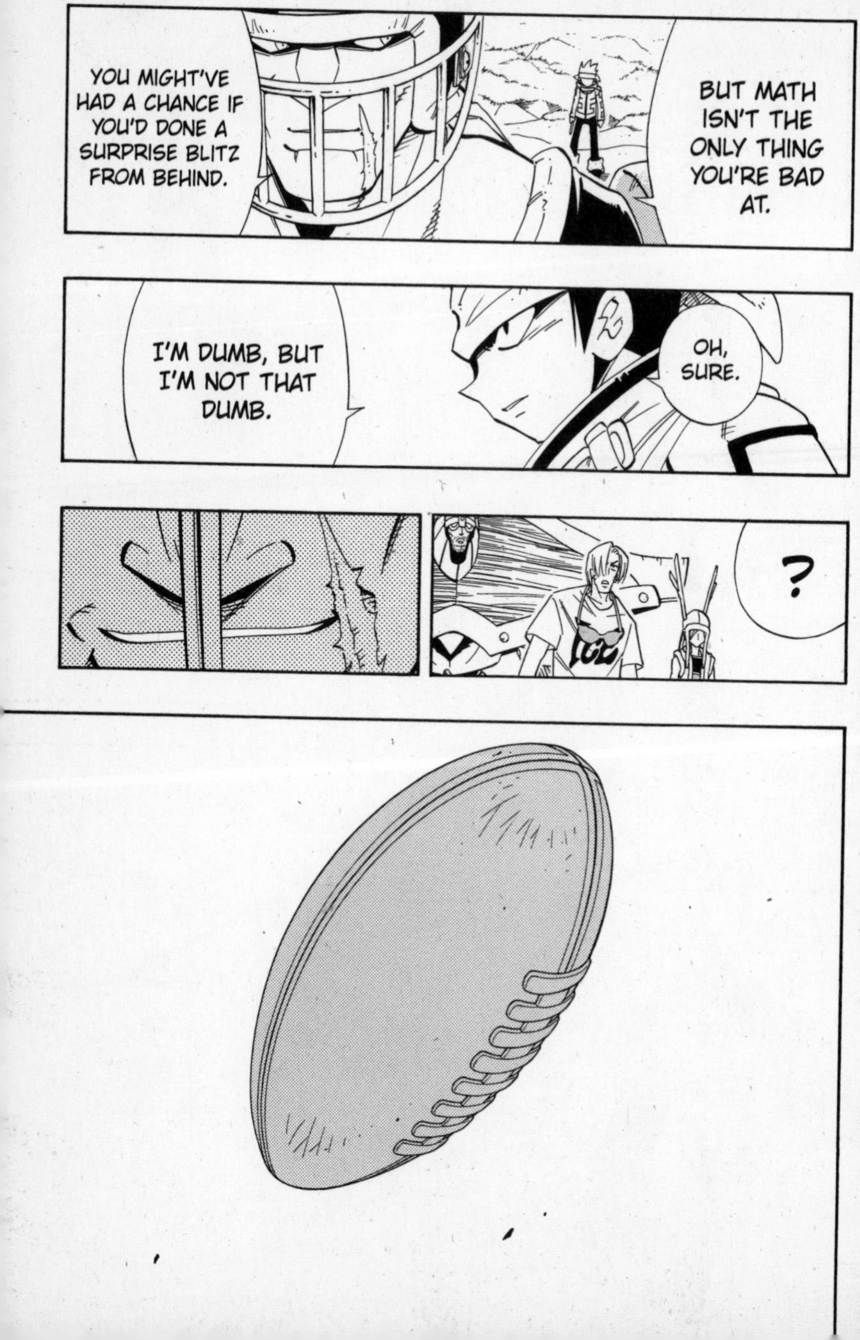

BUT MATH ISN'T THE ONLY THING YOU'RE BAD AT.
YOU MIGHT'VE HAD A CHANCE IF YOU'D DONE A SURPRISE BLITZ FROM BEHIND.
OH, SURE.
I'M DUMB, BUT I'M NOT THAT DUMB.
?

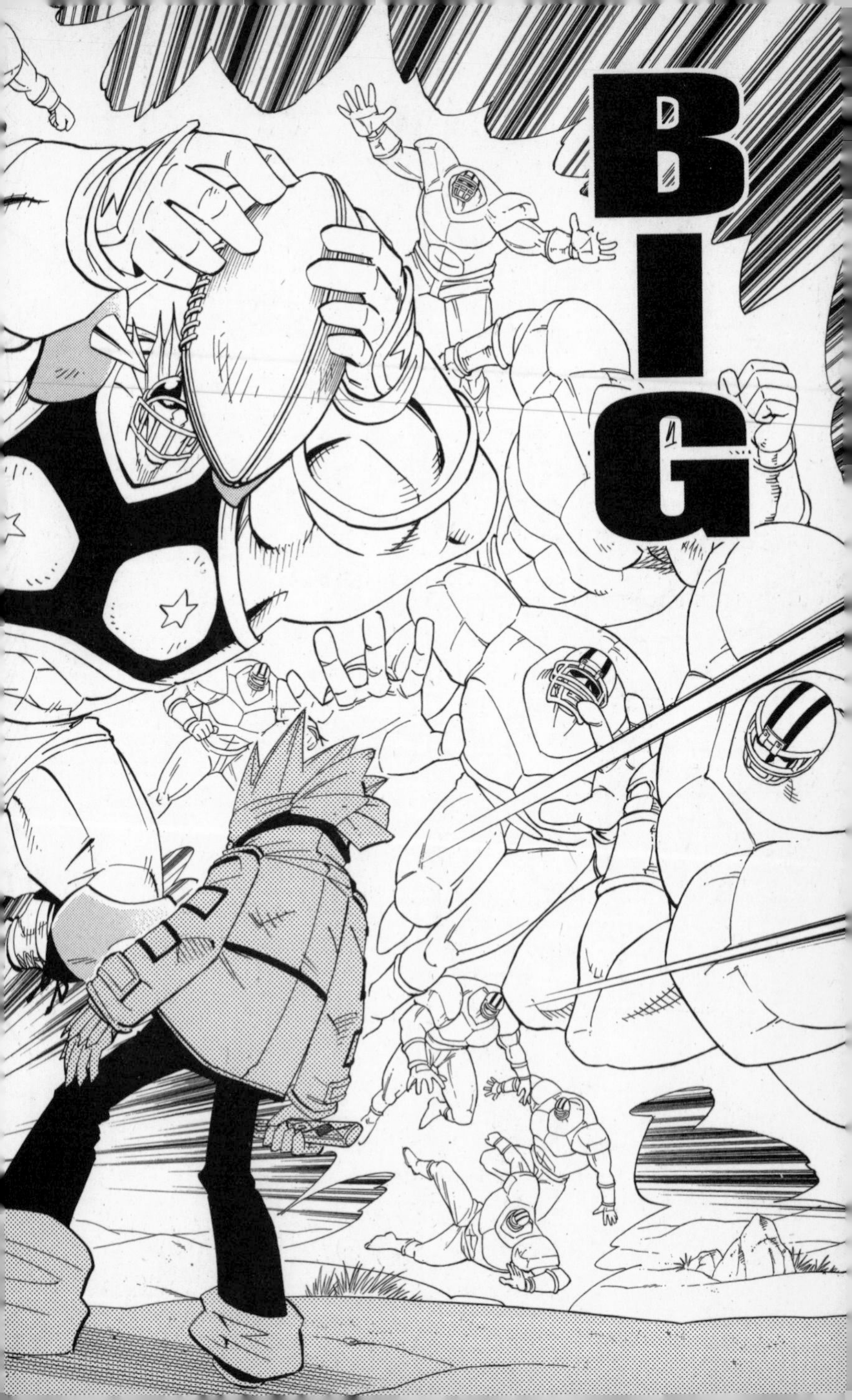
BIG

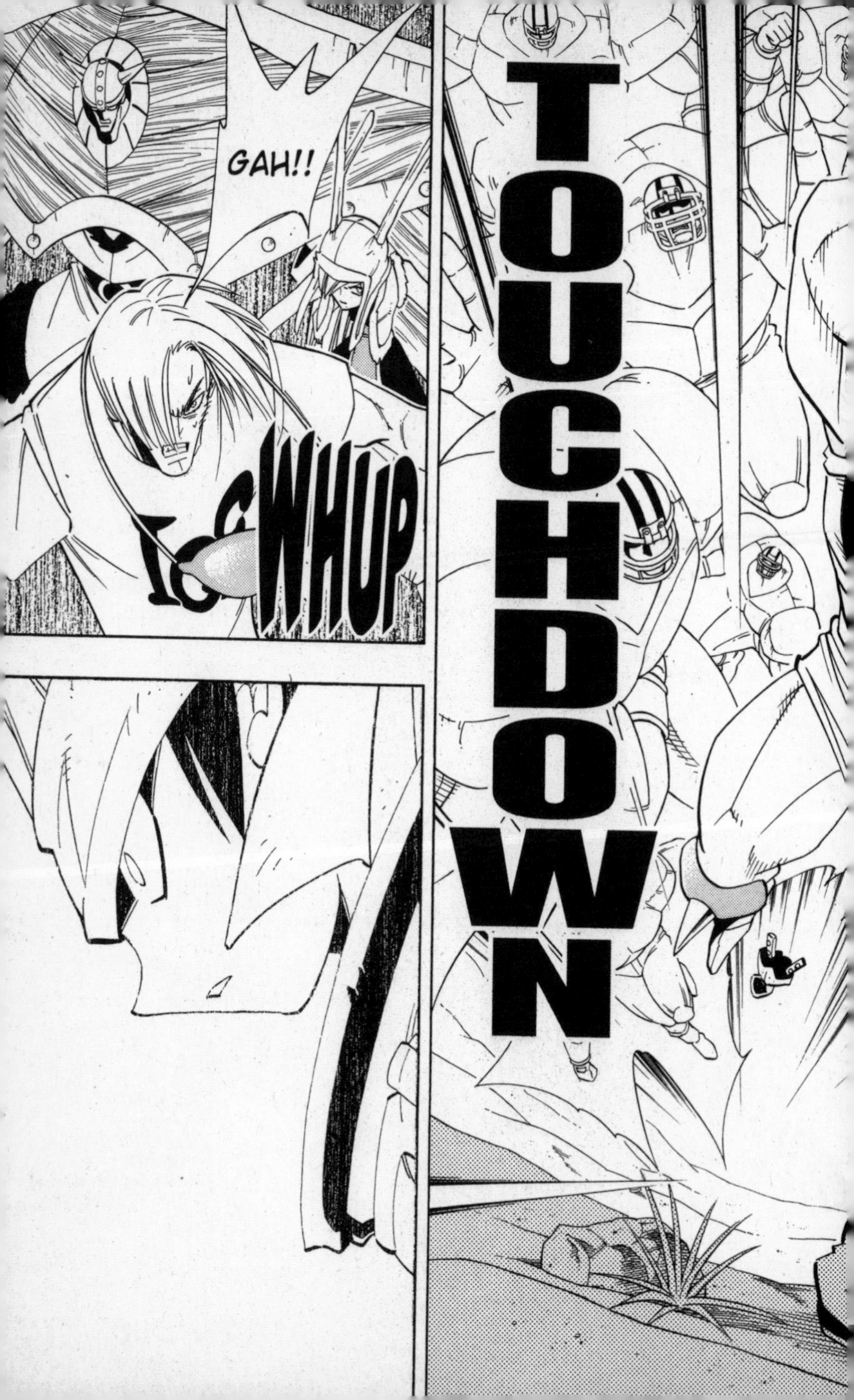
TOUCHDOWN
GAH!!
WHUP

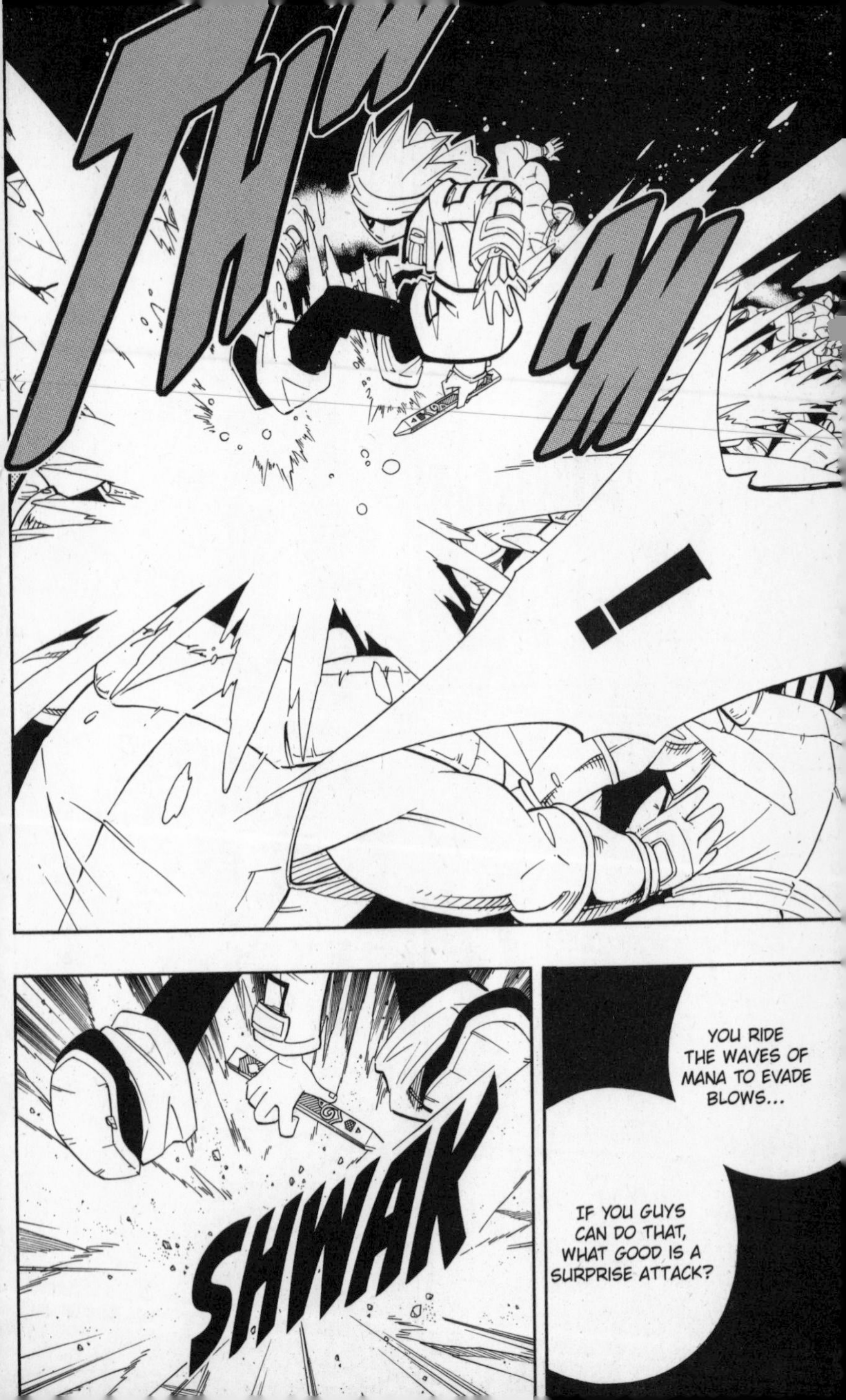
THWAM
!
YOU RIDE THE WAVES OF MANA TO EVADE BLOWS...
IF YOU GUYS CAN DO THAT, WHAT GOOD IS A SURPRISE ATTACK?
SHWAK

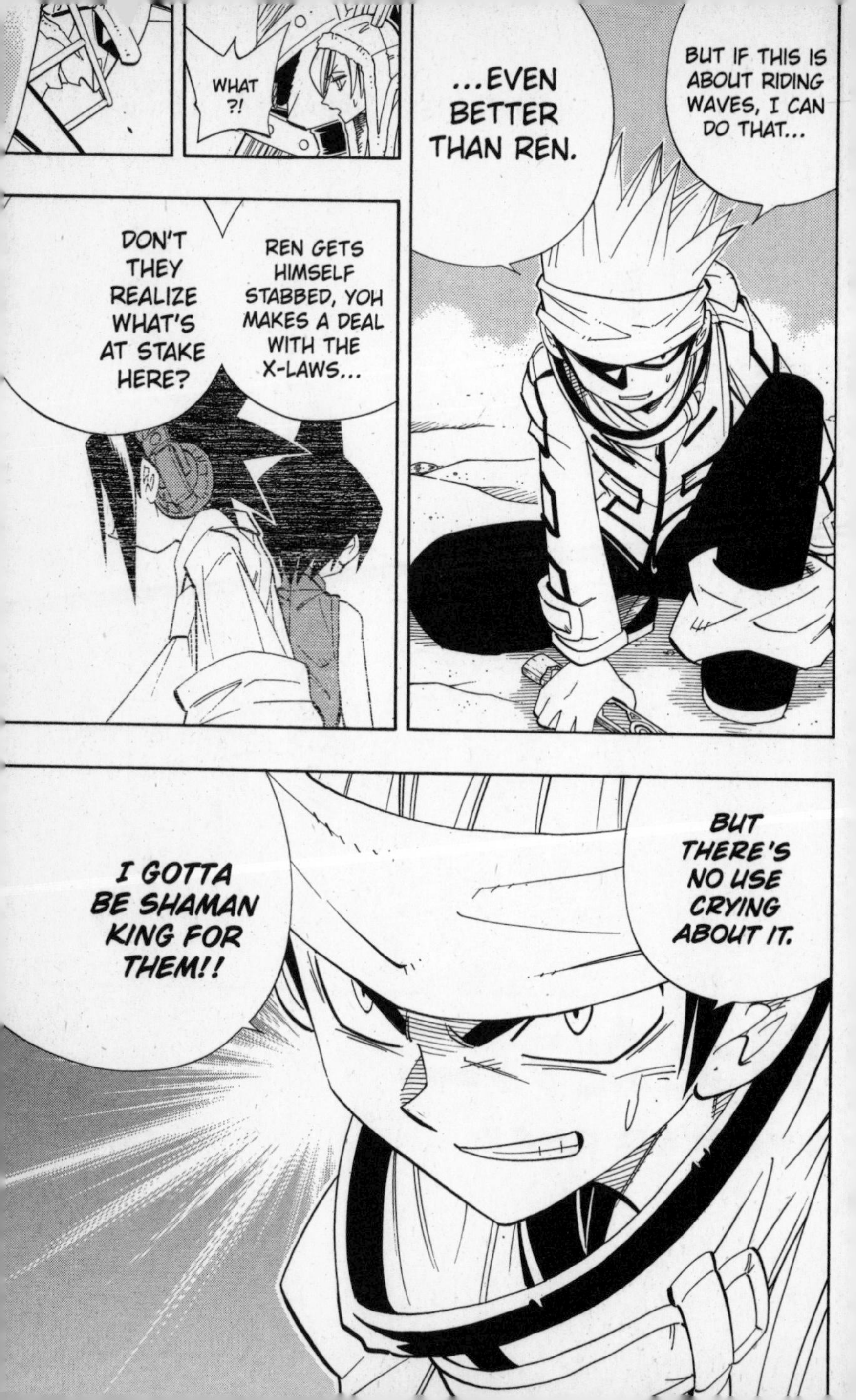
BUT IF THIS IS ABOUT RIDING WAVES, I CAN DO THAT...
...EVEN BETTER THAN REN.
WHAT ?!
REN GETS HIMSELF STABBED, YOH MAKES A DEAL WITH THE X-LAWS...
DON'T THEY REALIZE WHAT'S AT STAKE HERE?
BUT THERE'S NO USE CRYING ABOUT IT.
I GOTTA BE SHAMAN KING FOR THEM!!

SHAMAN KING CHARACTER FILE No.112

2001
(JAN)

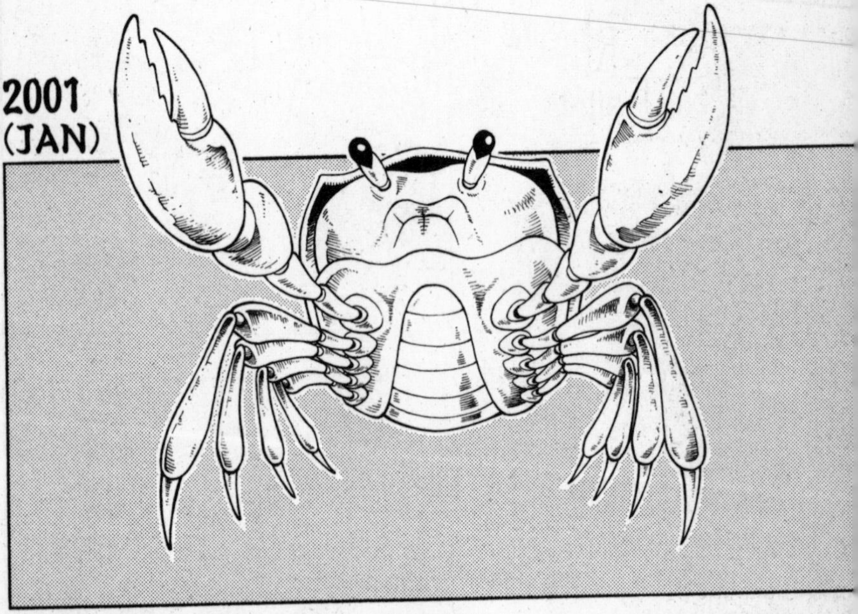

見えたカニ

SPOTTED CRAB

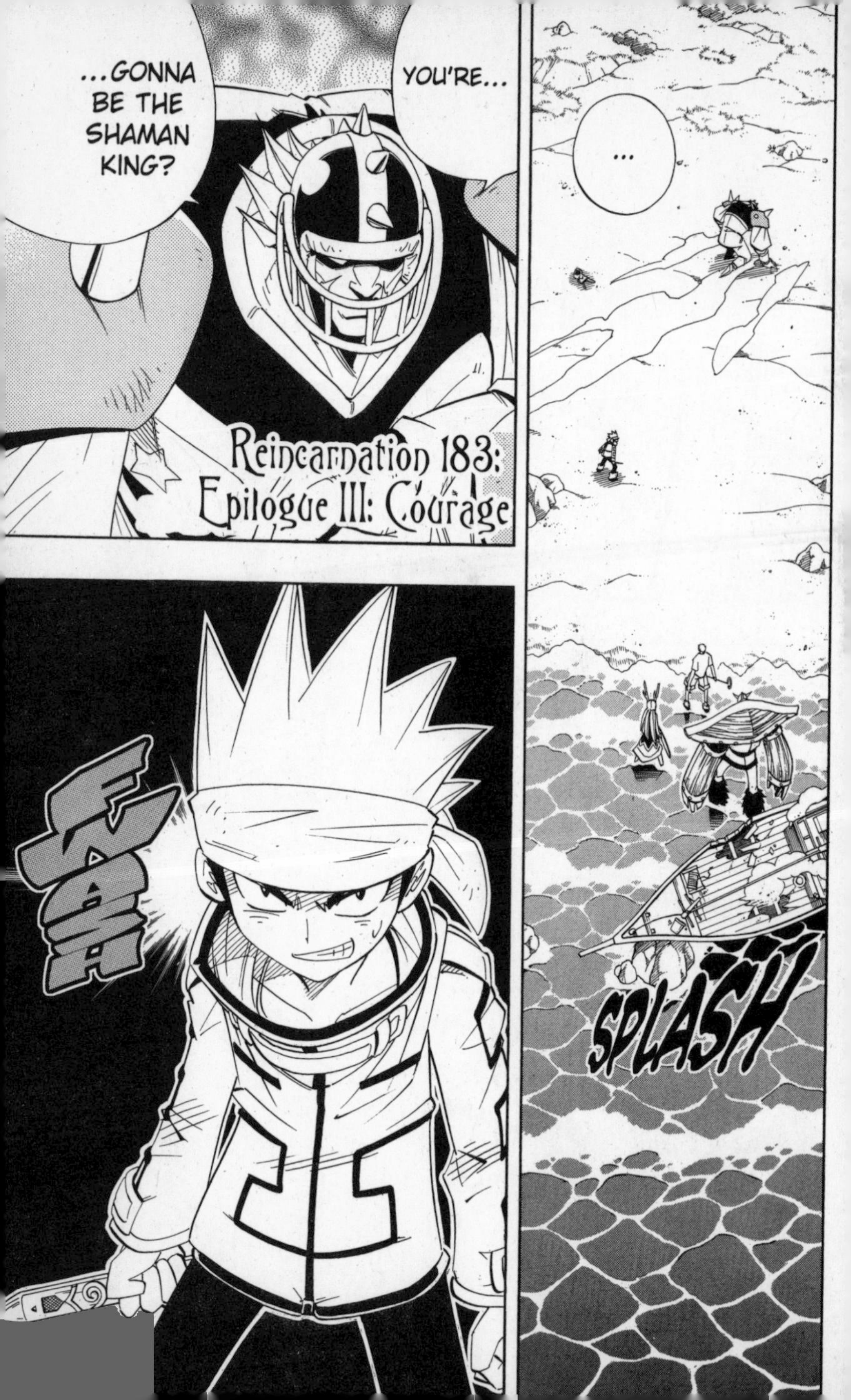
...
SPLASH
YOU'RE...
...GONNA BE THE SHAMAN KING?
Reincarnation 183: Epilogue III: Courage

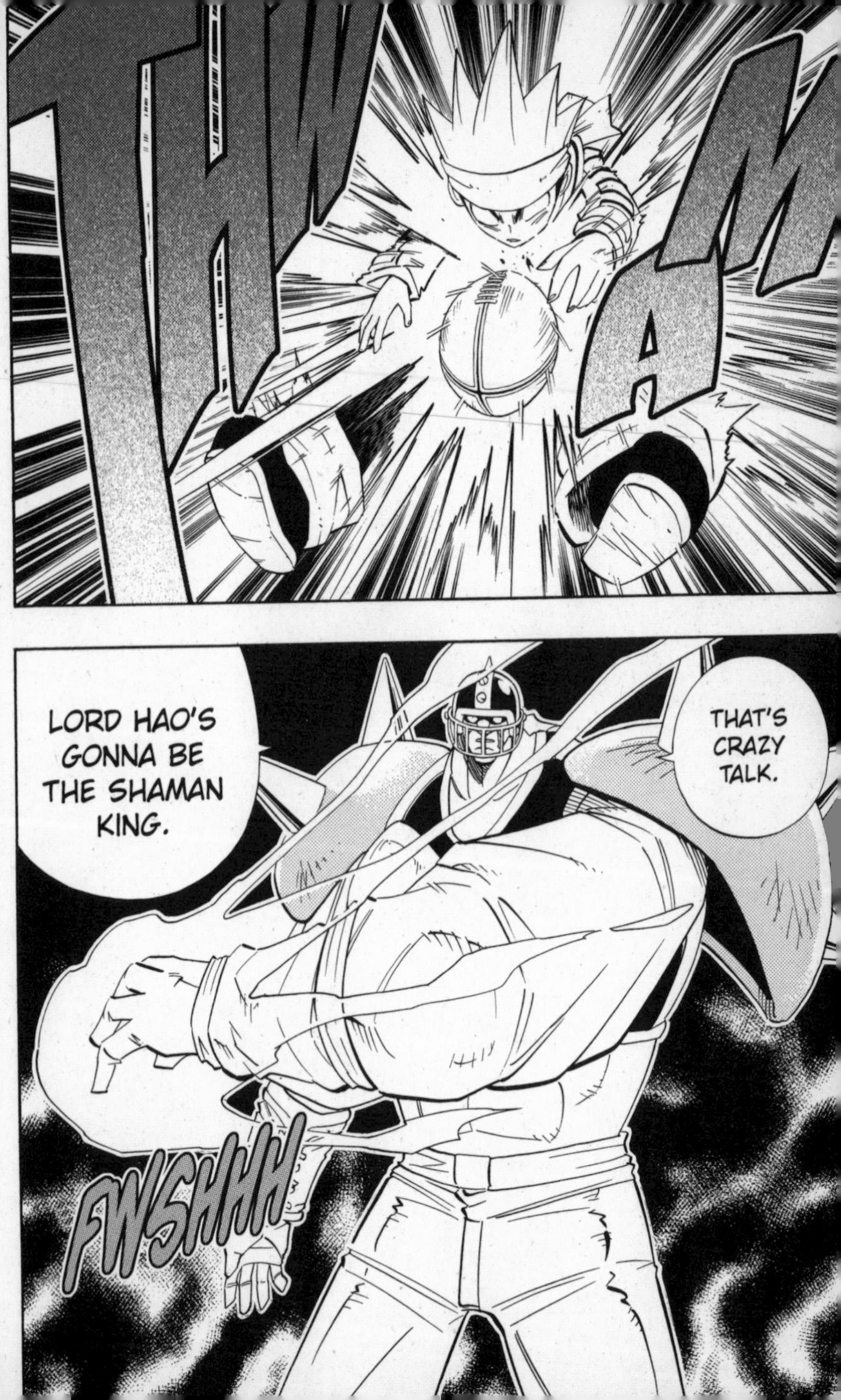
THWAM
THAT'S CRAZY TALK.
LORD HAO'S GONNA BE THE SHAMAN KING.
FWSHHH

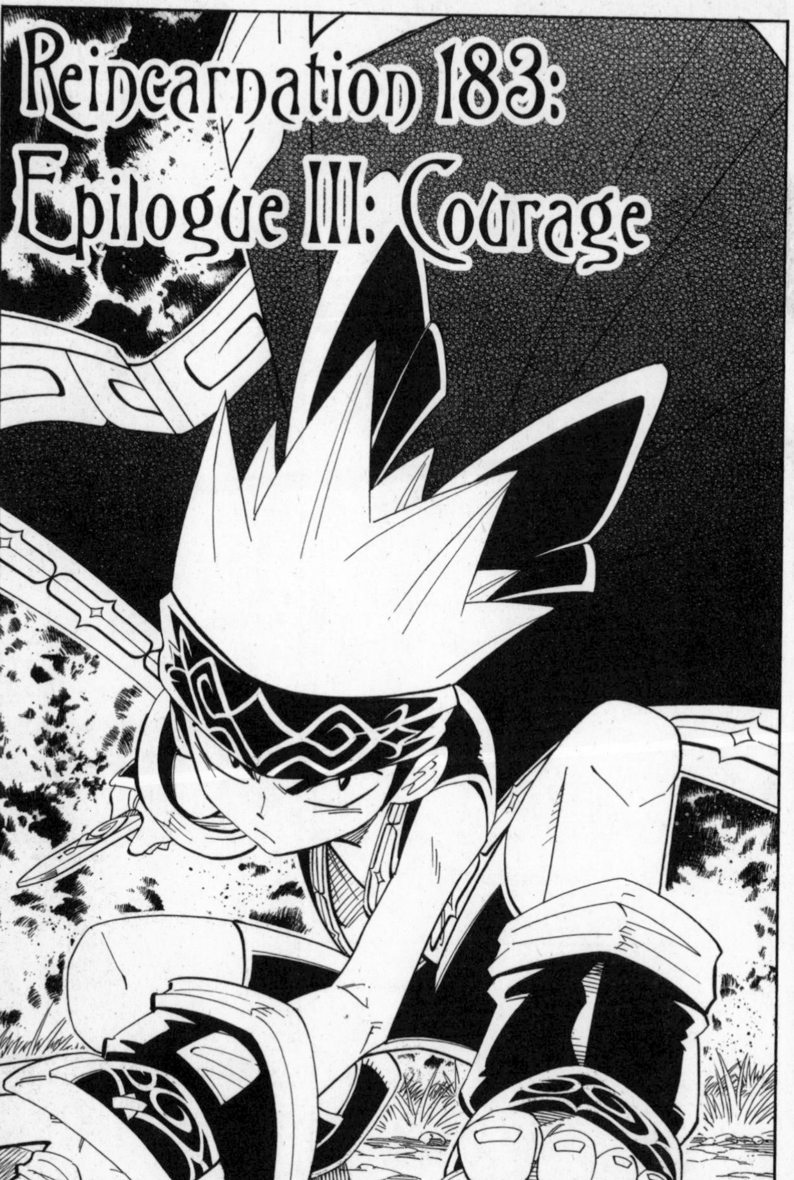
Reincarnation 183:
Epilogue III: Courage

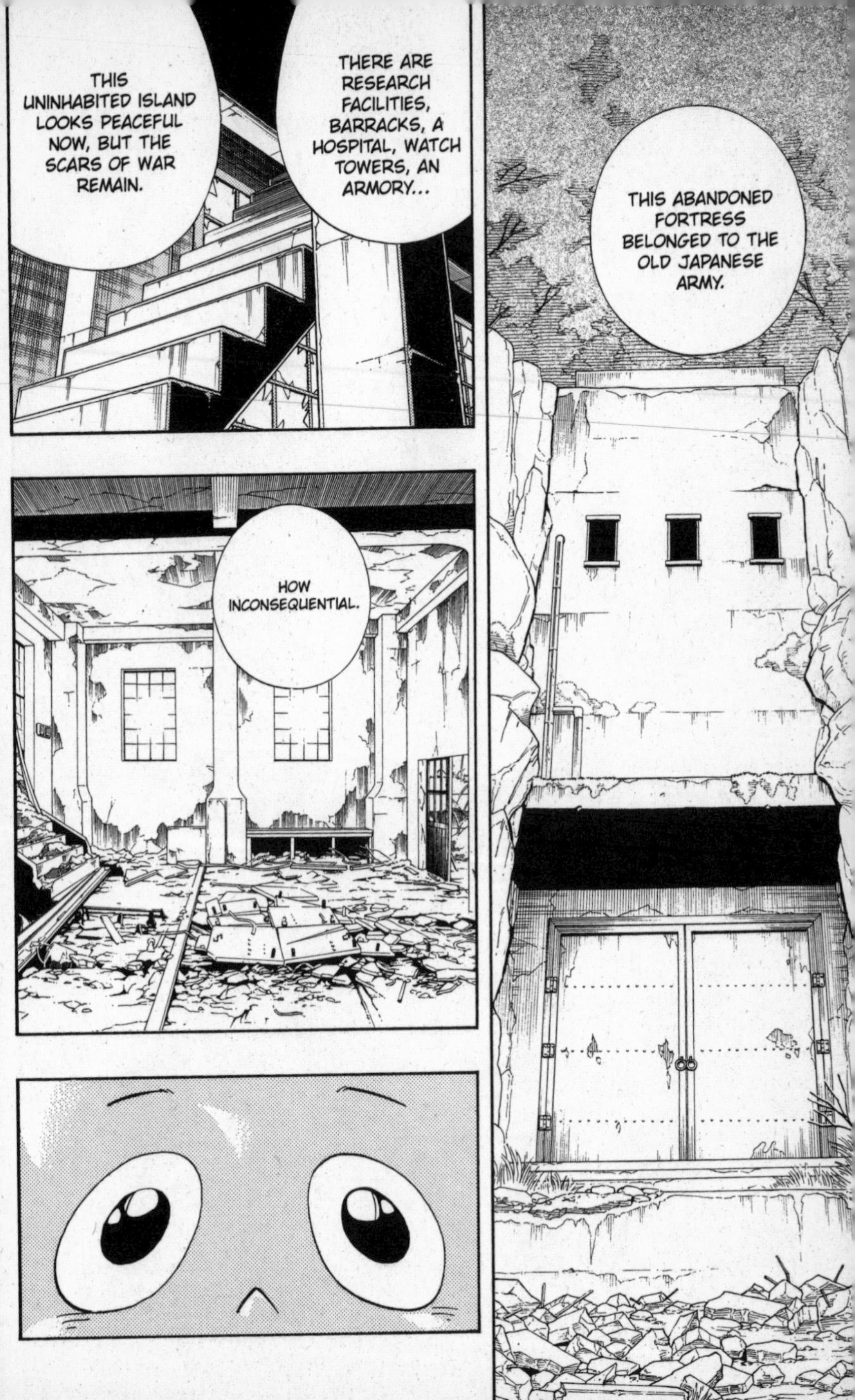
THIS ABANDONED FORTRESS BELONGED TO THE OLD JAPANESE ARMY.
THERE ARE RESEARCH FACILITIES, BARRACKS, A HOSPITAL, WATCH TOWERS, AN ARMORY...
THIS UNINHABITED ISLAND LOOKS PEACEFUL NOW, BUT THE SCARS OF WAR REMAIN.
HOW INCONSEQUENTIAL.

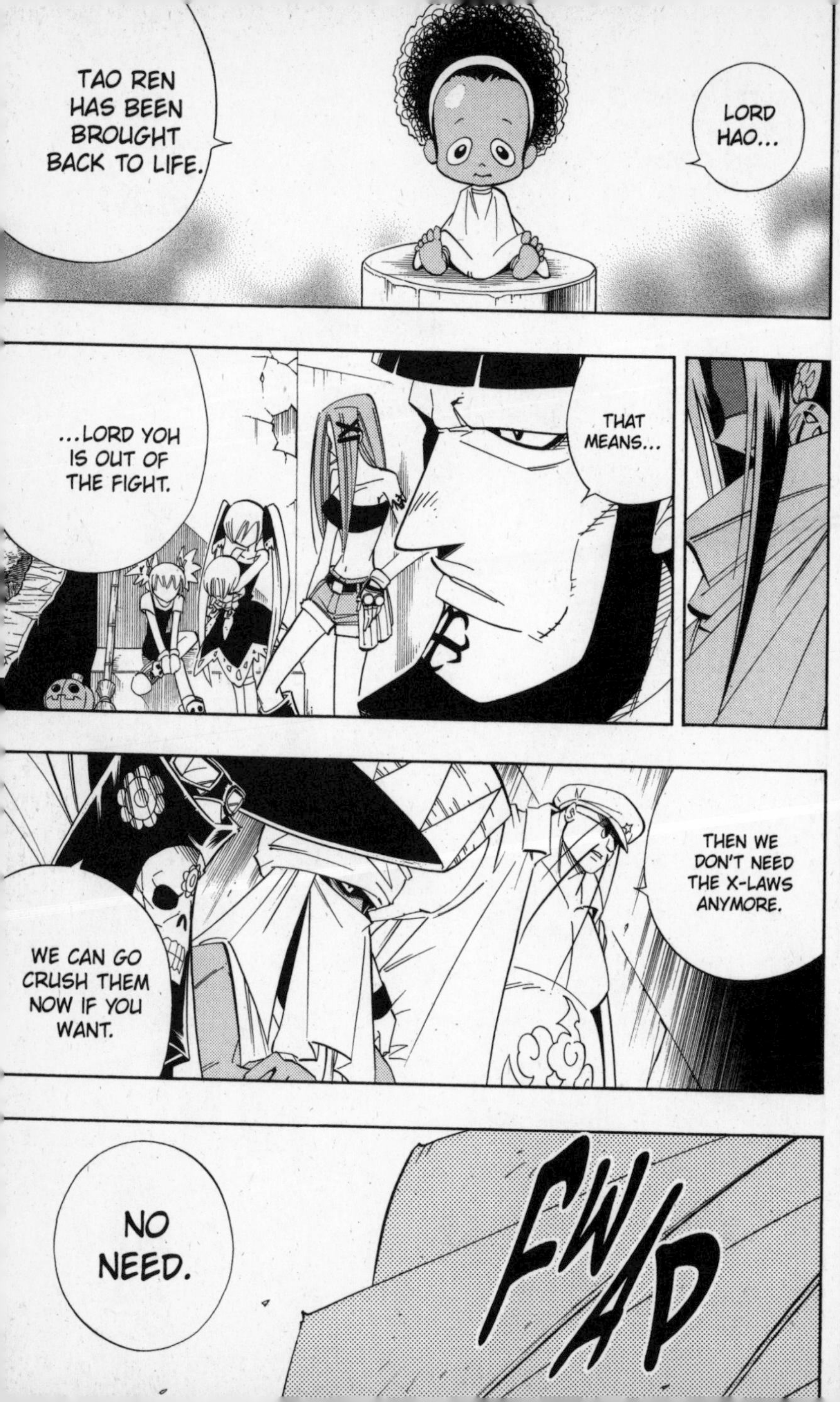
LORD HAO...
TAO REN HAS BEEN BROUGHT BACK TO LIFE.
THAT MEANS...
...LORD YOH IS OUT OF THE FIGHT.
THEN WE DON'T NEED THE X-LAWS ANYMORE.
WE CAN GO CRUSH THEM NOW IF YOU WANT.
FWAP
NO NEED.

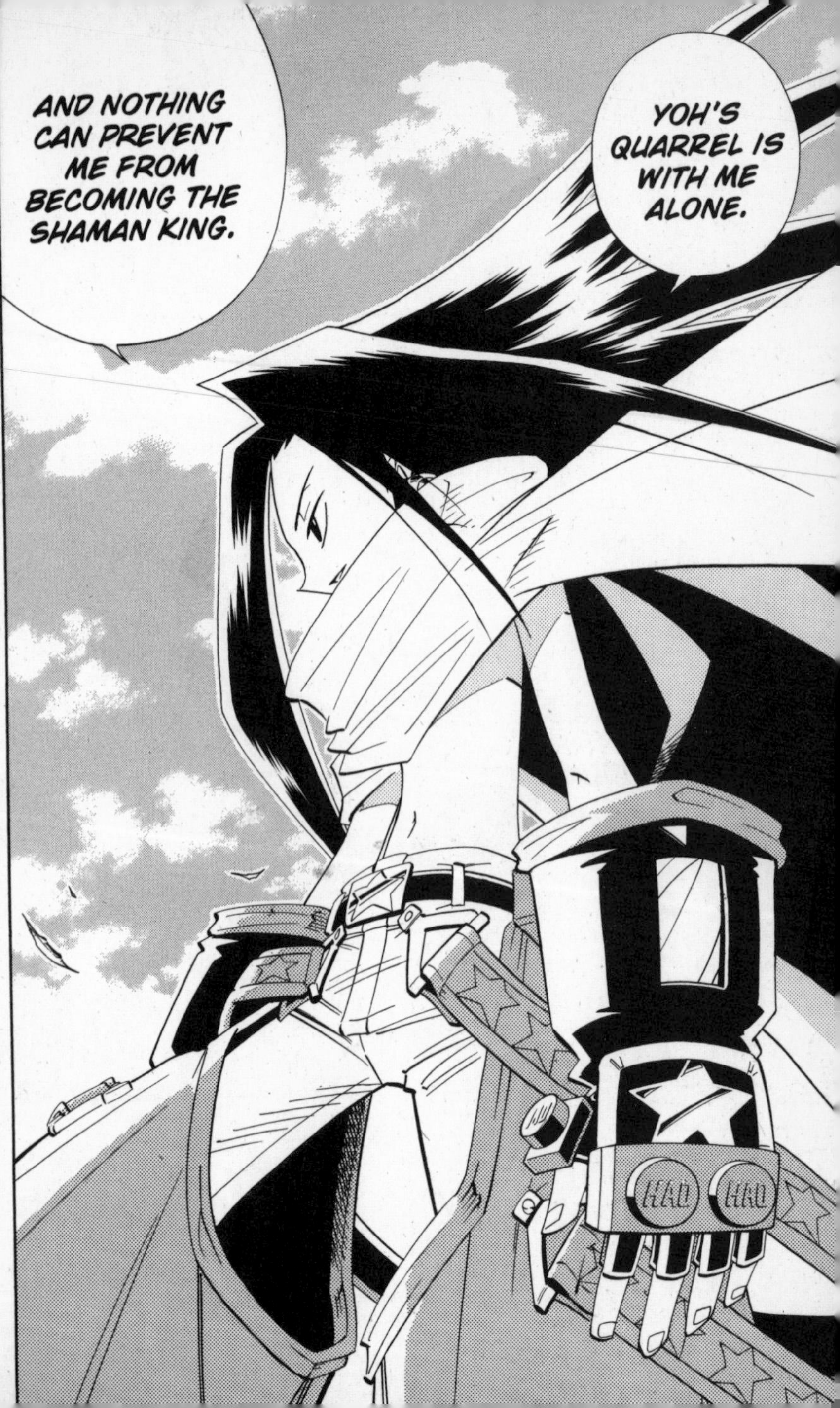
YOH'S QUARREL IS WITH ME ALONE.
AND NOTHING CAN PREVENT ME FROM BECOMING THE SHAMAN KING.
HAO
HAO

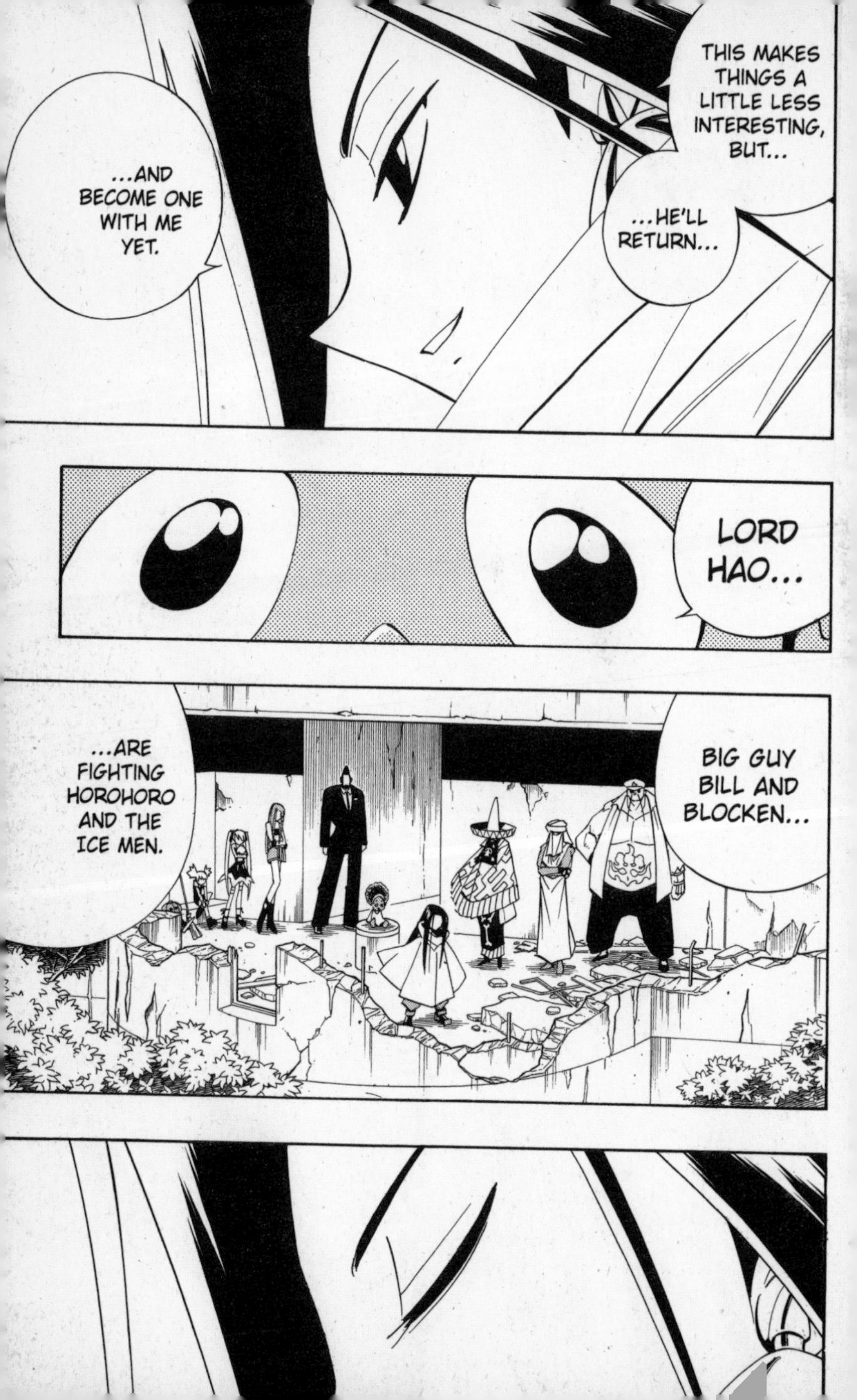
THIS MAKES THINGS A LITTLE LESS INTERESTING, BUT...
...HE'LL RETURN...
...AND BECOME ONE WITH ME YET.
LORD HAO...
BIG GUY BILL AND BLOCKEN...
...ARE FIGHTING HOROHORO AND THE ICE MEN.

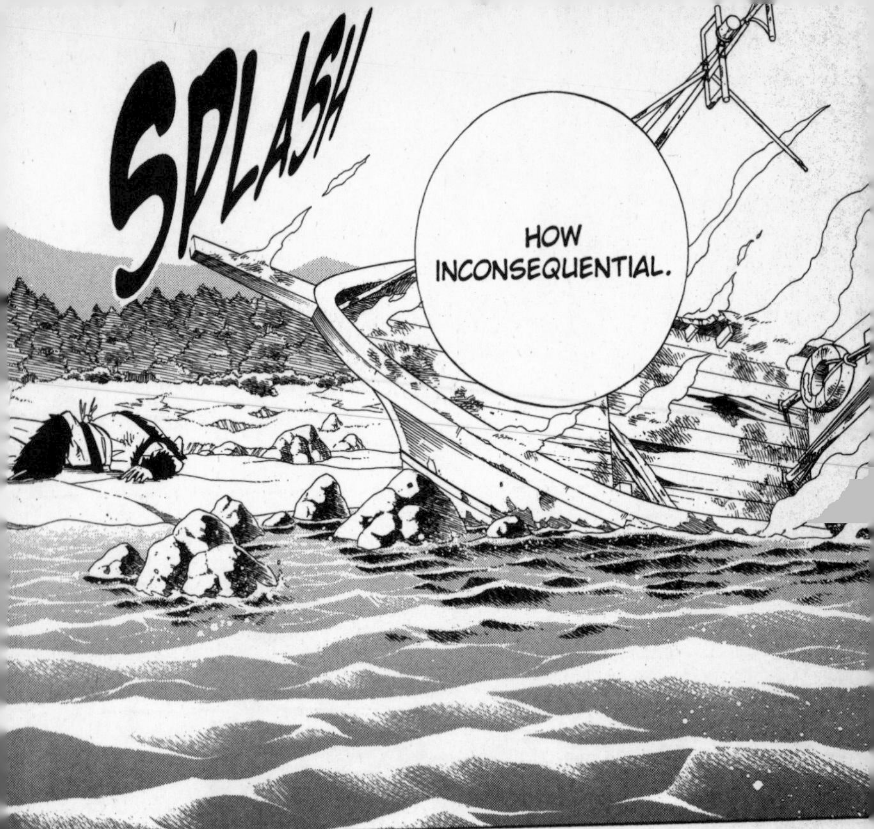
SPLASH
HOW INCONSEQUENTIAL.

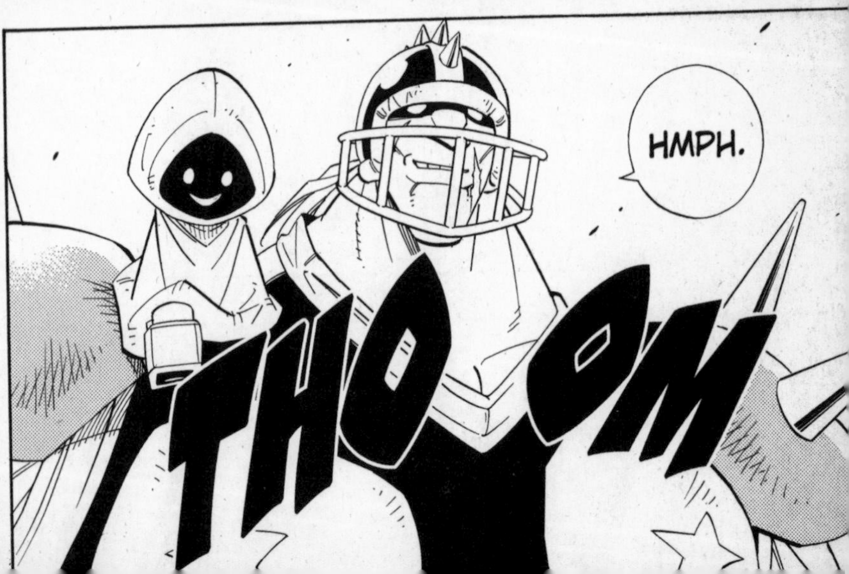
HMPH.
THOOM

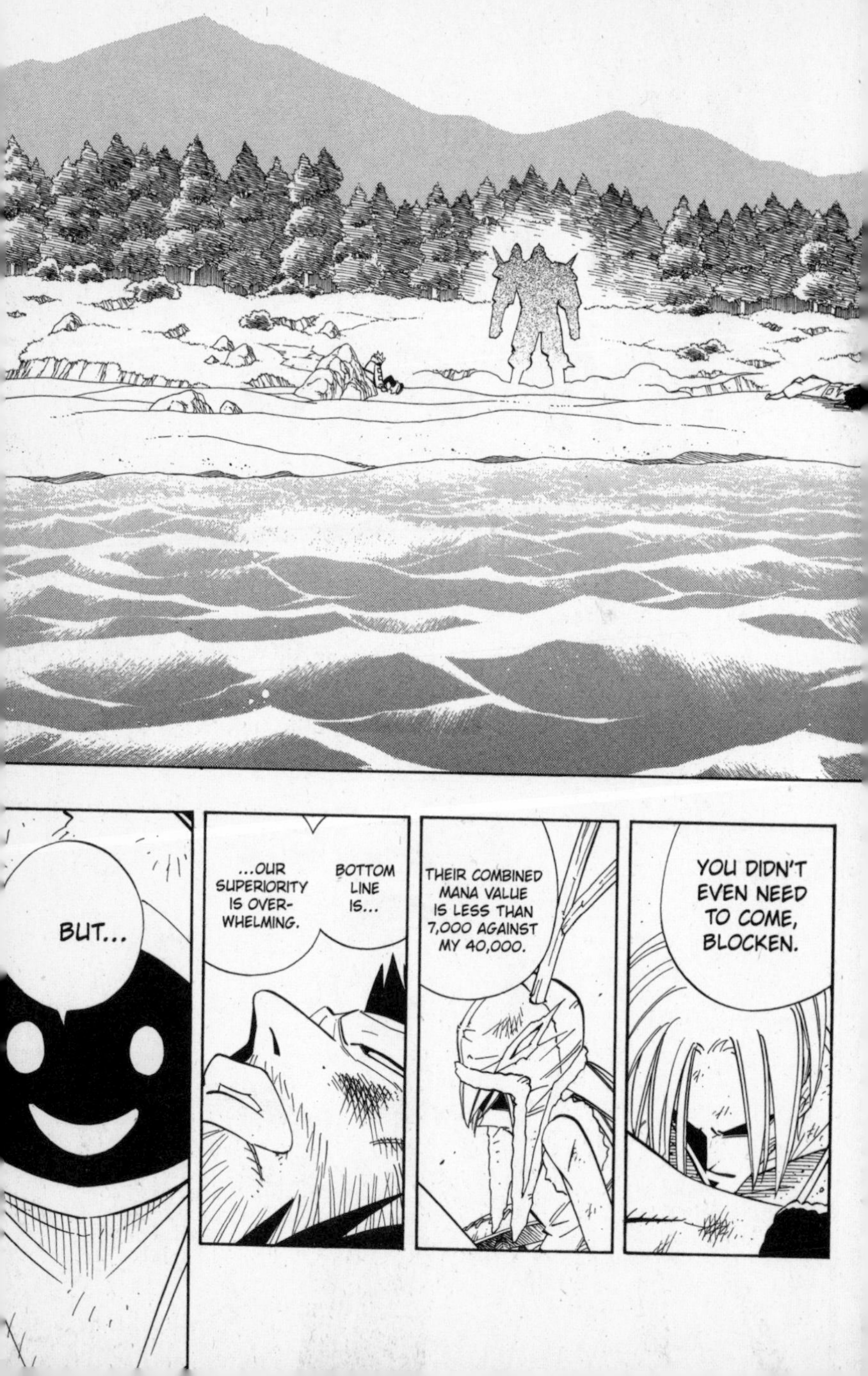
YOU DIDN'T EVEN NEED TO COME, BLOCKEN.
THEIR COMBINED MANA VALUE IS LESS THAN 7,000 AGAINST MY 40,000.
BOTTOM LINE IS...
...OUR SUPERIORITY IS OVER-WHELMING.
BUT...

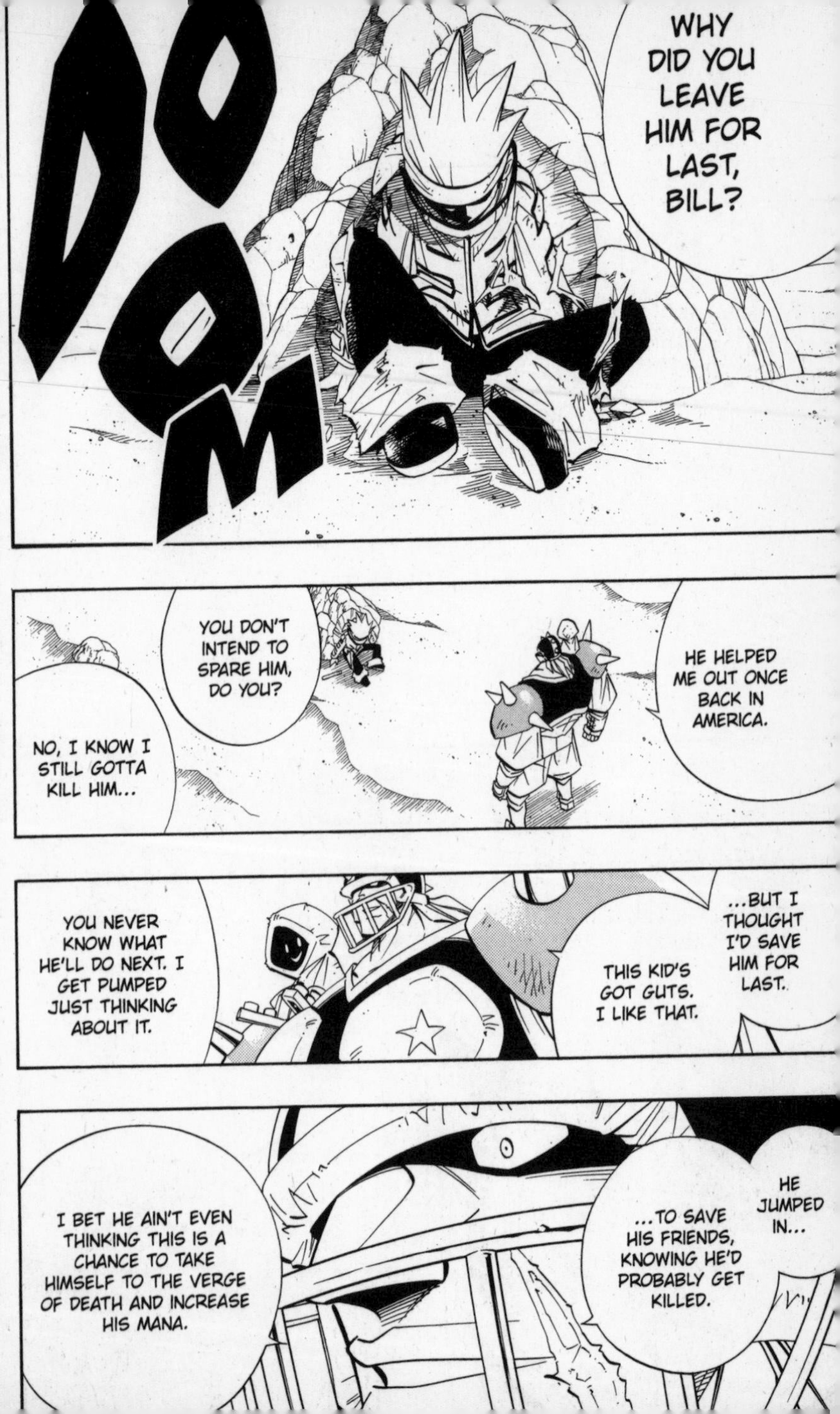
WHY DID YOU LEAVE HIM FOR LAST, BILL?
DOOM
HE HELPED ME OUT ONCE BACK IN AMERICA.
YOU DON'T INTEND TO SPARE HIM, DO YOU?
NO, I KNOW I STILL GOTTA KILL HIM...
...BUT I THOUGHT I'D SAVE HIM FOR LAST.
THIS KID'S GOT GUTS. I LIKE THAT.
YOU NEVER KNOW WHAT HE'LL DO NEXT. I GET PUMPED JUST THINKING ABOUT IT.
HE JUMPED IN...
...TO SAVE HIS FRIENDS, KNOWING HE'D PROBABLY GET KILLED.
I BET HE AIN'T EVEN THINKING THIS IS A CHANCE TO TAKE HIMSELF TO THE VERGE OF DEATH AND INCREASE HIS MANA.

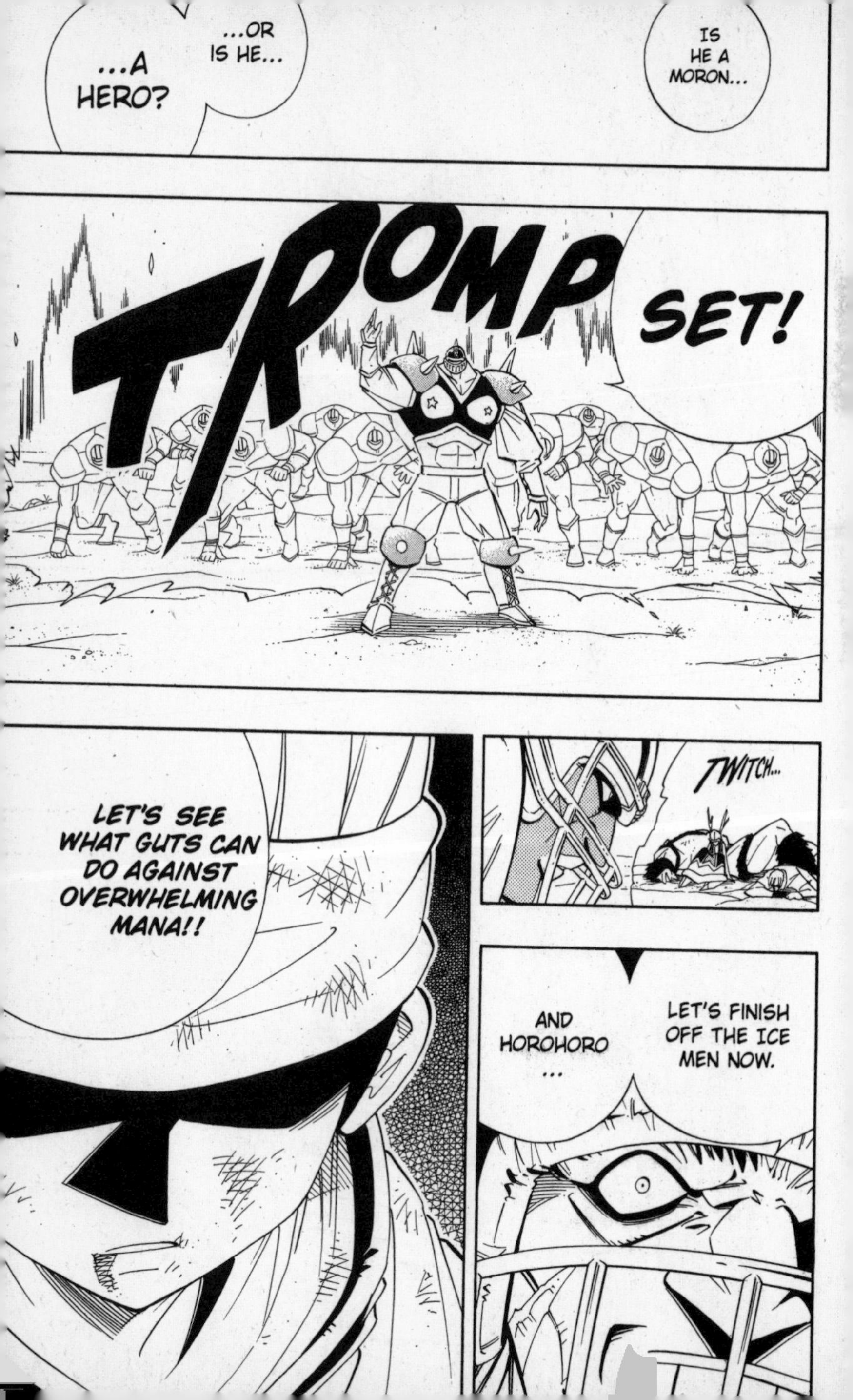
IS HE A MORON...
...OR IS HE...
...A HERO?
SET!
TROMP
TWITCH...
LET'S FINISH OFF THE ICE MEN NOW.
AND HOROHORO ...
LET'S SEE WHAT GUTS CAN DO AGAINST OVERWHELMING MANA!!

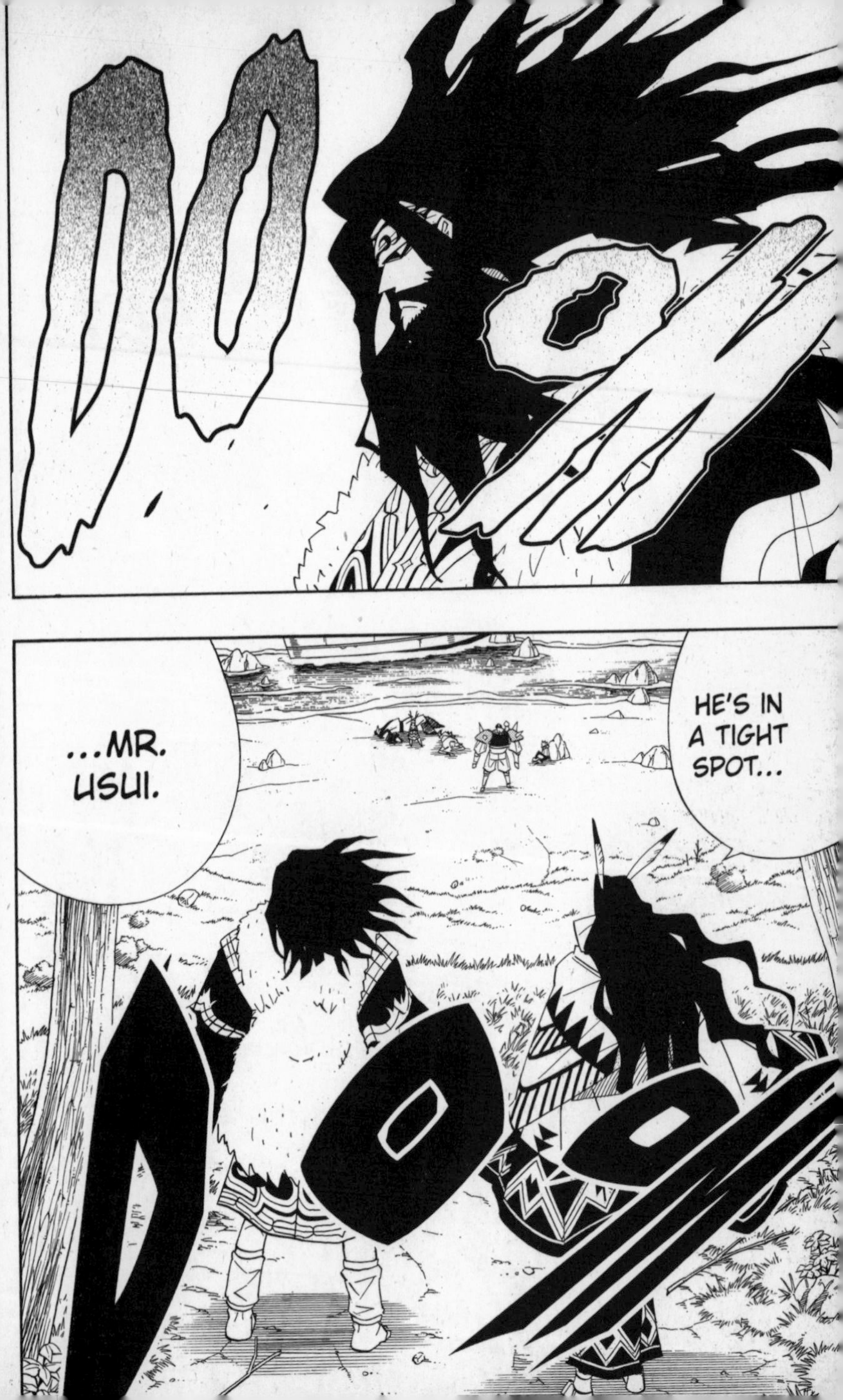
HE'S IN A TIGHT SPOT...
...MR. USUI.

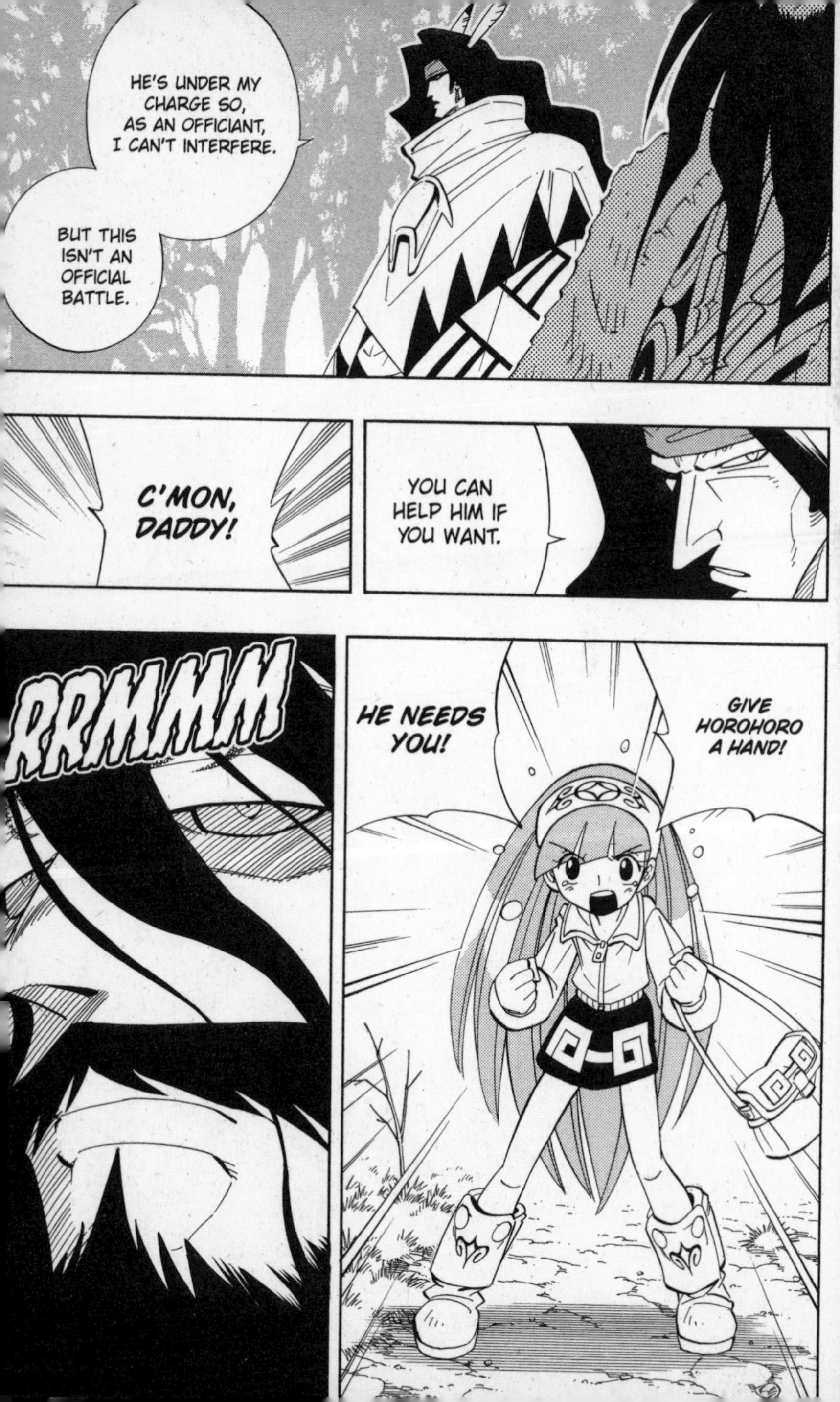
HE'S UNDER MY CHARGE SO, AS AN OFFICIANT, I CAN'T INTERFERE.
BUT THIS ISN'T AN OFFICIAL BATTLE.
YOU CAN HELP HIM IF YOU WANT.
C'MON, DADDY!
GIVE HOROHORO A HAND!
HE NEEDS YOU!
RRMMM

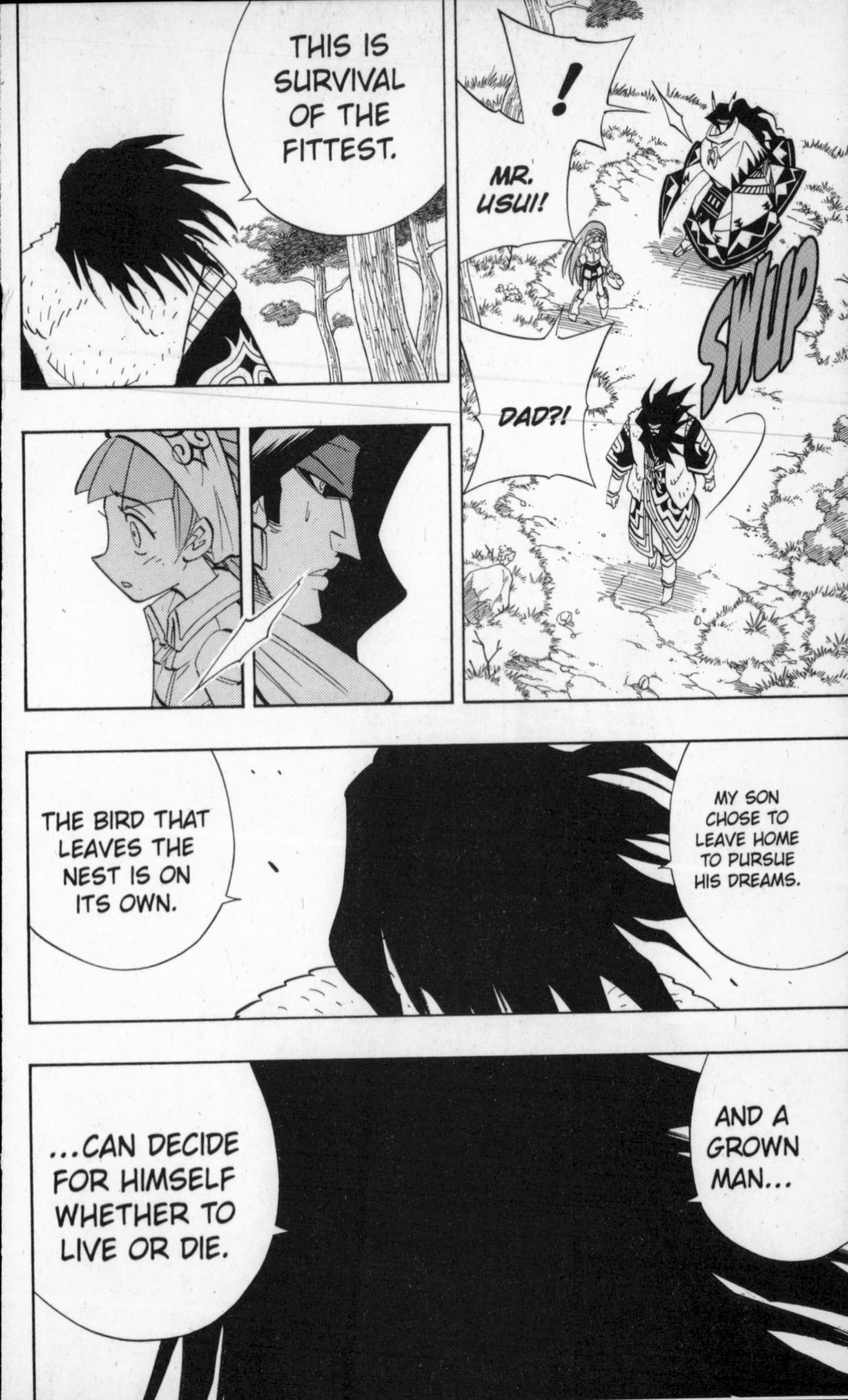
!
MR. USUI!
SHUP
DAD?!
THIS IS SURVIVAL OF THE FITTEST.
MY SON CHOSE TO LEAVE HOME TO PURSUE HIS DREAMS.
THE BIRD THAT LEAVES THE NEST IS ON ITS OWN.
AND A GROWN MAN...
...CAN DECIDE FOR HIMSELF WHETHER TO LIVE OR DIE.

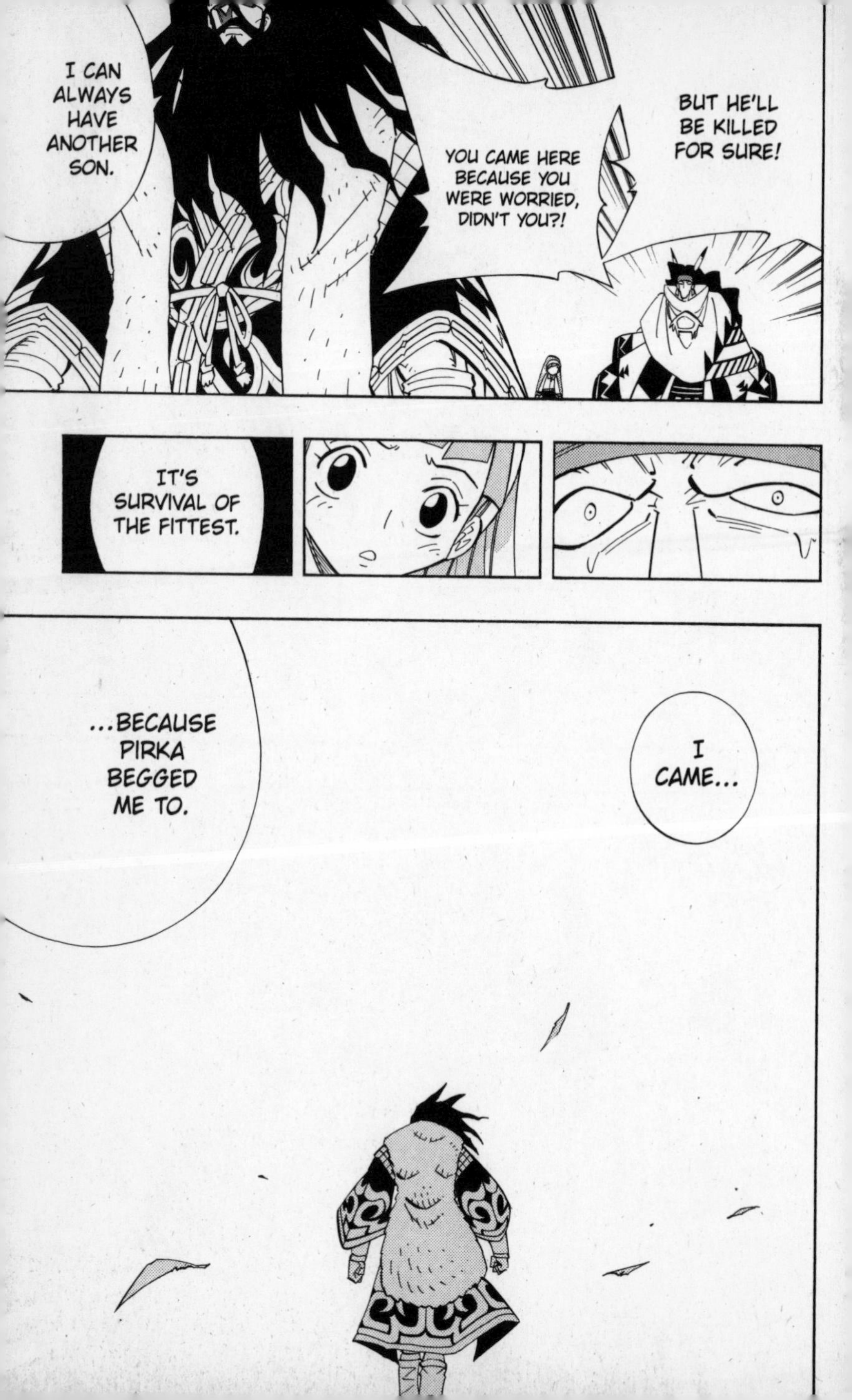
BUT HE'LL BE KILLED FOR SURE!
YOU CAME HERE BECAUSE YOU WERE WORRIED, DIDN'T YOU?!
I CAN ALWAYS HAVE ANOTHER SON.
IT'S SURVIVAL OF THE FITTEST.
I CAME...
...BECAUSE PIRKA BEGGED ME TO.

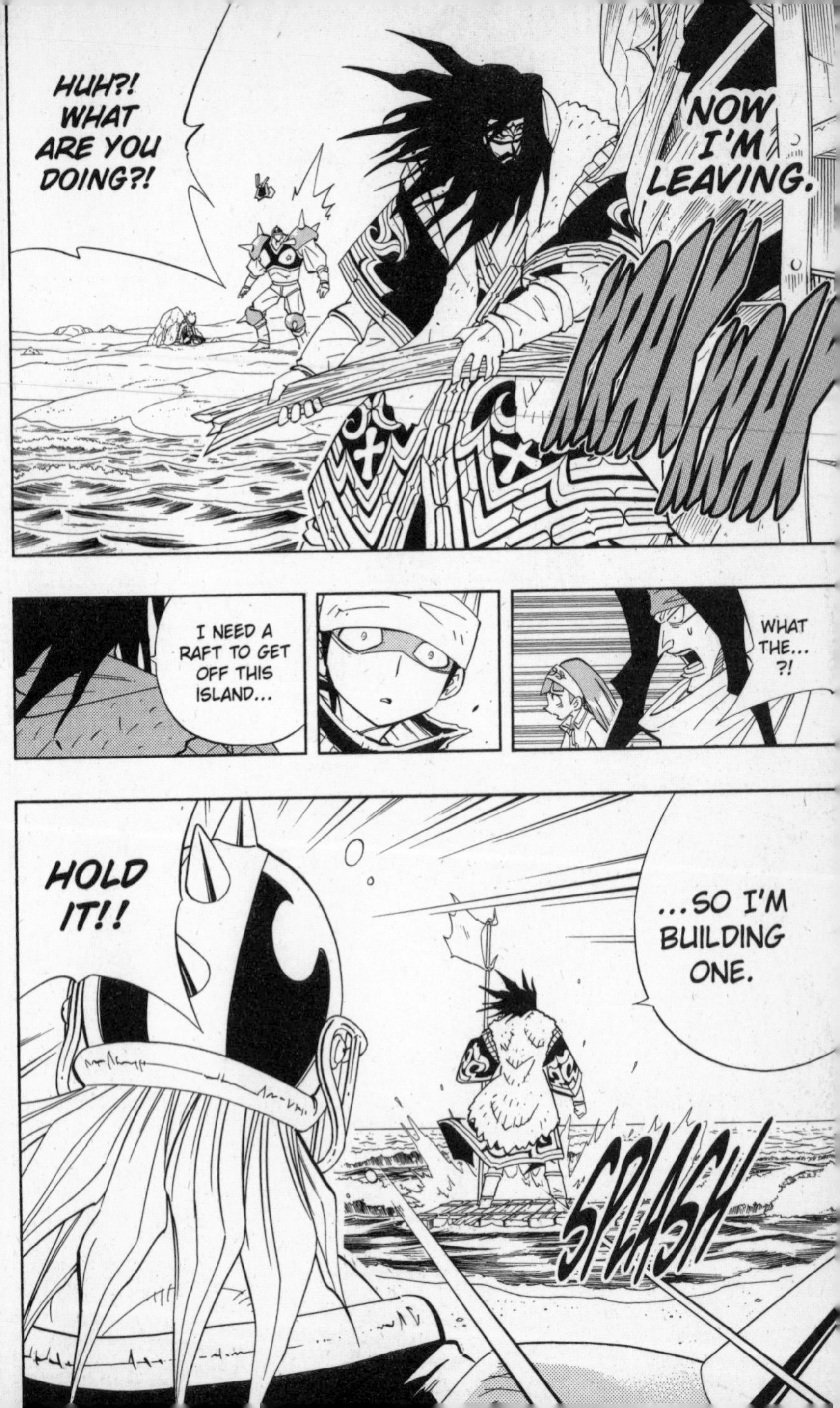
NOW I'M LEAVING.
HUH?! WHAT ARE YOU DOING?!
WHAT THE...?!
I NEED A RAFT TO GET OFF THIS ISLAND...
...SO I'M BUILDING ONE.
SPLASH
HOLD IT!!

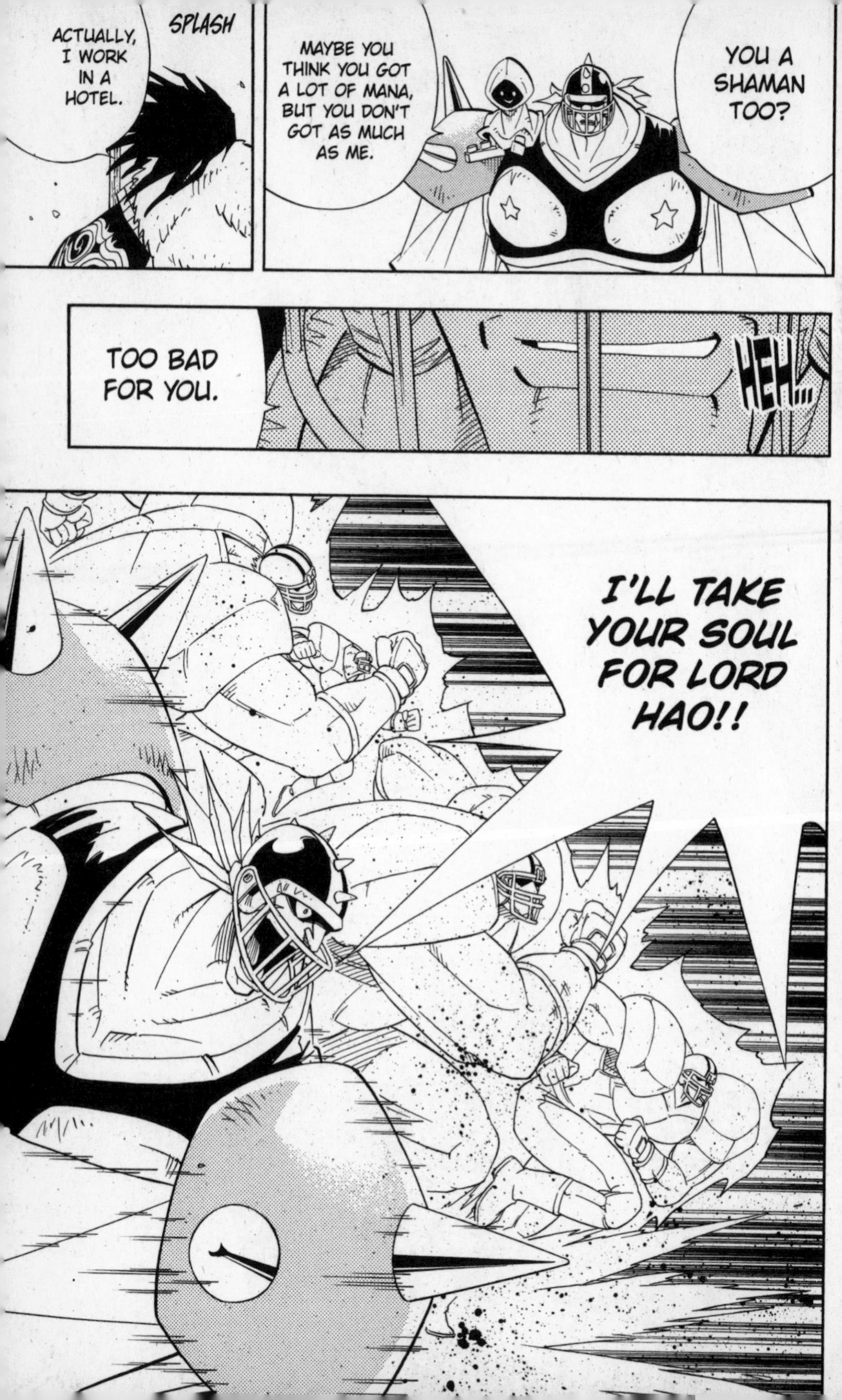
YOU A SHAMAN TOO?
MAYBE YOU THINK YOU GOT A LOT OF MANA, BUT YOU DON'T GOT AS MUCH AS ME.
SPLASH
ACTUALLY, I WORK IN A HOTEL.
HEH...
TOO BAD FOR YOU.
I'LL TAKE YOUR SOUL FOR LORD HAO!!

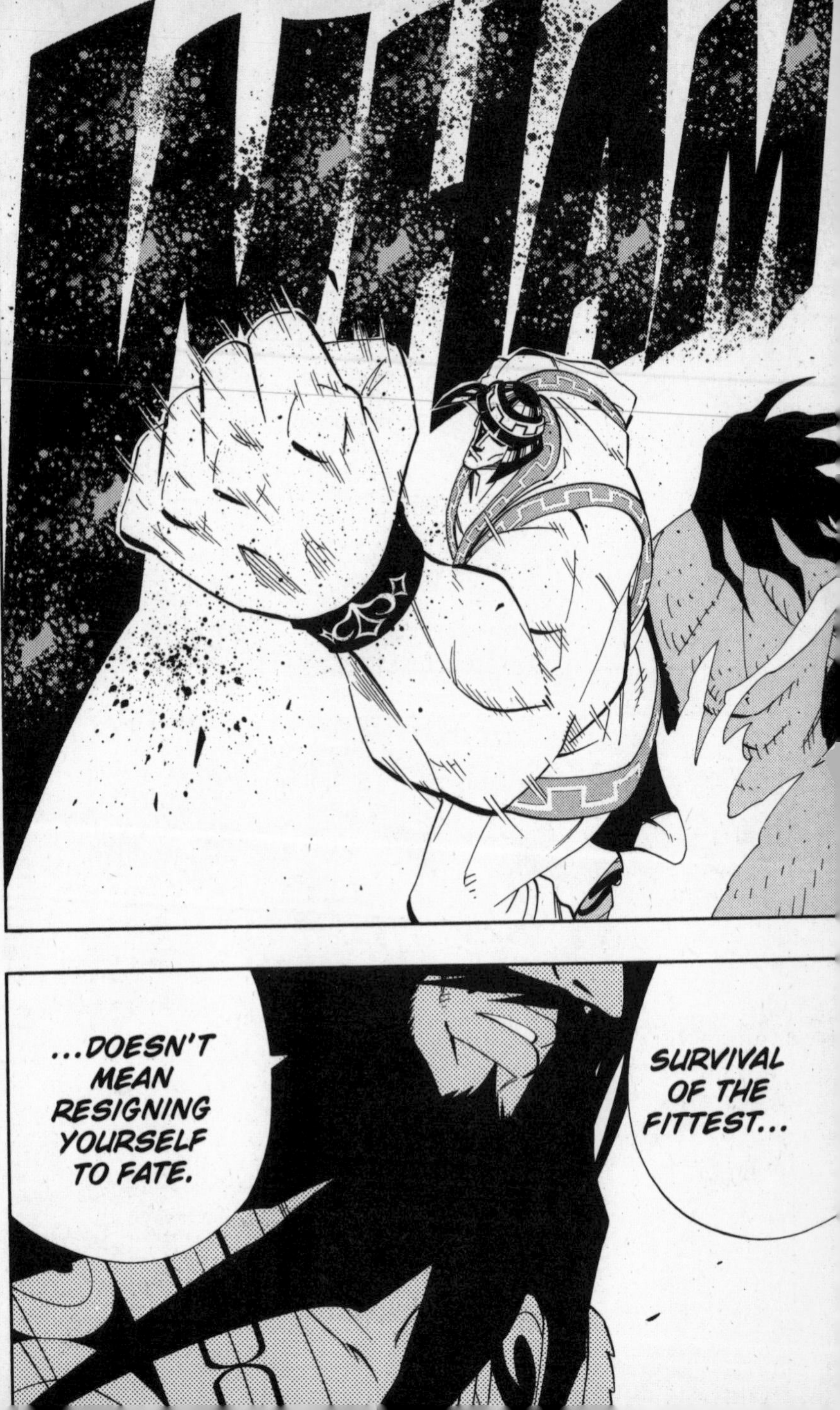
WHAM
SURVIVAL OF THE FITTEST...
...DOESN'T MEAN RESIGNING YOURSELF TO FATE.

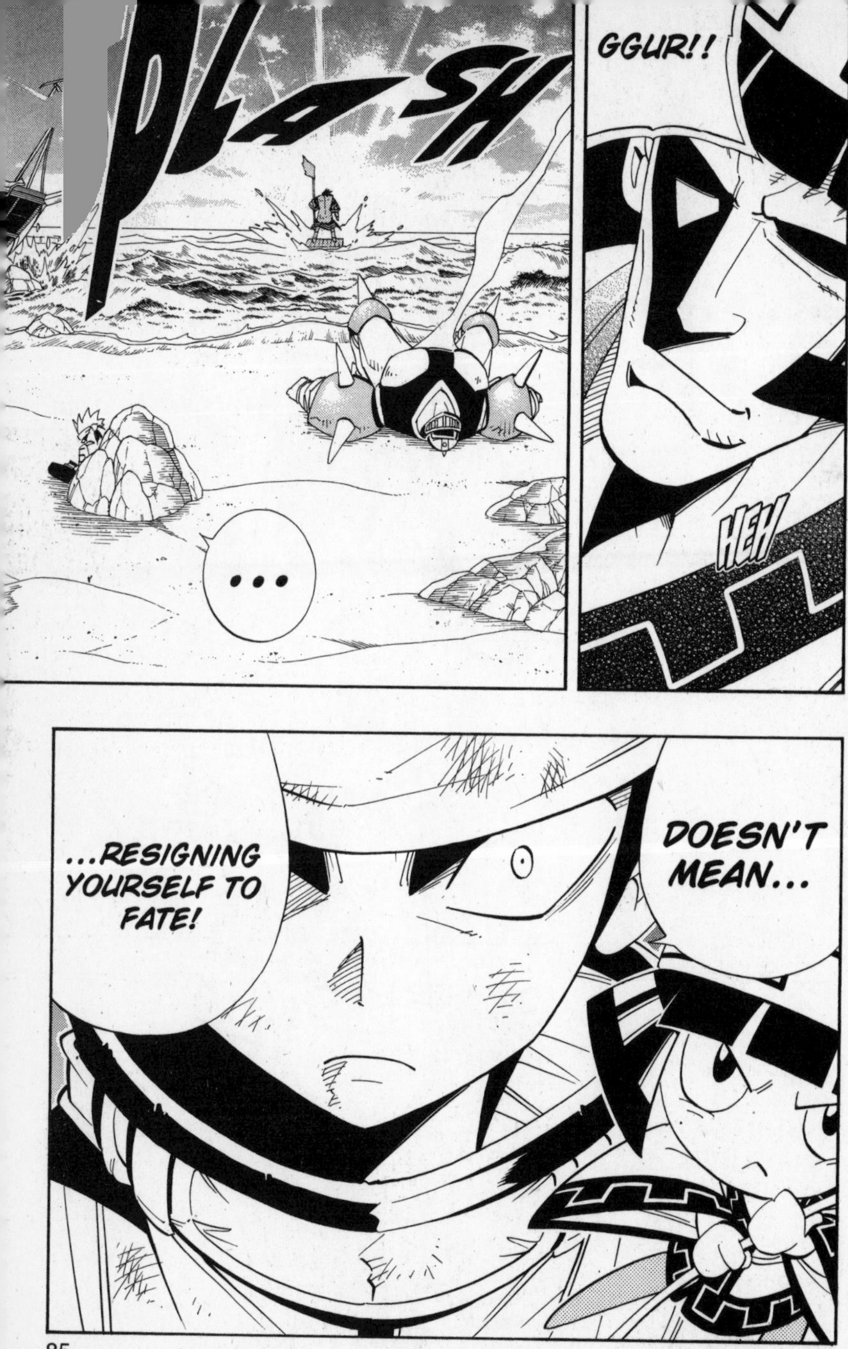

GGUR!!
HEH
PLASH
...
DOESN'T MEAN...
...RESIGNING YOURSELF TO FATE!

SHAMAN KING CHARACTER FILE No.113

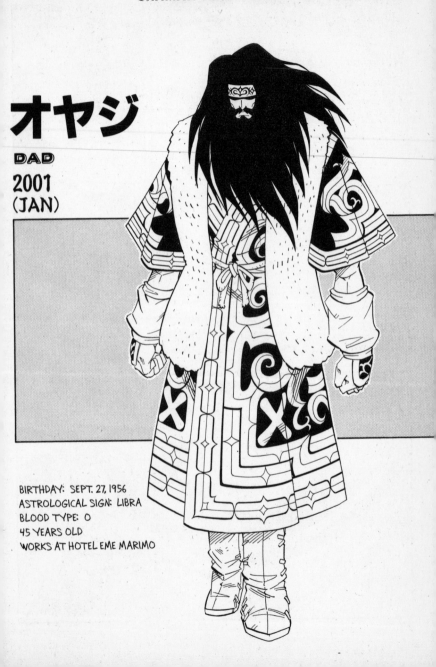

オヤジ

DAD

2001
(JAN)

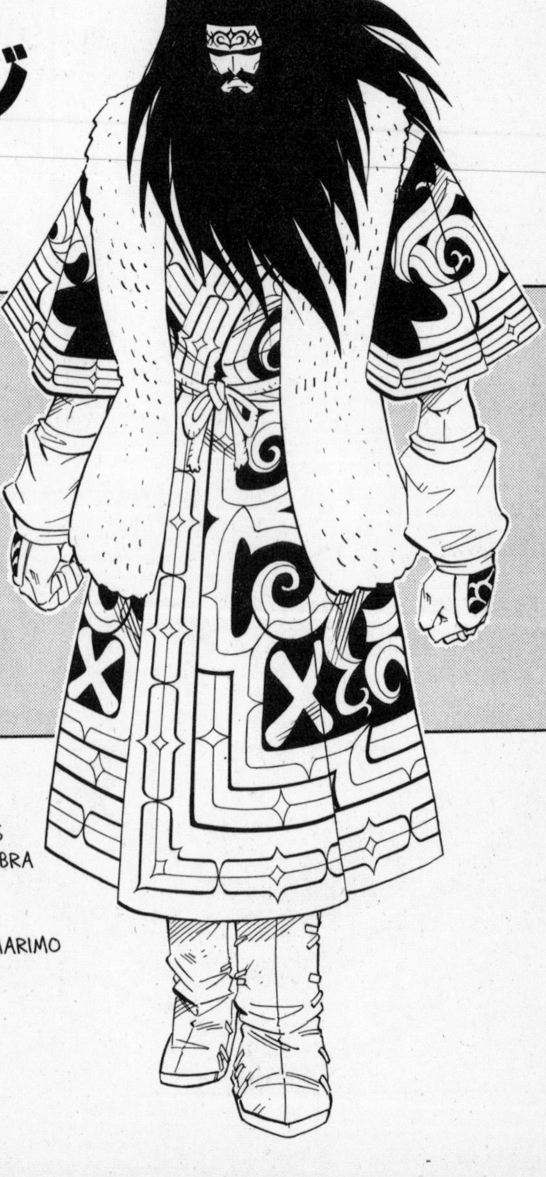

BIRTHDAY: SEPT. 27, 1956
ASTROLOGICAL SIGN: LIBRA
BLOOD TYPE: O
45 YEARS OLD
WORKS AT HOTEL EME MARIMO

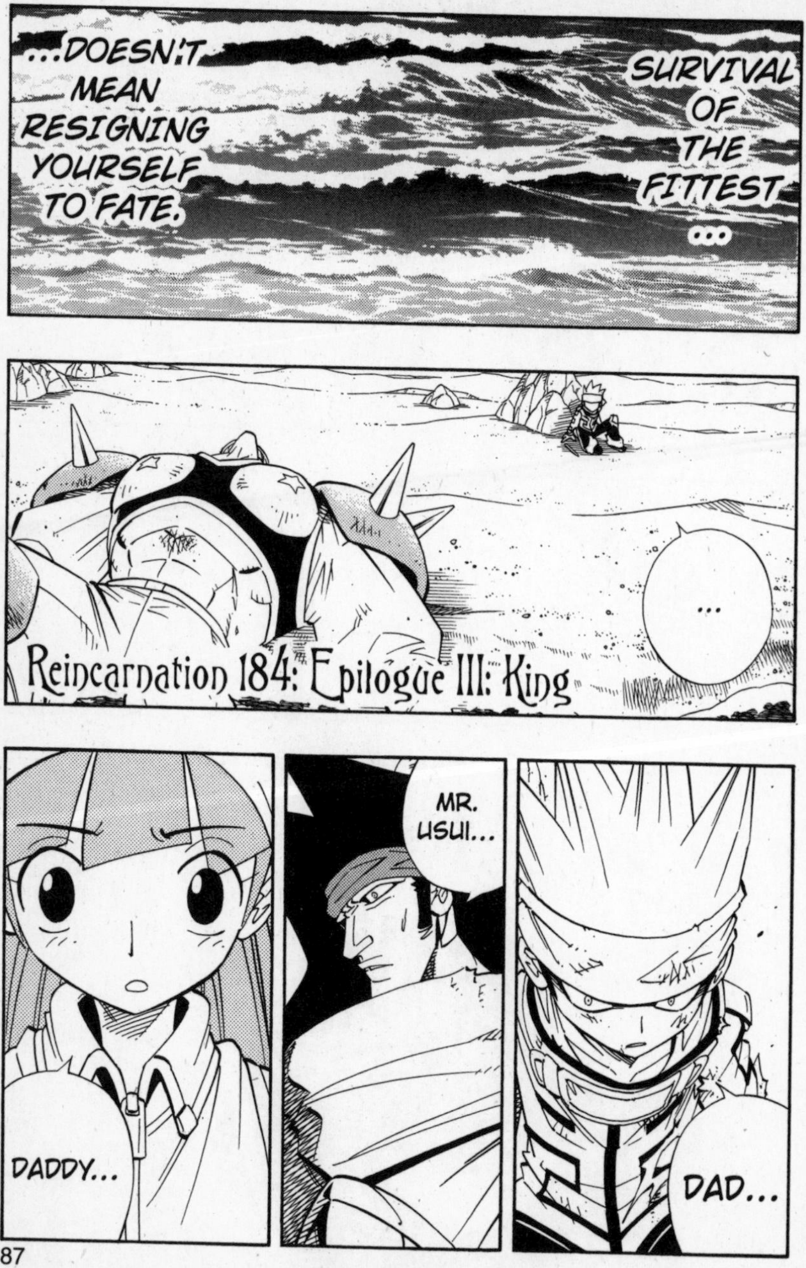
SURVIVAL OF THE FITTEST...
...DOESN'T MEAN RESIGNING YOURSELF TO FATE.
...
Reincarnation 184: Epilogue III: King
DAD...
MR. USUI...
DADDY...

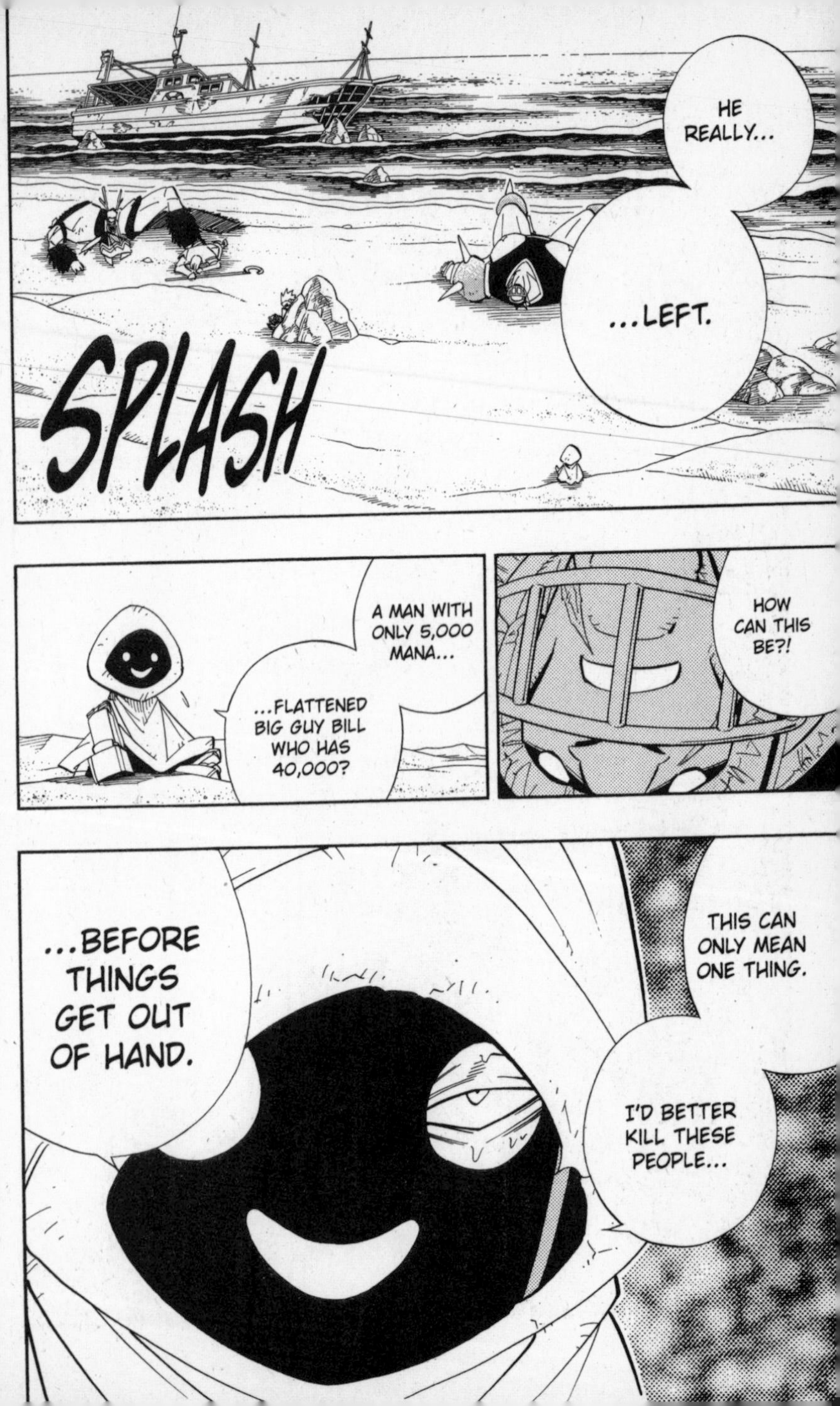

HE REALLY...
...LEFT.
SPLASH
HOW CAN THIS BE?!
A MAN WITH ONLY 5,000 MANA...
...FLATTENED BIG GUY BILL WHO HAS 40,000?
THIS CAN ONLY MEAN ONE THING.
I'D BETTER KILL THESE PEOPLE...
...BEFORE THINGS GET OUT OF HAND.

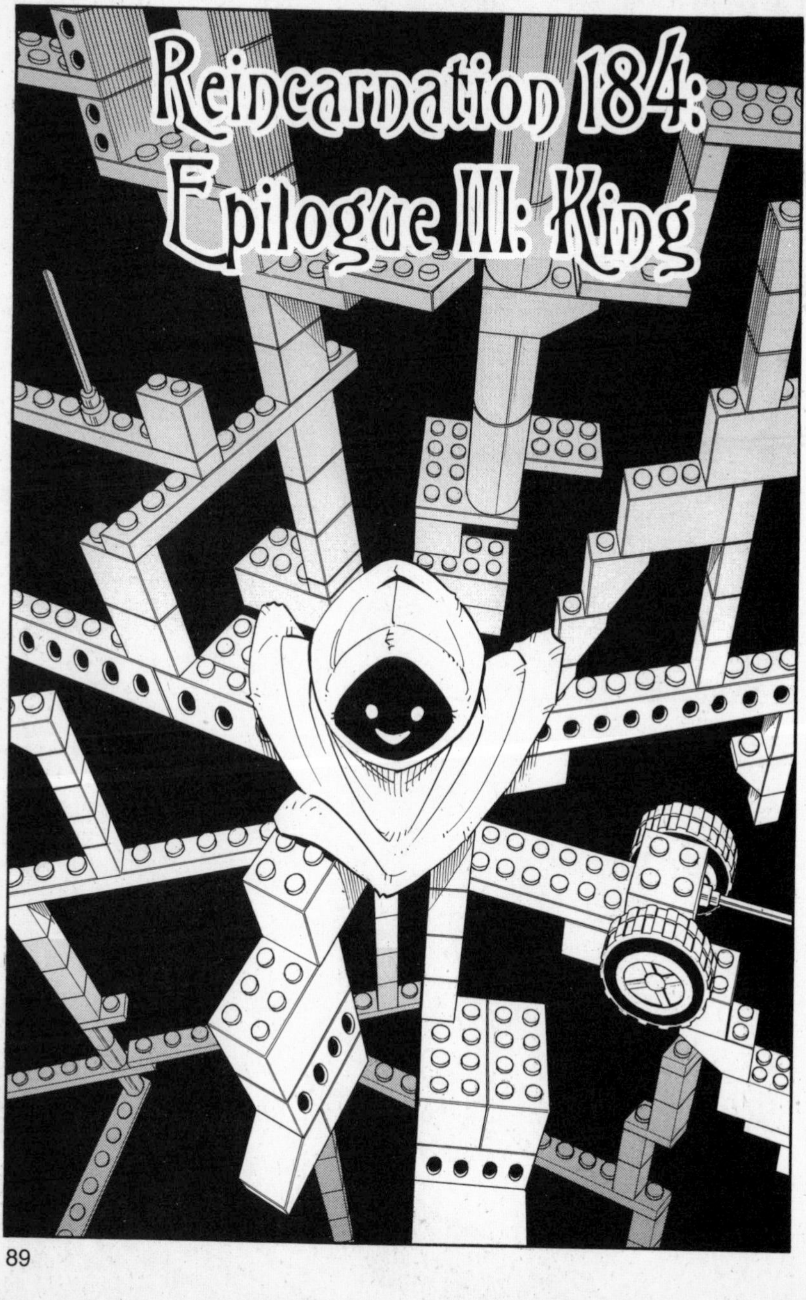
Reincarnation 184:
Epilogue III: King

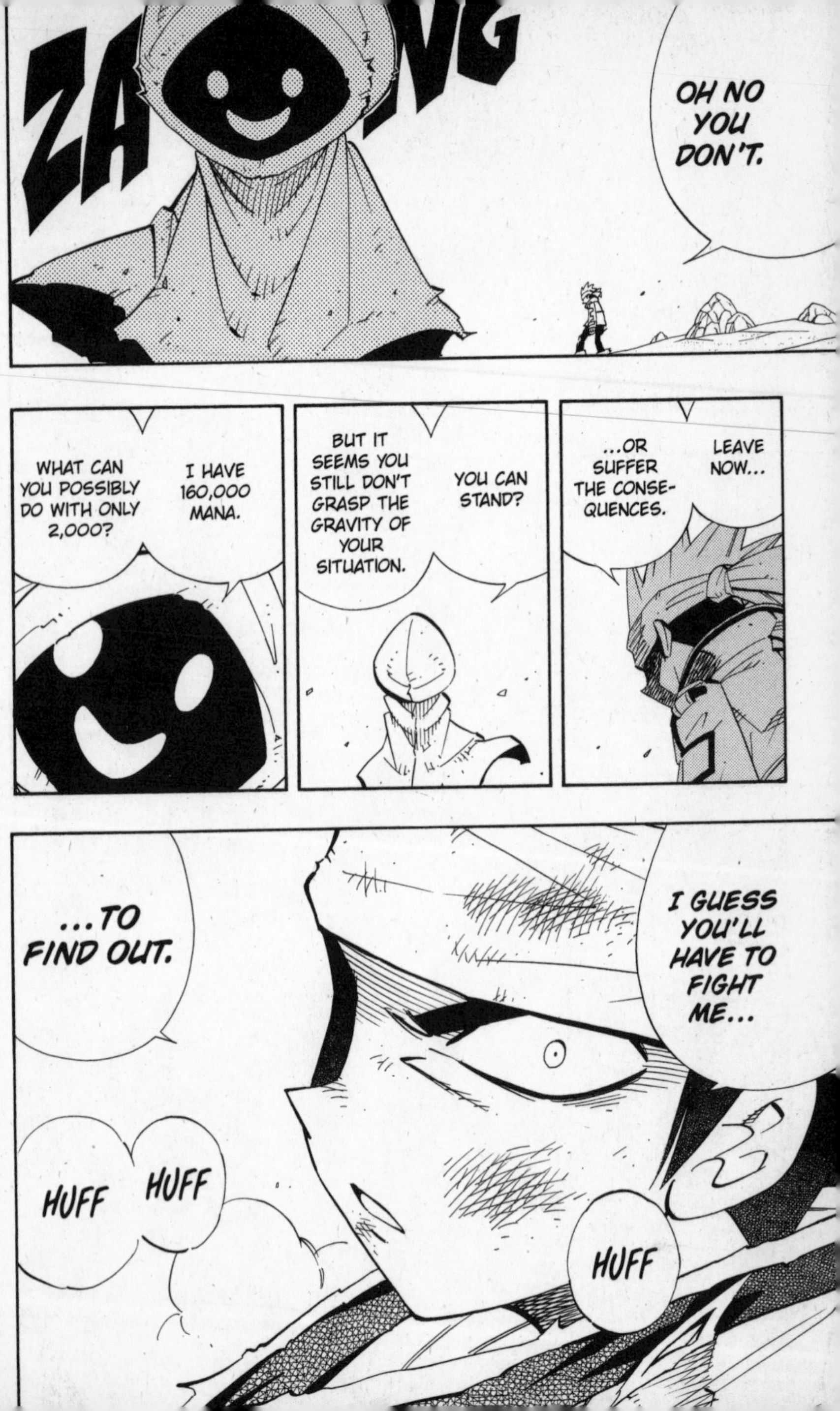
OH NO YOU DON'T.
ZA NG
LEAVE NOW...
...OR SUFFER THE CONSE-QUENCES.
YOU CAN STAND?
BUT IT SEEMS YOU STILL DON'T GRASP THE GRAVITY OF YOUR SITUATION.
I HAVE 160,000 MANA.
WHAT CAN YOU POSSIBLY DO WITH ONLY 2,000?
I GUESS YOU'LL HAVE TO FIGHT ME...
...TO FIND OUT.
HUFF
HUFF
HUFF

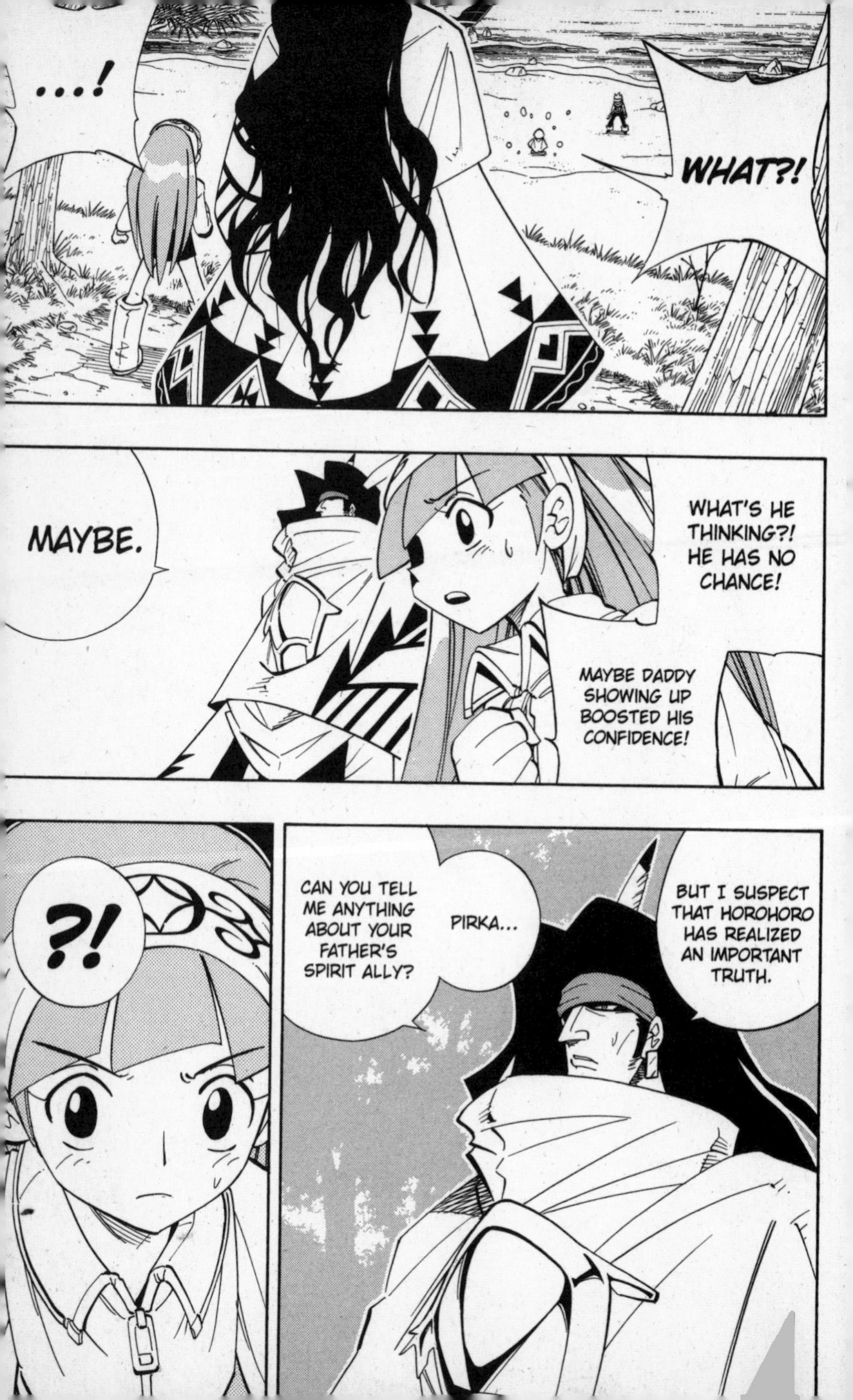
WHAT?!
...!
WHAT'S HE THINKING?! HE HAS NO CHANCE!
MAYBE DADDY SHOWING UP BOOSTED HIS CONFIDENCE!
MAYBE.
BUT I SUSPECT THAT HOROHORO HAS REALIZED AN IMPORTANT TRUTH.
PIRKA...
CAN YOU TELL ME ANYTHING ABOUT YOUR FATHER'S SPIRIT ALLY?
?!

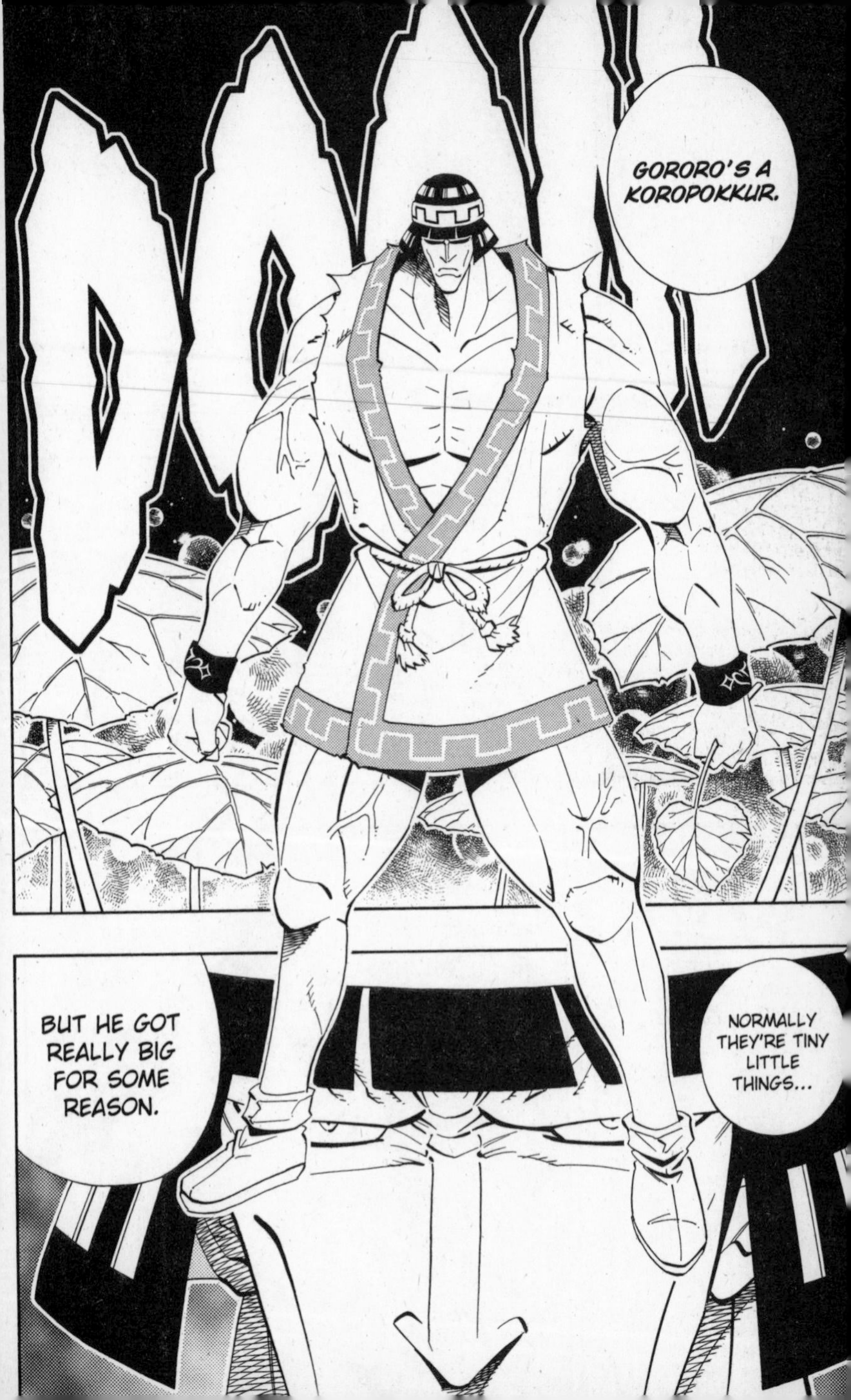
GORORO'S A KOROPOKKUR.
NORMALLY THEY'RE TINY LITTLE THINGS...
BUT HE GOT REALLY BIG FOR SOME REASON.

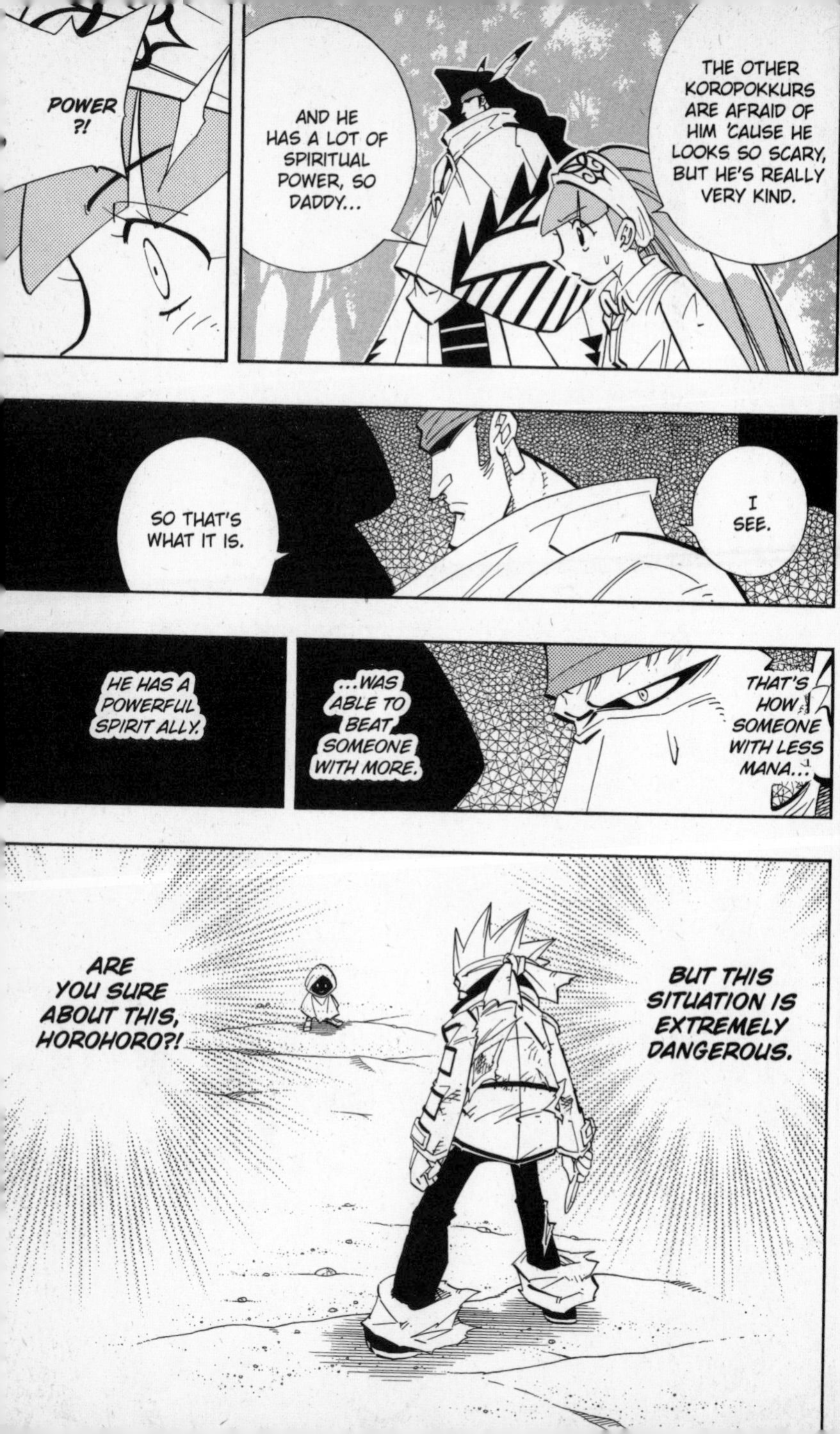
THE OTHER KOROPOKKURS ARE AFRAID OF HIM 'CAUSE HE LOOKS SO SCARY, BUT HE'S REALLY VERY KIND.
AND HE HAS A LOT OF SPIRITUAL POWER, SO DADDY...
POWER ?!
I SEE.
SO THAT'S WHAT IT IS.
THAT'S HOW SOMEONE WITH LESS MANA...
...WAS ABLE TO BEAT SOMEONE WITH MORE.
HE HAS A POWERFUL SPIRIT ALLY.
BUT THIS SITUATION IS EXTREMELY DANGEROUS.
ARE YOU SURE ABOUT THIS, HOROHORO?!

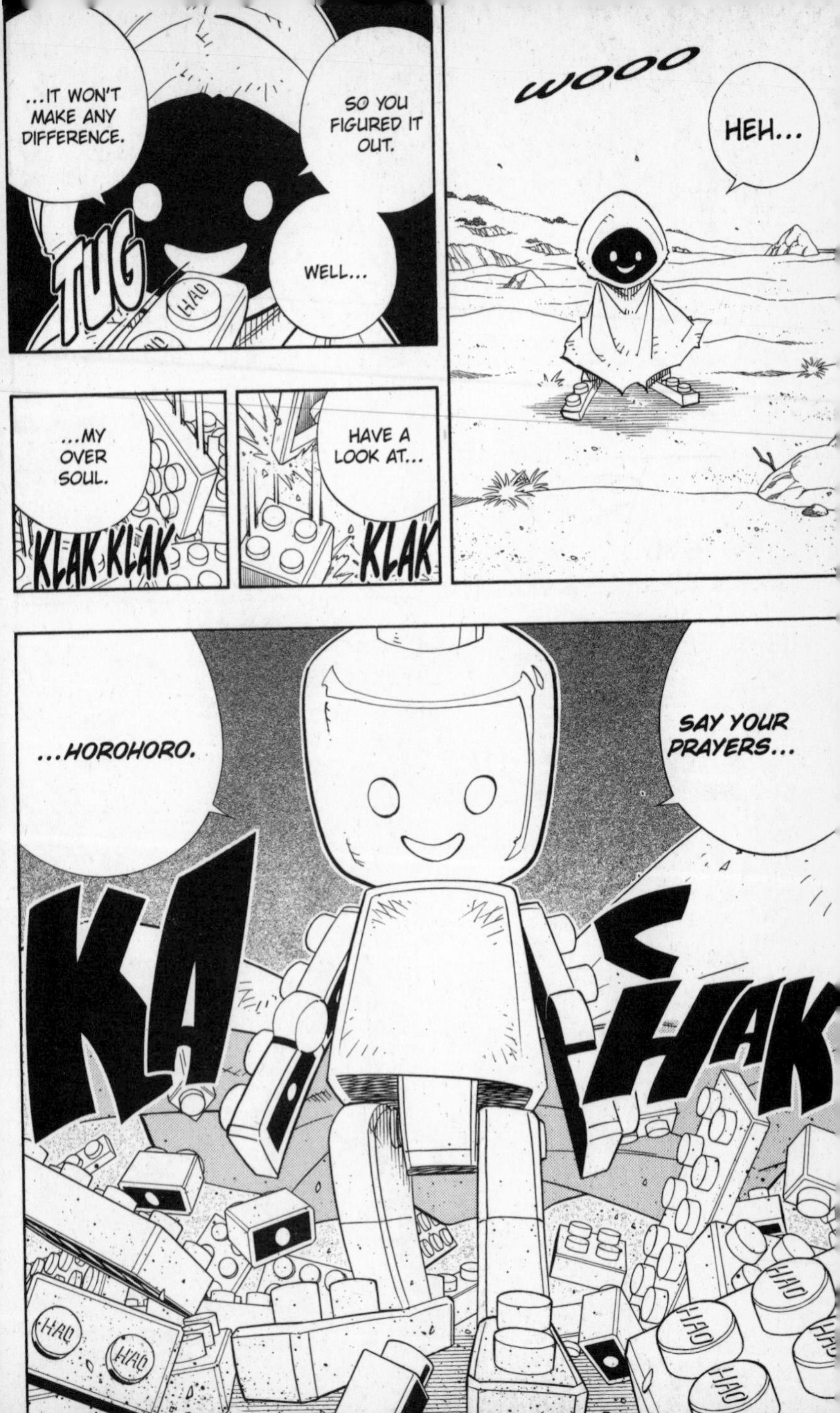
WOOO
HEH...
SO YOU FIGURED IT OUT.
WELL...
...IT WON'T MAKE ANY DIFFERENCE.
TUG
HAO
HAVE A LOOK AT...
KLAK
...MY OVER SOUL.
KLAK KLAK
SAY YOUR PRAYERS...
...HOROHORO.
KACHAK
HAO

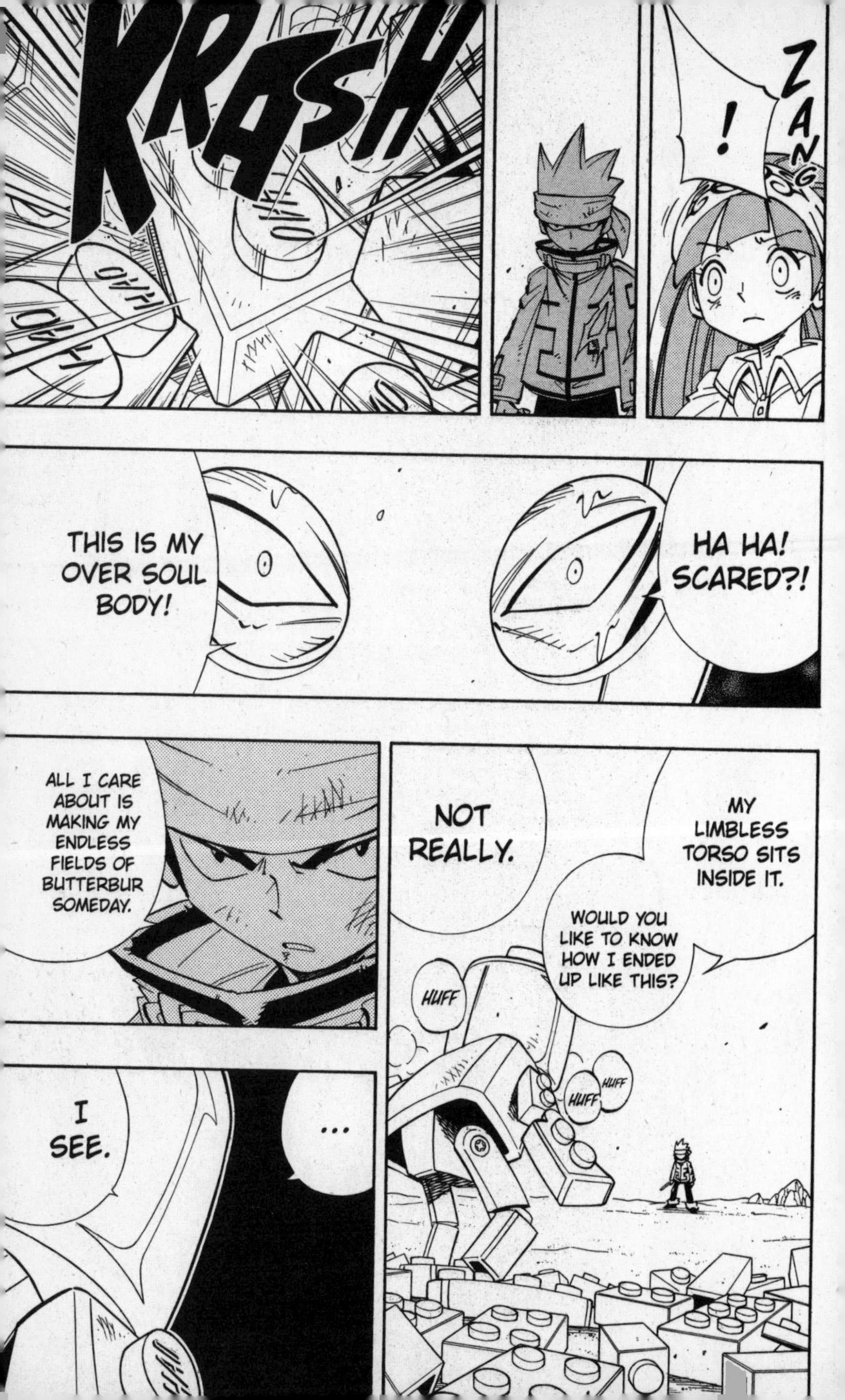
ZANG
!
KRASH
HA HA! SCARED?!
THIS IS MY OVER SOUL BODY!
MY LIMBLESS TORSO SITS INSIDE IT.
NOT REALLY.
WOULD YOU LIKE TO KNOW HOW I ENDED UP LIKE THIS?
HUFF
HUFF
HUFF
ALL I CARE ABOUT IS MAKING MY ENDLESS FIELDS OF BUTTERBUR SOMEDAY.
...
I SEE.

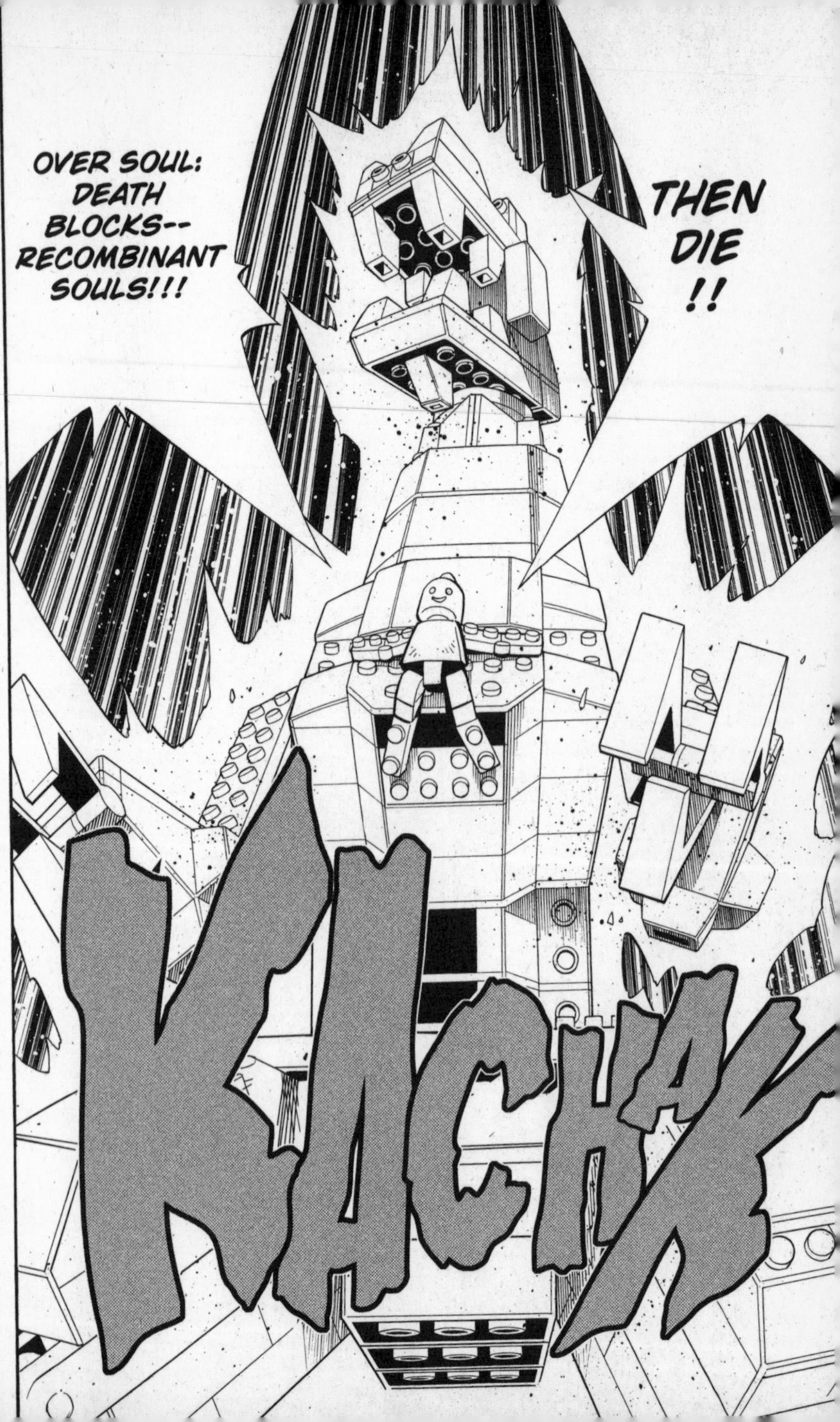
THEN DIE !!
OVER SOUL: DEATH BLOCKS-- RECOMBINANT SOULS!!!
KACHAK

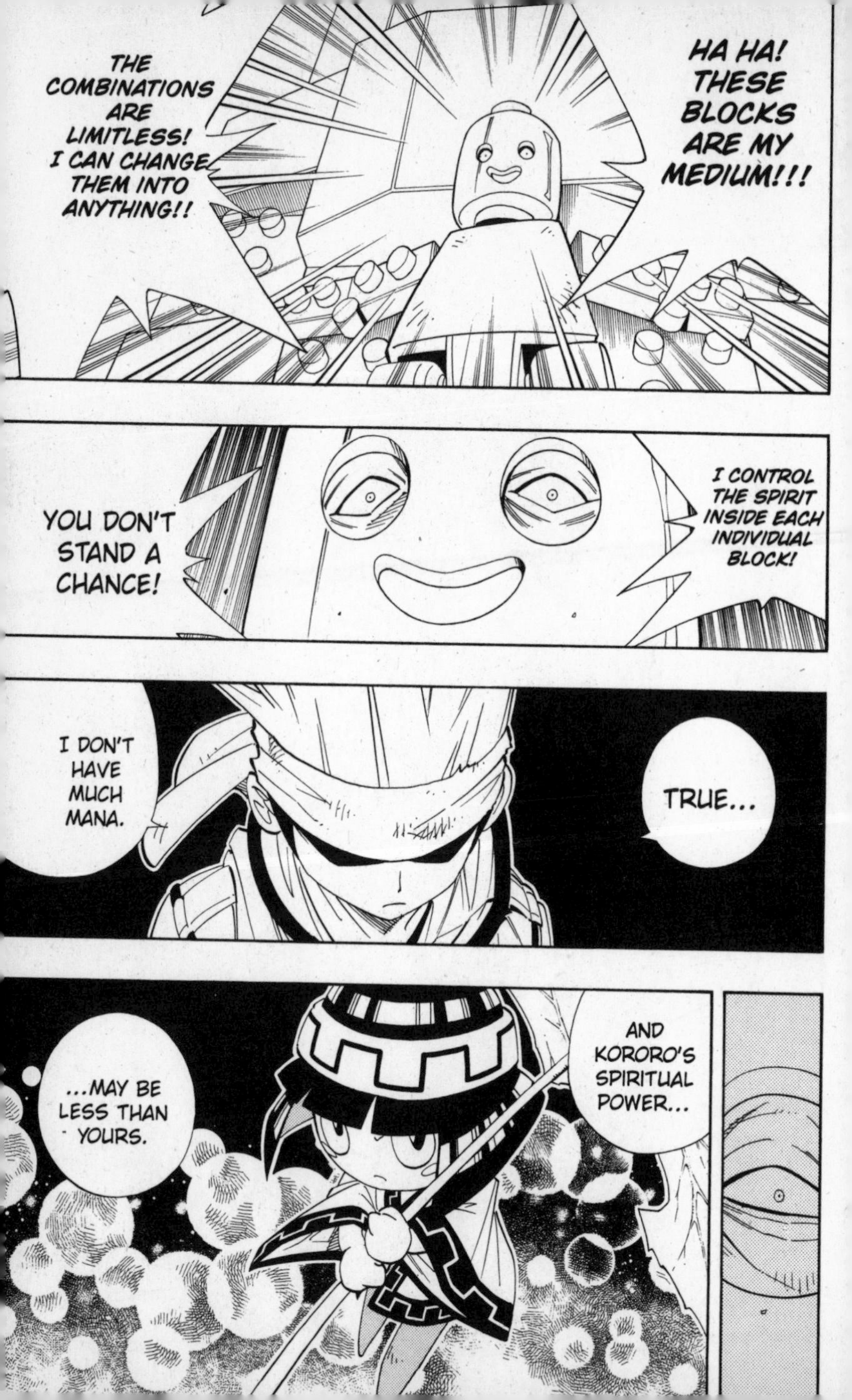
HA HA! THESE BLOCKS ARE MY MEDIUM!!!
THE COMBINATIONS ARE LIMITLESS! I CAN CHANGE THEM INTO ANYTHING!!
I CONTROL THE SPIRIT INSIDE EACH INDIVIDUAL BLOCK!
YOU DON'T STAND A CHANCE!
TRUE...
I DON'T HAVE MUCH MANA.
AND KORORO'S SPIRITUAL POWER...
...MAY BE LESS THAN YOURS.

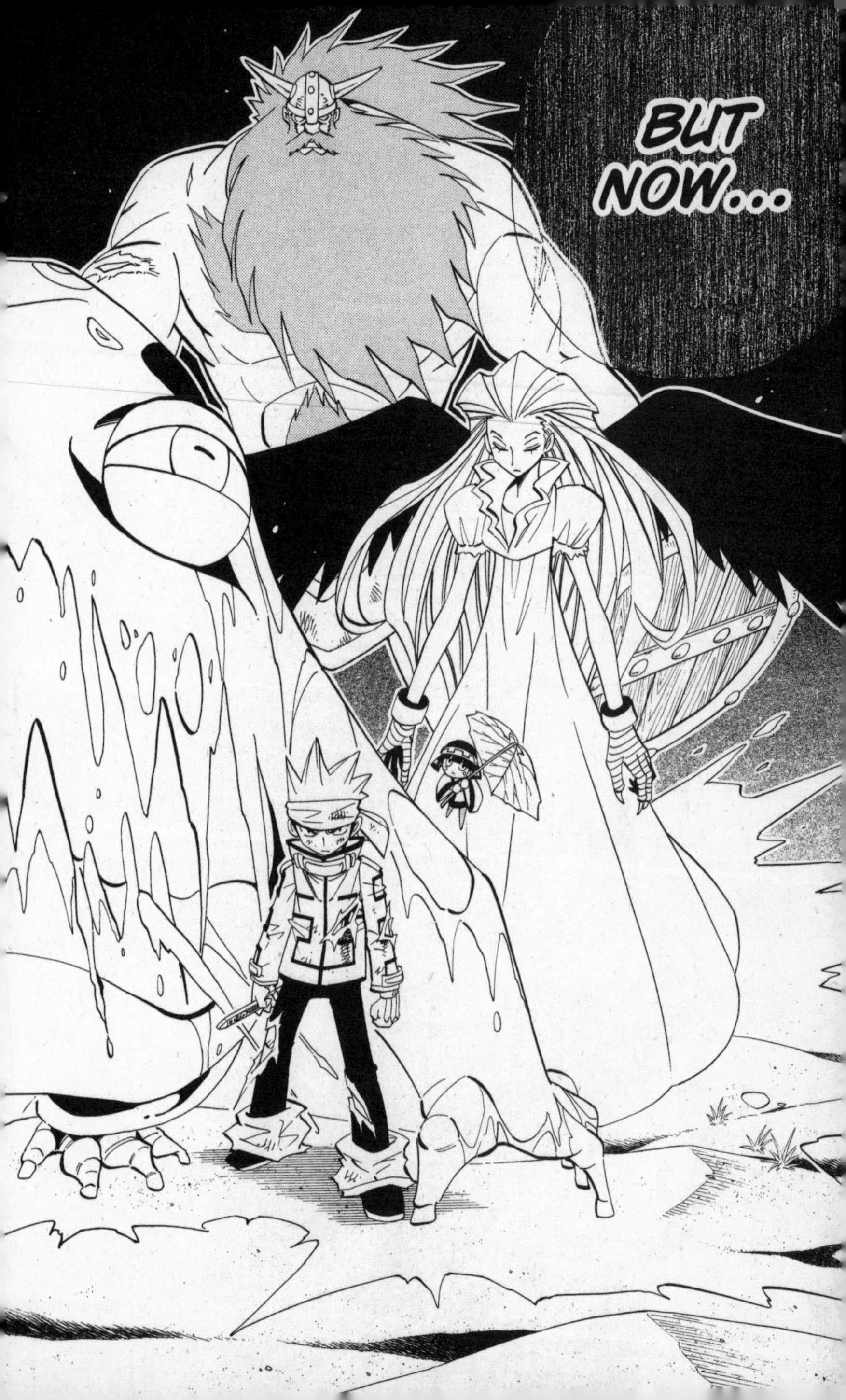
BUT NOW...

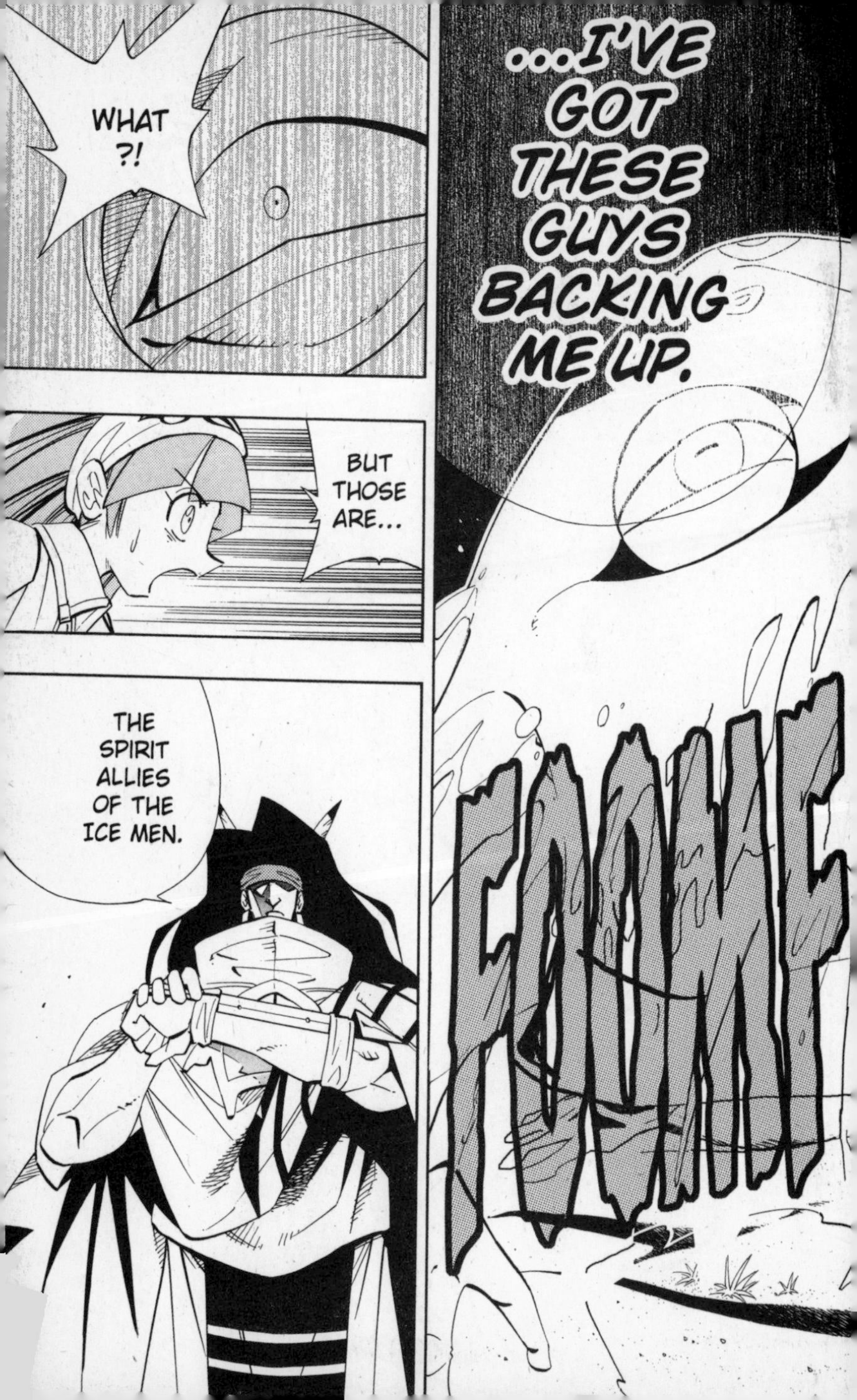
...I'VE GOT THESE GUYS BACKING ME UP.
WHAT ?!
BUT THOSE ARE...
THE SPIRIT ALLIES OF THE ICE MEN.

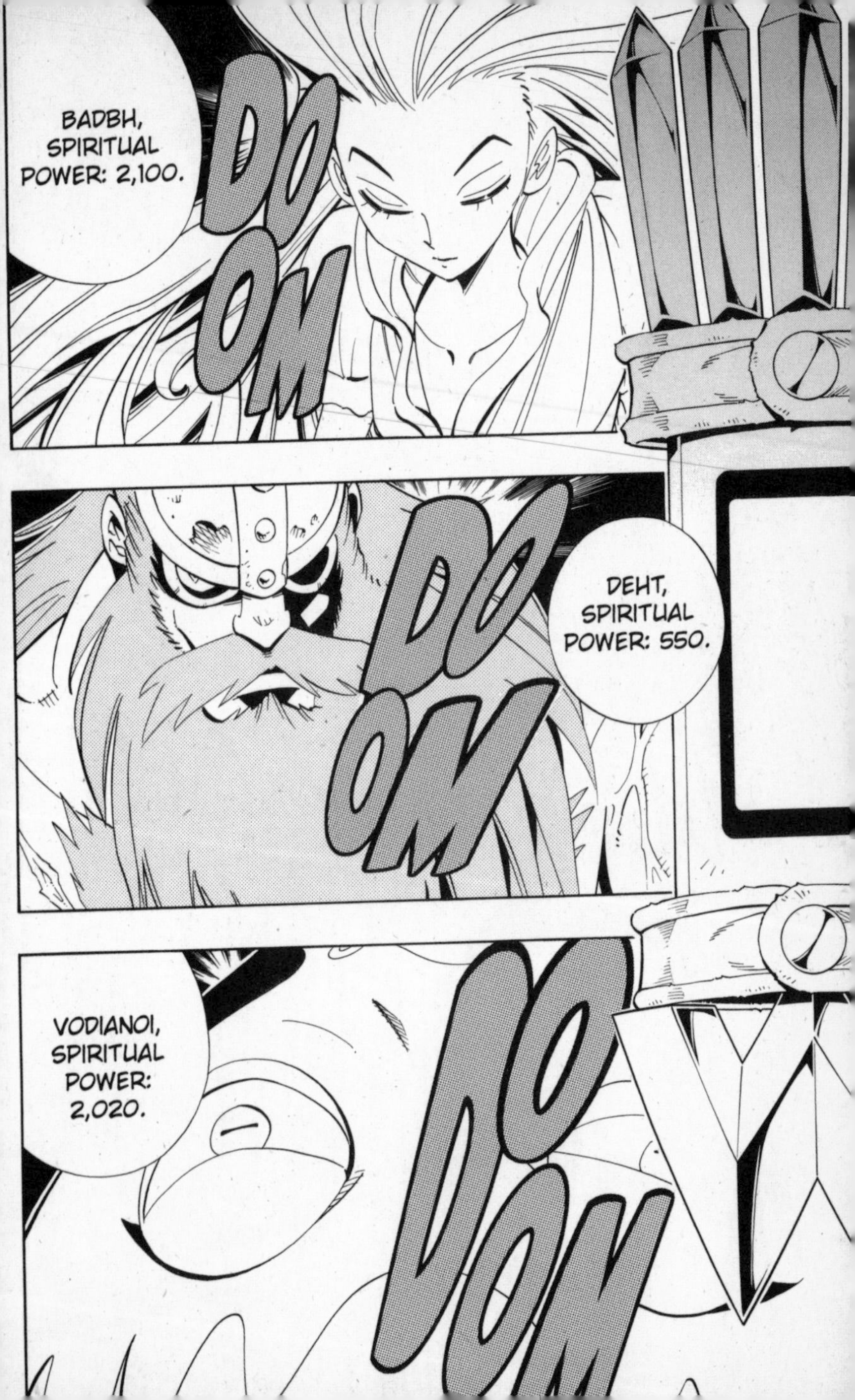
BADBH, SPIRITUAL POWER: 2,100.
DOOM
DEHT, SPIRITUAL POWER: 550.
DOOM
VODIANOI, SPIRITUAL POWER: 2,020.
DODOOM

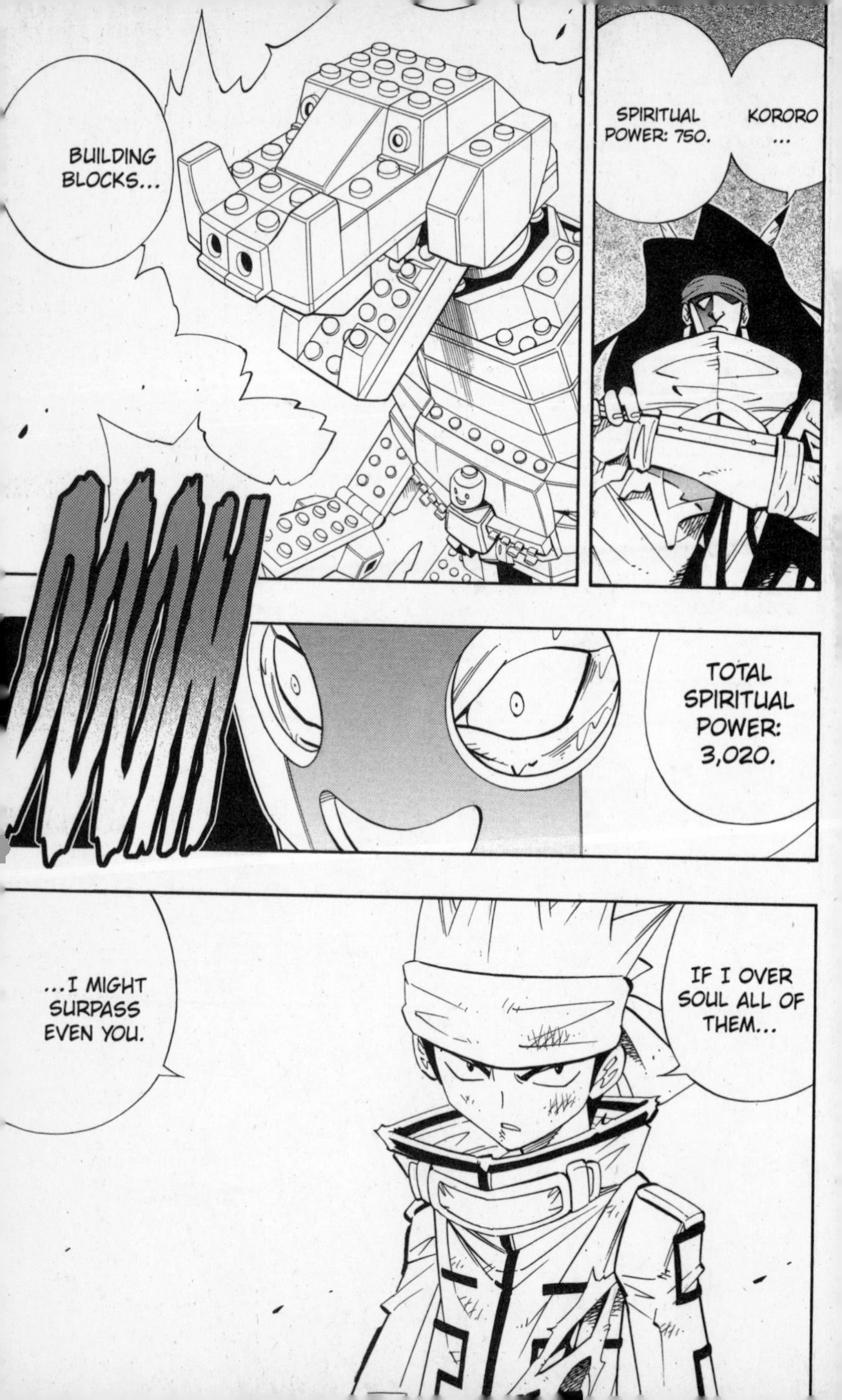
KORORO ...
SPIRITUAL POWER: 750.
BUILDING BLOCKS...
TOTAL SPIRITUAL POWER: 3,020.
IF I OVER SOUL ALL OF THEM...
...I MIGHT SURPASS EVEN YOU.

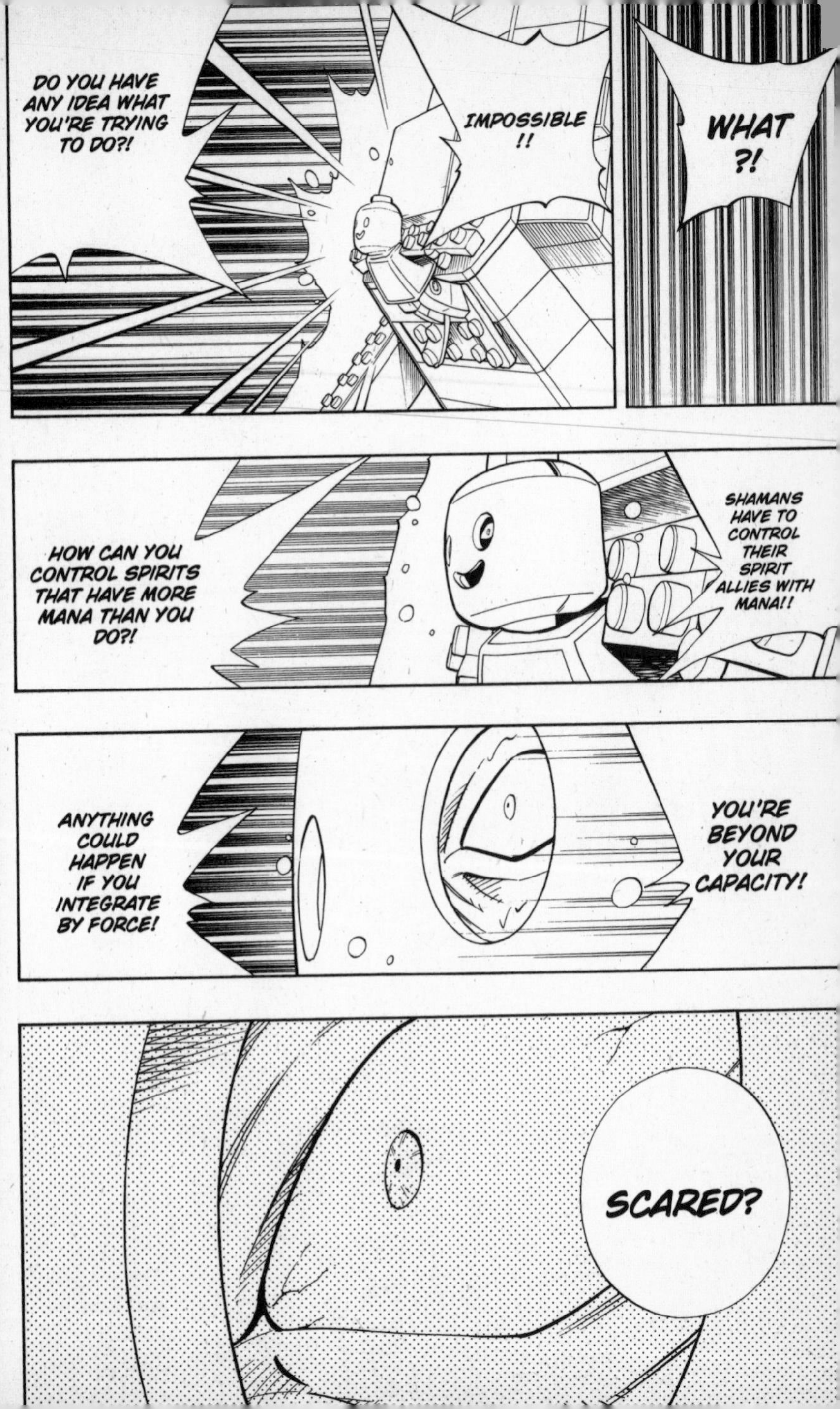
WHAT?!
IMPOSSIBLE!!
DO YOU HAVE ANY IDEA WHAT YOU'RE TRYING TO DO?!
SHAMANS HAVE TO CONTROL THEIR SPIRIT ALLIES WITH MANA!!
HOW CAN YOU CONTROL SPIRITS THAT HAVE MORE MANA THAN YOU DO?!
YOU'RE BEYOND YOUR CAPACITY!
ANYTHING COULD HAPPEN IF YOU INTEGRATE BY FORCE!
SCARED?

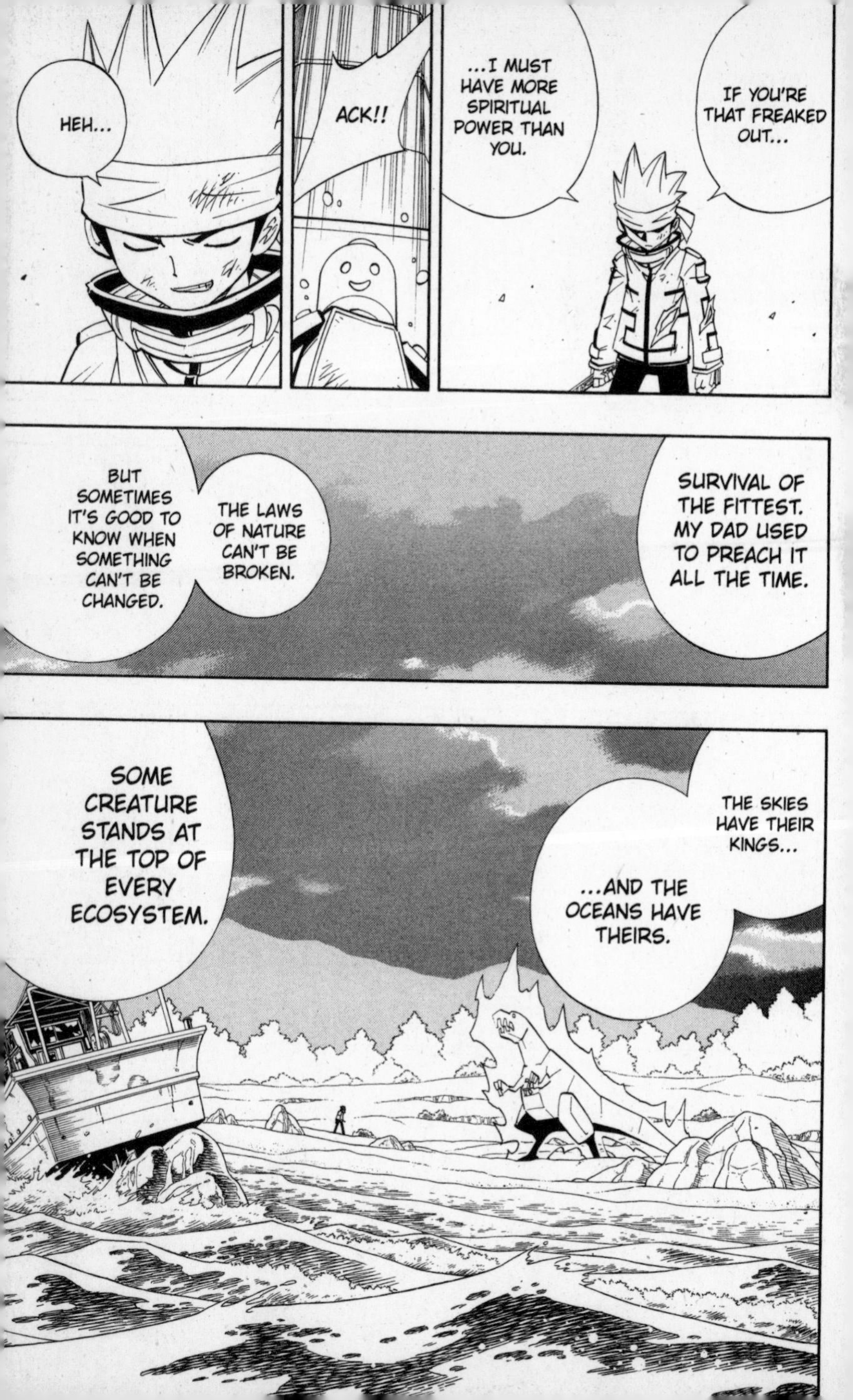
IF YOU'RE THAT FREAKED OUT...
...I MUST HAVE MORE SPIRITUAL POWER THAN YOU.
ACK!!
HEH...
SURVIVAL OF THE FITTEST. MY DAD USED TO PREACH IT ALL THE TIME.
THE LAWS OF NATURE CAN'T BE BROKEN.
BUT SOMETIMES IT'S GOOD TO KNOW WHEN SOMETHING CAN'T BE CHANGED.
THE SKIES HAVE THEIR KINGS...
...AND THE OCEANS HAVE THEIRS.
SOME CREATURE STANDS AT THE TOP OF EVERY ECOSYSTEM.

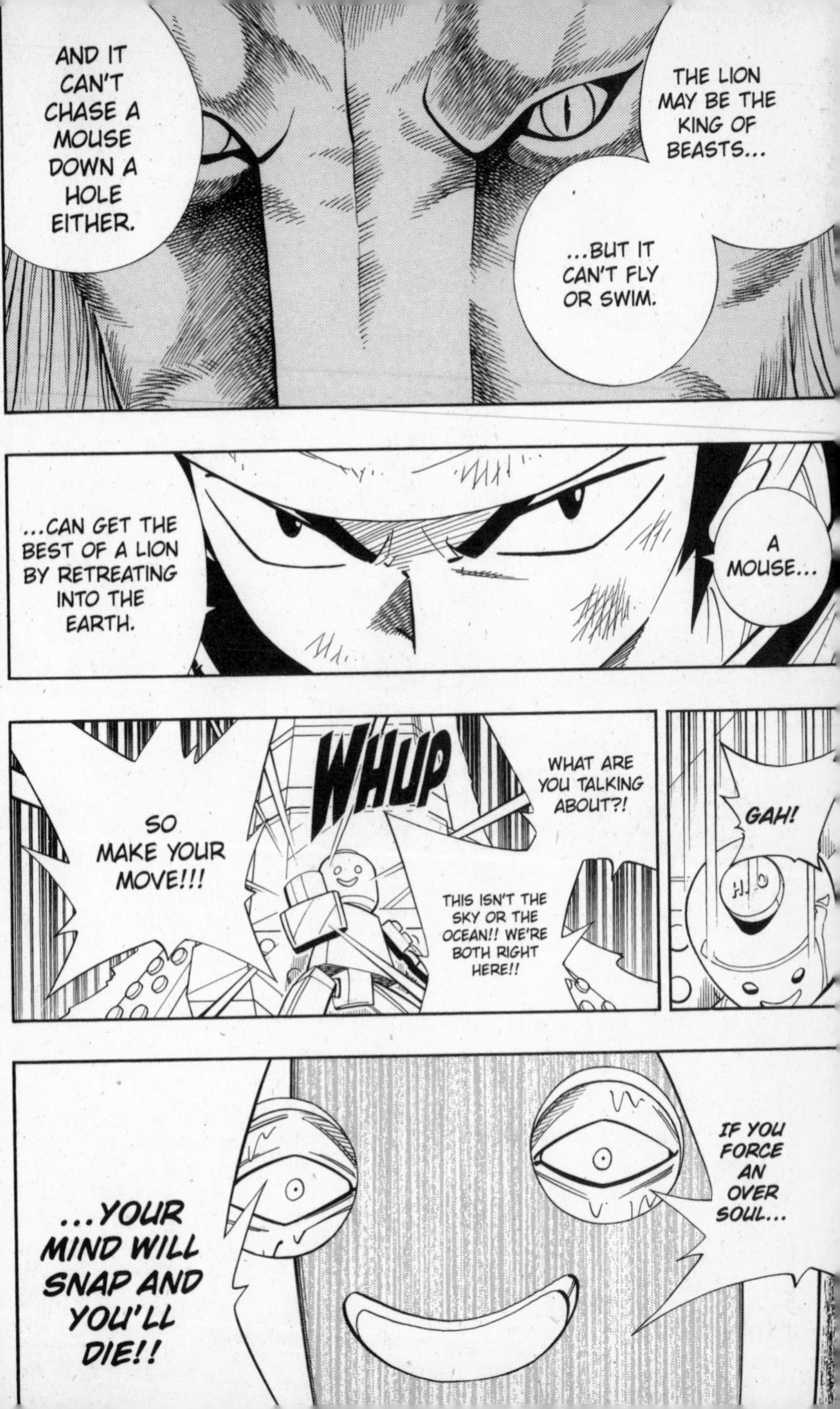
THE LION MAY BE THE KING OF BEASTS...
...BUT IT CAN'T FLY OR SWIM.
AND IT CAN'T CHASE A MOUSE DOWN A HOLE EITHER.
A MOUSE...
...CAN GET THE BEST OF A LION BY RETREATING INTO THE EARTH.
GAH!
WHAT ARE YOU TALKING ABOUT?!
WHUP
THIS ISN'T THE SKY OR THE OCEAN!! WE'RE BOTH RIGHT HERE!!
SO MAKE YOUR MOVE!!!
IF YOU FORCE AN OVER SOUL...
...YOUR MIND WILL SNAP AND YOU'LL DIE!!

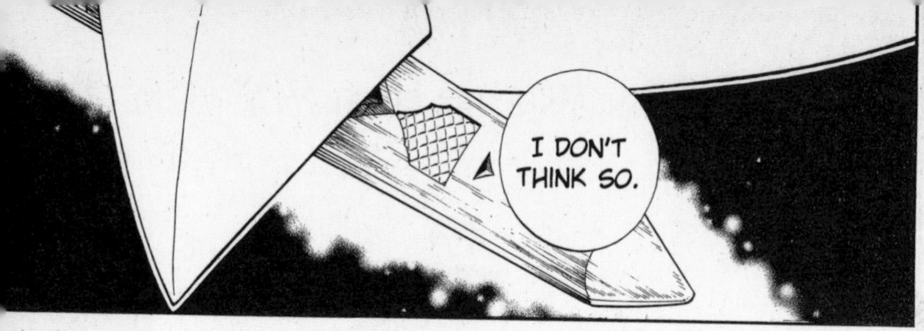
I DON'T THINK SO.

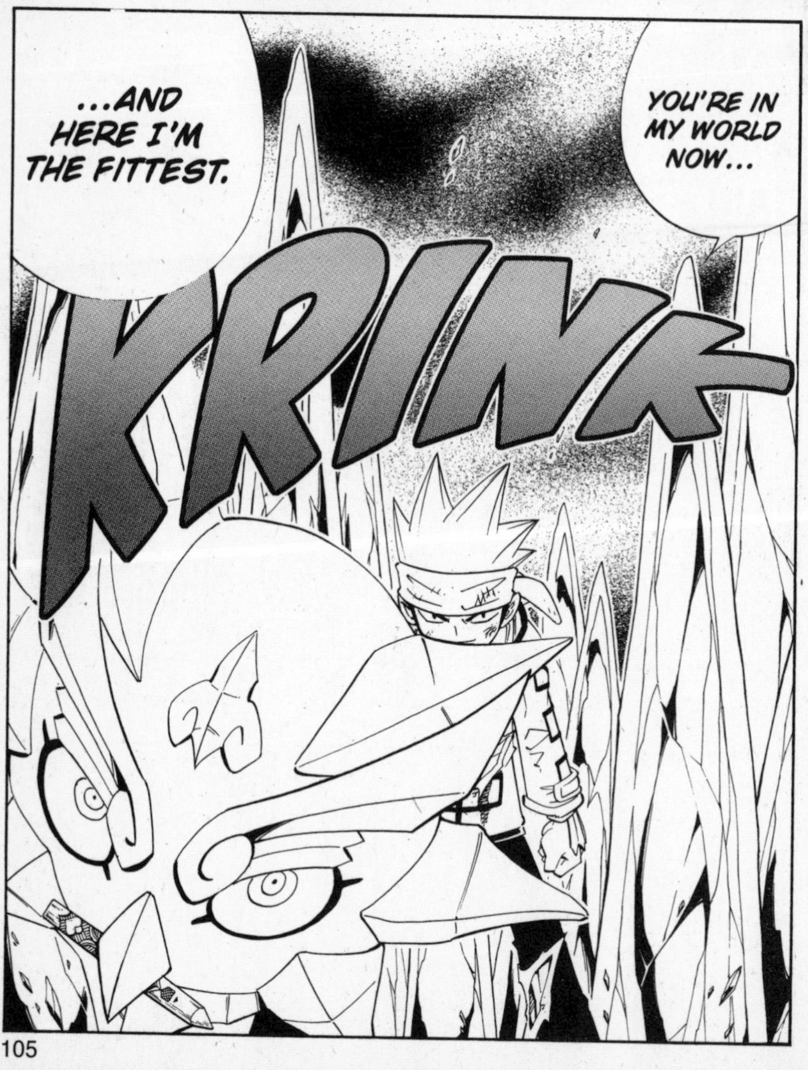
YOU'RE IN MY WORLD NOW...
...AND HERE I'M THE FITTEST.
KRINK

SHAMAN KING CHARACTER FILE No.114

ゴロロ

GORORO

2001
(JAN)

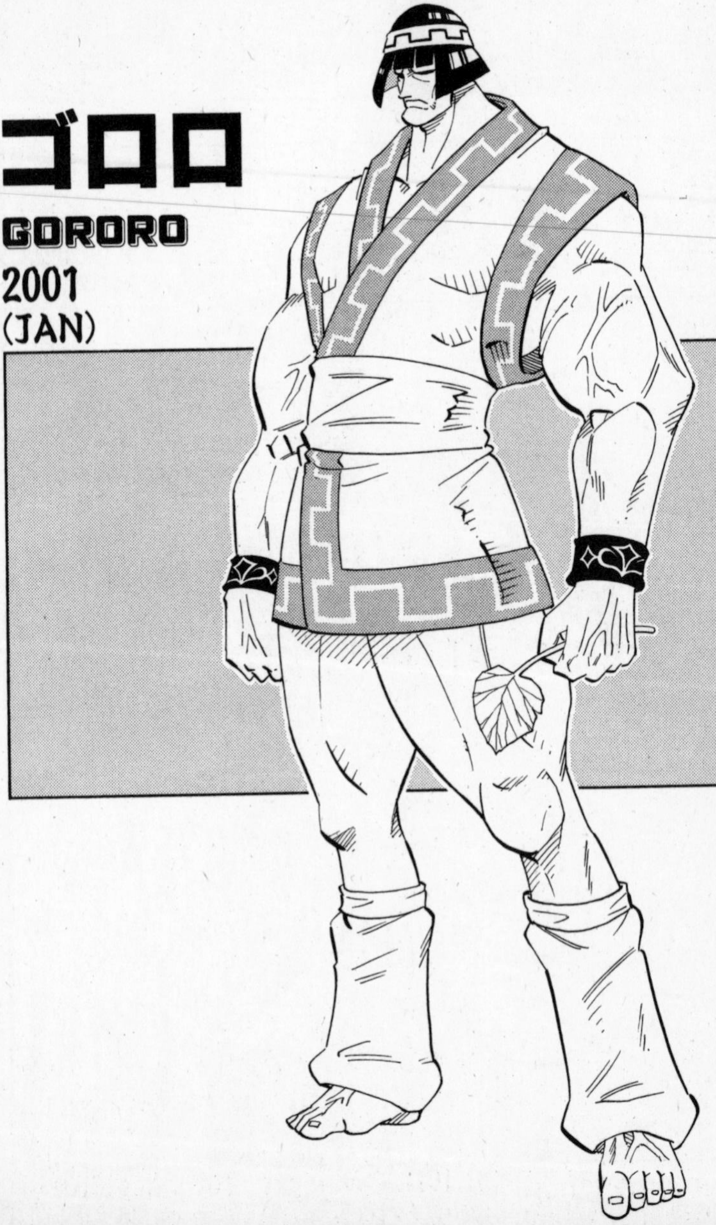

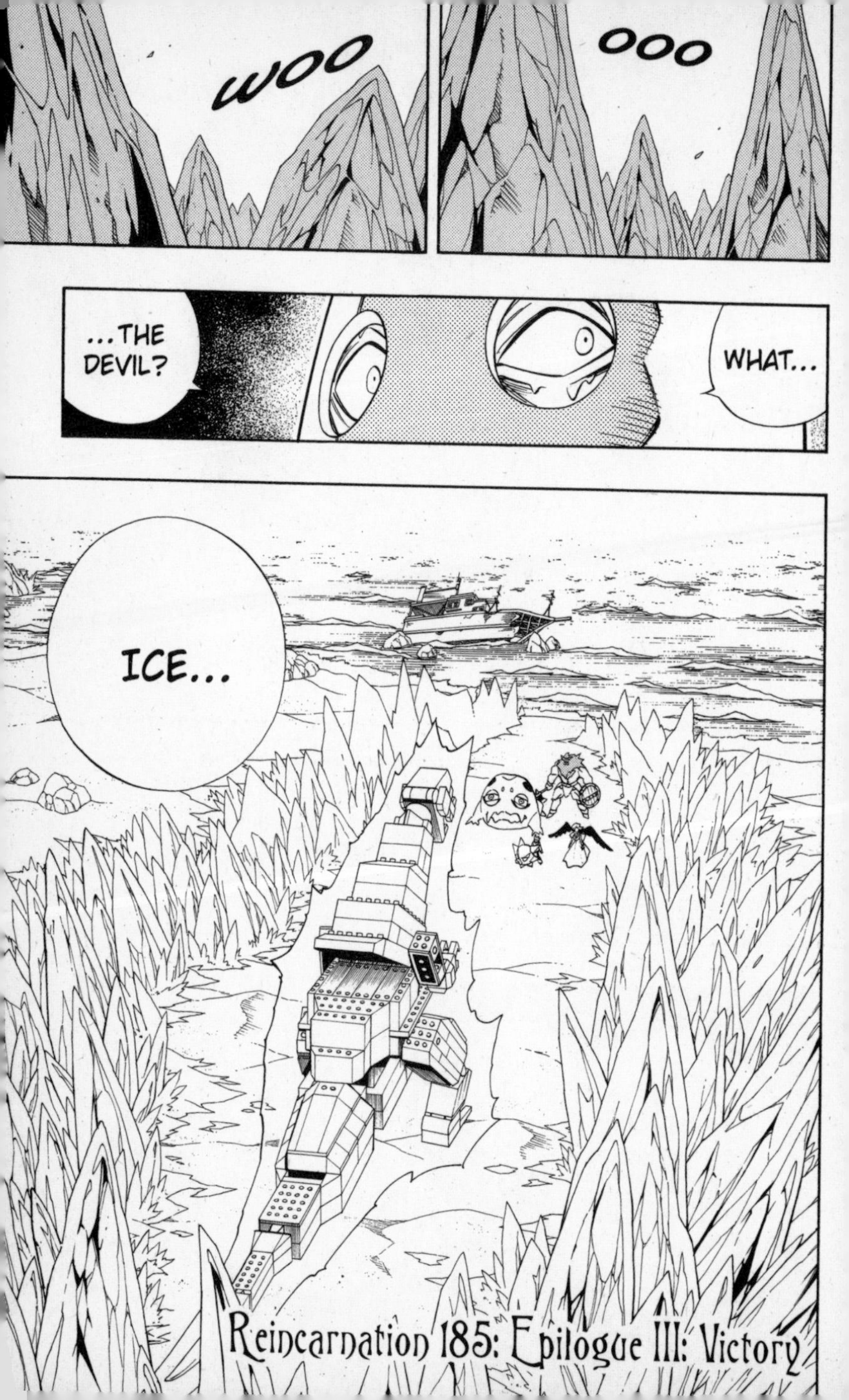
OOO
WOO
WHAT...
...THE DEVIL?
ICE...

Reincarnation 185: Epilogue III: Victory

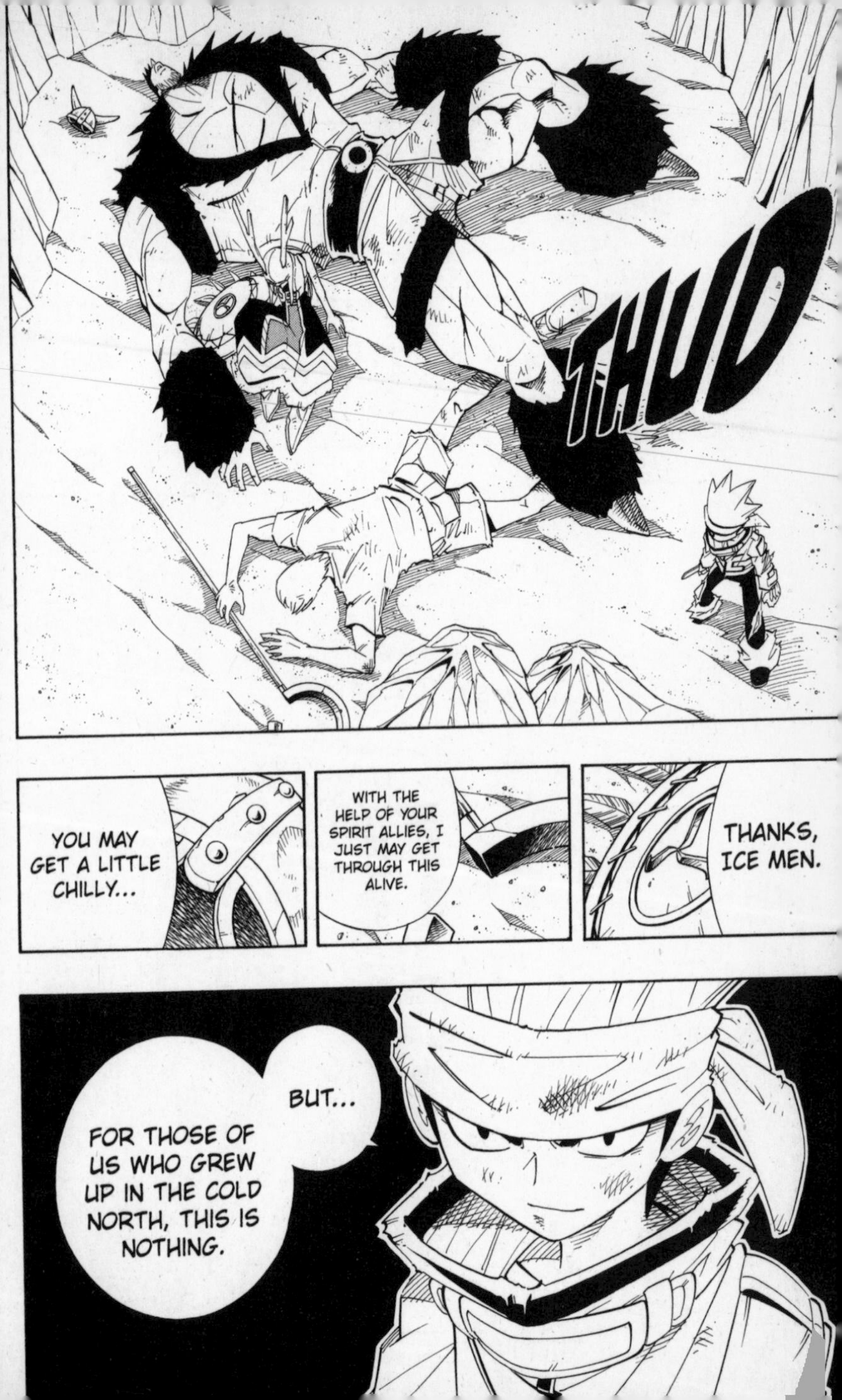
THUD
THANKS, ICE MEN.
WITH THE HELP OF YOUR SPIRIT ALLIES, I JUST MAY GET THROUGH THIS ALIVE.
YOU MAY GET A LITTLE CHILLY...
BUT...
FOR THOSE OF US WHO GREW UP IN THE COLD NORTH, THIS IS NOTHING.

Reincarnation 185: Epilogue III: Victory

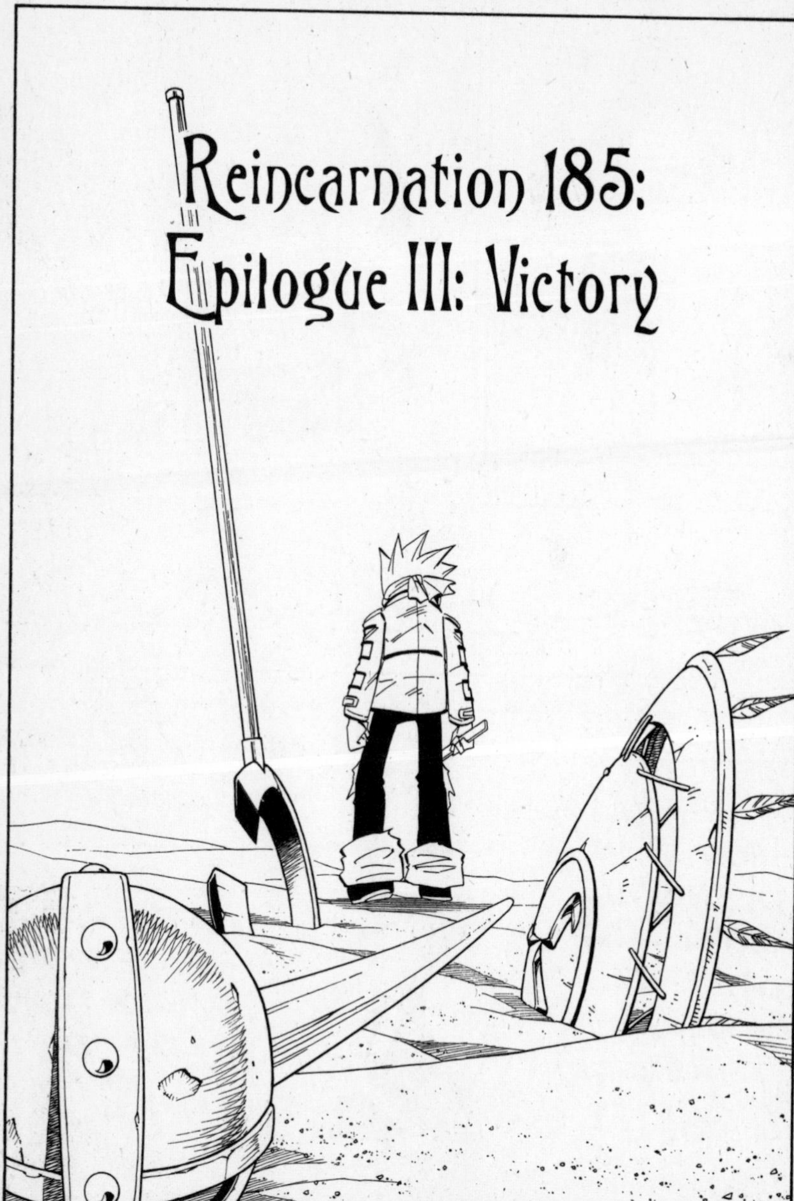

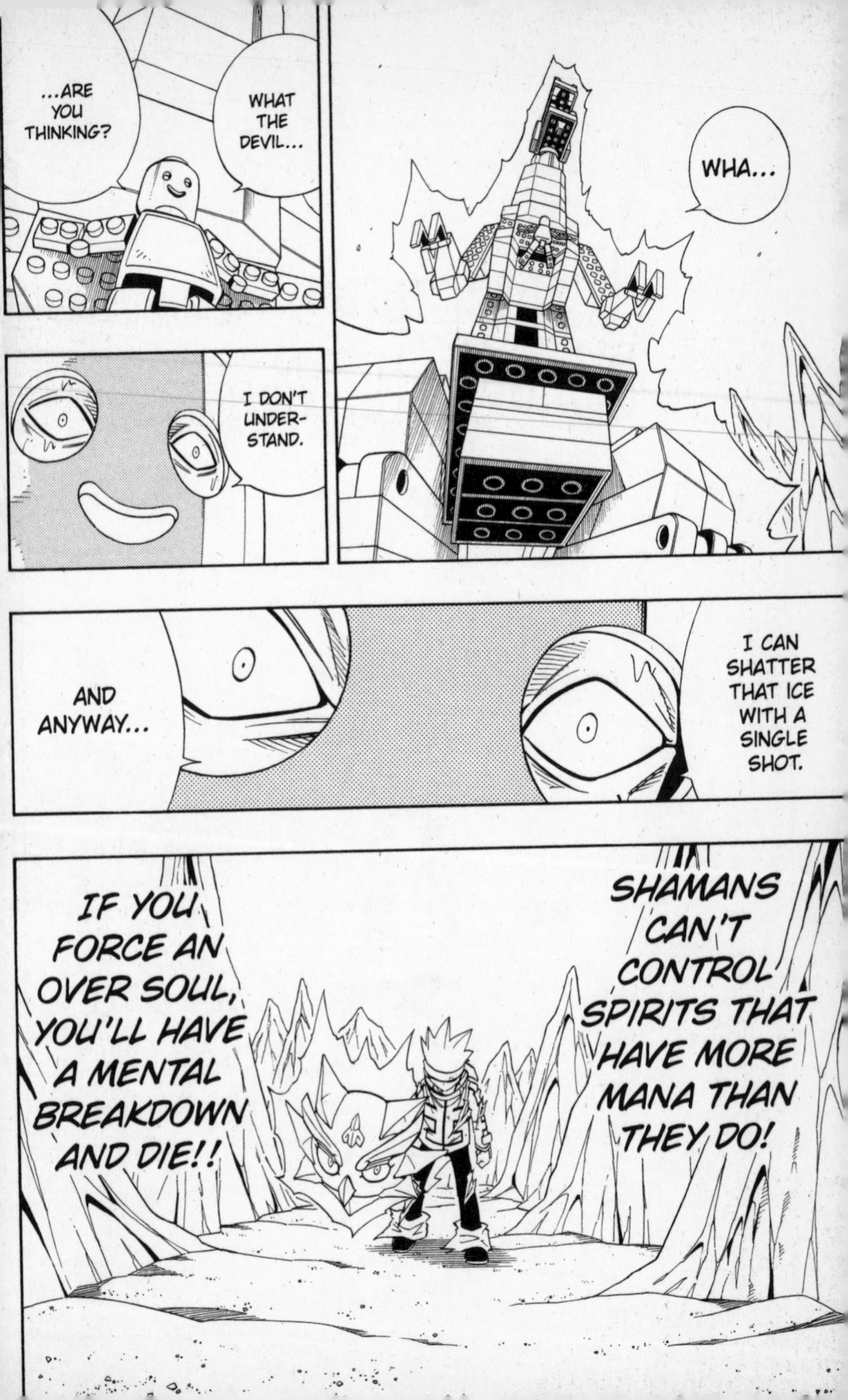
WHA...
WHAT THE DEVIL...
...ARE YOU THINKING?
I DON'T UNDER-STAND.
I CAN SHATTER THAT ICE WITH A SINGLE SHOT.
AND ANYWAY...
SHAMANS CAN'T CONTROL SPIRITS THAT HAVE MORE MANA THAN THEY DO!
IF YOU FORCE AN OVER SOUL, YOU'LL HAVE A MENTAL BREAKDOWN AND DIE!!

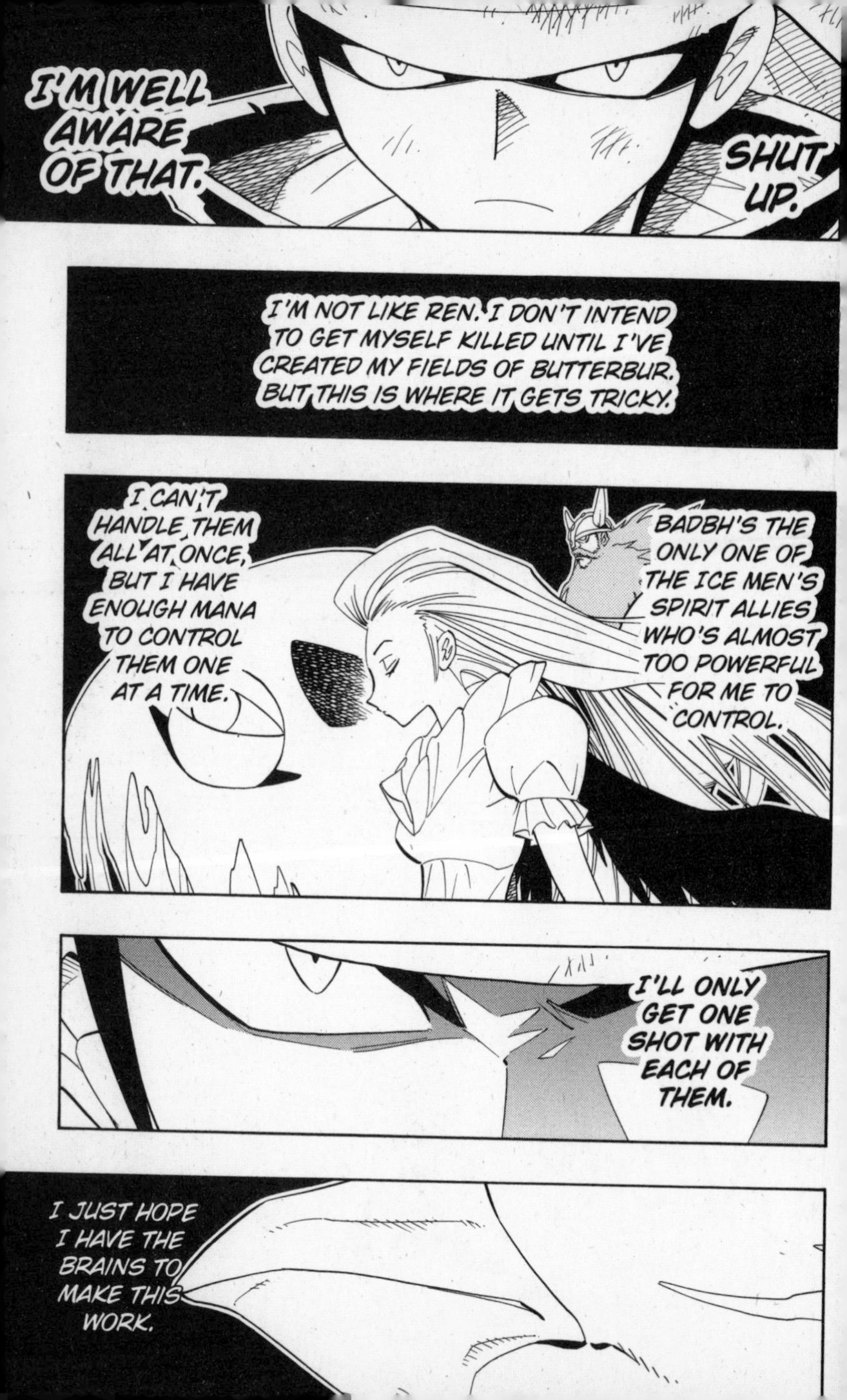
SHUT UP.
I'M WELL AWARE OF THAT.
I'M NOT LIKE REN. I DON'T INTEND TO GET MYSELF KILLED UNTIL I'VE CREATED MY FIELDS OF BUTTERBUR. BUT THIS IS WHERE IT GETS TRICKY.
BADBH'S THE ONLY ONE OF THE ICE MEN'S SPIRIT ALLIES WHO'S ALMOST TOO POWERFUL FOR ME TO CONTROL.
I CAN'T HANDLE THEM ALL AT ONCE, BUT I HAVE ENOUGH MANA TO CONTROL THEM ONE AT A TIME.
I'LL ONLY GET ONE SHOT WITH EACH OF THEM.
I JUST HOPE I HAVE THE BRAINS TO MAKE THIS WORK.

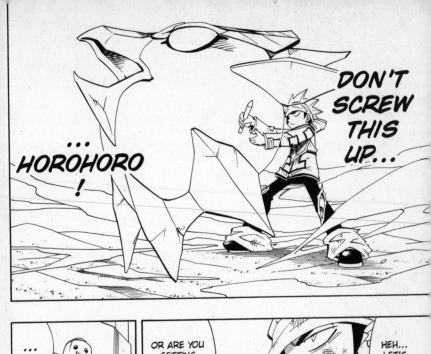

DON'T SCREW THIS UP...
...HOROHORO!
HEH... LET'S FINISH THIS.
OR ARE YOU GETTING COLD FEET?
...
HEH ...
BILL...
HUFF
HUFF
HUFF
THIS KID CAN'T BE A HERO.
HE'S TOO RECKLESS. HE WON'T LIVE LONG ENOUGH TO REALIZE HIS POTENTIAL.
KLAK

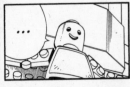

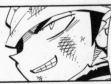

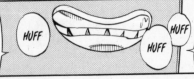

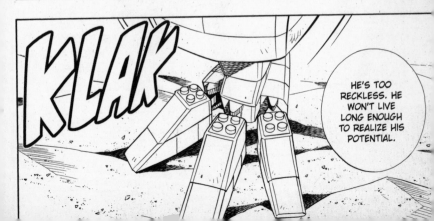

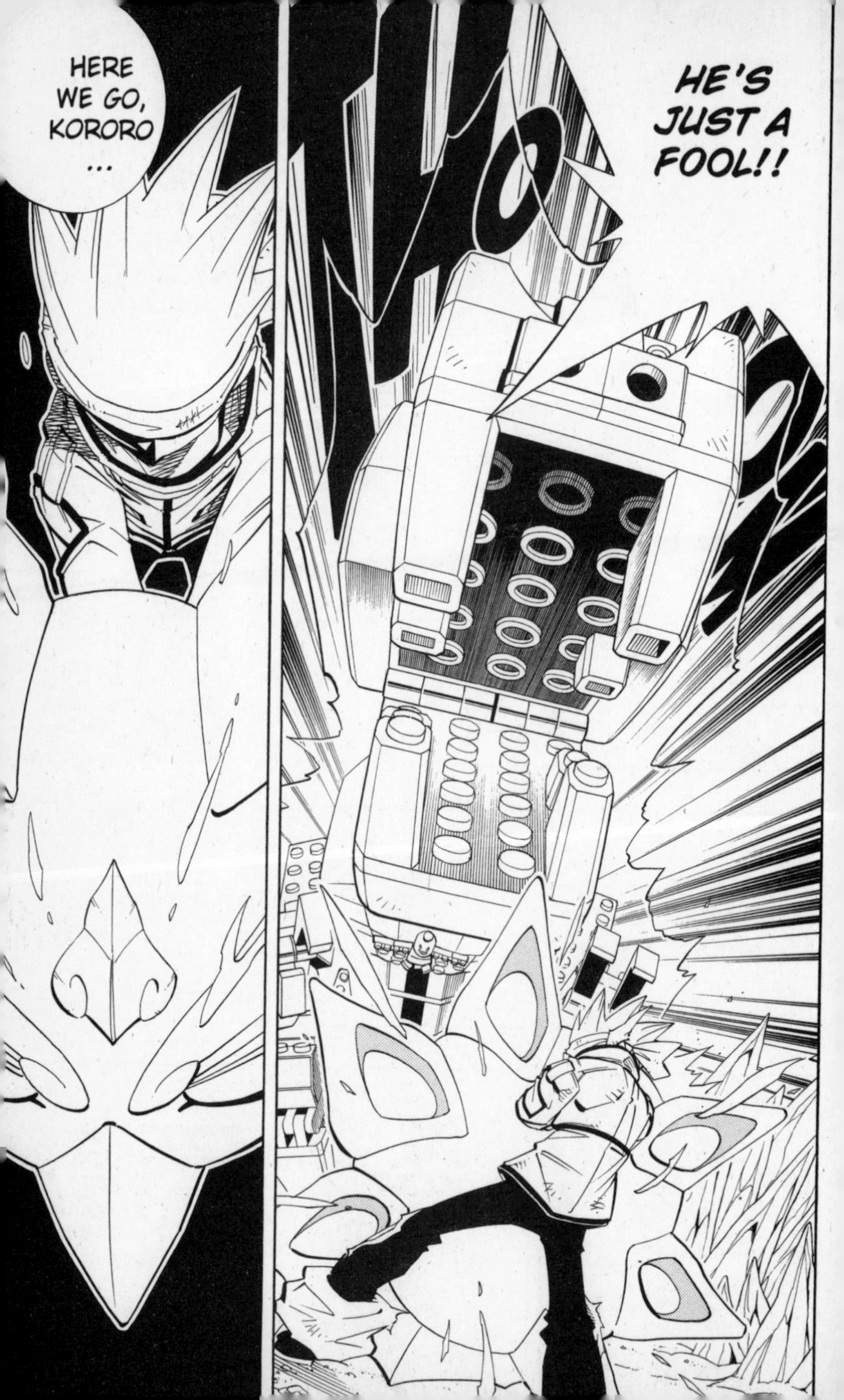
HE'S JUST A FOOL!!
HERE WE GO, KORORO ...

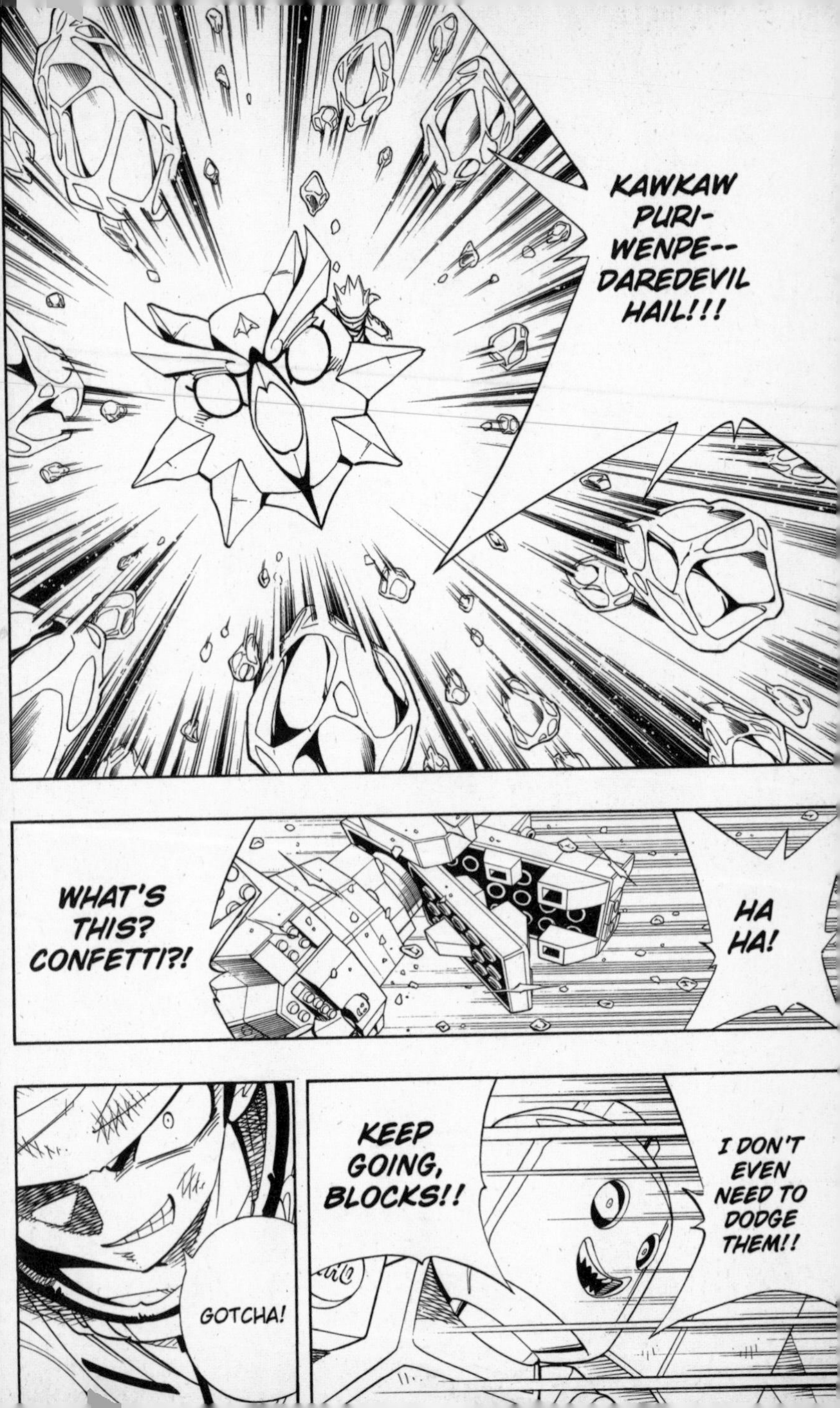
KAWKAW PURI-WENPE-- DAREDEVIL HAIL!!!
HA HA!
WHAT'S THIS? CONFETTI?!
I DON'T EVEN NEED TO DODGE THEM!!
KEEP GOING, BLOCKS!!
GOTCHA!

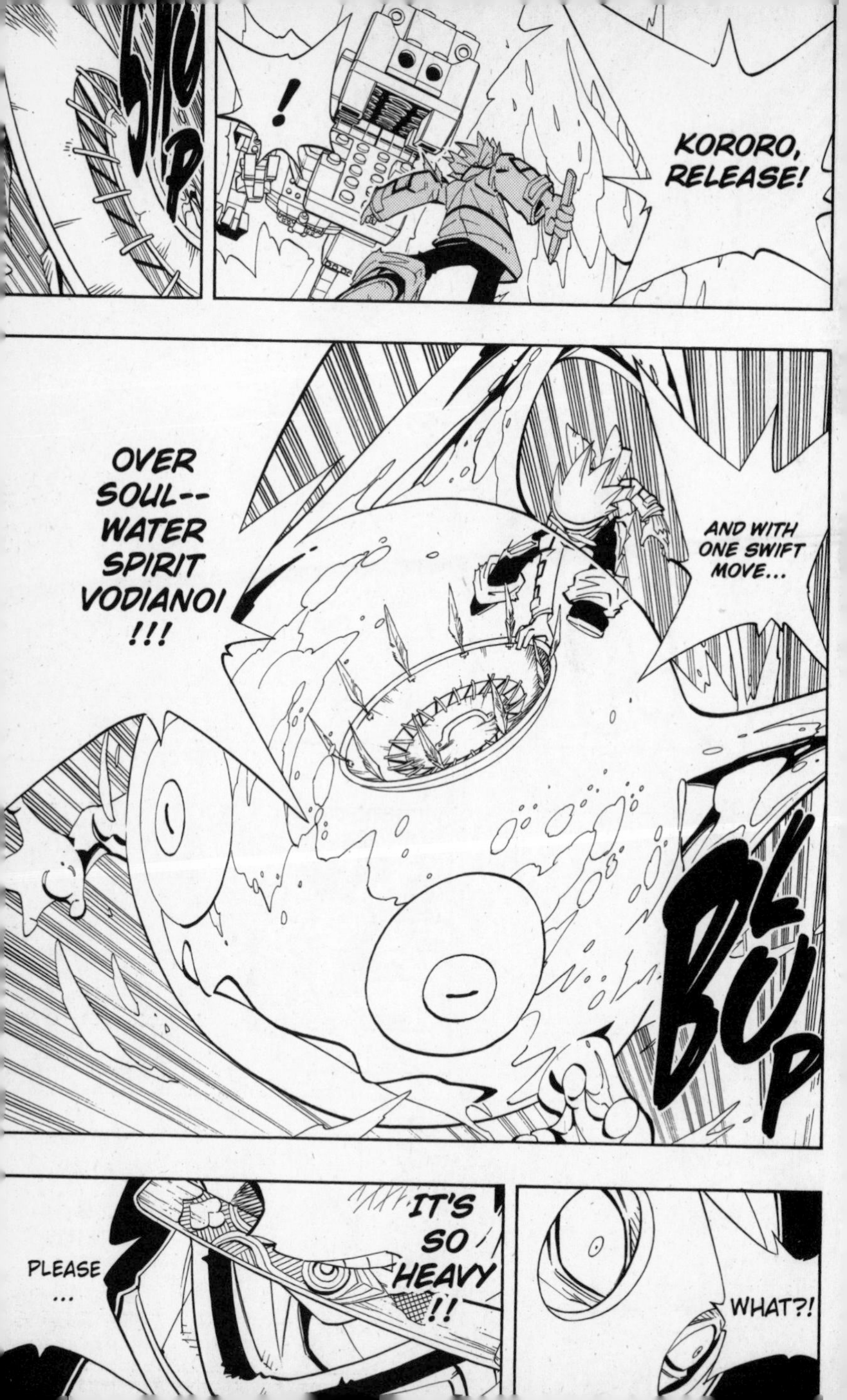
KORORO, RELEASE!
!
SNAP
AND WITH ONE SWIFT MOVE...
OVER SOUL-- WATER SPIRIT VODIANOI !!!
BLOOP
WHAT?!
IT'S SO HEAVY !!
PLEASE ...

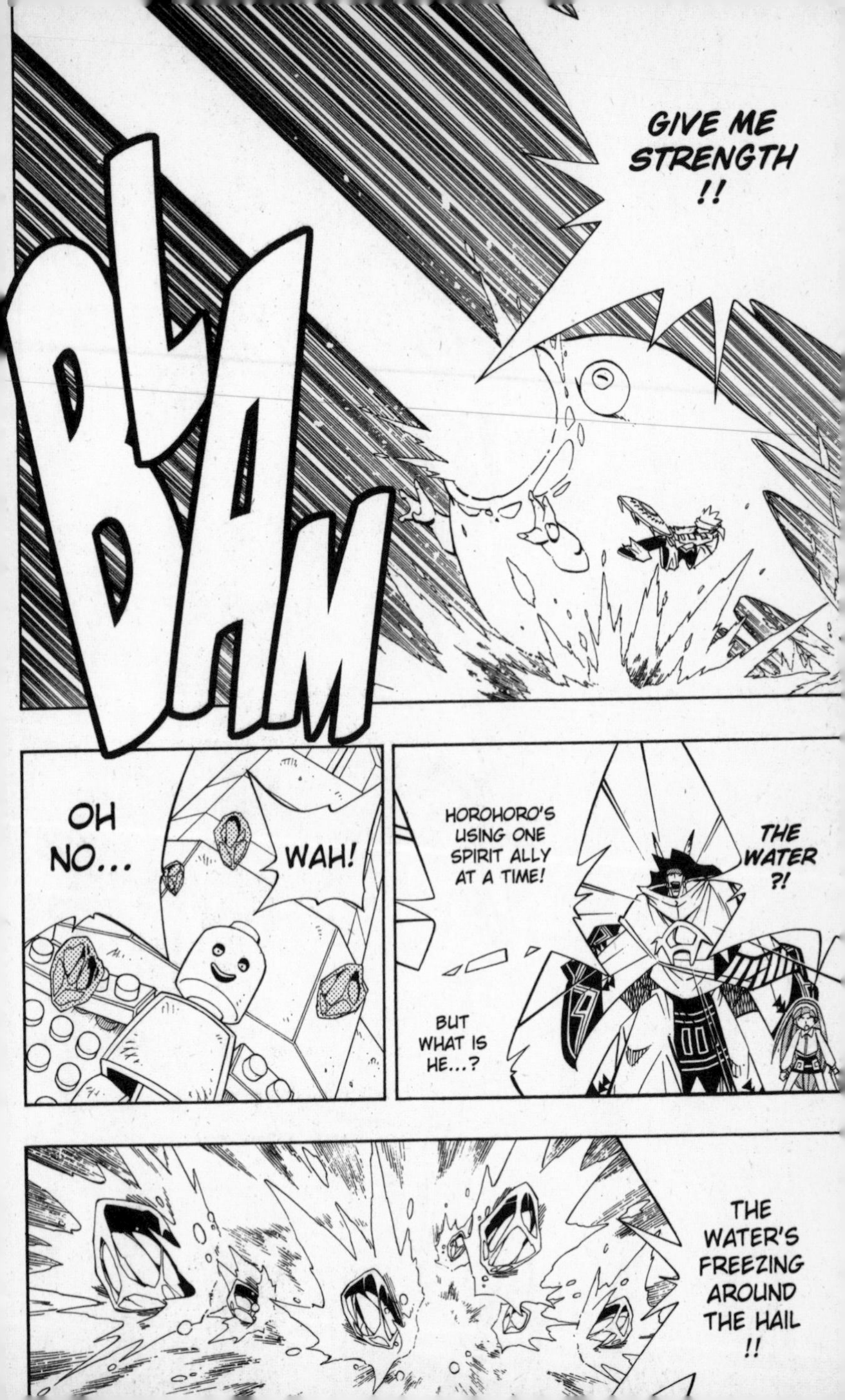
GIVE ME STRENGTH!!
BLAM
THE WATER?!
HOROHORO'S USING ONE SPIRIT ALLY AT A TIME!
BUT WHAT IS HE...?
WAH!
OH NO...
THE WATER'S FREEZING AROUND THE HAIL!!

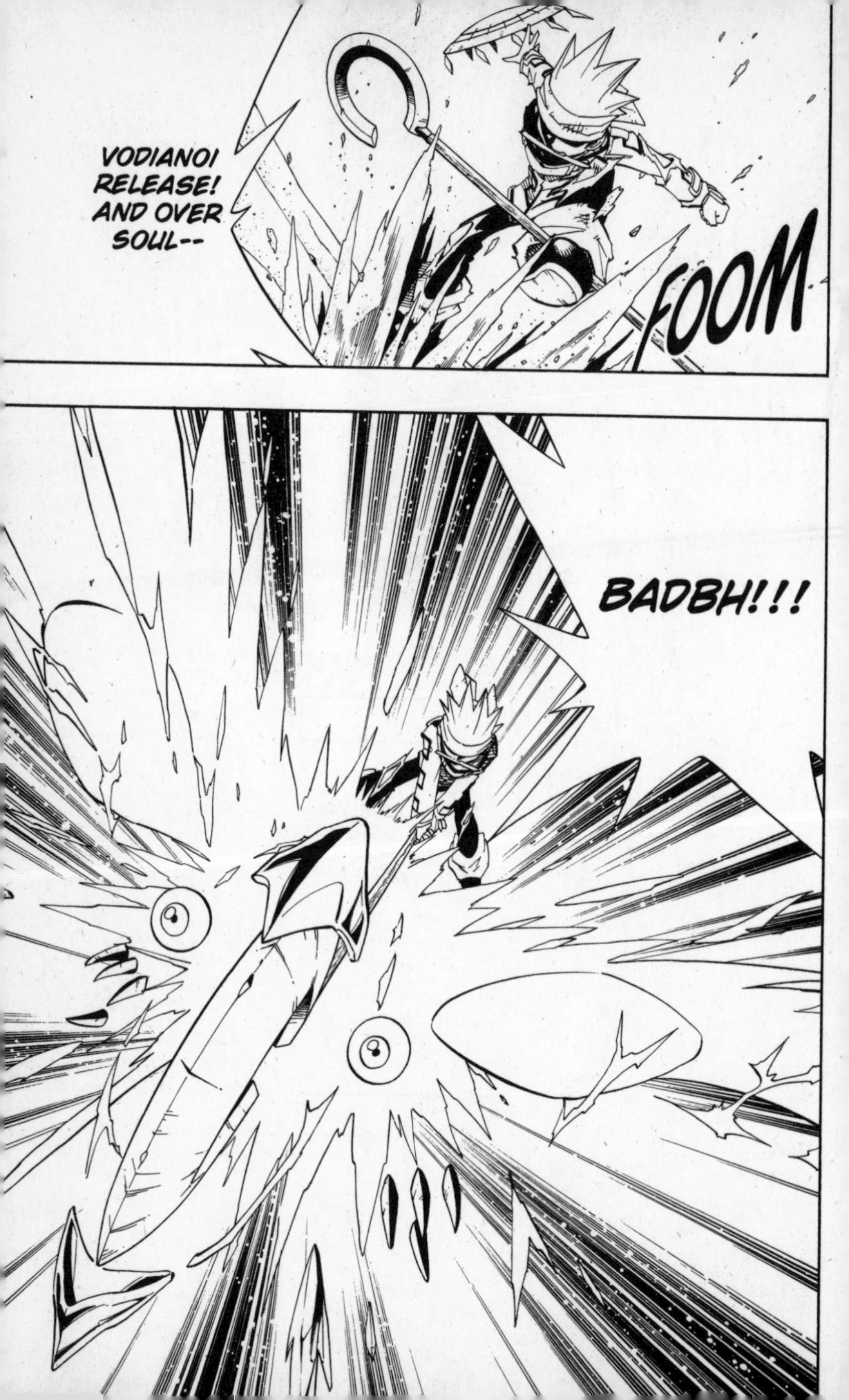

FOOM
VODIANOI RELEASE! AND OVER SOUL--
BADBH!!!

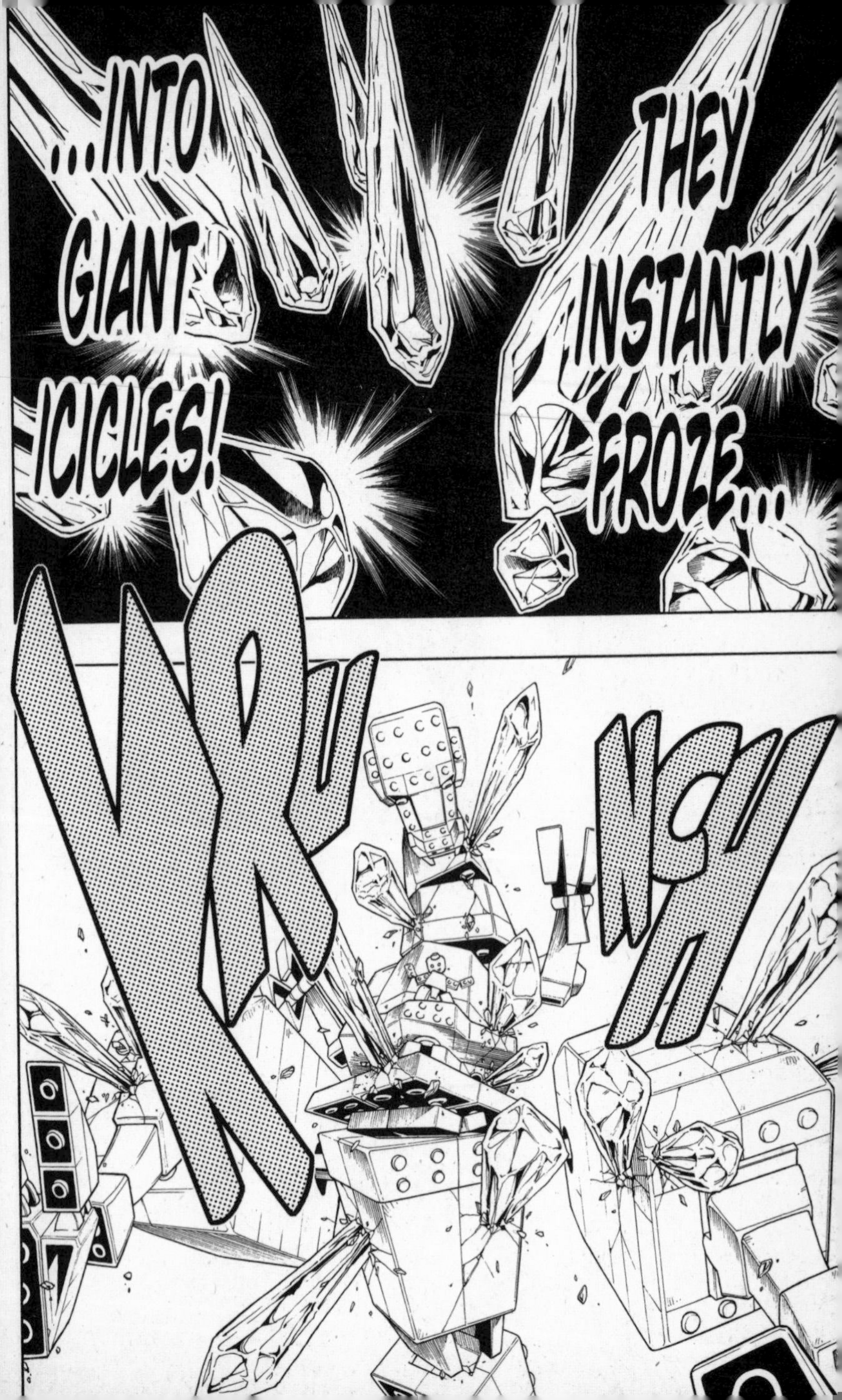
THEY INSTANTLY FROZE...
...INTO GIANT ICICLES!
KRUNCH

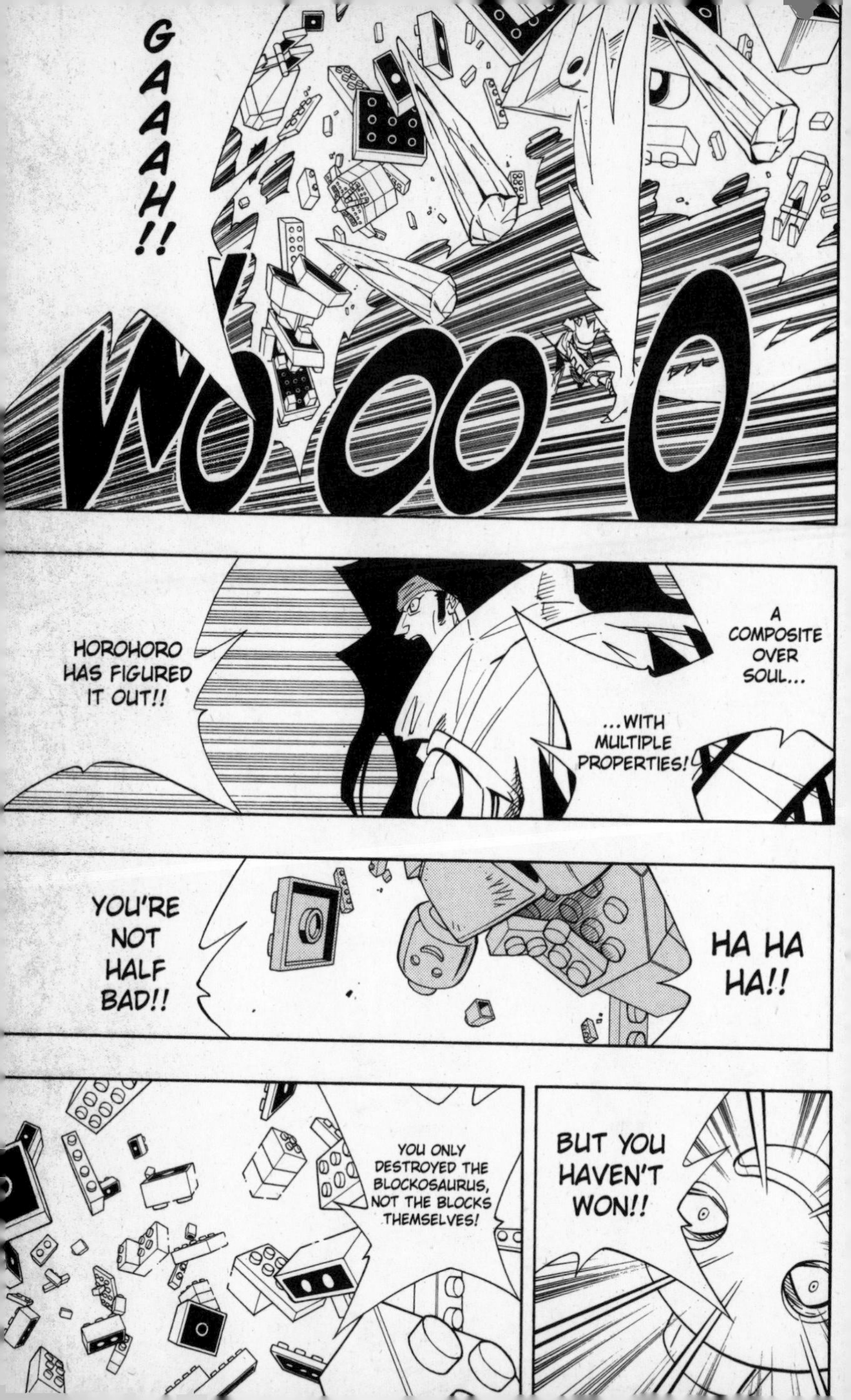
GAAAAH!!
A COMPOSITE OVER SOUL...
...WITH MULTIPLE PROPERTIES!
HOROHORO HAS FIGURED IT OUT!!
HA HA HA!!
YOU'RE NOT HALF BAD!!
BUT YOU HAVEN'T WON!!
YOU ONLY DESTROYED THE BLOCKOSAURUS, NOT THE BLOCKS THEMSELVES!

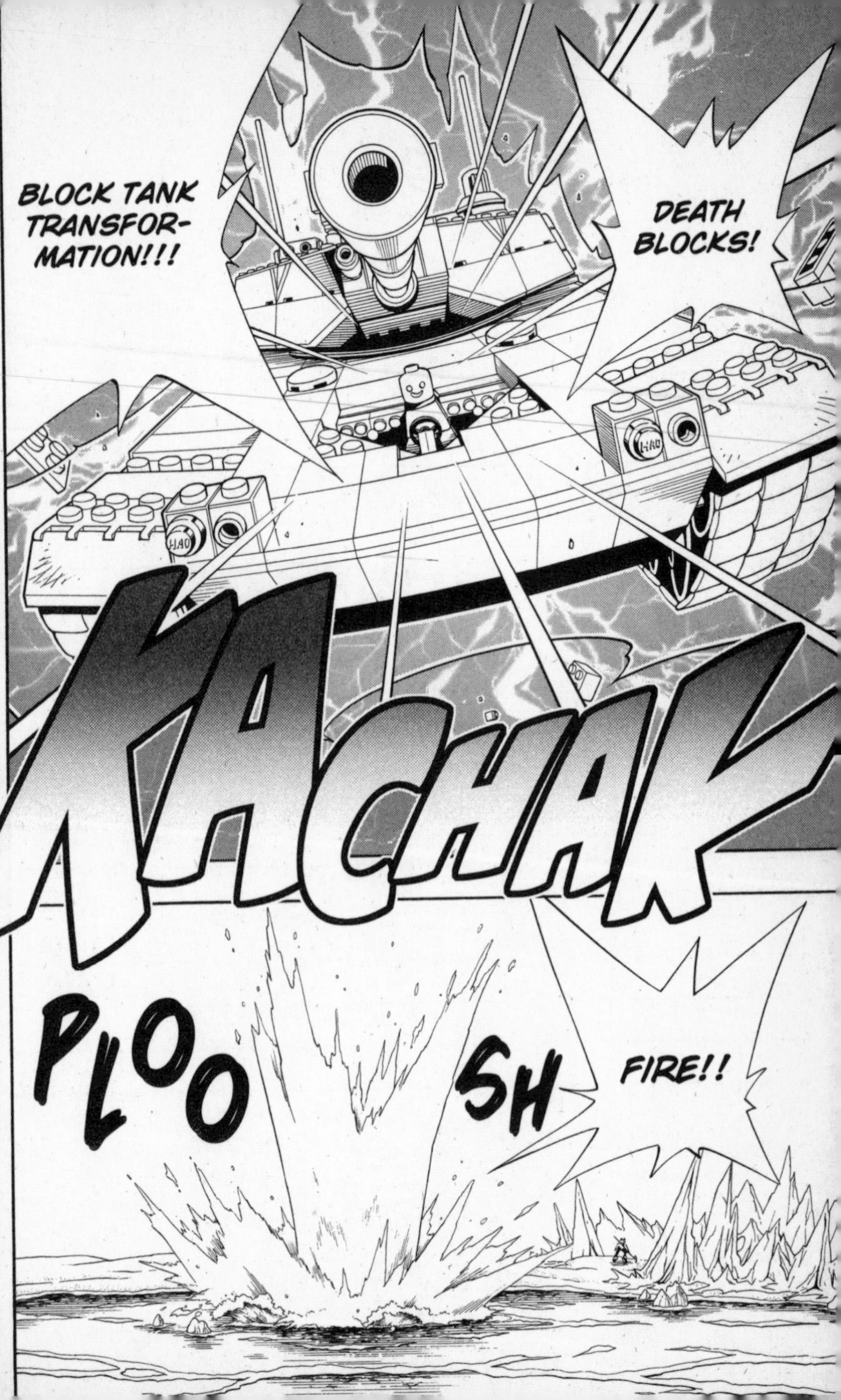
DEATH BLOCKS!
BLOCK TANK TRANSFOR-MATION!!!
KACHAK
FIRE!!
PLOOSH

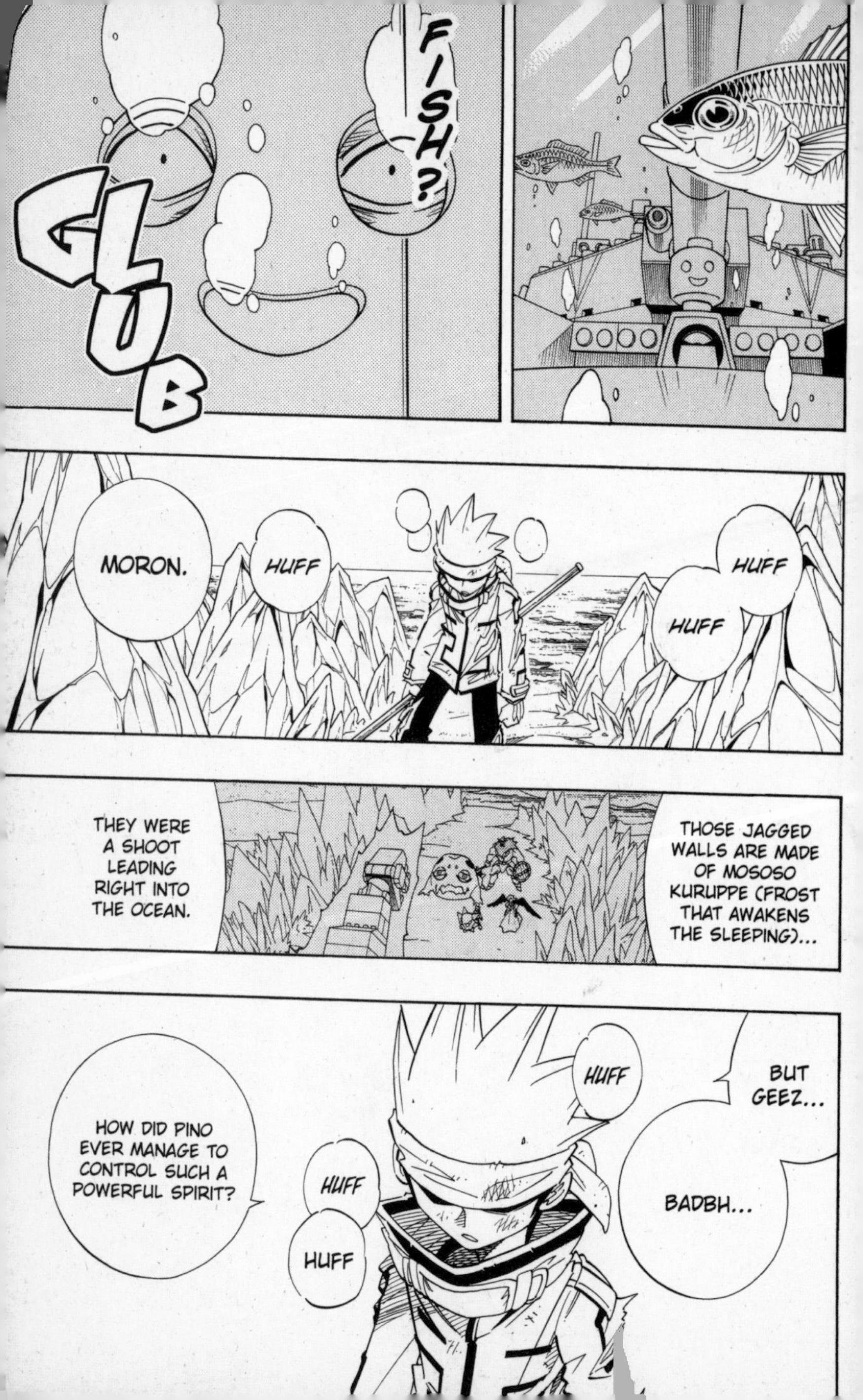

GLUB
FISH?
HUFF
HUFF
HUFF
MORON.
THOSE JAGGED WALLS ARE MADE OF MOSOSO KURUPPE (FROST THAT AWAKENS THE SLEEPING)...
THEY WERE A SHOOT LEADING RIGHT INTO THE OCEAN.
BUT GEEZ...
HUFF
BADBH...
HUFF
HUFF
HOW DID PINO EVER MANAGE TO CONTROL SUCH A POWERFUL SPIRIT?

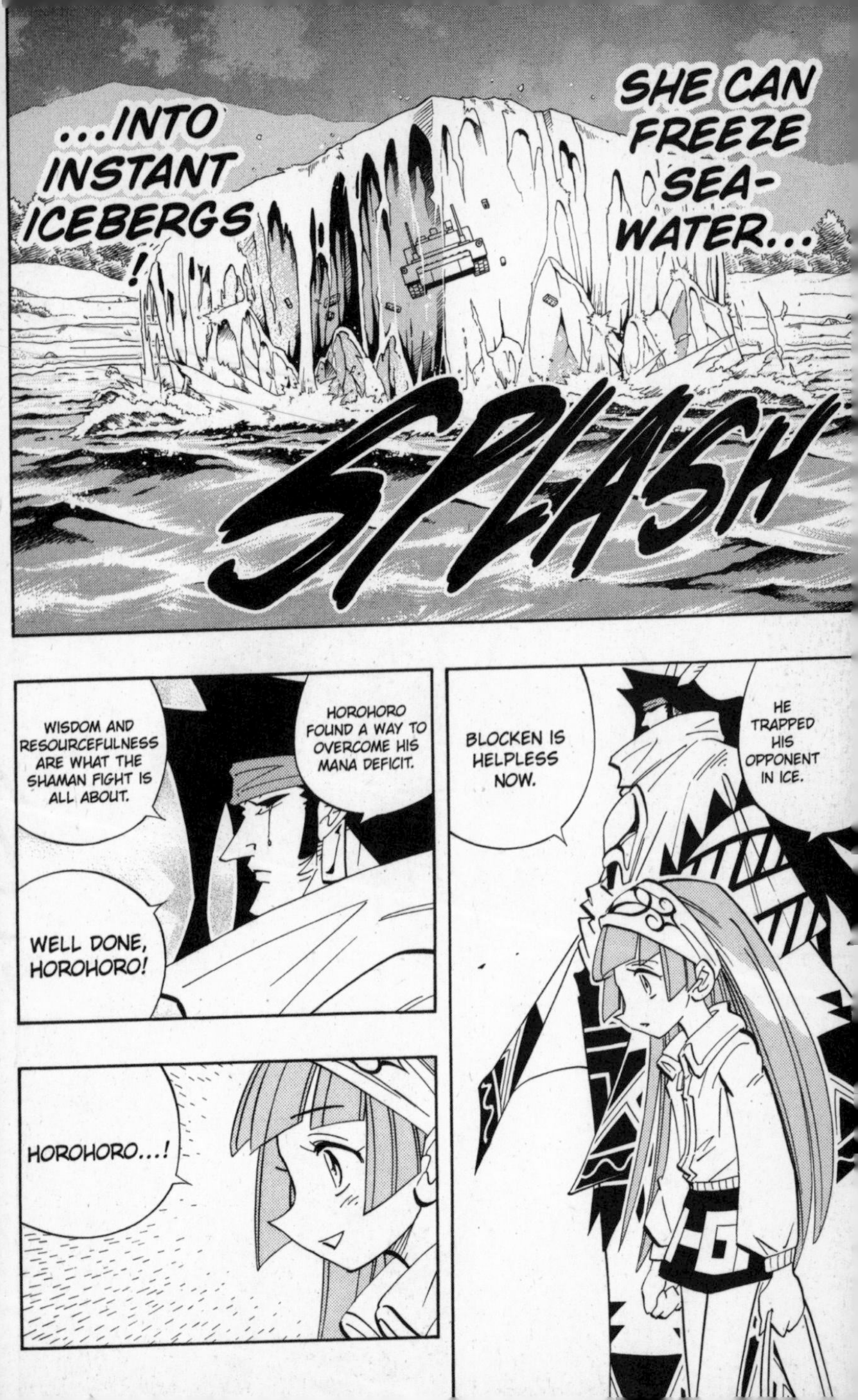
SHE CAN FREEZE SEA-WATER...
...INTO INSTANT ICEBERGS!
SPLASH
HE TRAPPED HIS OPPONENT IN ICE.
BLOCKEN IS HELPLESS NOW.
HOROHORO FOUND A WAY TO OVERCOME HIS MANA DEFICIT.
WISDOM AND RESOURCEFULNESS ARE WHAT THE SHAMAN FIGHT IS ALL ABOUT.
WELL DONE, HOROHORO!
HOROHORO...!

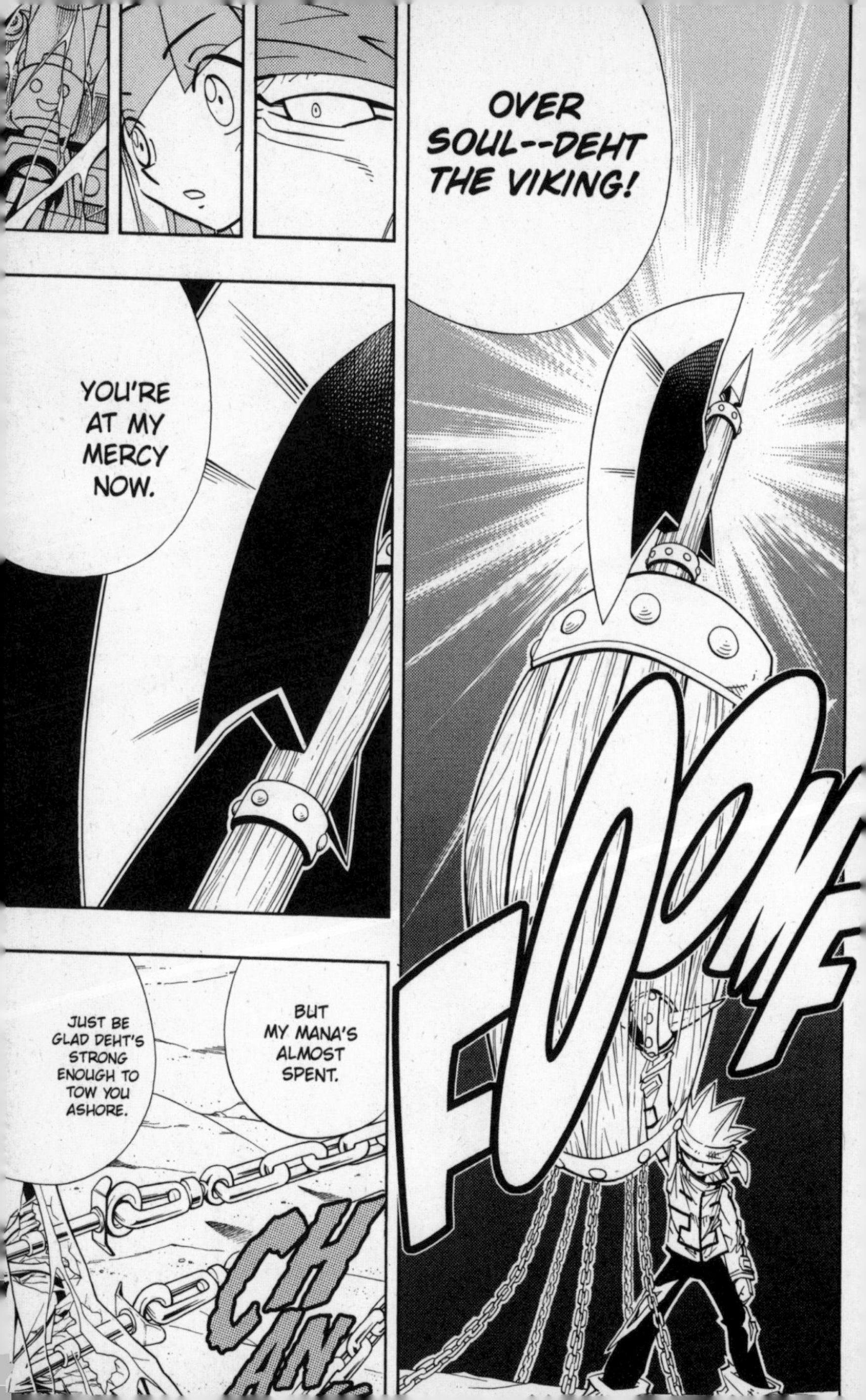
OVER SOUL--DEHT THE VIKING!
FOOMF
YOU'RE AT MY MERCY NOW.
BUT MY MANA'S ALMOST SPENT.
JUST BE GLAD DEHT'S STRONG ENOUGH TO TOW YOU ASHORE.

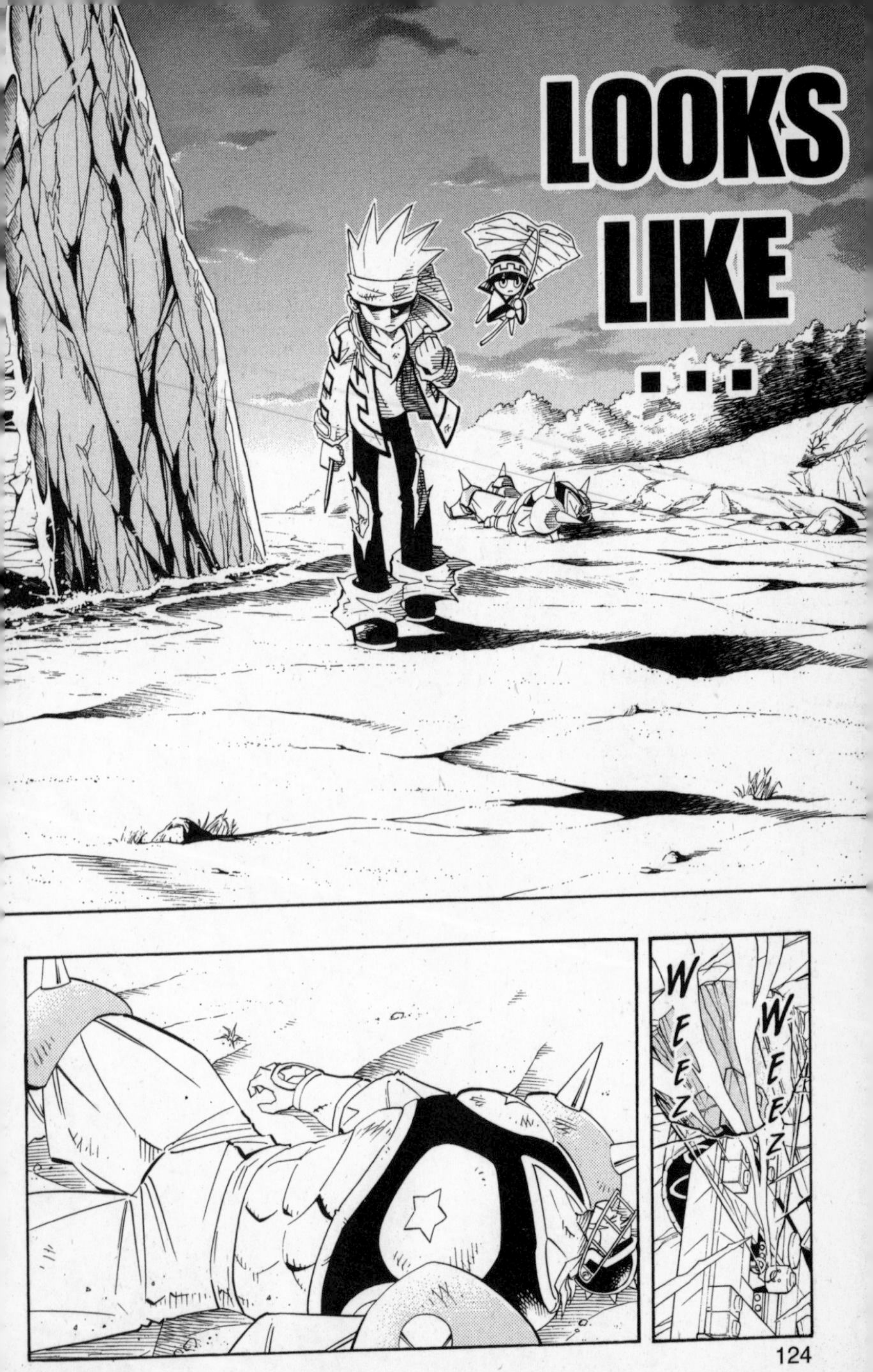
LOOKS LIKE
...
WEEZ
WEEZ

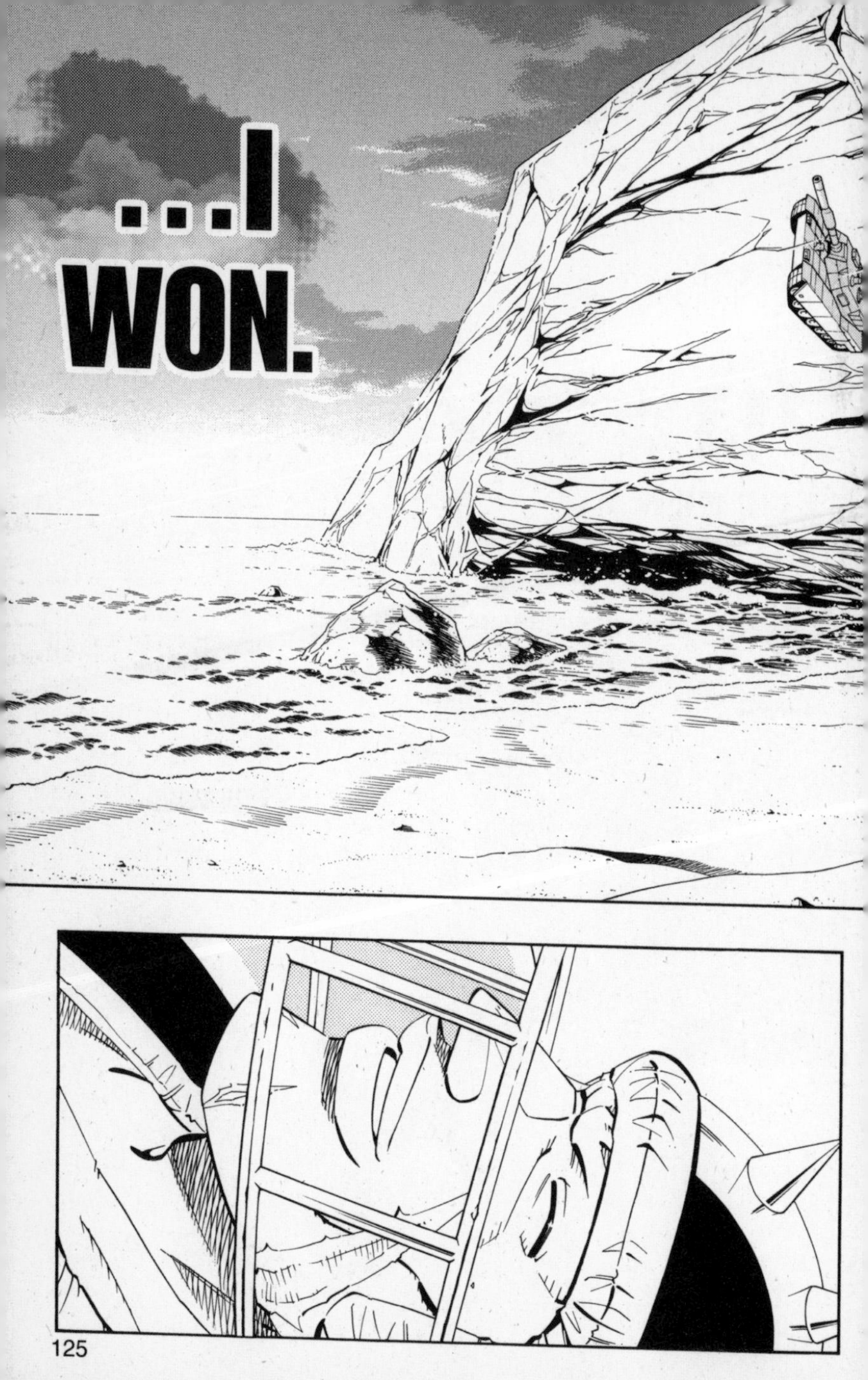
...I WON.

SHAMAN KING CHARACTER FILE No.115

ブロッケン

BLOCKEN

2001
(JAN)

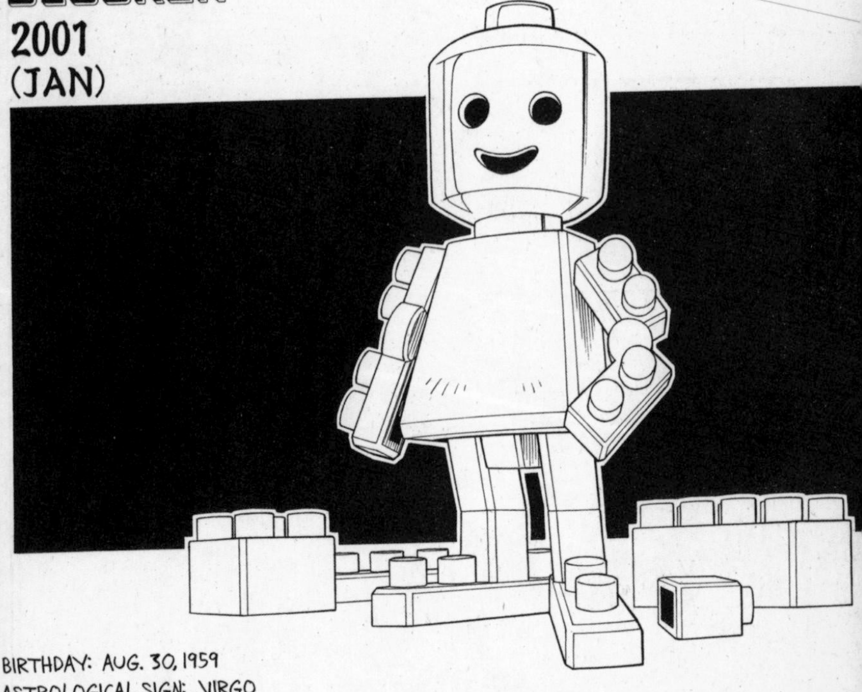

BIRTHDAY: AUG. 30, 1959
ASTROLOGICAL SIGN: VIRGO
BLOOD TYPE: B
42 YEARS OLD

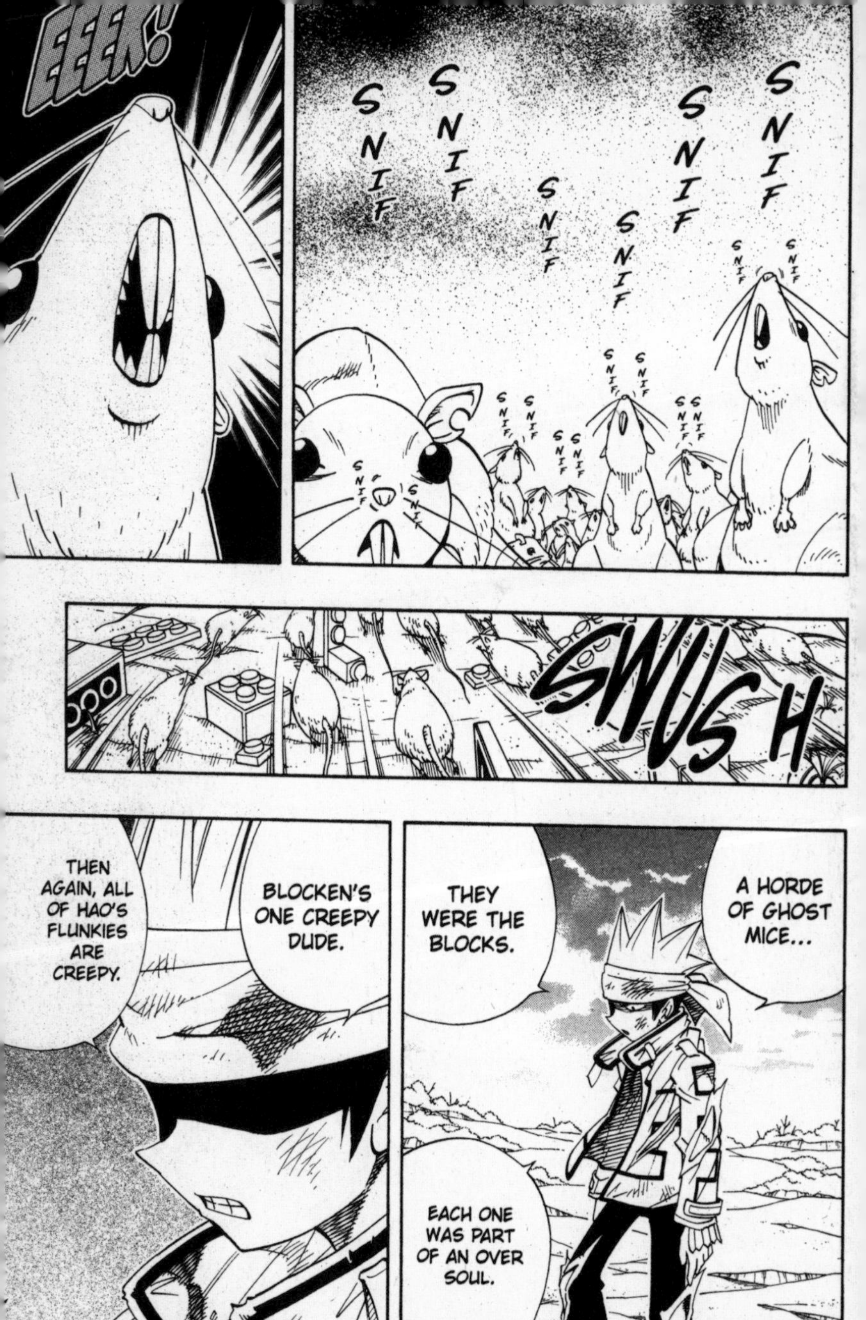
SNIF SNIF SNIF SNIF SNIF SNIF
SNIF SNIF
SNIF SNIF
SNIF SNIF
SNIF SNIF
SNIF SNIF
SNIF SNIF
EEEK!
SWUSH
A HORDE OF GHOST MICE...
THEY WERE THE BLOCKS.
EACH ONE WAS PART OF AN OVER SOUL.
BLOCKEN'S ONE CREEPY DUDE.
THEN AGAIN, ALL OF HAO'S FLUNKIES ARE CREEPY.

Reincarnation 186: Epilogue IV

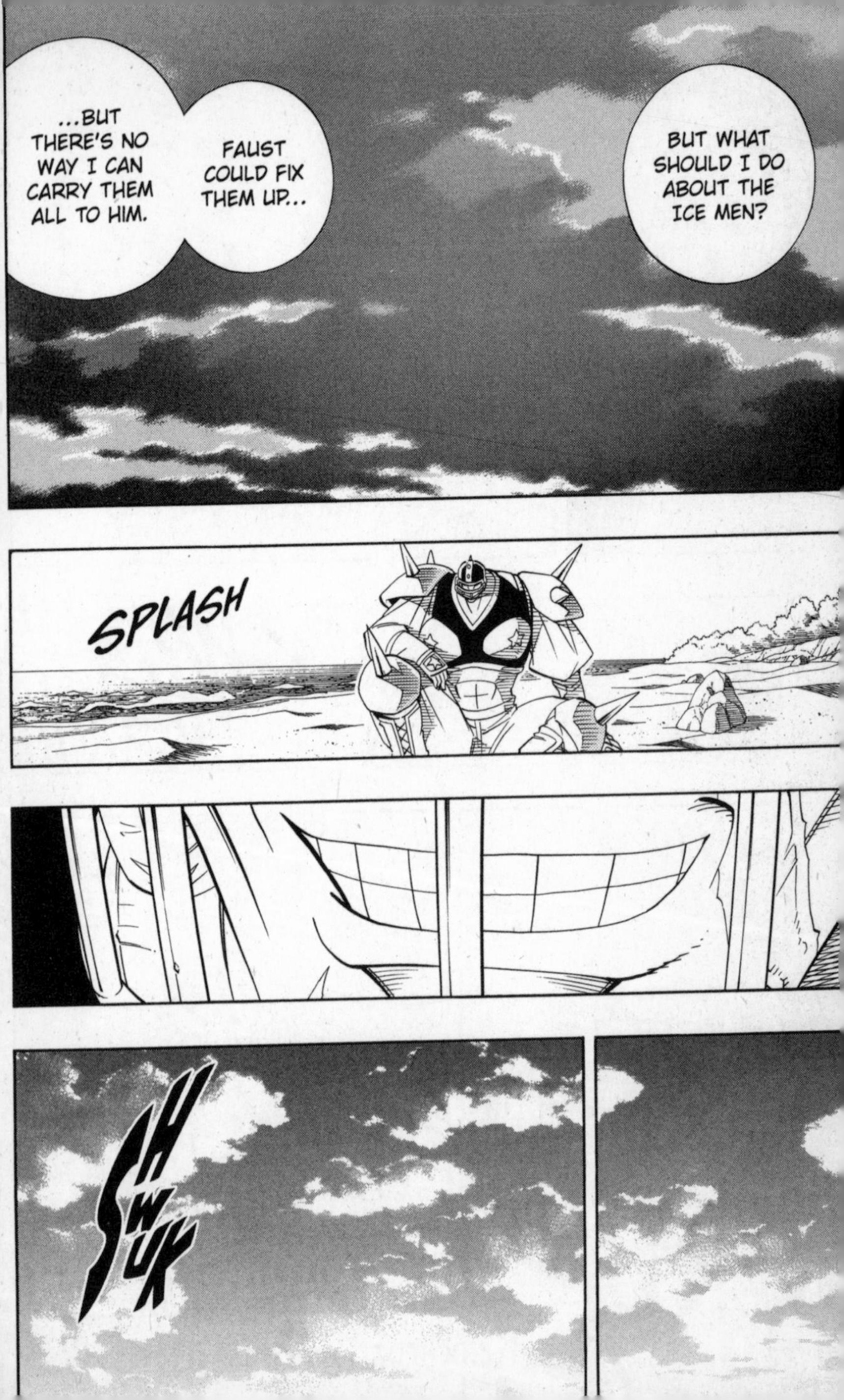
BUT WHAT SHOULD I DO ABOUT THE ICE MEN?
FAUST COULD FIX THEM UP...
...BUT THERE'S NO WAY I CAN CARRY THEM ALL TO HIM.
SPLASH
SHWUK

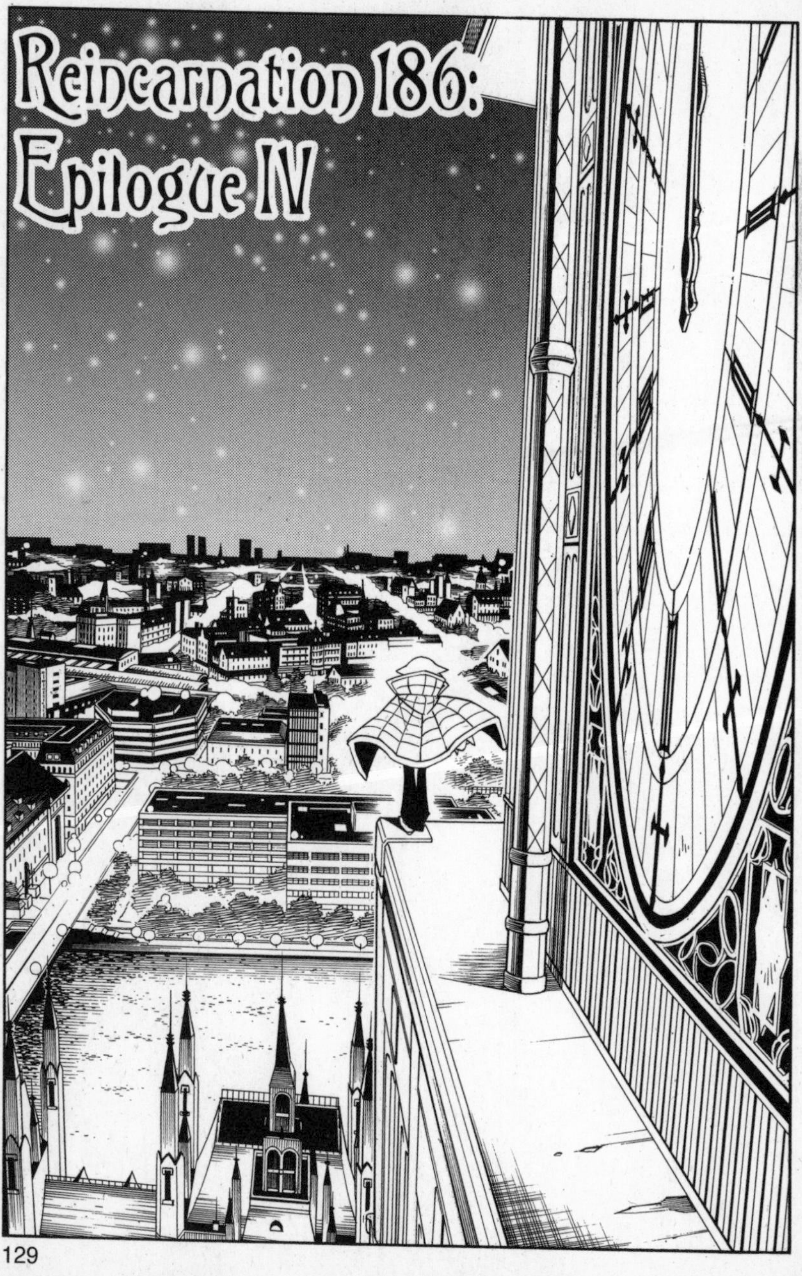
Reincarnation 186:
Epilogue IV

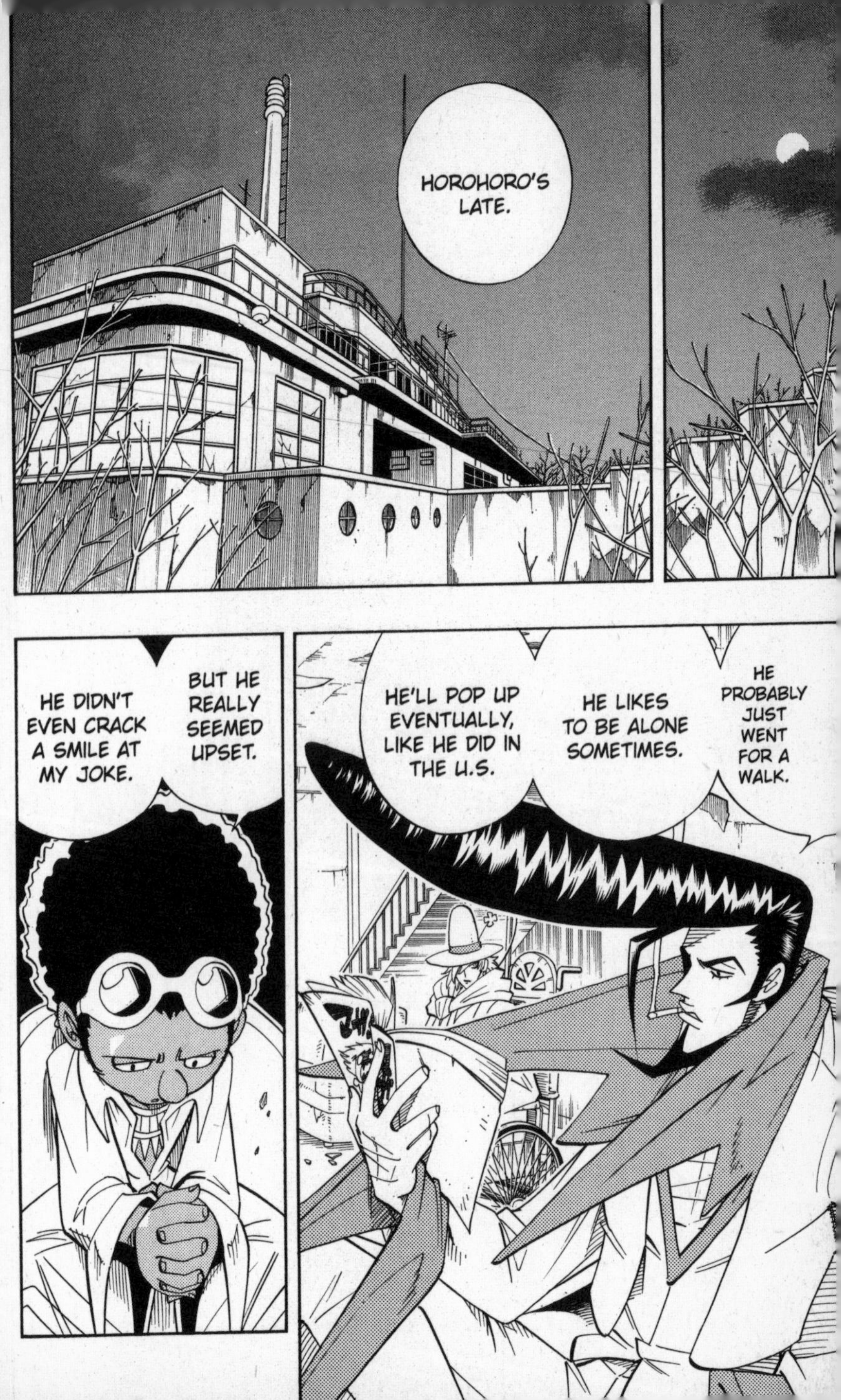
HOROHORO'S LATE.
HE PROBABLY JUST WENT FOR A WALK.
HE LIKES TO BE ALONE SOMETIMES.
HE'LL POP UP EVENTUALLY, LIKE HE DID IN THE U.S.
BUT HE REALLY SEEMED UPSET.
HE DIDN'T EVEN CRACK A SMILE AT MY JOKE.

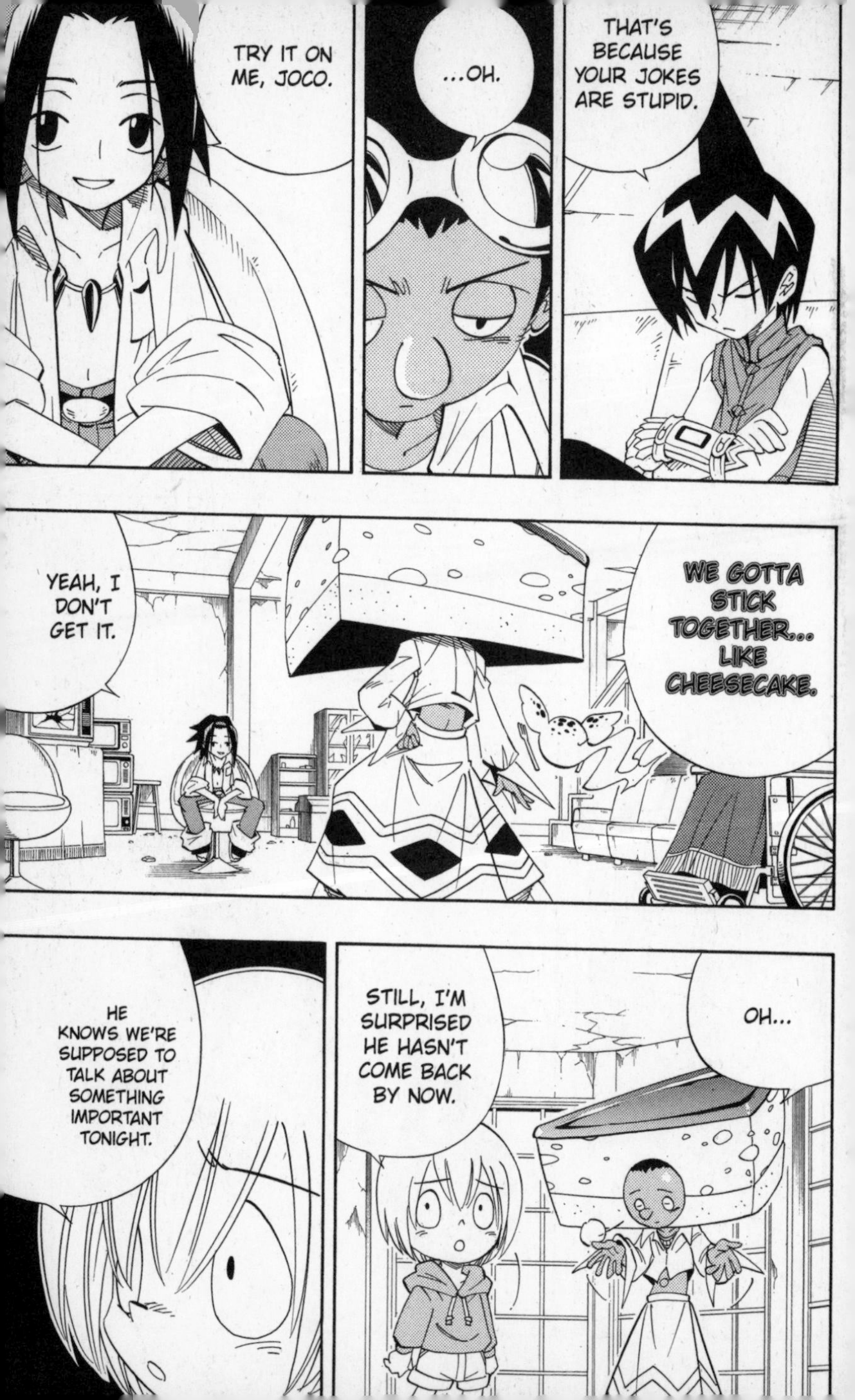
THAT'S BECAUSE YOUR JOKES ARE STUPID.
...OH.
TRY IT ON ME, JOCO.
WE GOTTA STICK TOGETHER... LIKE CHEESECAKE.
YEAH, I DON'T GET IT.
OH...
STILL, I'M SURPRISED HE HASN'T COME BACK BY NOW.
HE KNOWS WE'RE SUPPOSED TO TALK ABOUT SOMETHING IMPORTANT TONIGHT.

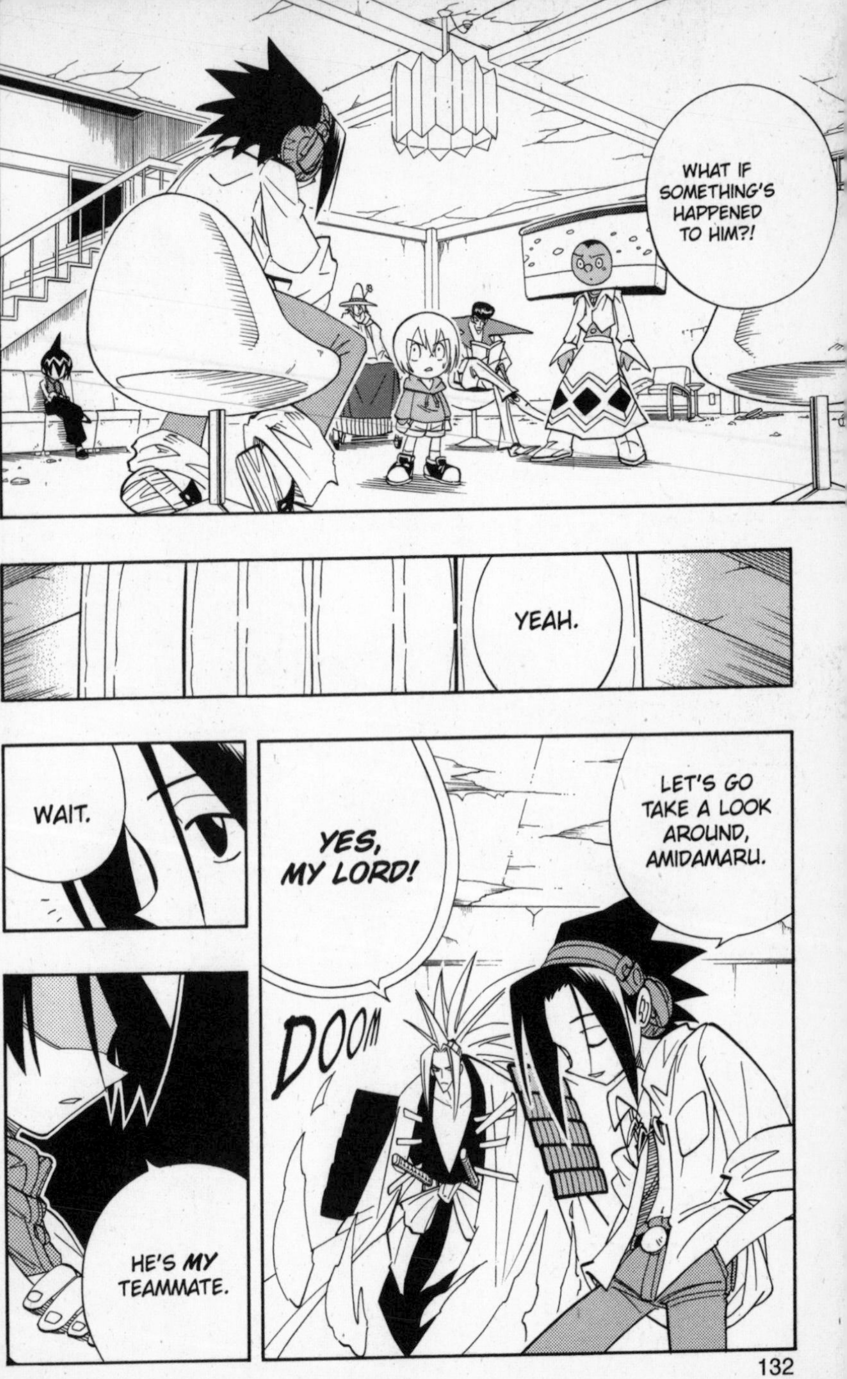
WHAT IF SOMETHING'S HAPPENED TO HIM?!
YEAH.
LET'S GO TAKE A LOOK AROUND, AMIDAMARU.
YES, MY LORD!
DOOM
WAIT.
HE'S *MY* TEAMMATE.

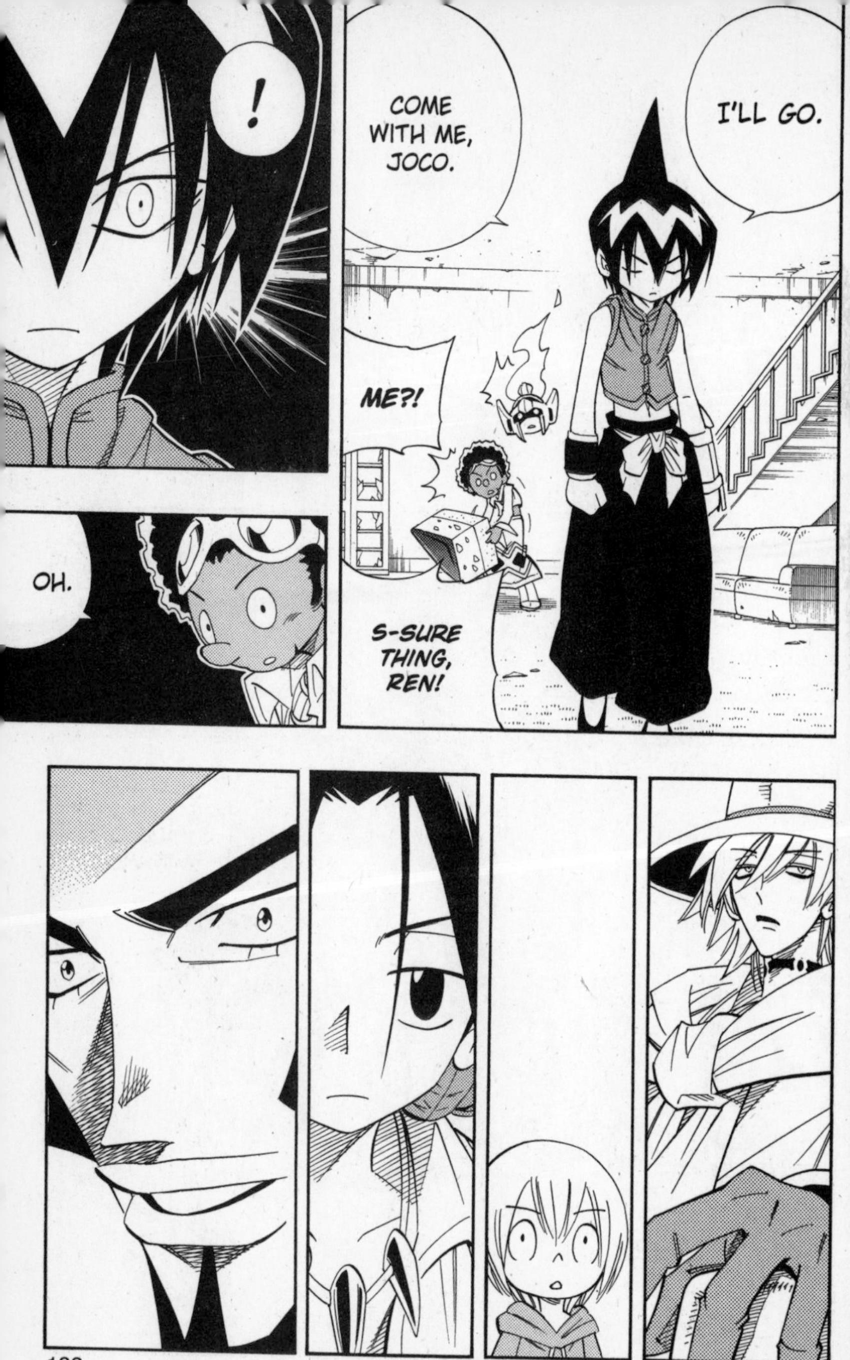
I'LL GO.
COME WITH ME, JOCO.
ME?!
S-SURE THING, REN!
!
OH.

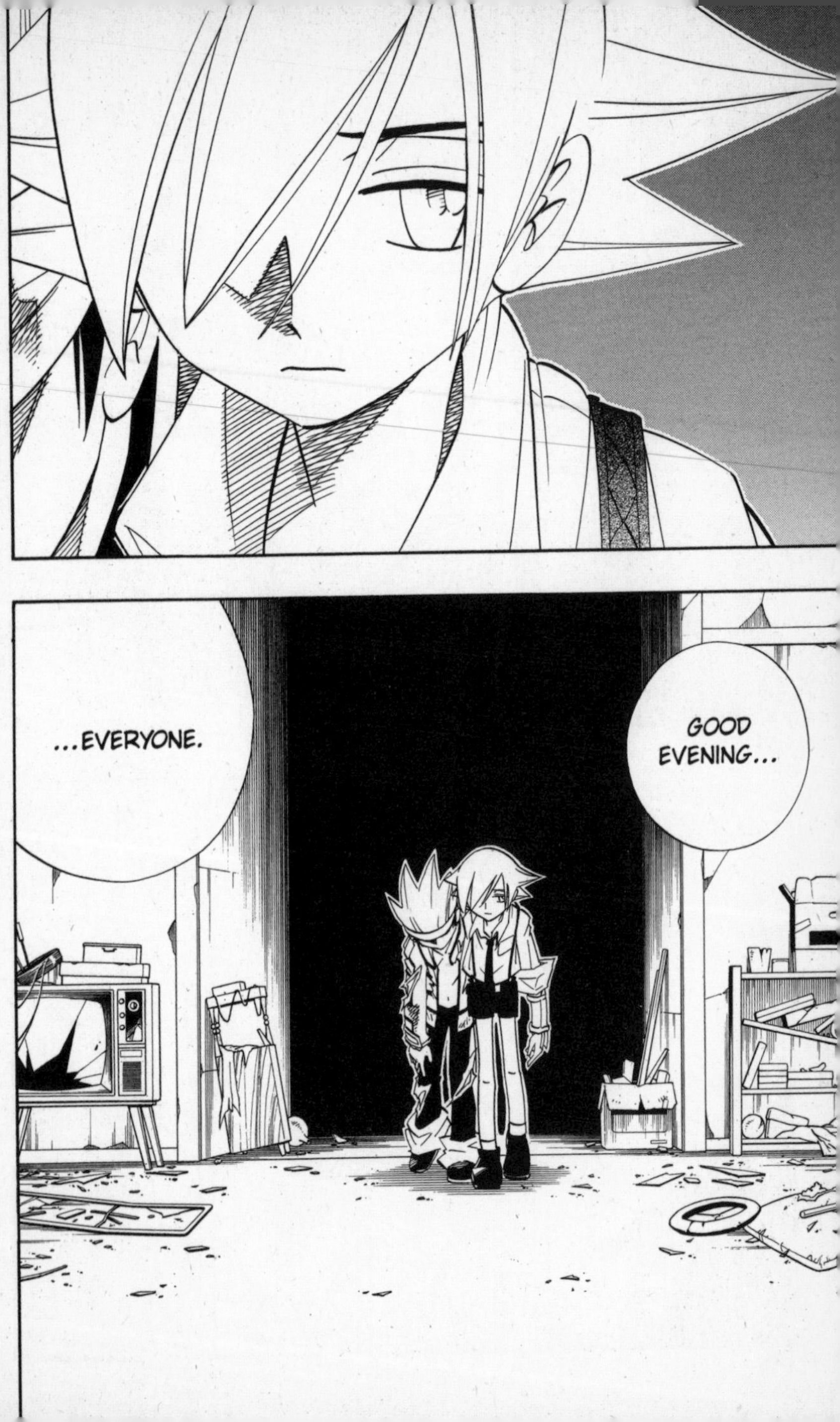
GOOD EVENING...
...EVERYONE.

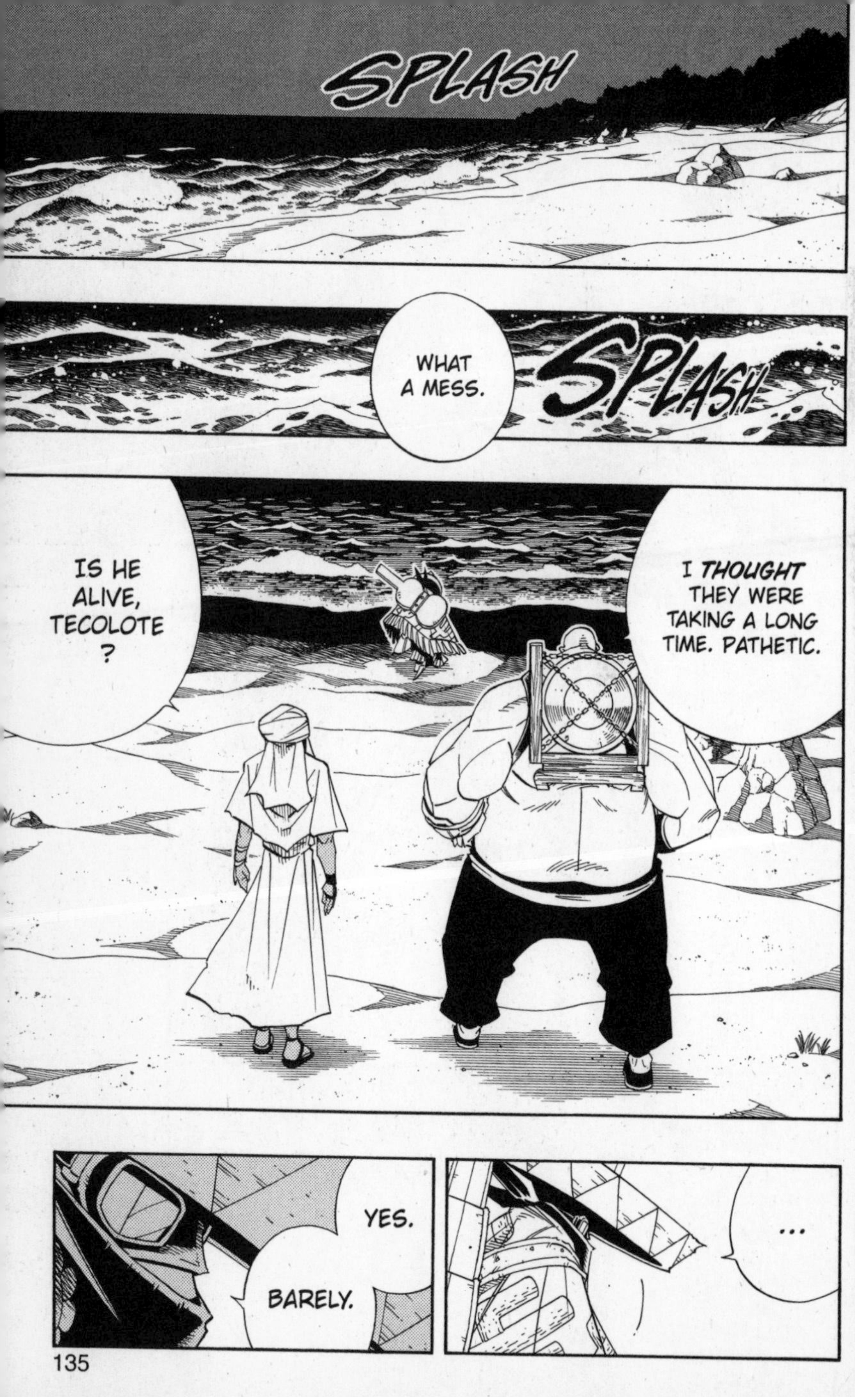
SPLASH
SPLASH
WHAT A MESS.
I *THOUGHT* THEY WERE TAKING A LONG TIME. PATHETIC.
IS HE ALIVE, TECOLOTE ?
...
YES.
BARELY.

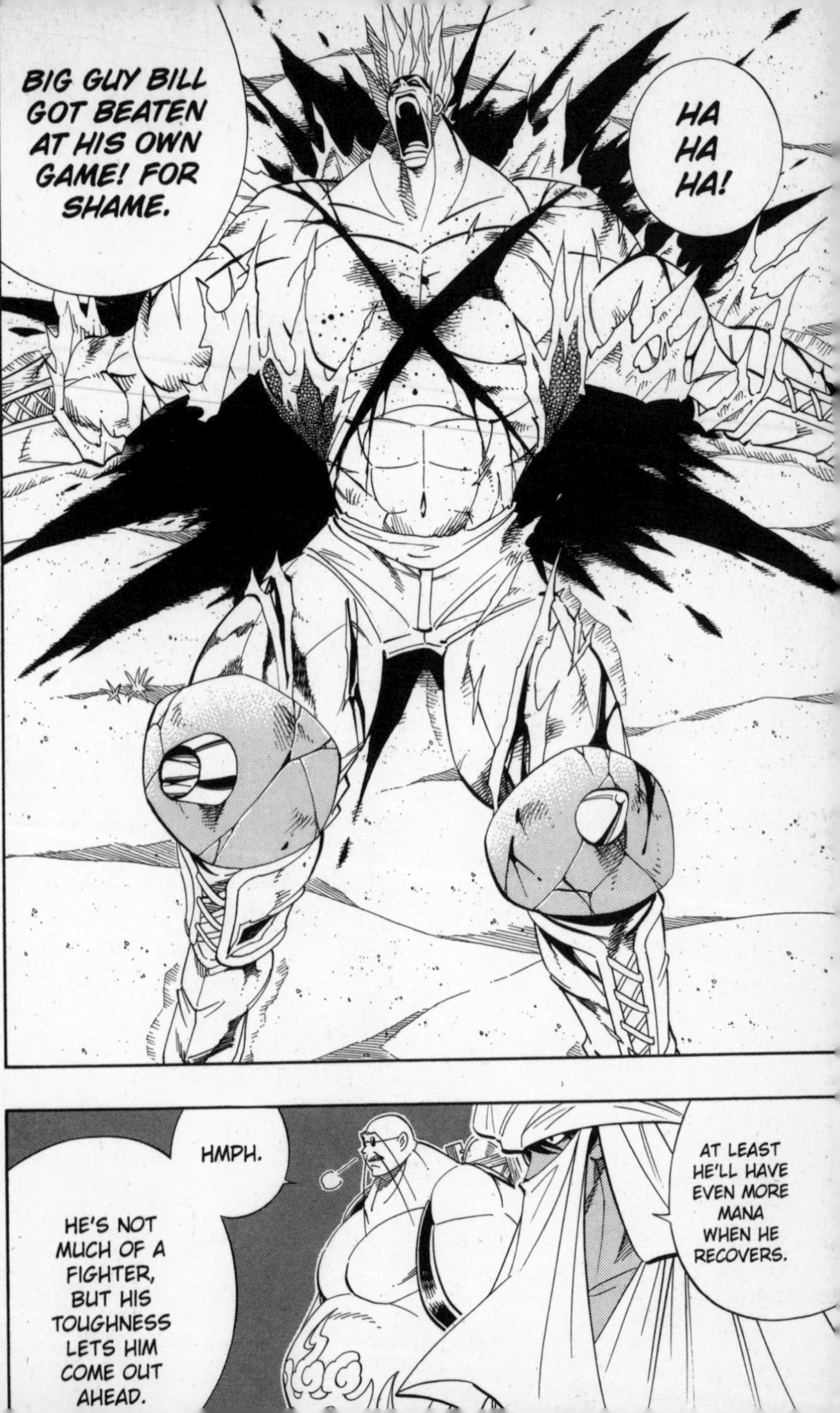
HA HA HA!
BIG GUY BILL GOT BEATEN AT HIS OWN GAME! FOR SHAME.
AT LEAST HE'LL HAVE EVEN MORE MANA WHEN HE RECOVERS.
HMPH.
HE'S NOT MUCH OF A FIGHTER, BUT HIS TOUGHNESS LETS HIM COME OUT AHEAD.

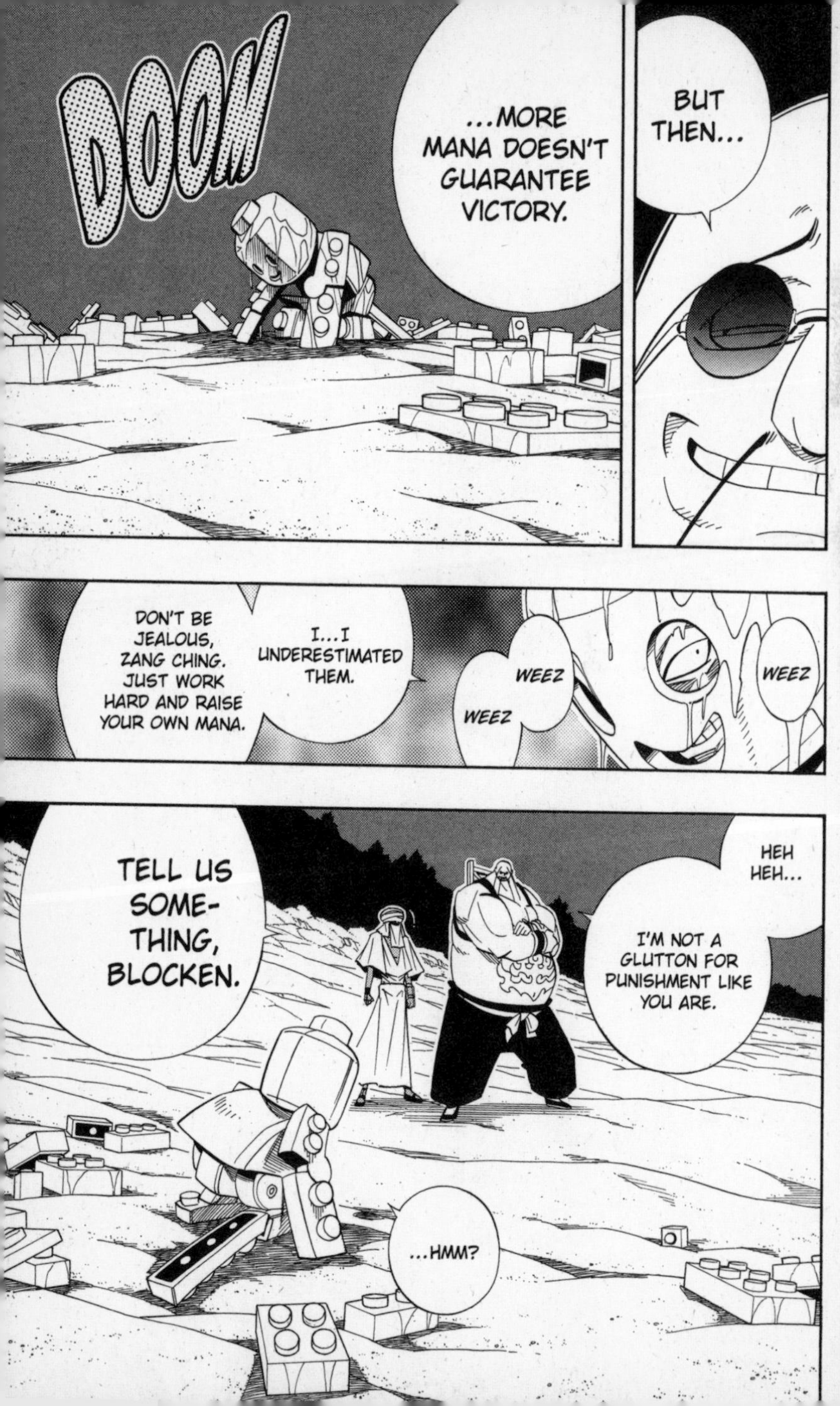
BUT THEN...
...MORE MANA DOESN'T GUARANTEE VICTORY.
DOOM
WEEZ
WEEZ
WEEZ
I...I UNDERESTIMATED THEM.
DON'T BE JEALOUS, ZANG CHING. JUST WORK HARD AND RAISE YOUR OWN MANA.
HEH HEH...
I'M NOT A GLUTTON FOR PUNISHMENT LIKE YOU ARE.
TELL US SOME-THING, BLOCKEN.
...HMM?

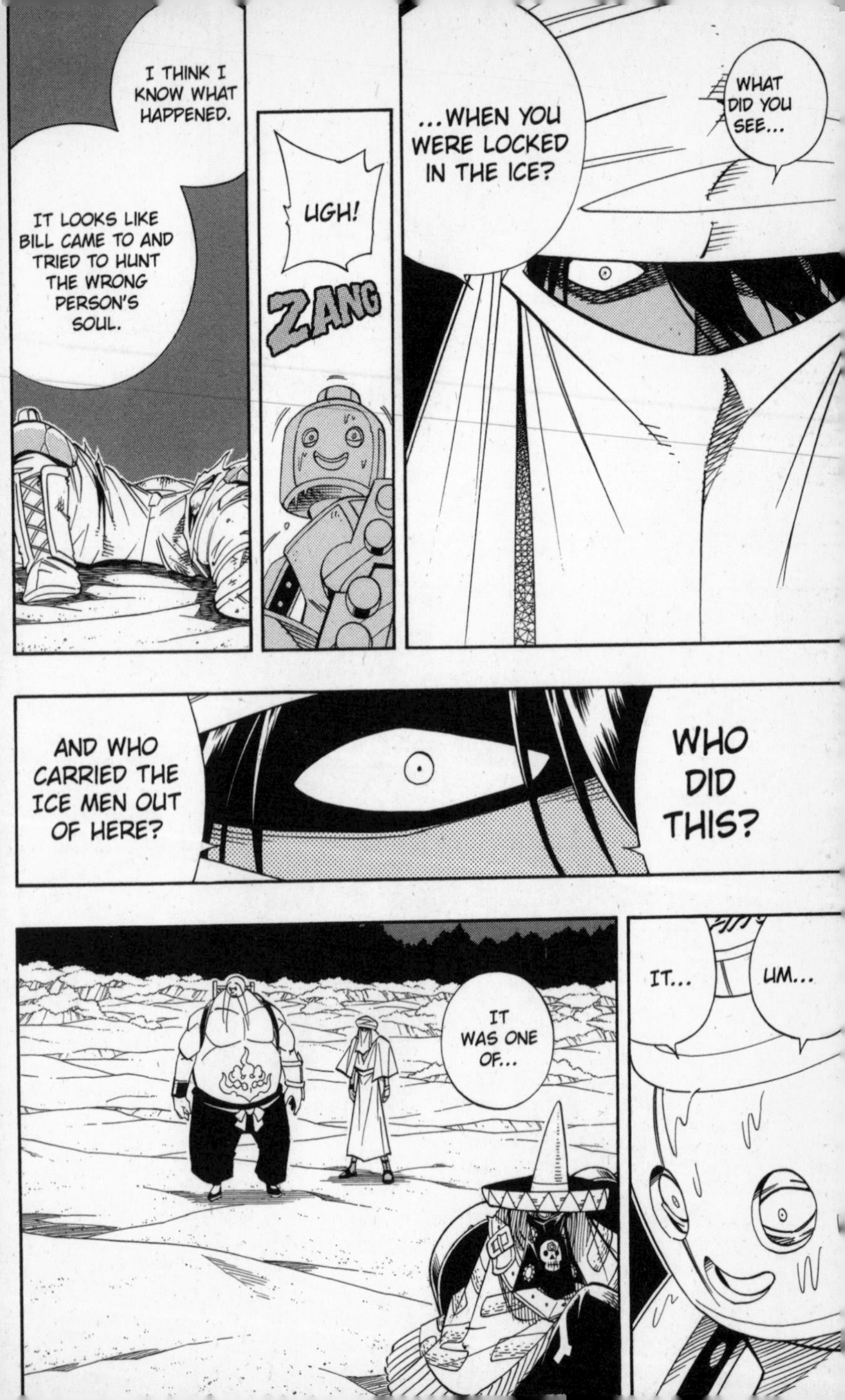
WHAT DID YOU SEE...
...WHEN YOU WERE LOCKED IN THE ICE?
UGH!
ZANG
I THINK I KNOW WHAT HAPPENED.
IT LOOKS LIKE BILL CAME TO AND TRIED TO HUNT THE WRONG PERSON'S SOUL.
WHO DID THIS?
AND WHO CARRIED THE ICE MEN OUT OF HERE?
UM...
IT...
IT WAS ONE OF...

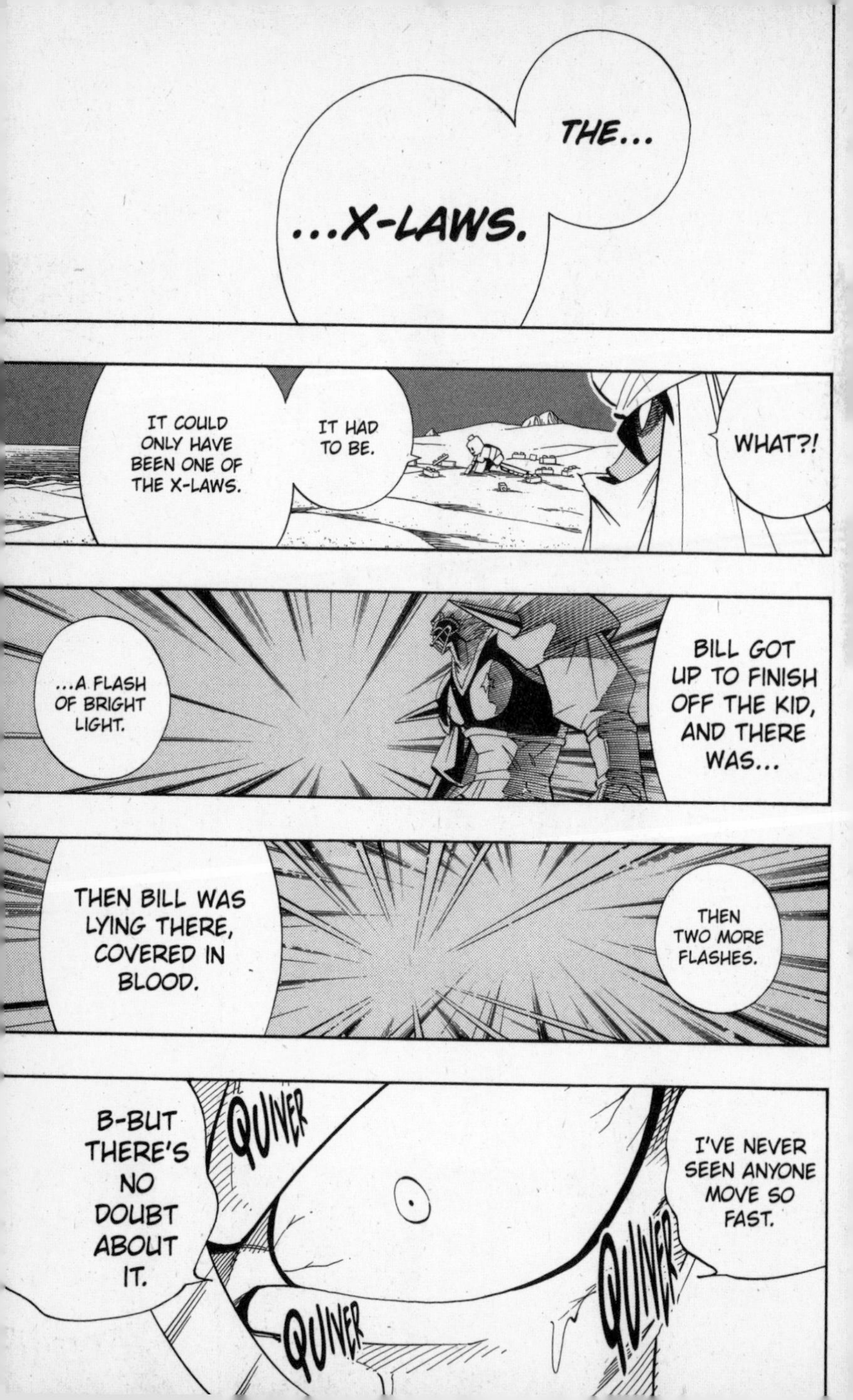
THE...
...X-LAWS.
WHAT?!
IT HAD TO BE.
IT COULD ONLY HAVE BEEN ONE OF THE X-LAWS.
BILL GOT UP TO FINISH OFF THE KID, AND THERE WAS...
...A FLASH OF BRIGHT LIGHT.
THEN TWO MORE FLASHES.
THEN BILL WAS LYING THERE, COVERED IN BLOOD.
I'VE NEVER SEEN ANYONE MOVE SO FAST.
QUIVER
QUIVER
QUIVER
B-BUT THERE'S NO DOUBT ABOUT IT.

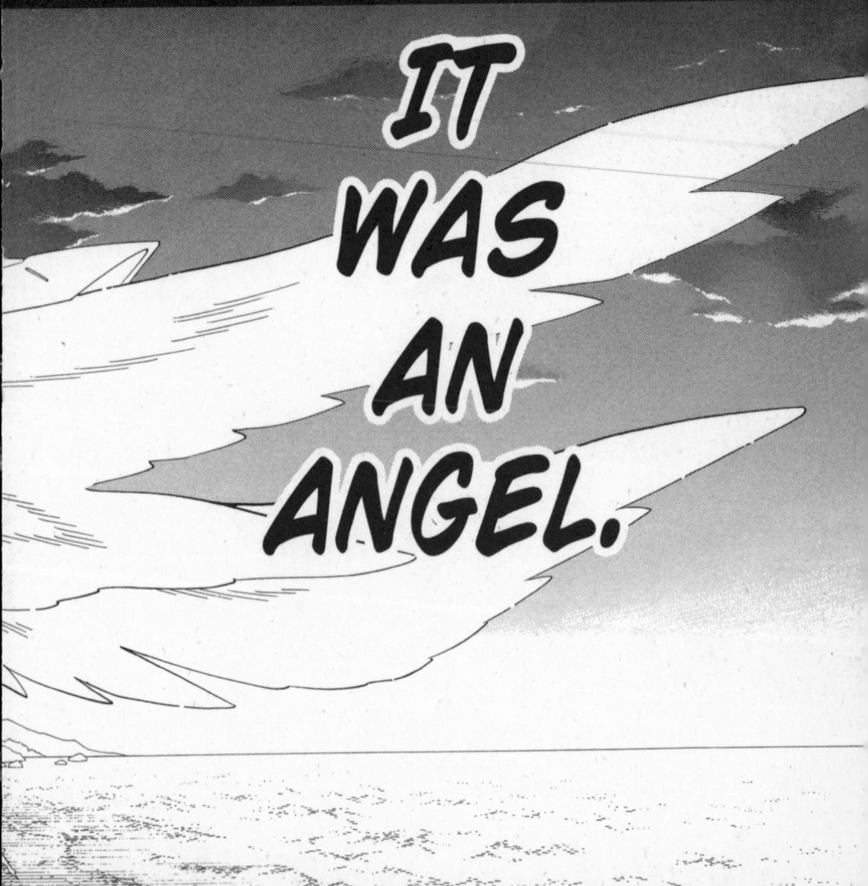
IT WAS AN ANGEL.

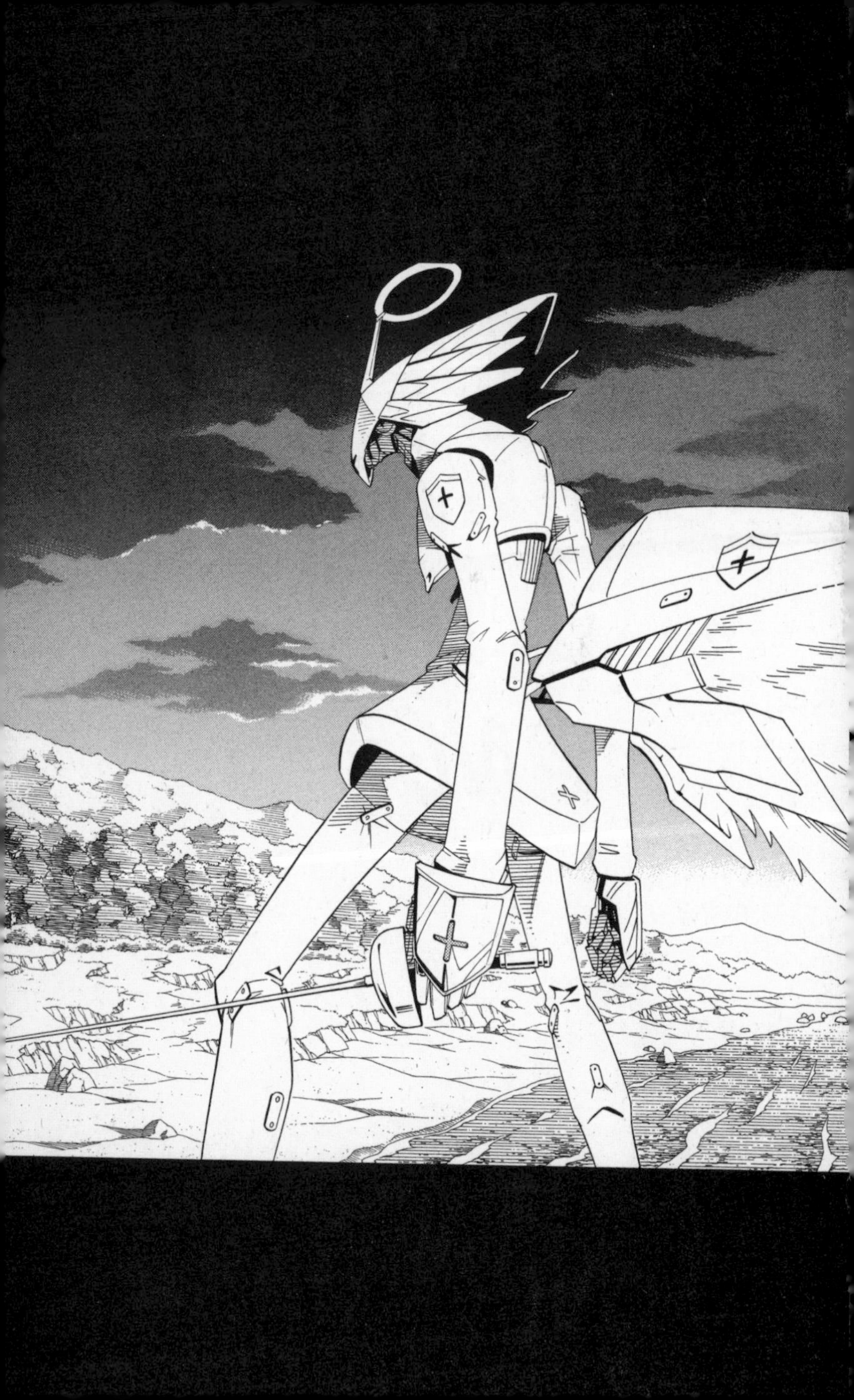

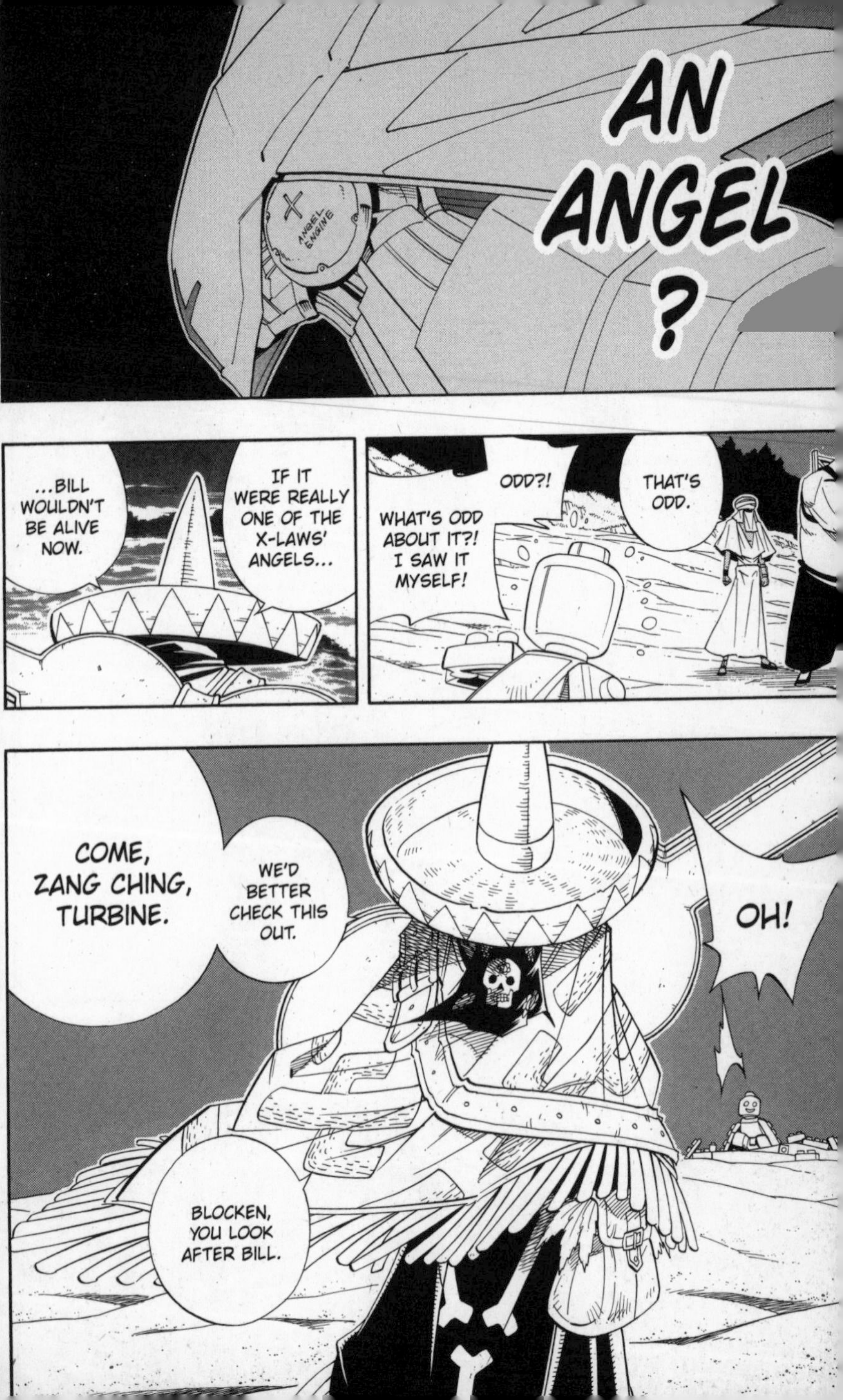
AN ANGEL ?
ANGEL ENGINE
THAT'S ODD.
ODD?!
WHAT'S ODD ABOUT IT?! I SAW IT MYSELF!
IF IT WERE REALLY ONE OF THE X-LAWS' ANGELS...
...BILL WOULDN'T BE ALIVE NOW.
OH!
WE'D BETTER CHECK THIS OUT.
COME, ZANG CHING, TURBINE.
BLOCKEN, YOU LOOK AFTER BILL.

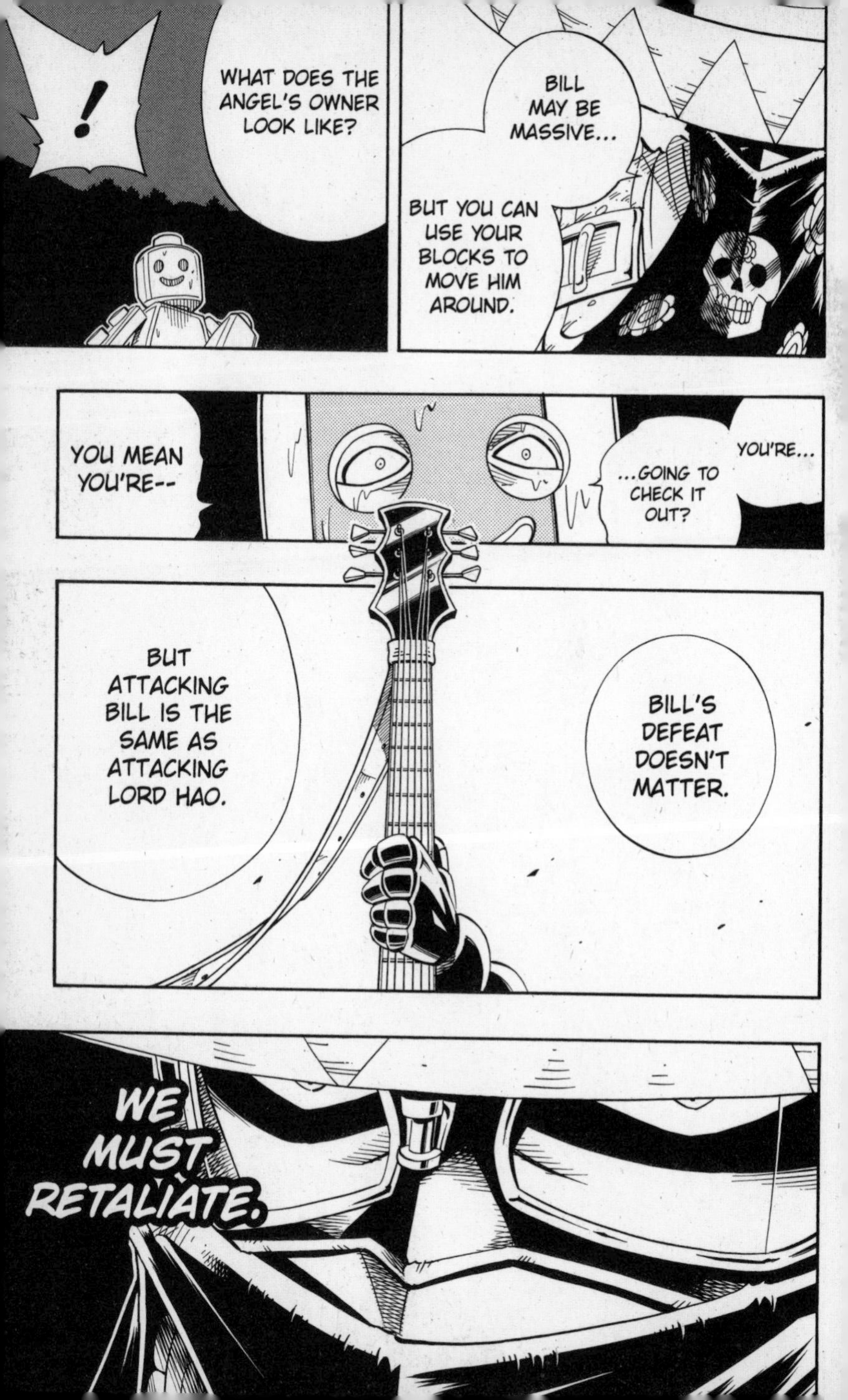
BILL MAY BE MASSIVE...
BUT YOU CAN USE YOUR BLOCKS TO MOVE HIM AROUND.
WHAT DOES THE ANGEL'S OWNER LOOK LIKE?
!
YOU'RE...
...GOING TO CHECK IT OUT?
YOU MEAN YOU'RE--
BILL'S DEFEAT DOESN'T MATTER.
BUT ATTACKING BILL IS THE SAME AS ATTACKING LORD HAO.
WE MUST RETALIATE.

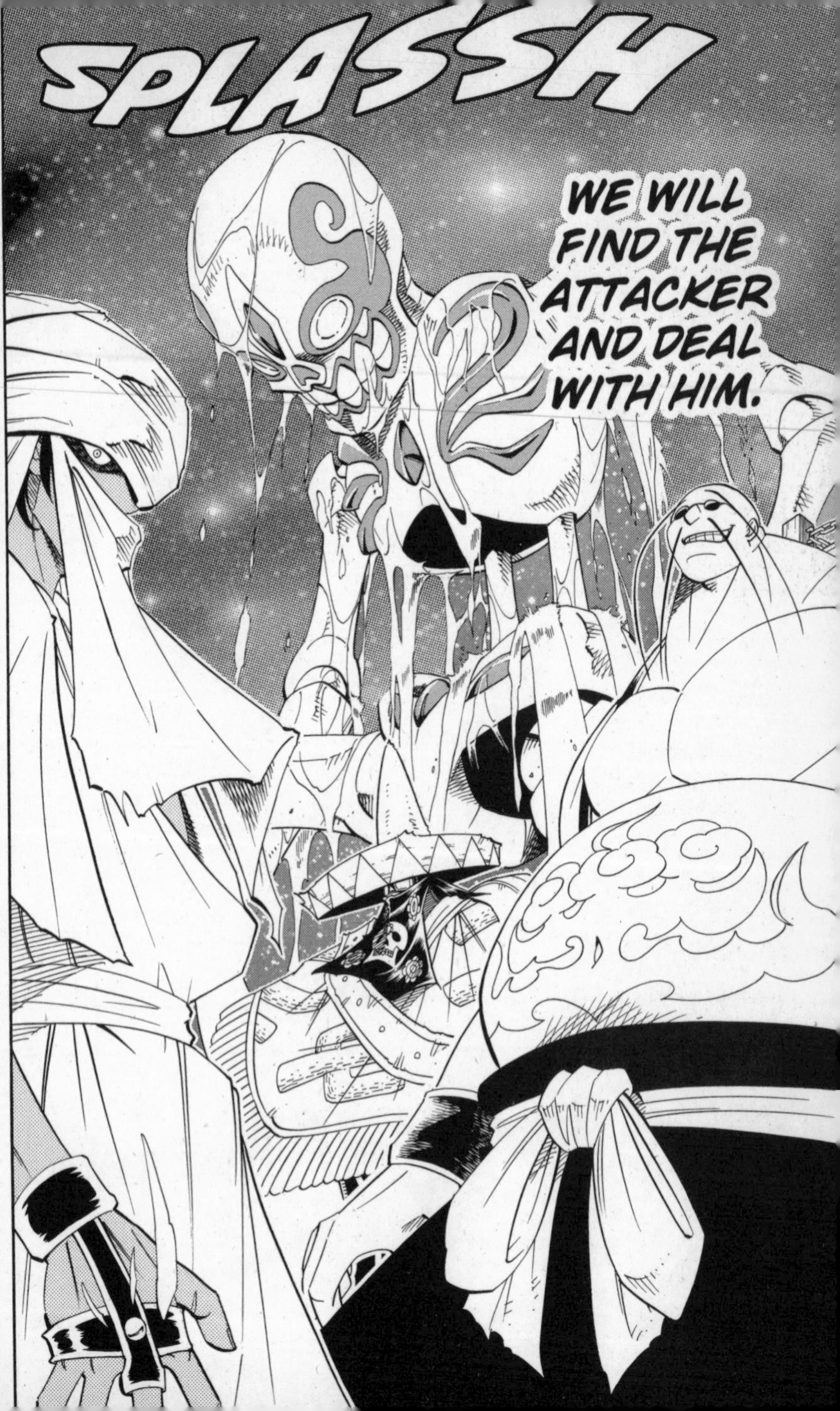
SPLASSH
WE WILL FIND THE ATTACKER AND DEAL WITH HIM.

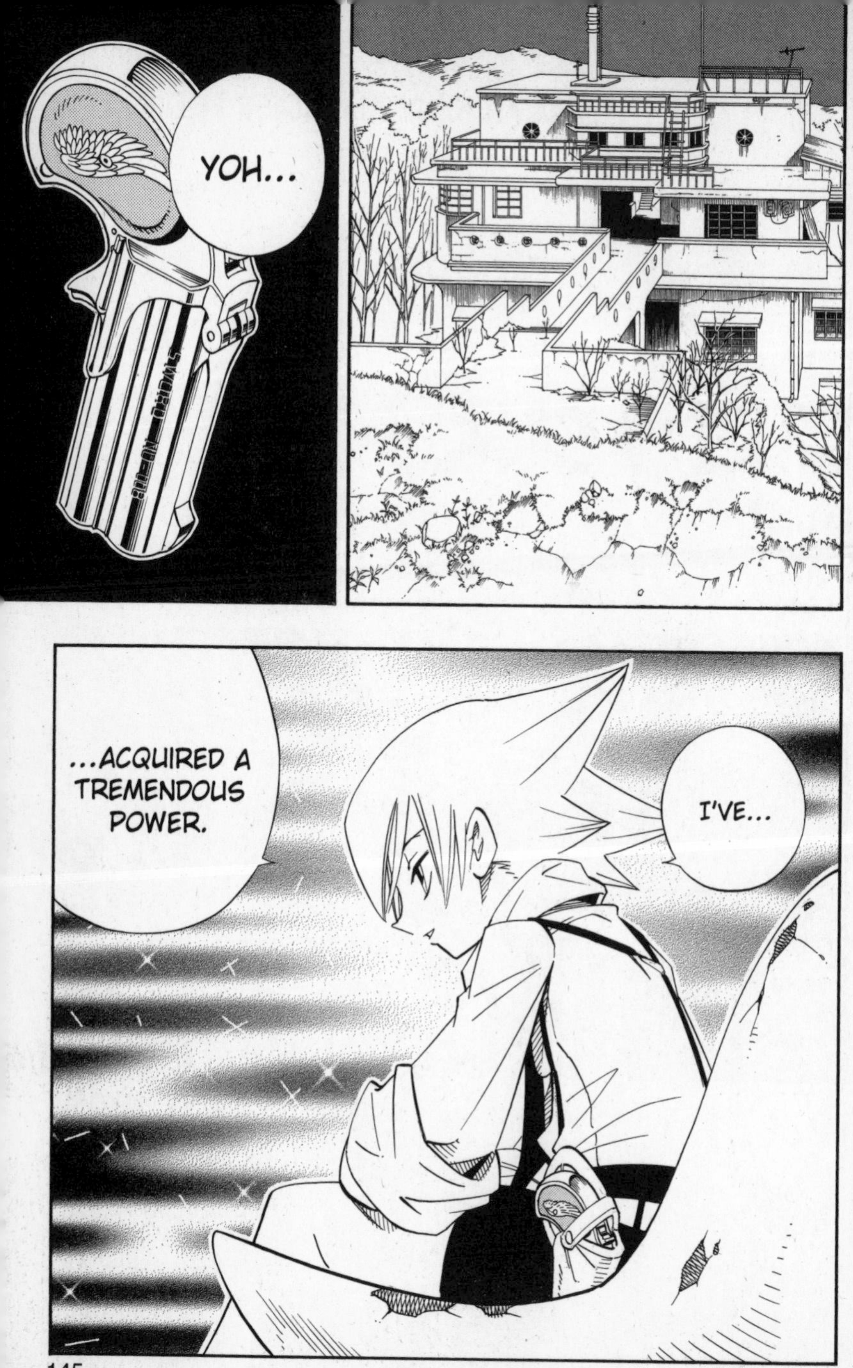
YOH...
I'VE...
...ACQUIRED A TREMENDOUS POWER.

SHAMAN KING CHARACTER FILE No.116

ブロックス

BLOCK

2001
(JAN)

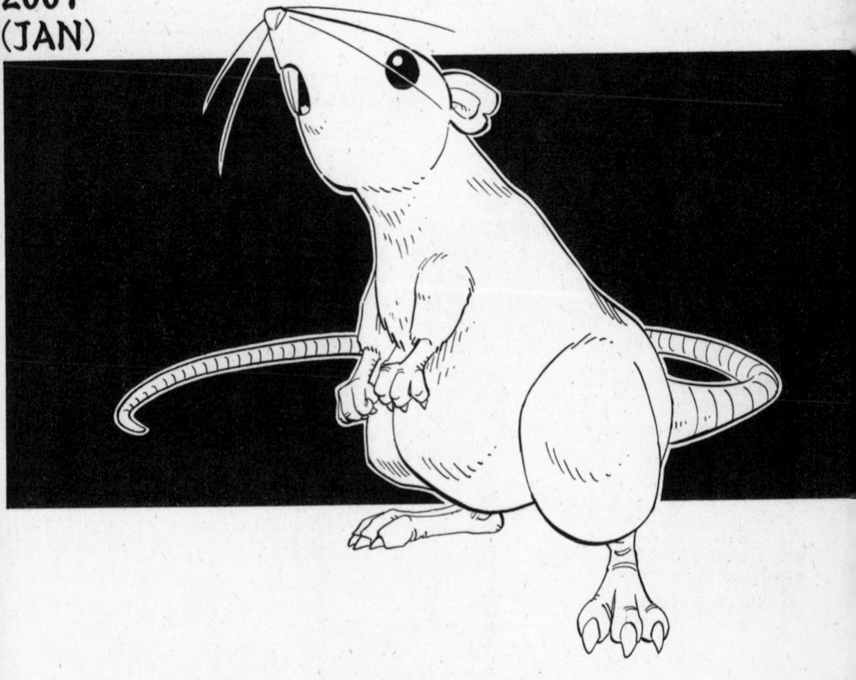

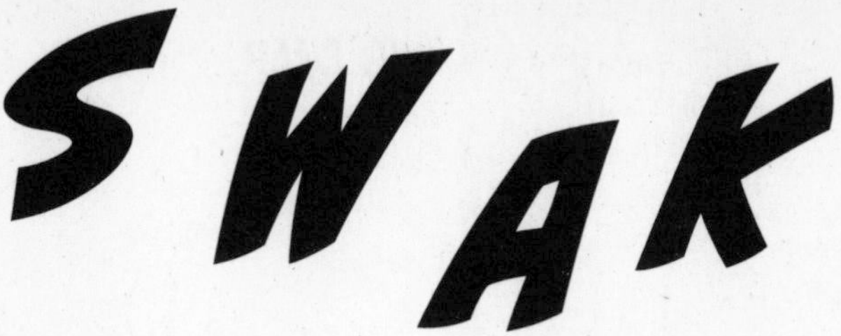
SWAK

Reincarnation 187: Epilogue IV: Boy

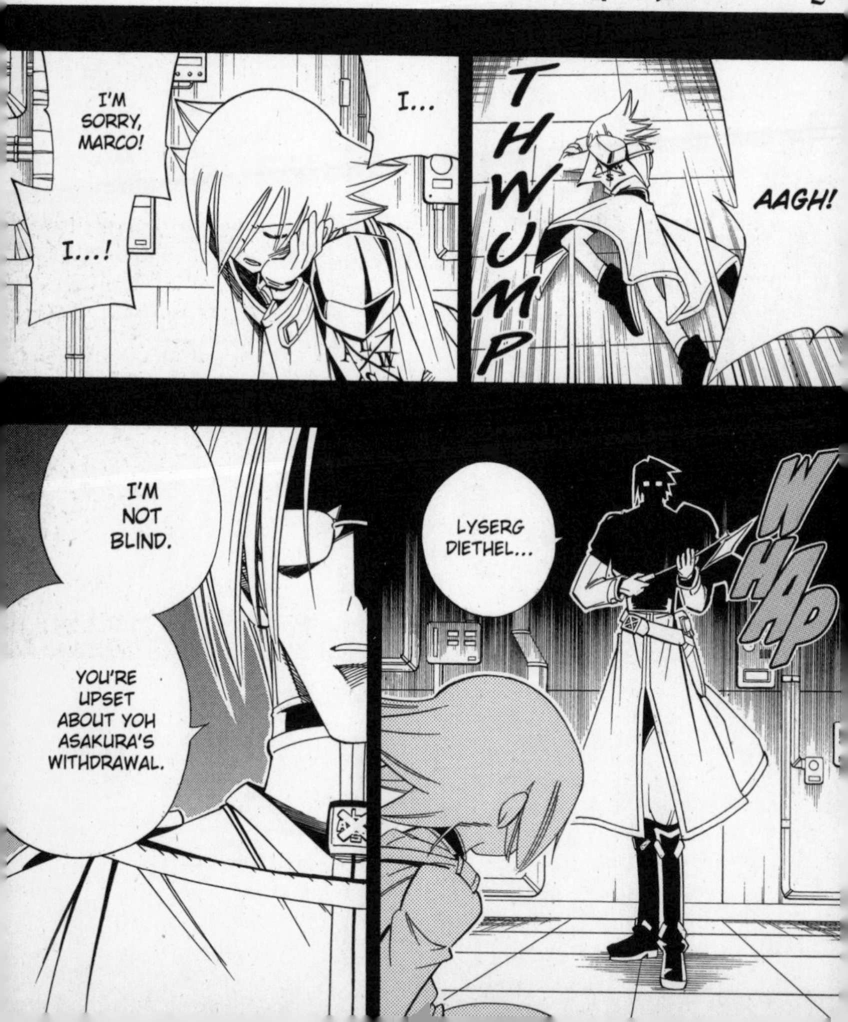
THWUMP
AAGH!
I...
I'M SORRY, MARCO!
I...!
LYSERG DIETHEL...
WHAP
I'M NOT BLIND.
YOU'RE UPSET ABOUT YOH ASAKURA'S WITHDRAWAL.

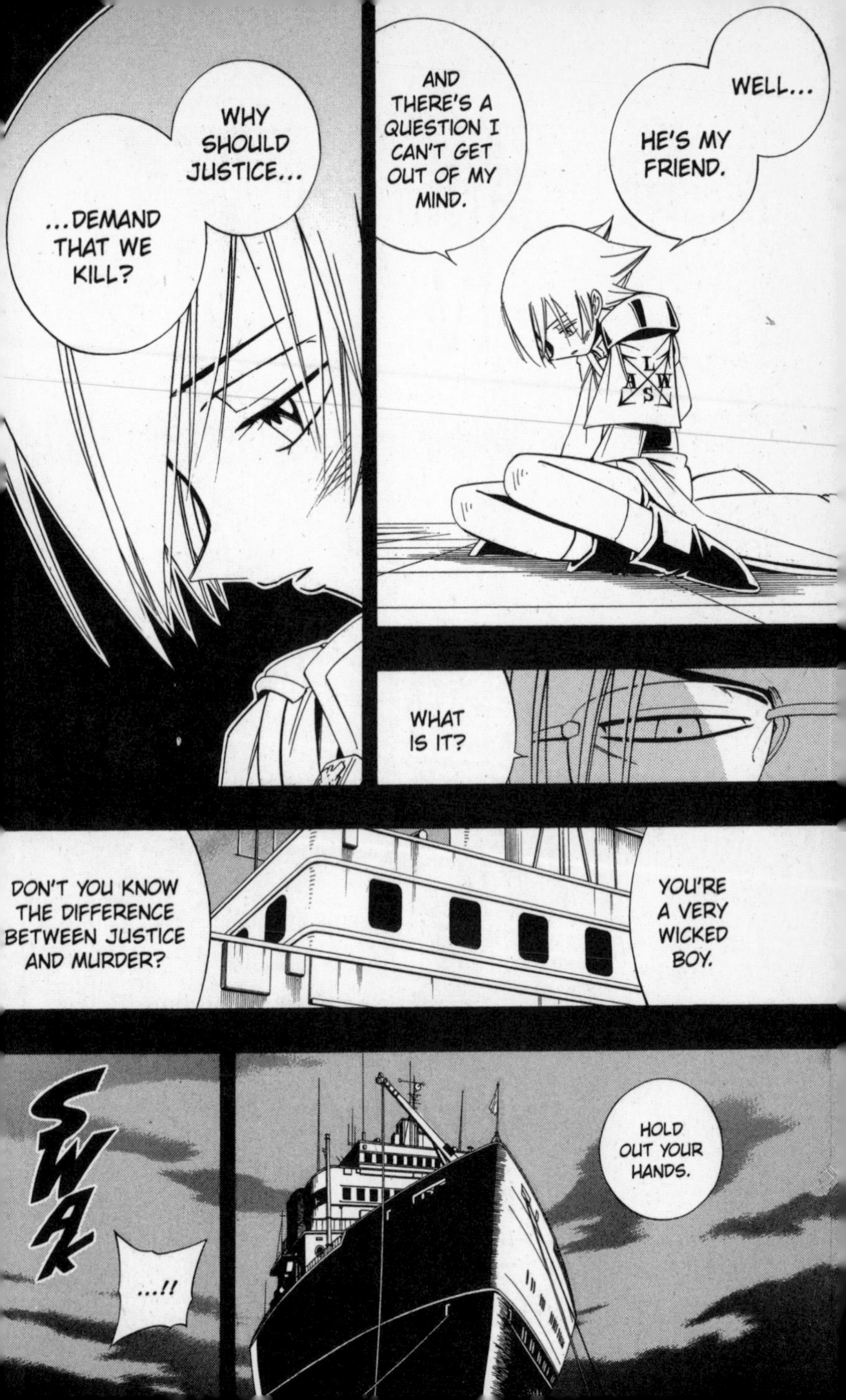
WELL...
HE'S MY FRIEND.
AND THERE'S A QUESTION I CAN'T GET OUT OF MY MIND.
WHAT IS IT?
WHY SHOULD JUSTICE...
...DEMAND THAT WE KILL?
YOU'RE A VERY WICKED BOY.
DON'T YOU KNOW THE DIFFERENCE BETWEEN JUSTICE AND MURDER?
HOLD OUT YOUR HANDS.
SWAK
...!!

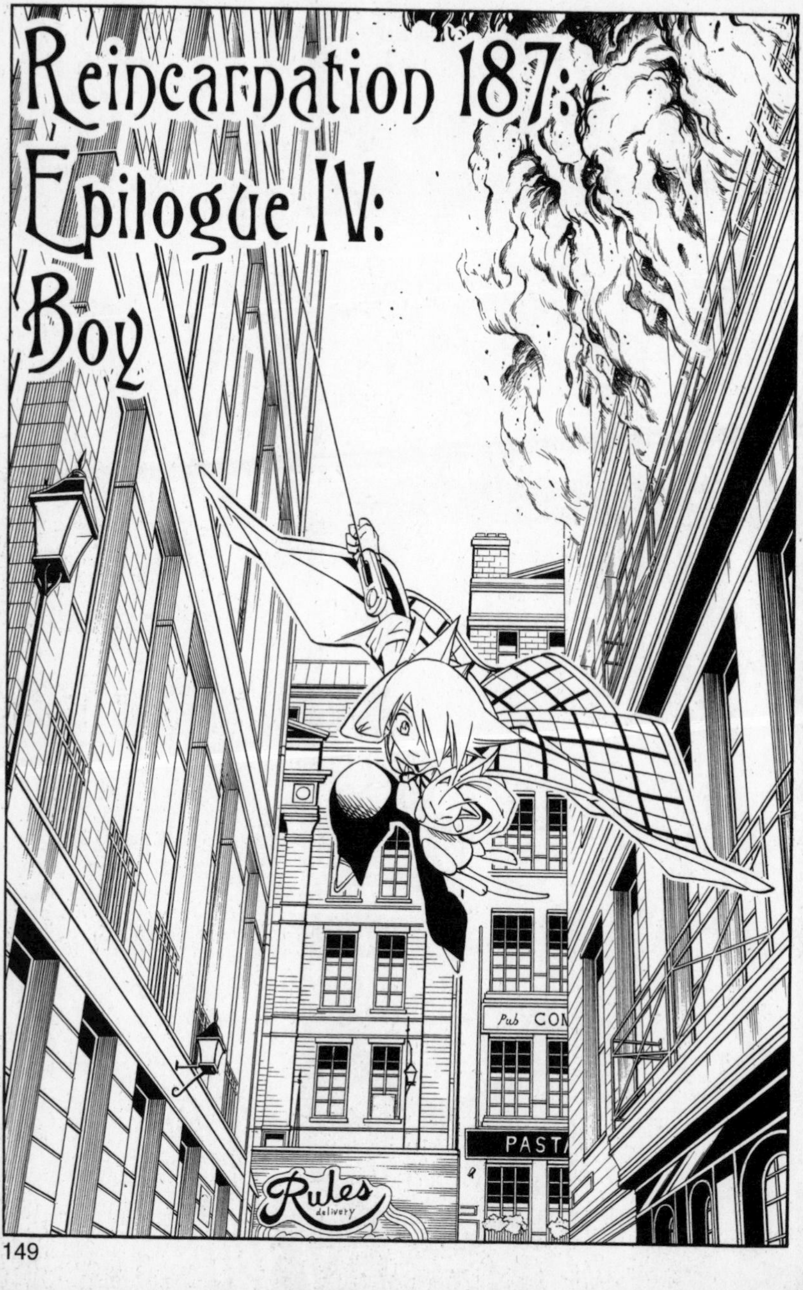
Reincarnation 187:
Epilogue IV:
Boy
Pub COM
PASTA
Rules
delivery

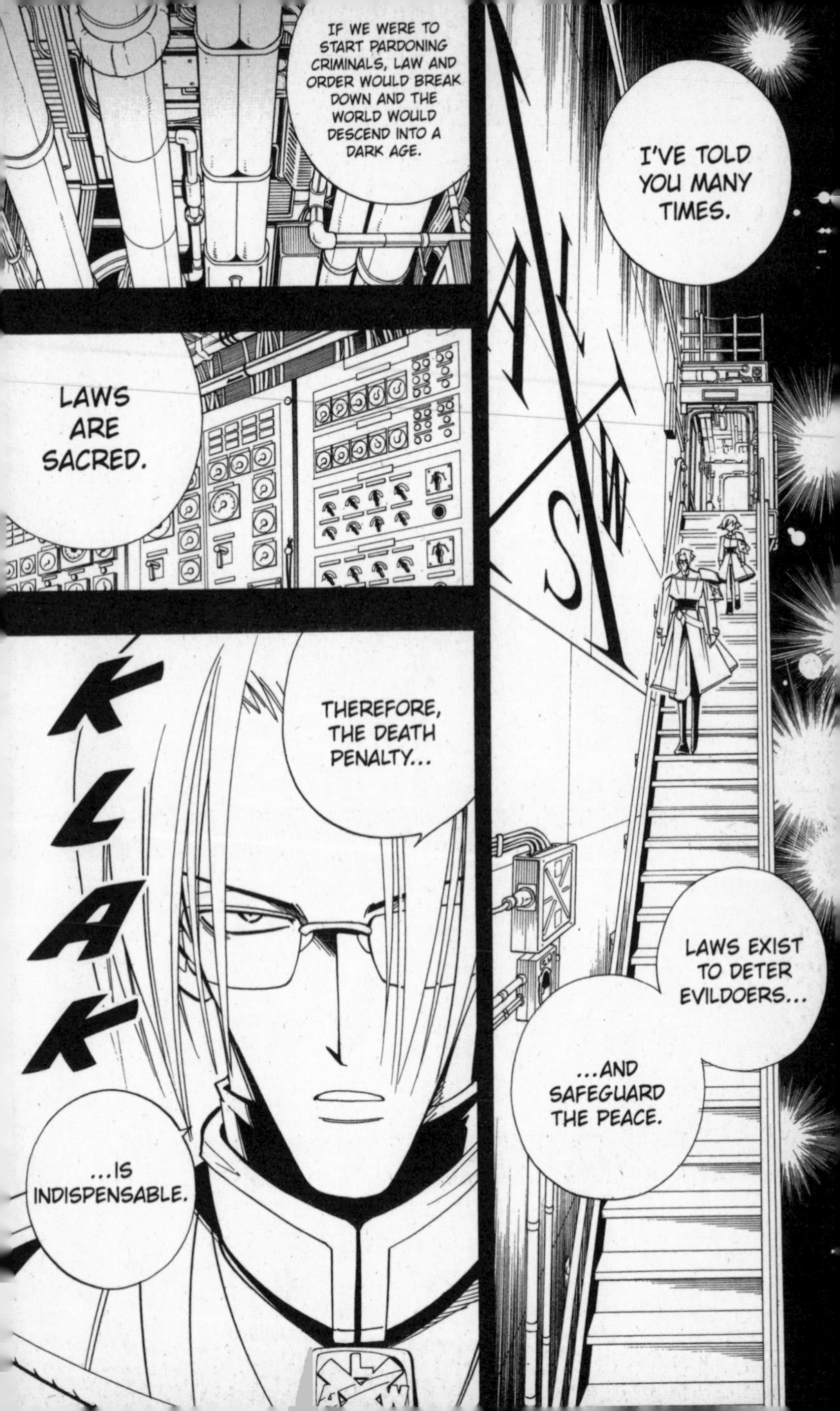
I'VE TOLD YOU MANY TIMES.
LAWS EXIST TO DETER EVILDOERS...
...AND SAFEGUARD THE PEACE.
IF WE WERE TO START PARDONING CRIMINALS, LAW AND ORDER WOULD BREAK DOWN AND THE WORLD WOULD DESCEND INTO A DARK AGE.
LAWS ARE SACRED.
THEREFORE, THE DEATH PENALTY...
KLAK
...IS INDISPENSABLE.

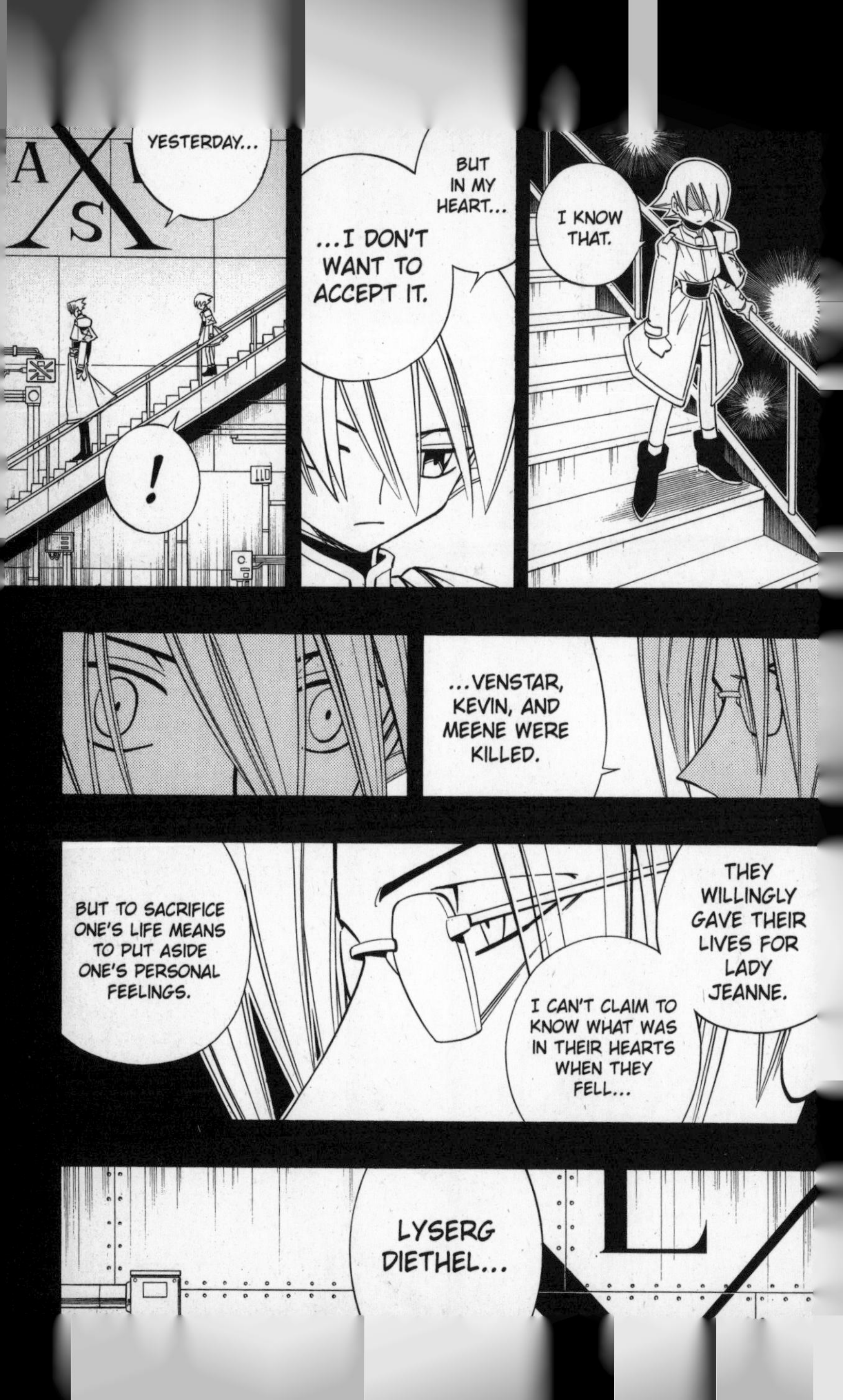
I KNOW THAT.
BUT IN MY HEART...
...I DON'T WANT TO ACCEPT IT.
YESTERDAY...
!
...VENSTAR, KEVIN, AND MEENE WERE KILLED.
THEY WILLINGLY GAVE THEIR LIVES FOR LADY JEANNE.
I CAN'T CLAIM TO KNOW WHAT WAS IN THEIR HEARTS WHEN THEY FELL...
BUT TO SACRIFICE ONE'S LIFE MEANS TO PUT ASIDE ONE'S PERSONAL FEELINGS.
LYSERG DIETHEL...

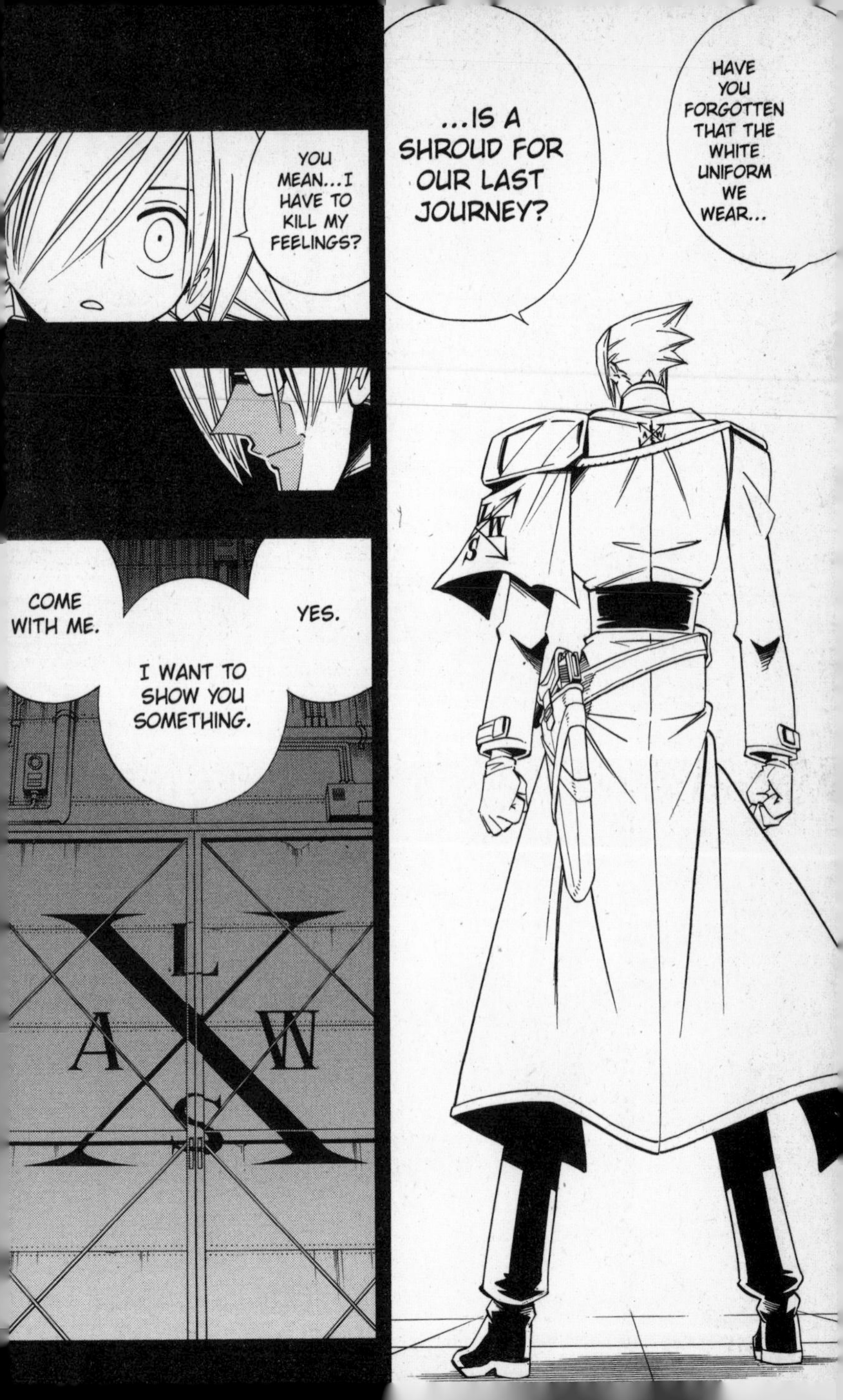
HAVE YOU FORGOTTEN THAT THE WHITE UNIFORM WE WEAR...
...IS A SHROUD FOR OUR LAST JOURNEY?
YOU MEAN...I HAVE TO KILL MY FEELINGS?
YES.
COME WITH ME.
I WANT TO SHOW YOU SOMETHING.
L
A
W
S

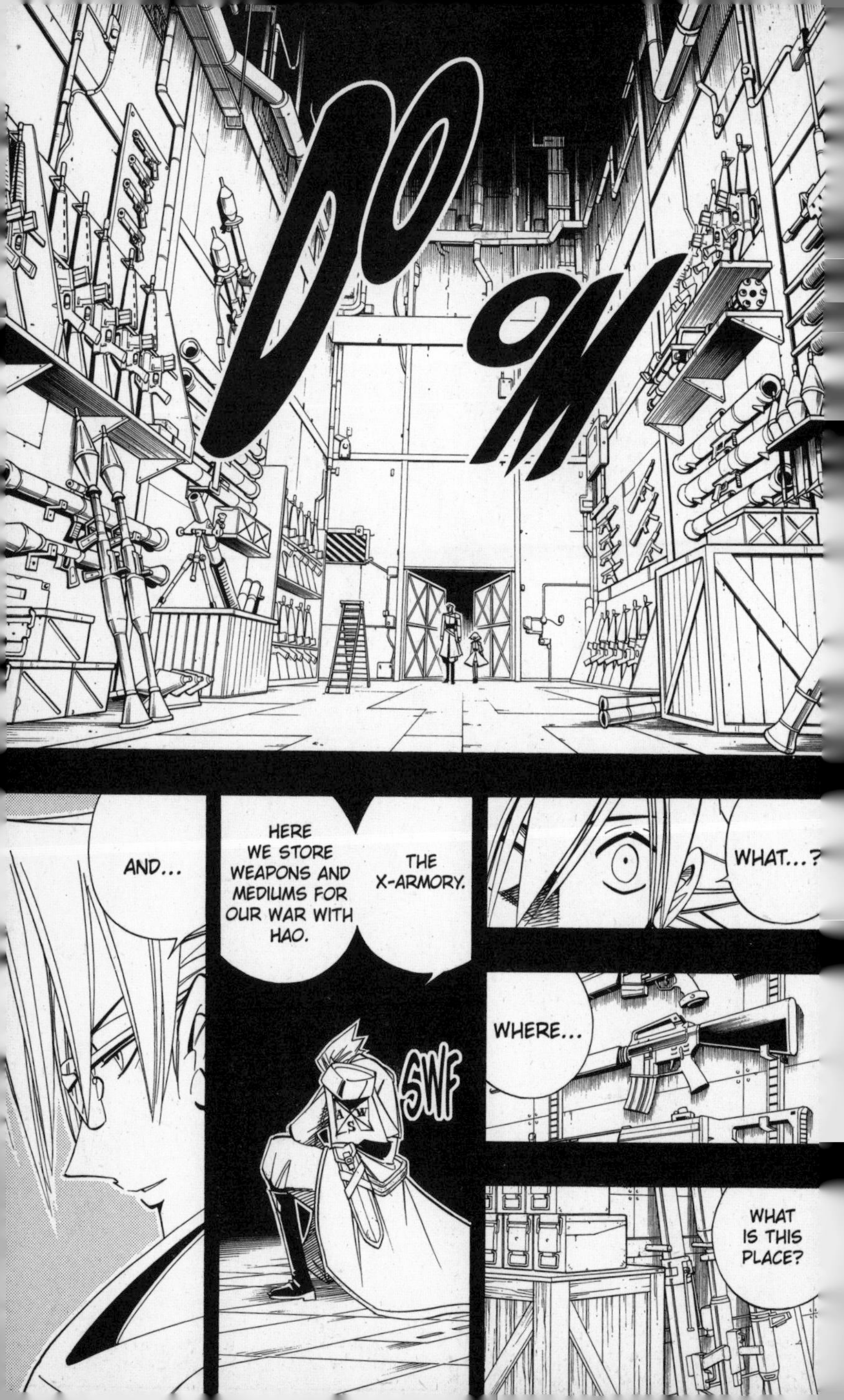
WHAT...?
WHERE...
WHAT IS THIS PLACE?
THE X-ARMORY.
HERE WE STORE WEAPONS AND MEDIUMS FOR OUR WAR WITH HAO.
SWF
AND...

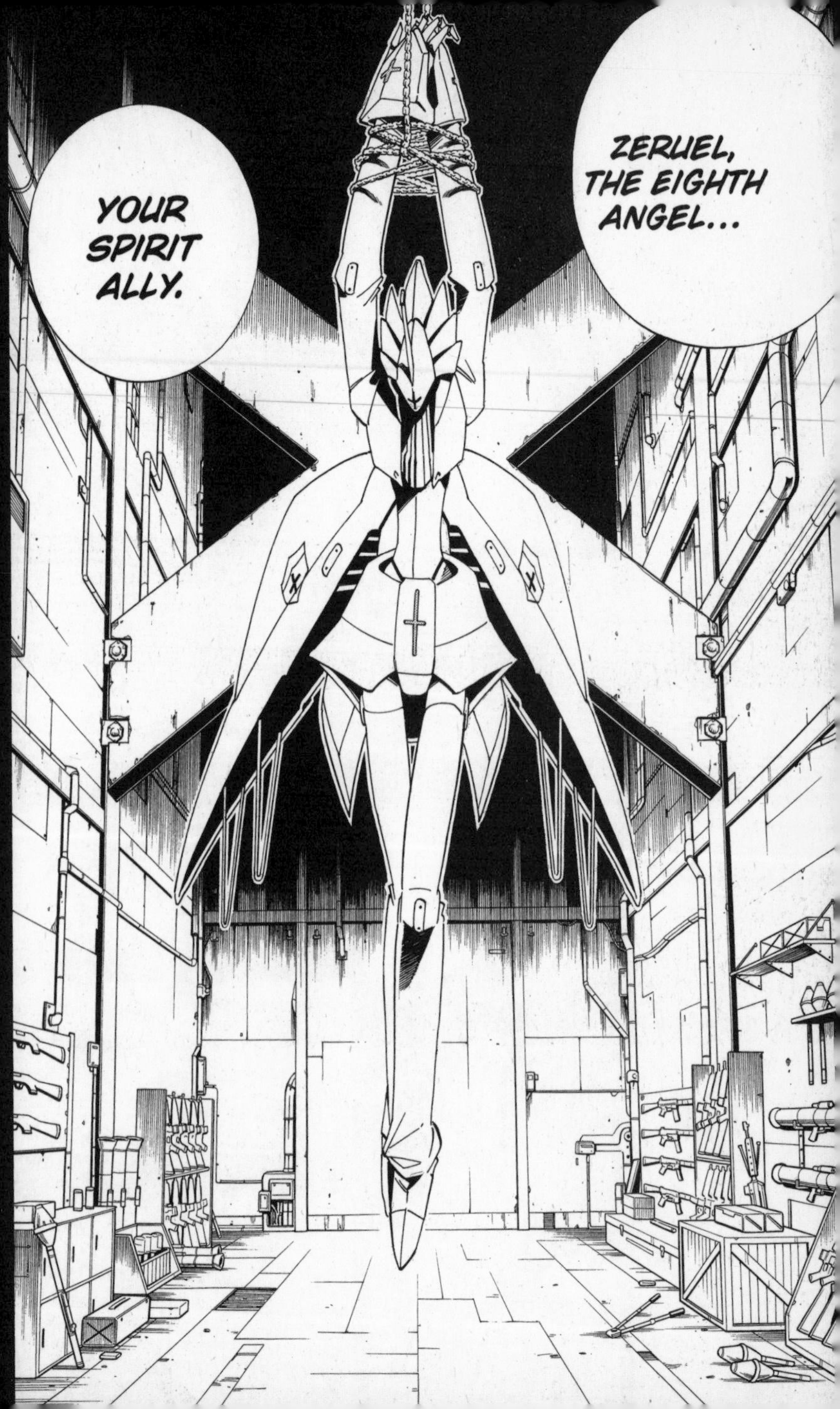
ZERUEL, THE EIGHTH ANGEL...
YOUR SPIRIT ALLY.

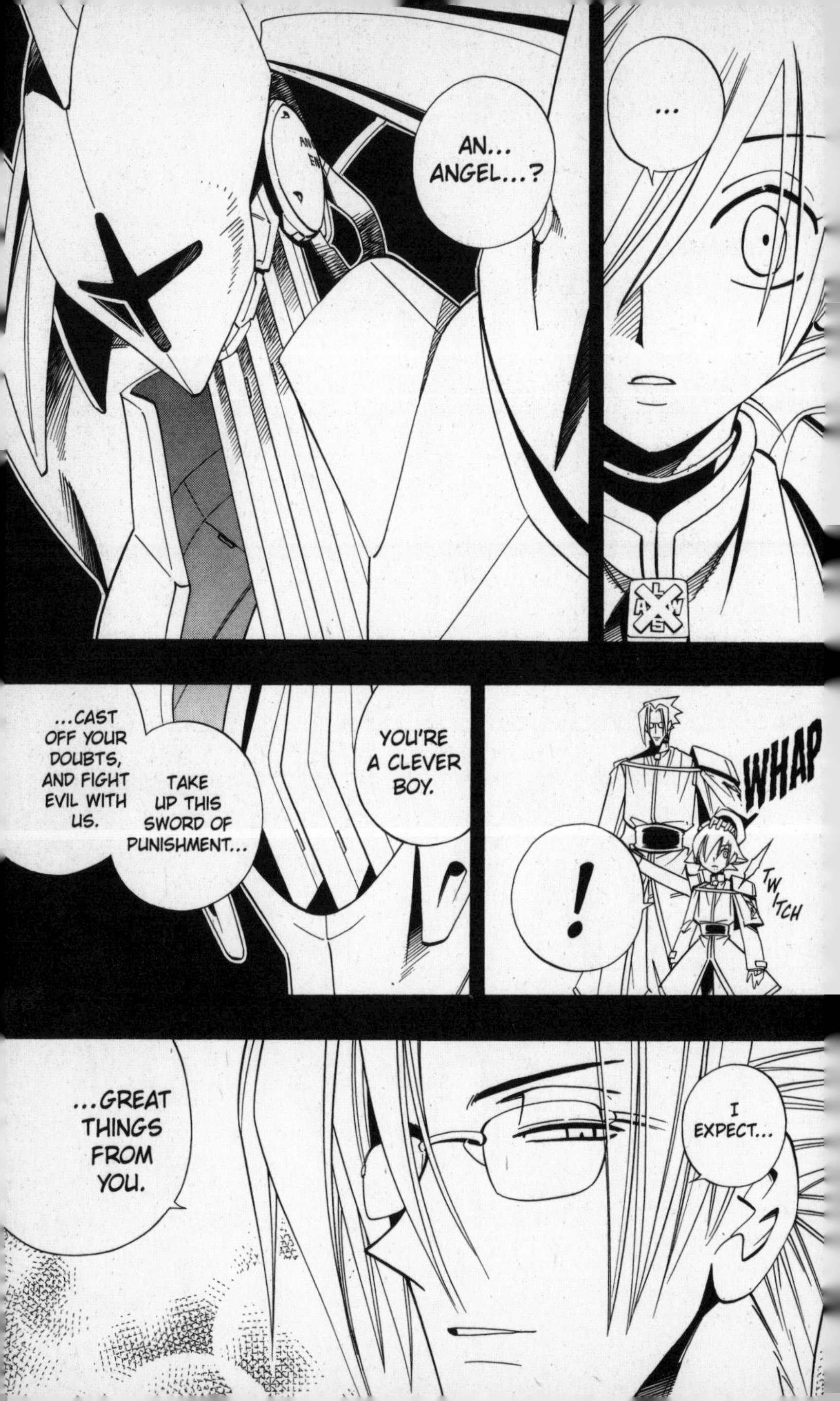
...
AN... ANGEL...?
WHAP
TWITCH
!
YOU'RE A CLEVER BOY.
TAKE UP THIS SWORD OF PUNISHMENT...
...CAST OFF YOUR DOUBTS, AND FIGHT EVIL WITH US.
I EXPECT...
...GREAT THINGS FROM YOU.

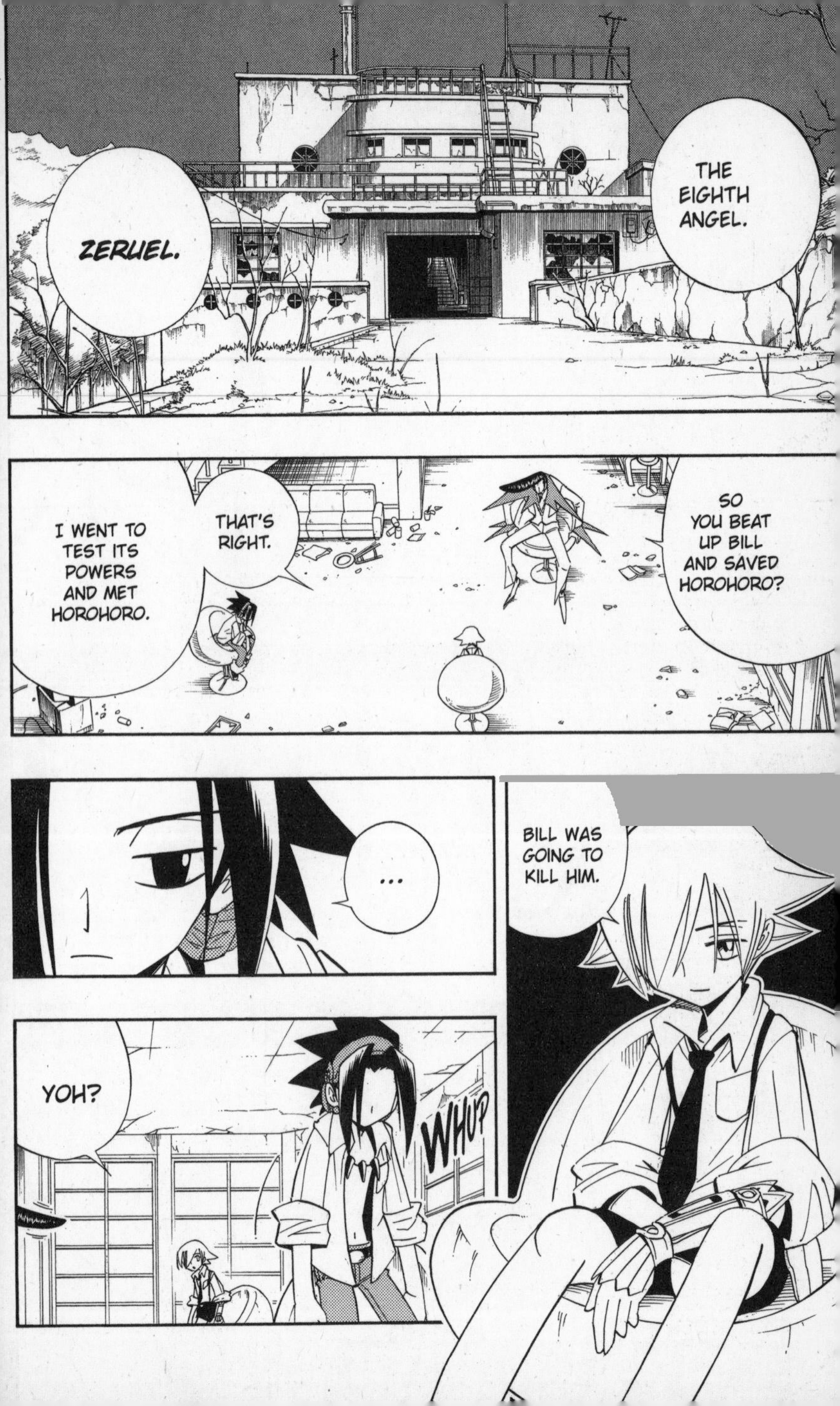
THE EIGHTH ANGEL.
ZERUEL.
SO YOU BEAT UP BILL AND SAVED HOROHORO?
THAT'S RIGHT.
I WENT TO TEST ITS POWERS AND MET HOROHORO.
BILL WAS GOING TO KILL HIM.
...
YOH?
WHUP

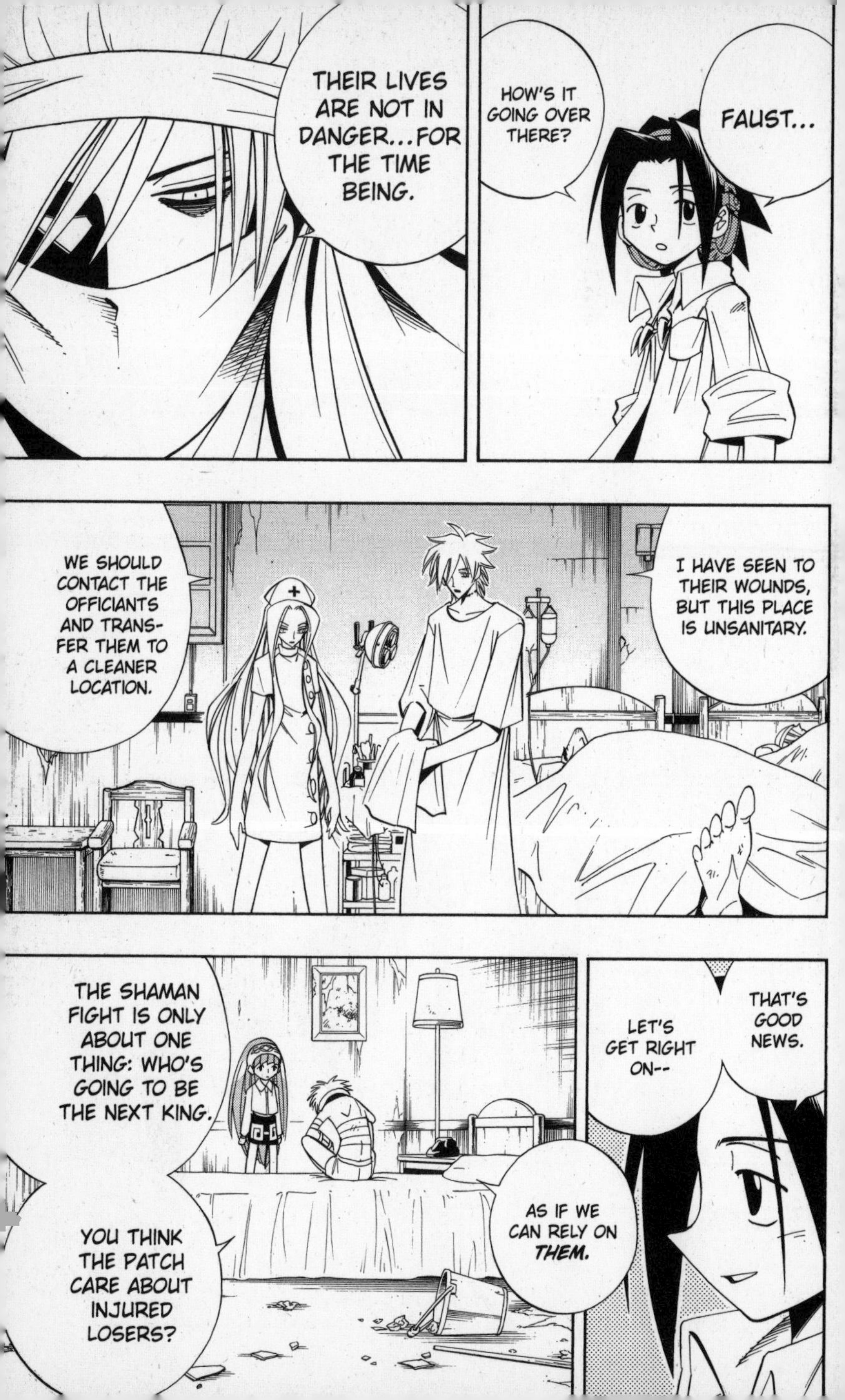
FAUST...
HOW'S IT GOING OVER THERE?
THEIR LIVES ARE NOT IN DANGER...FOR THE TIME BEING.
I HAVE SEEN TO THEIR WOUNDS, BUT THIS PLACE IS UNSANITARY.
WE SHOULD CONTACT THE OFFICIANTS AND TRANS-FER THEM TO A CLEANER LOCATION.
THAT'S GOOD NEWS.
LET'S GET RIGHT ON--
AS IF WE CAN RELY ON *THEM.*
THE SHAMAN FIGHT IS ONLY ABOUT ONE THING: WHO'S GOING TO BE THE NEXT KING.
YOU THINK THE PATCH CARE ABOUT INJURED LOSERS?

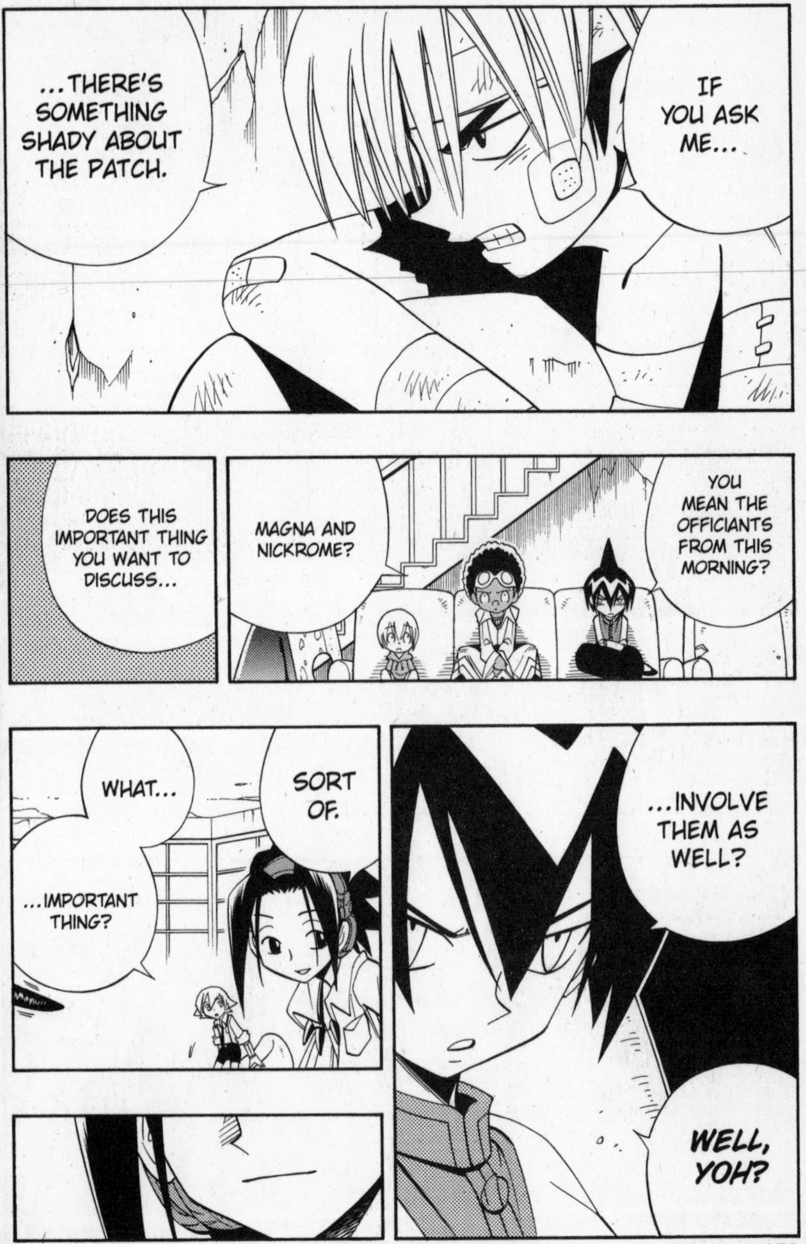
IF YOU ASK ME...
...THERE'S SOMETHING SHADY ABOUT THE PATCH.
YOU MEAN THE OFFICIANTS FROM THIS MORNING?
MAGNA AND NICKROME?
DOES THIS IMPORTANT THING YOU WANT TO DISCUSS...
...INVOLVE THEM AS WELL?
WELL, YOH?
SORT OF.
WHAT...
...IMPORTANT THING?

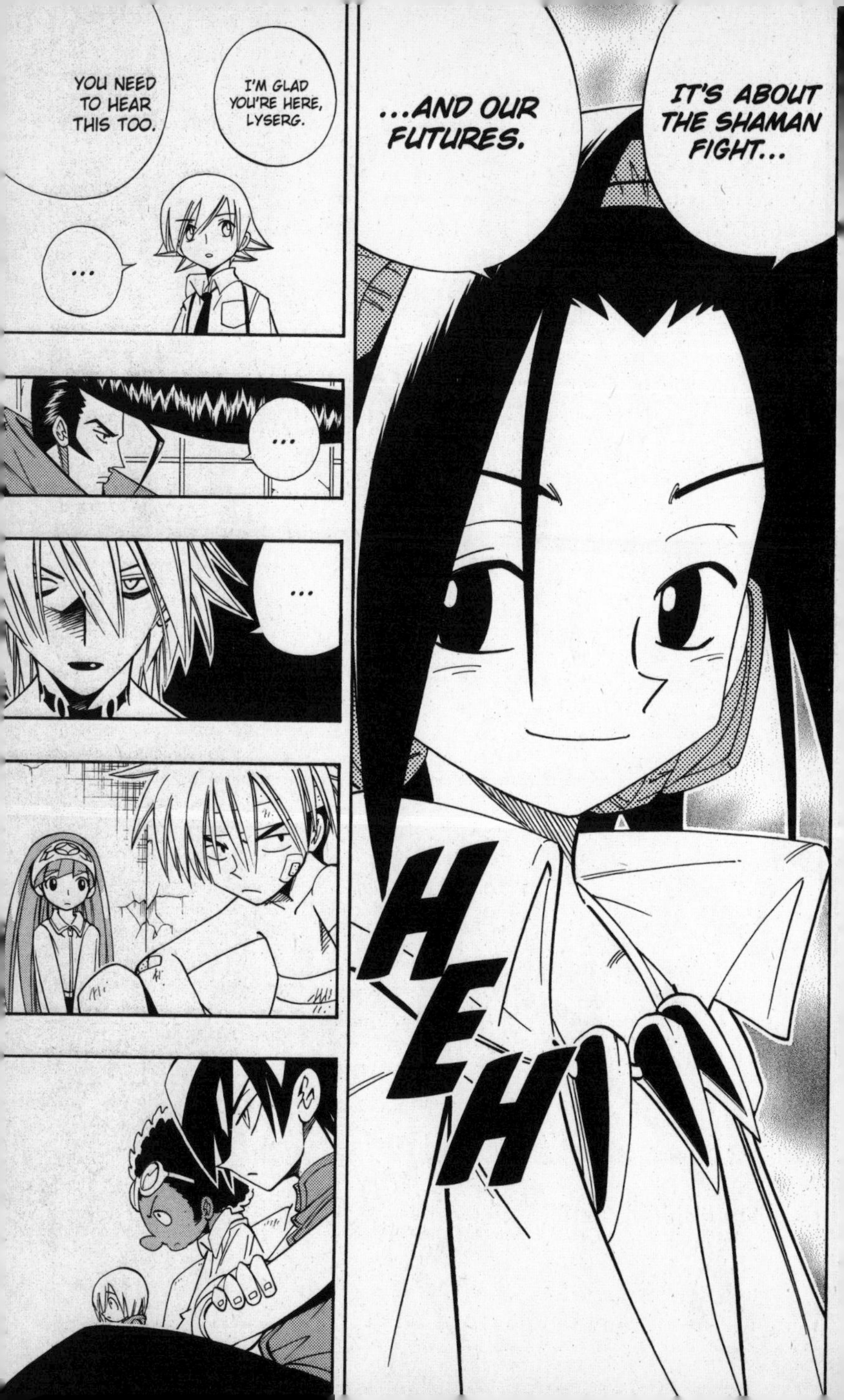
IT'S ABOUT THE SHAMAN FIGHT...
...AND OUR FUTURES.
HEH
I'M GLAD YOU'RE HERE, LYSERG.
YOU NEED TO HEAR THIS TOO.
...
...
...

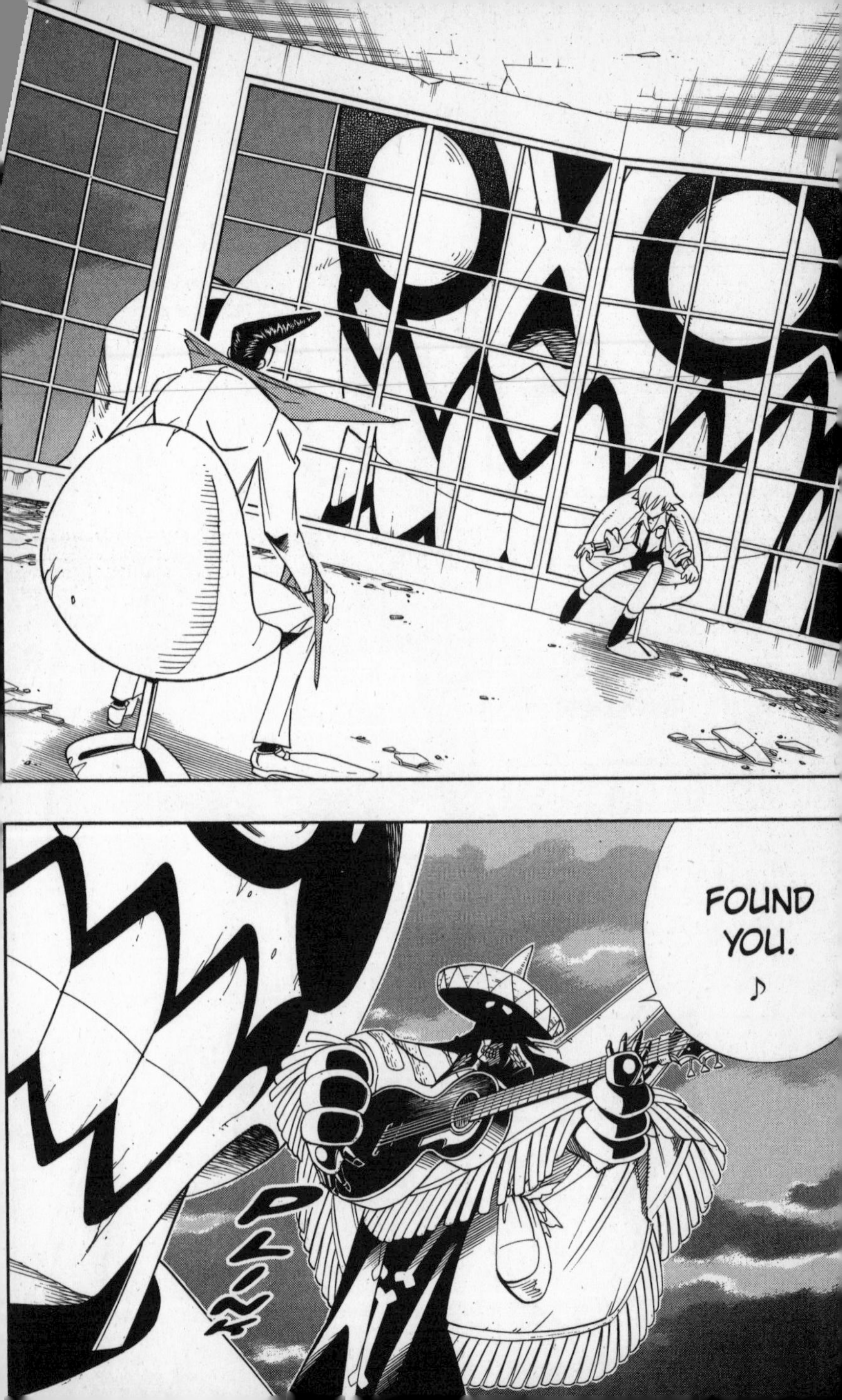
FOUND YOU. ♪

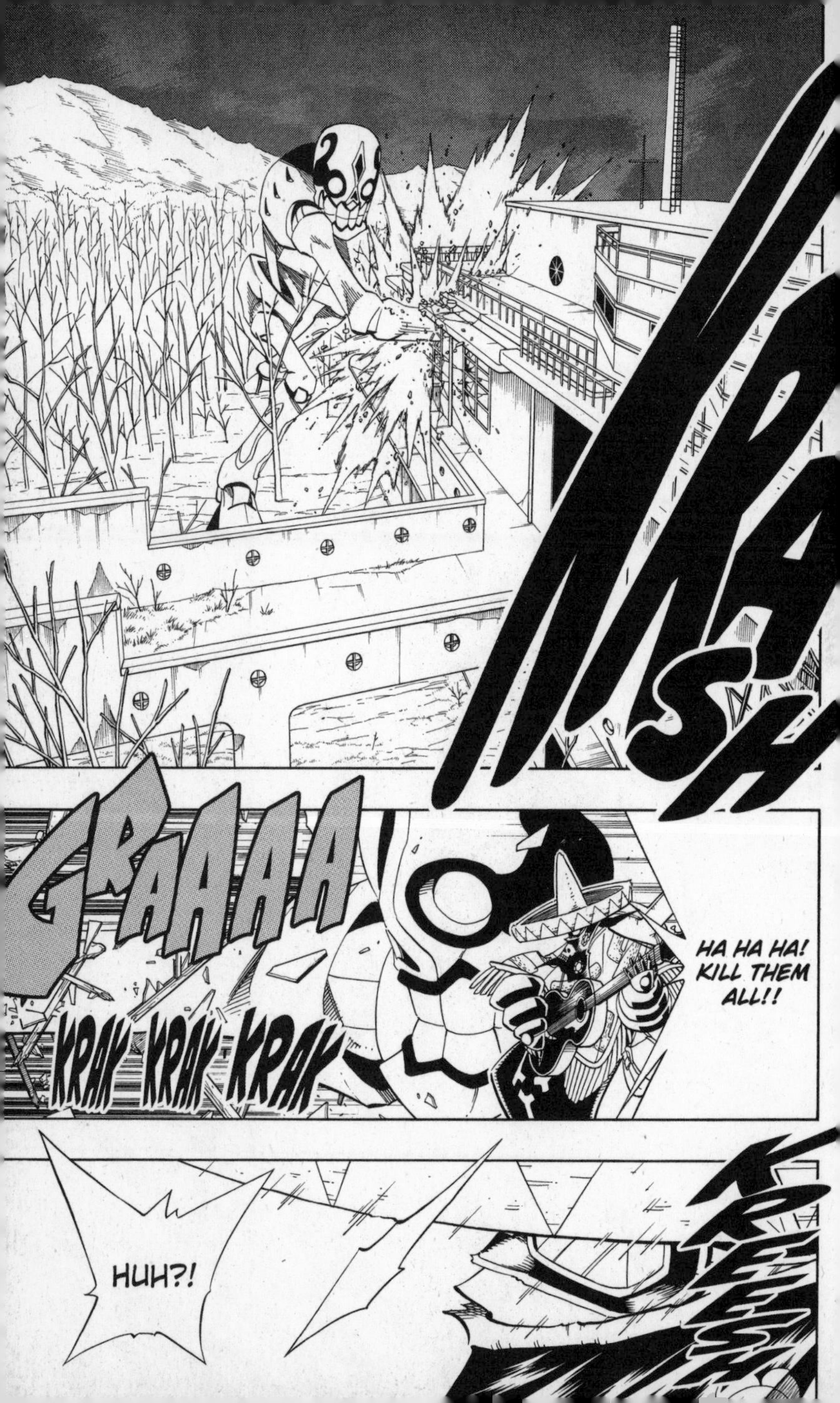
GRAAAA
HA HA HA! KILL THEM ALL!!
KRAK KRAK KRAK
HUH?!

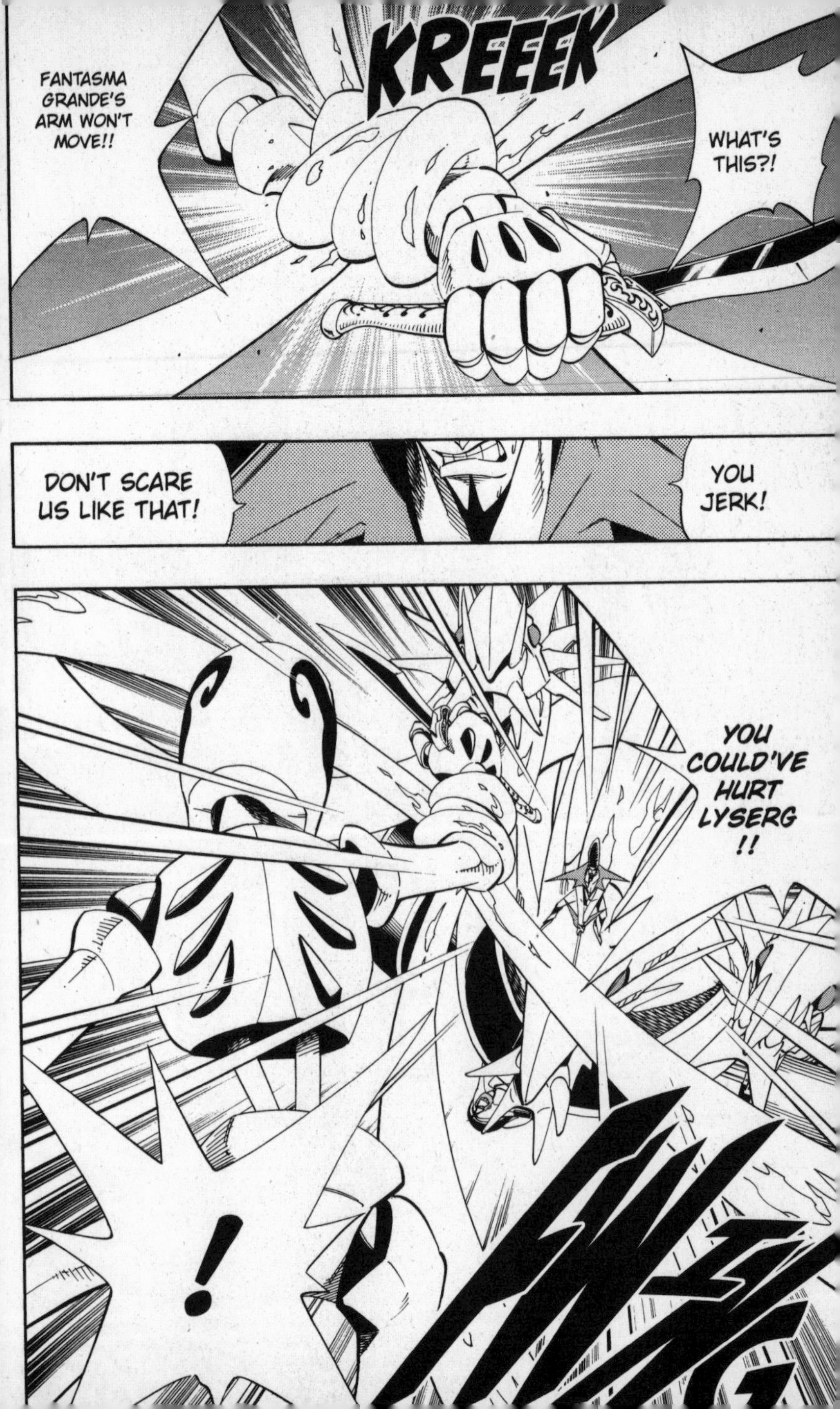
KREEEK
WHAT'S THIS?!
FANTASMA GRANDE'S ARM WON'T MOVE!!
YOU JERK!
DON'T SCARE US LIKE THAT!
YOU COULD'VE HURT LYSERG !!
!

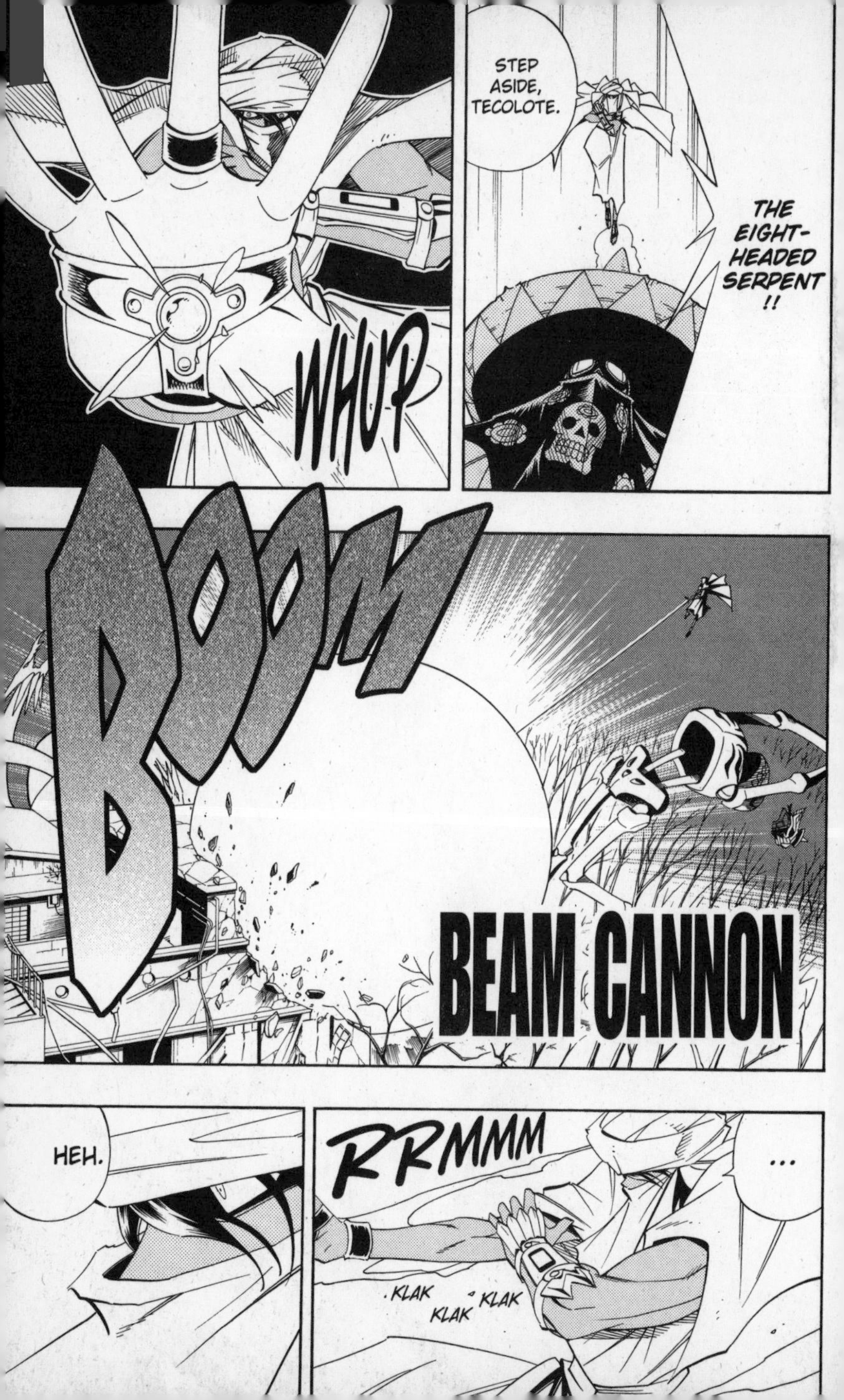
STEP ASIDE, TECOLOTE.
THE EIGHT-HEADED SERPENT!!
WHUP
BOOM
BEAM CANNON
...
RRMMM
KLAK
KLAK
KLAK
HEH.

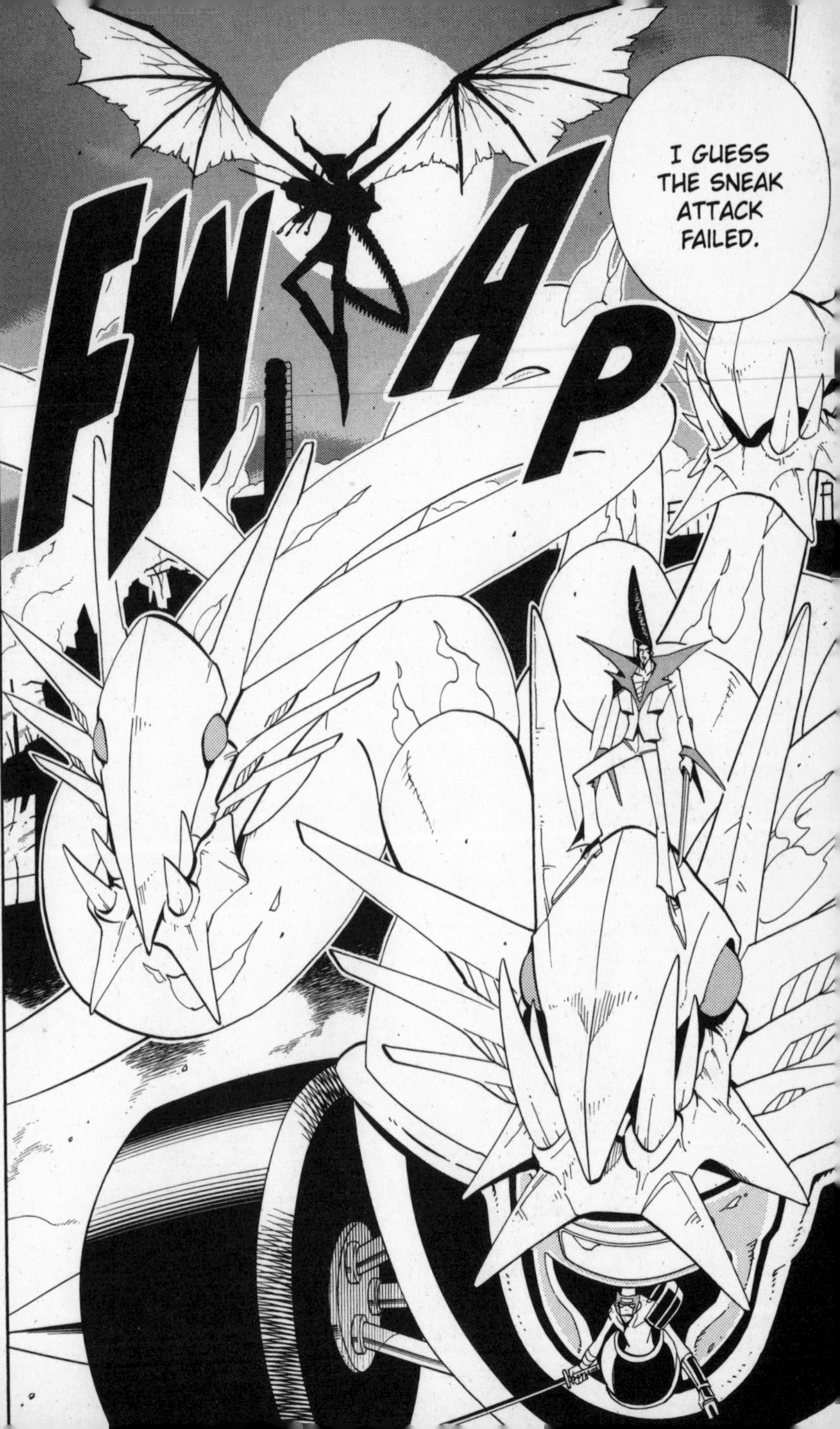
I GUESS THE SNEAK ATTACK FAILED.
FWAP

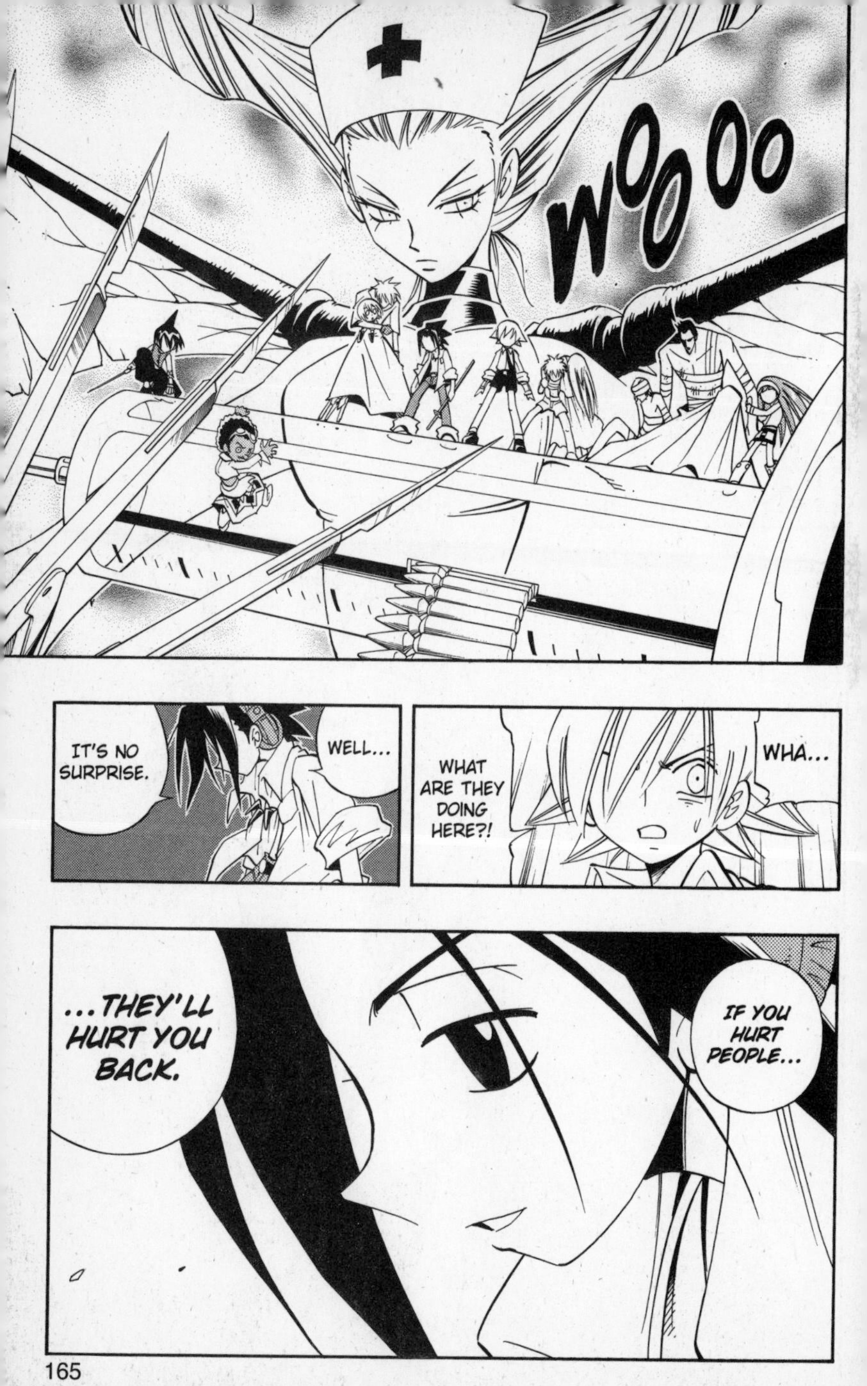
WOOOO
WHA...
WHAT ARE THEY DOING HERE?!
WELL...
IT'S NO SURPRISE.
IF YOU HURT PEOPLE...
...THEY'LL HURT YOU BACK.

SHAMAN KING CHARACTER FILE No.117

ゼルエル

ZERUEL

2001
(JAN)

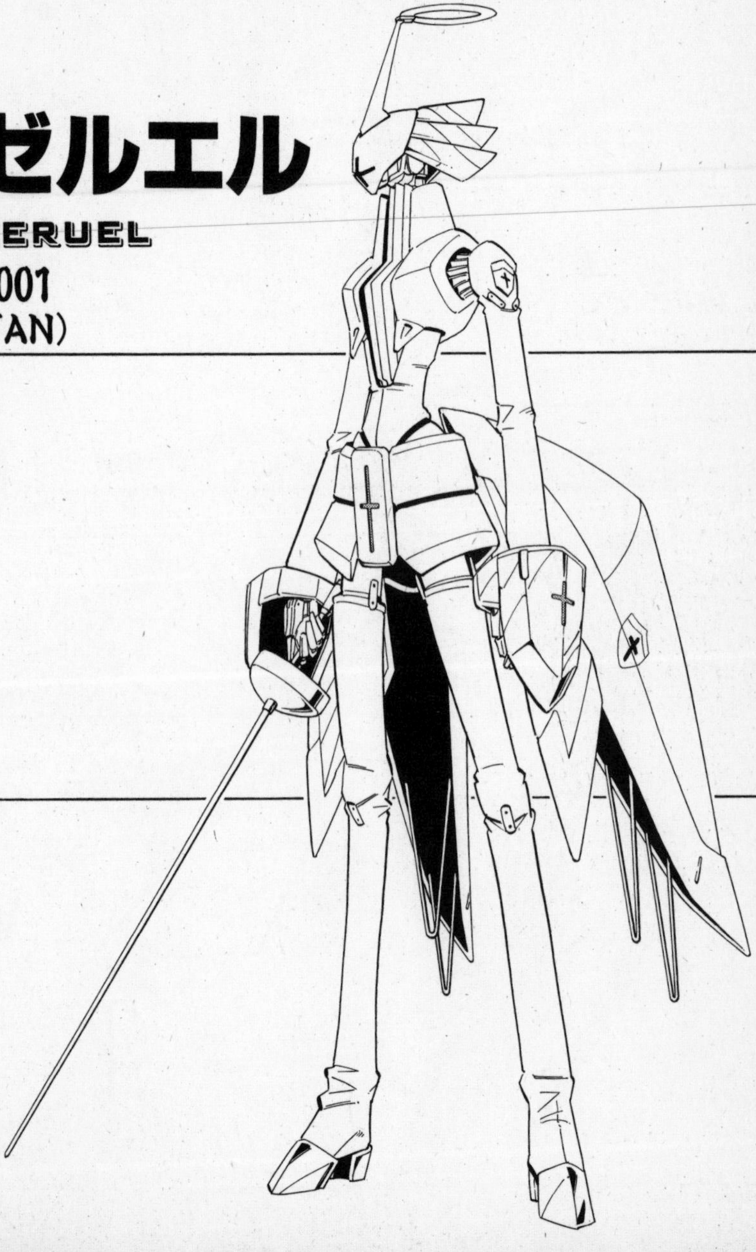

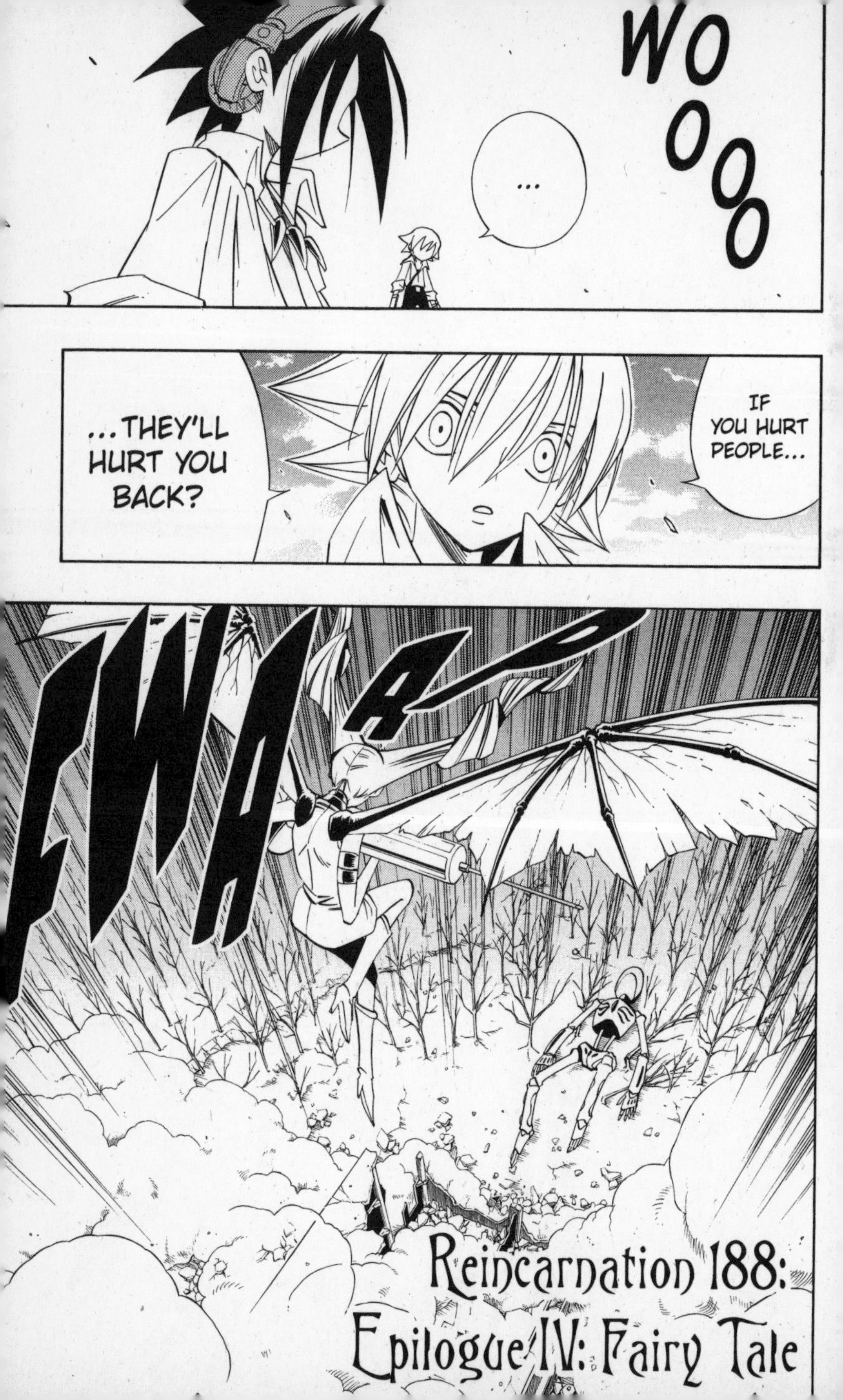
WOOOO
...
IF YOU HURT PEOPLE...
...THEY'LL HURT YOU BACK?
FWAP
Reincarnation 188:
Epilogue IV: Fairy Tale

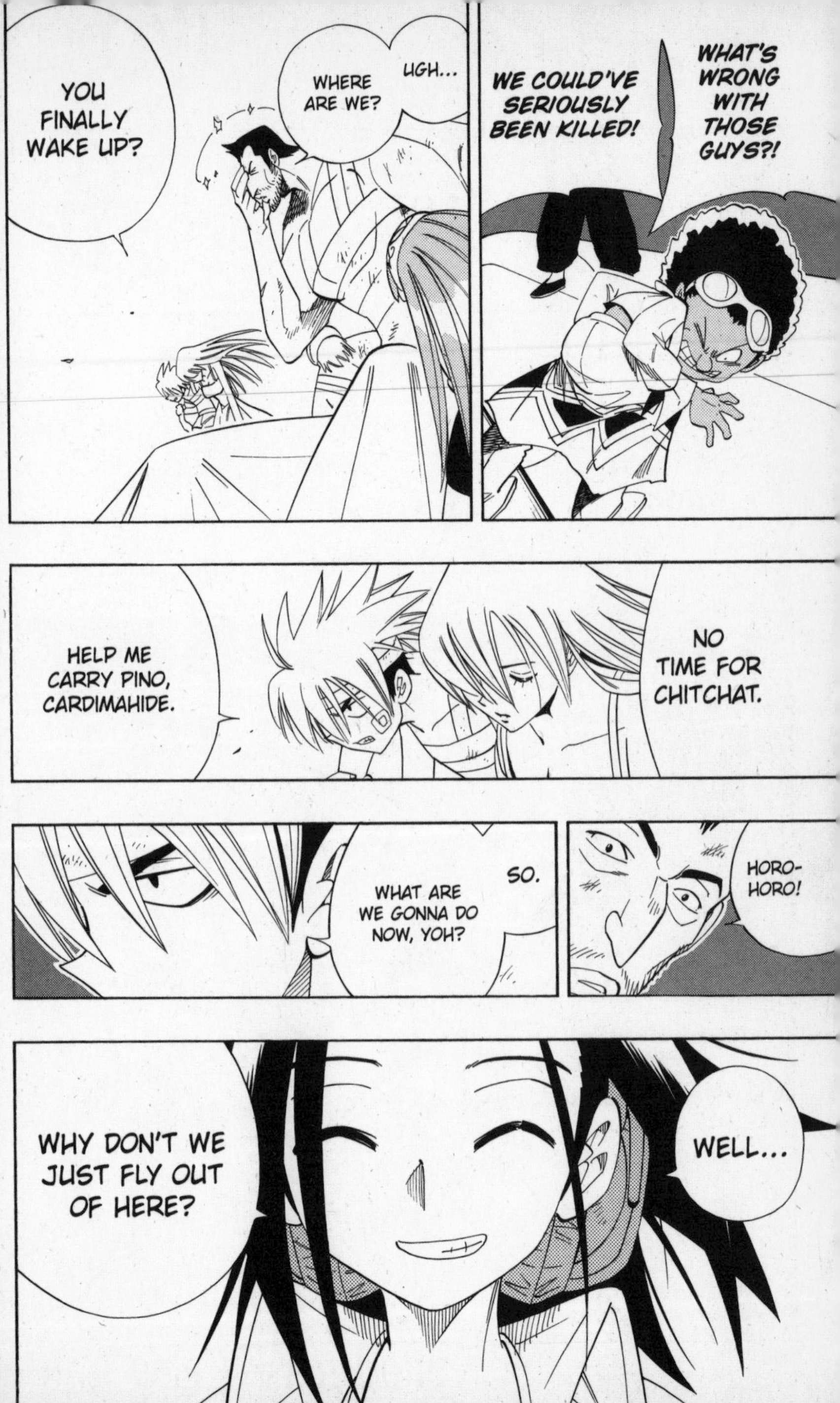
WHAT'S WRONG WITH THOSE GUYS?!
WE COULD'VE SERIOUSLY BEEN KILLED!
UGH...
WHERE ARE WE?
YOU FINALLY WAKE UP?
NO TIME FOR CHITCHAT.
HELP ME CARRY PINO, CARDIMAHIDE.
HORO-HORO!
SO.
WHAT ARE WE GONNA DO NOW, YOH?
WELL...
WHY DON'T WE JUST FLY OUT OF HERE?

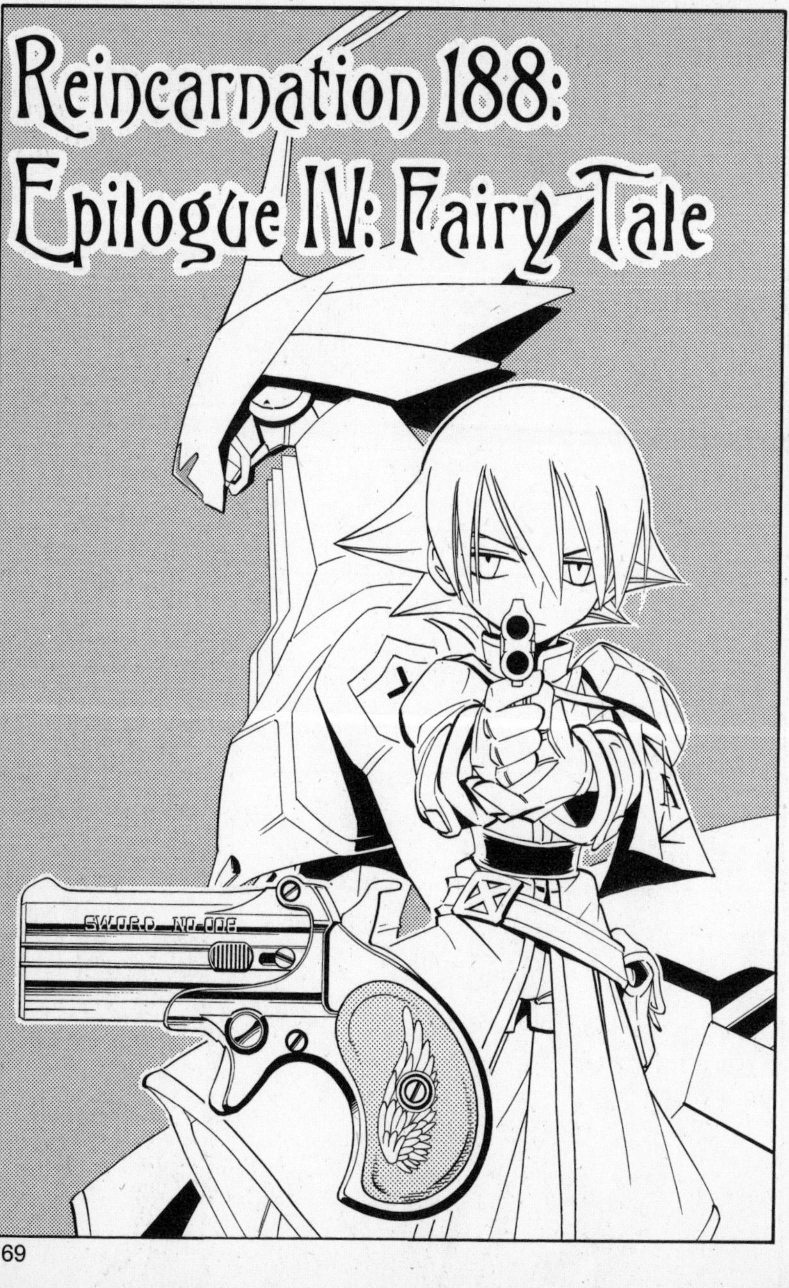
Reincarnation 188:
Epilogue IV: Fairy Tale
SWORD NO.006

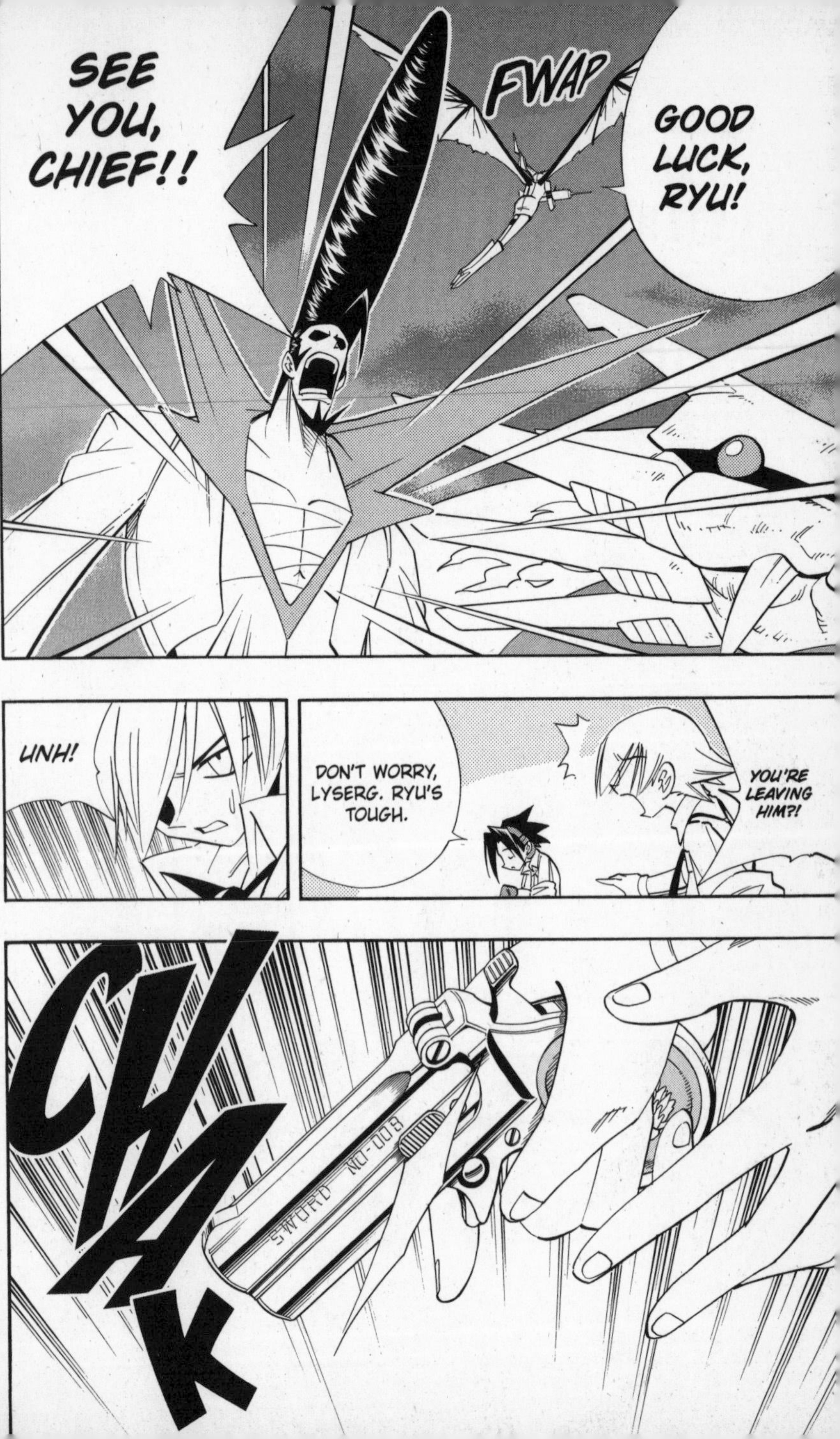
GOOD LUCK, RYU!
FWAP
SEE YOU, CHIEF!!
YOU'RE LEAVING HIM?!
DON'T WORRY, LYSERG. RYU'S TOUGH.
UNH!
CHAK
SWORD NO-008

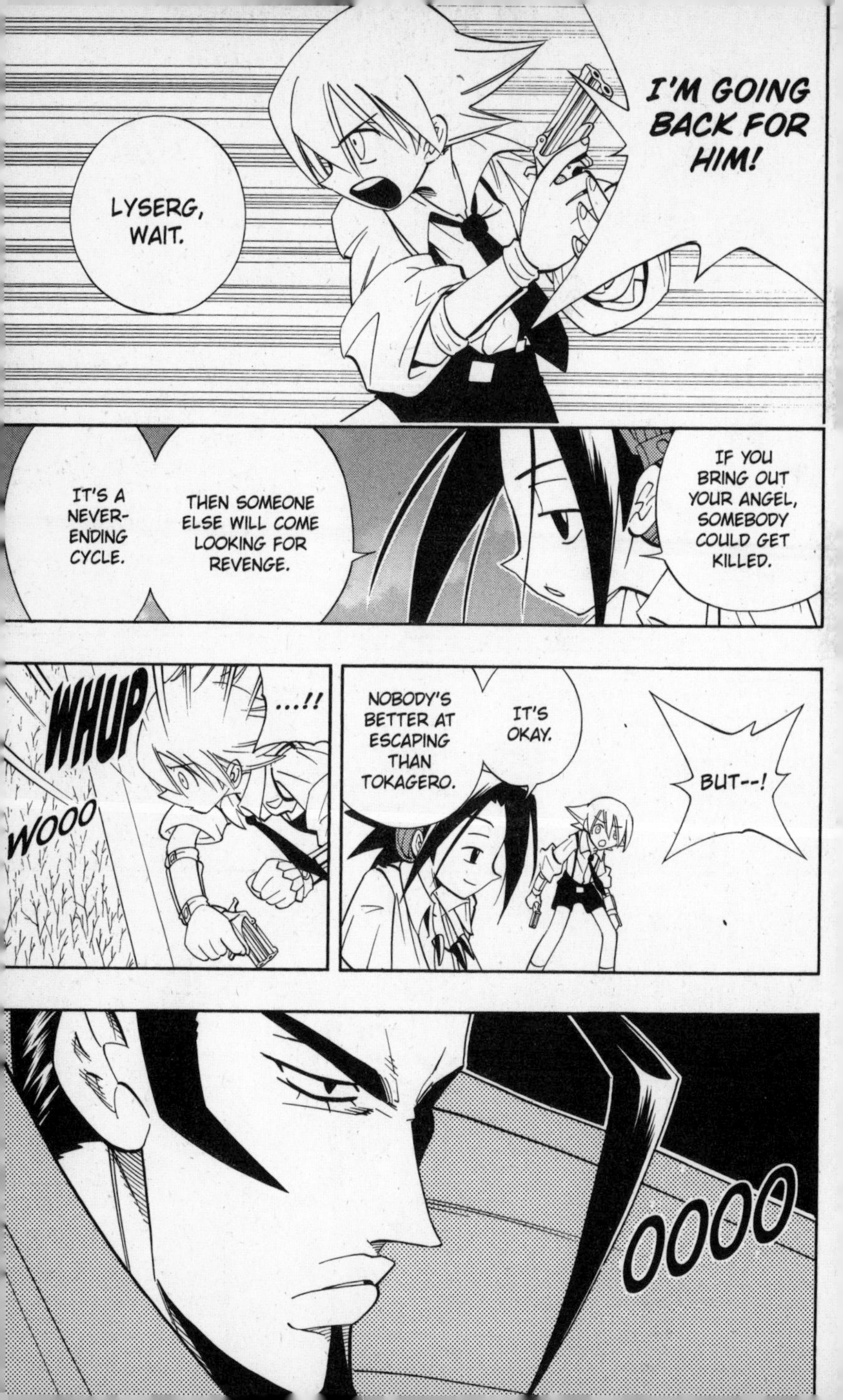
I'M GOING BACK FOR HIM!
LYSERG, WAIT.
IF YOU BRING OUT YOUR ANGEL, SOMEBODY COULD GET KILLED.
THEN SOMEONE ELSE WILL COME LOOKING FOR REVENGE.
IT'S A NEVER-ENDING CYCLE.
BUT--!
IT'S OKAY.
NOBODY'S BETTER AT ESCAPING THAN TOKAGERO.
...!!
WHUP
WOOO
OOOO

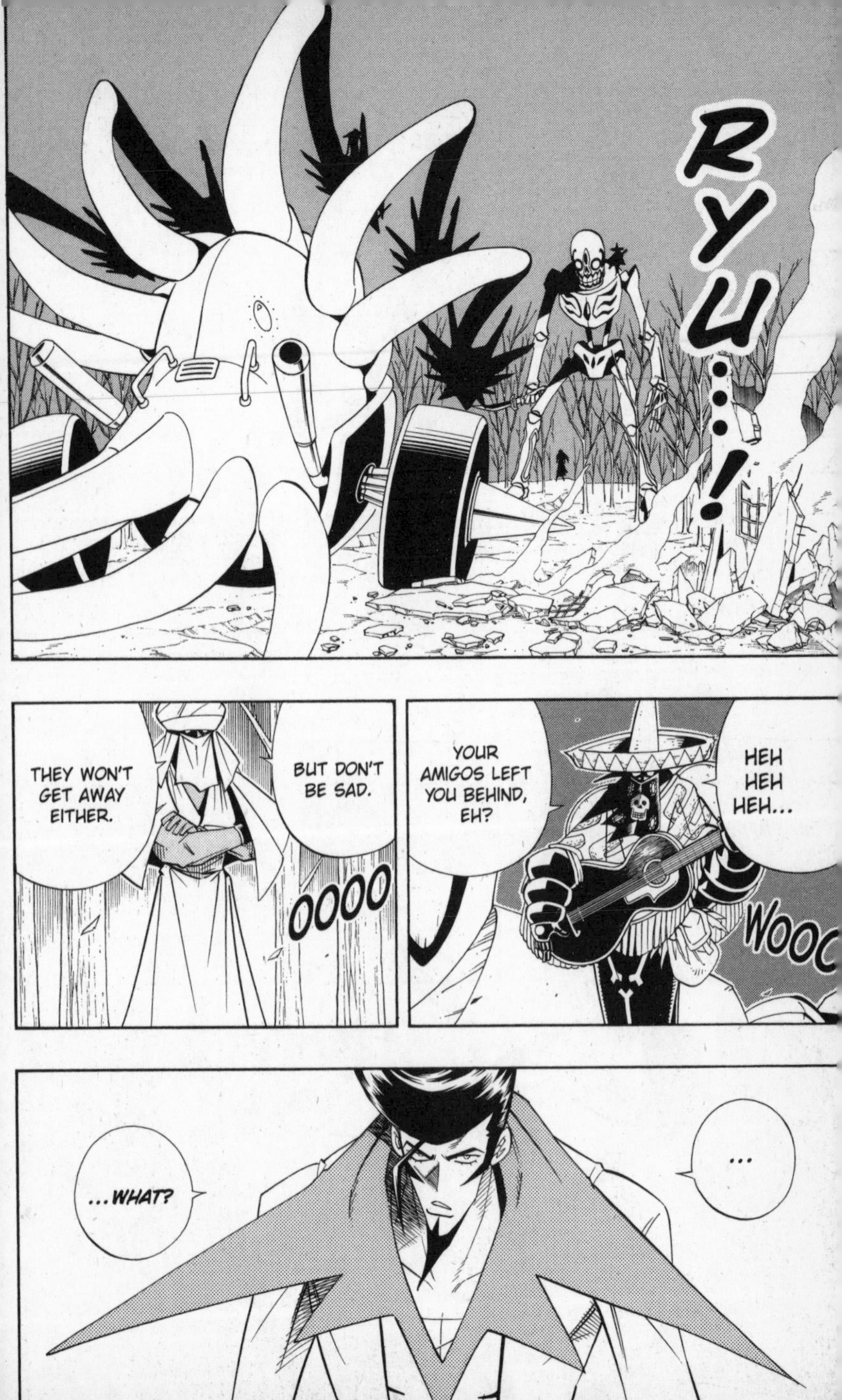
RYU...!
HEH HEH HEH...
YOUR AMIGOS LEFT YOU BEHIND, EH?
BUT DON'T BE SAD.
THEY WON'T GET AWAY EITHER.
OOOO
...
...WHAT?

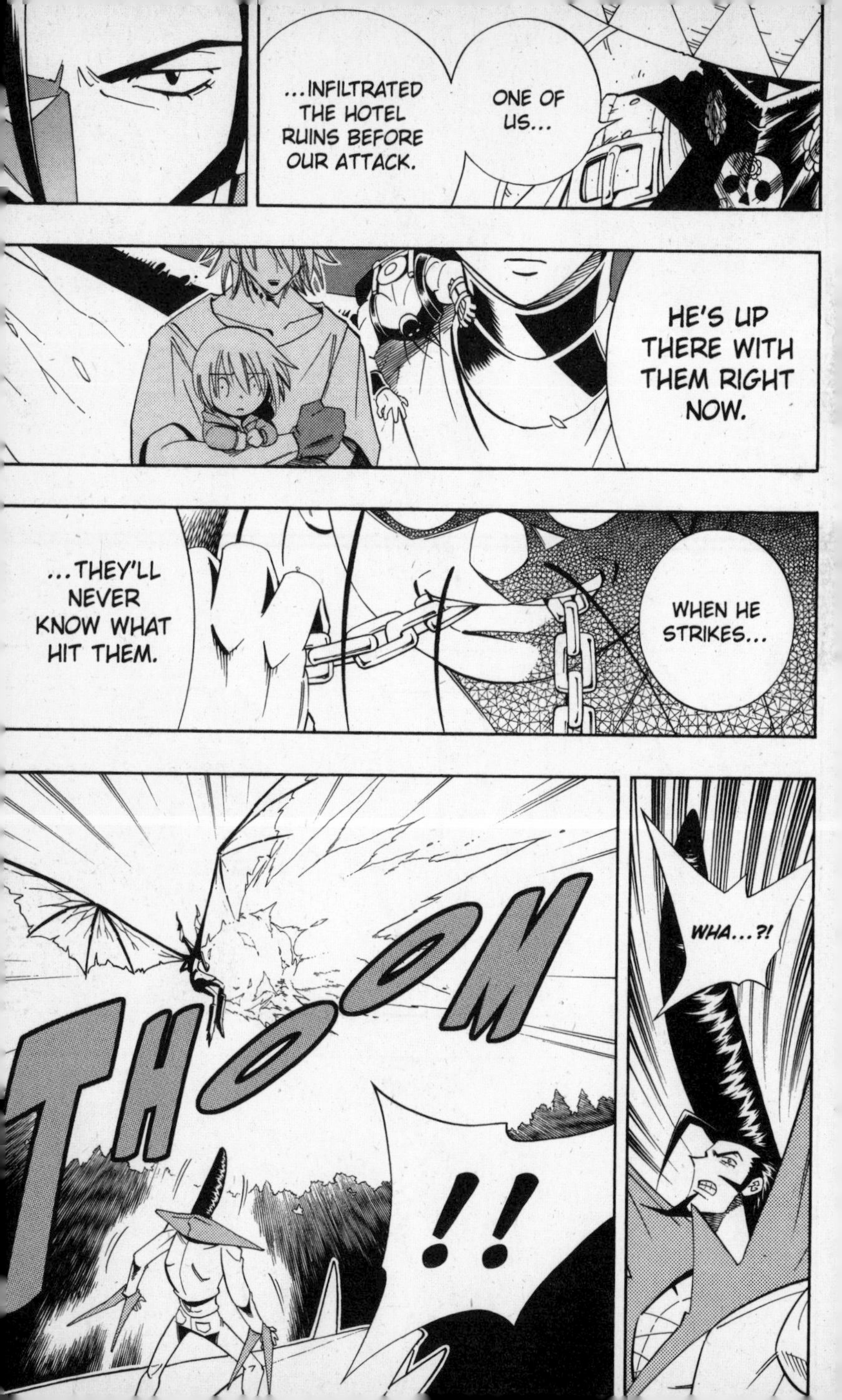
ONE OF US...
...INFILTRATED THE HOTEL RUINS BEFORE OUR ATTACK.
HE'S UP THERE WITH THEM RIGHT NOW.
WHEN HE STRIKES...
...THEY'LL NEVER KNOW WHAT HIT THEM.
WHA...?!
THOOM
!!

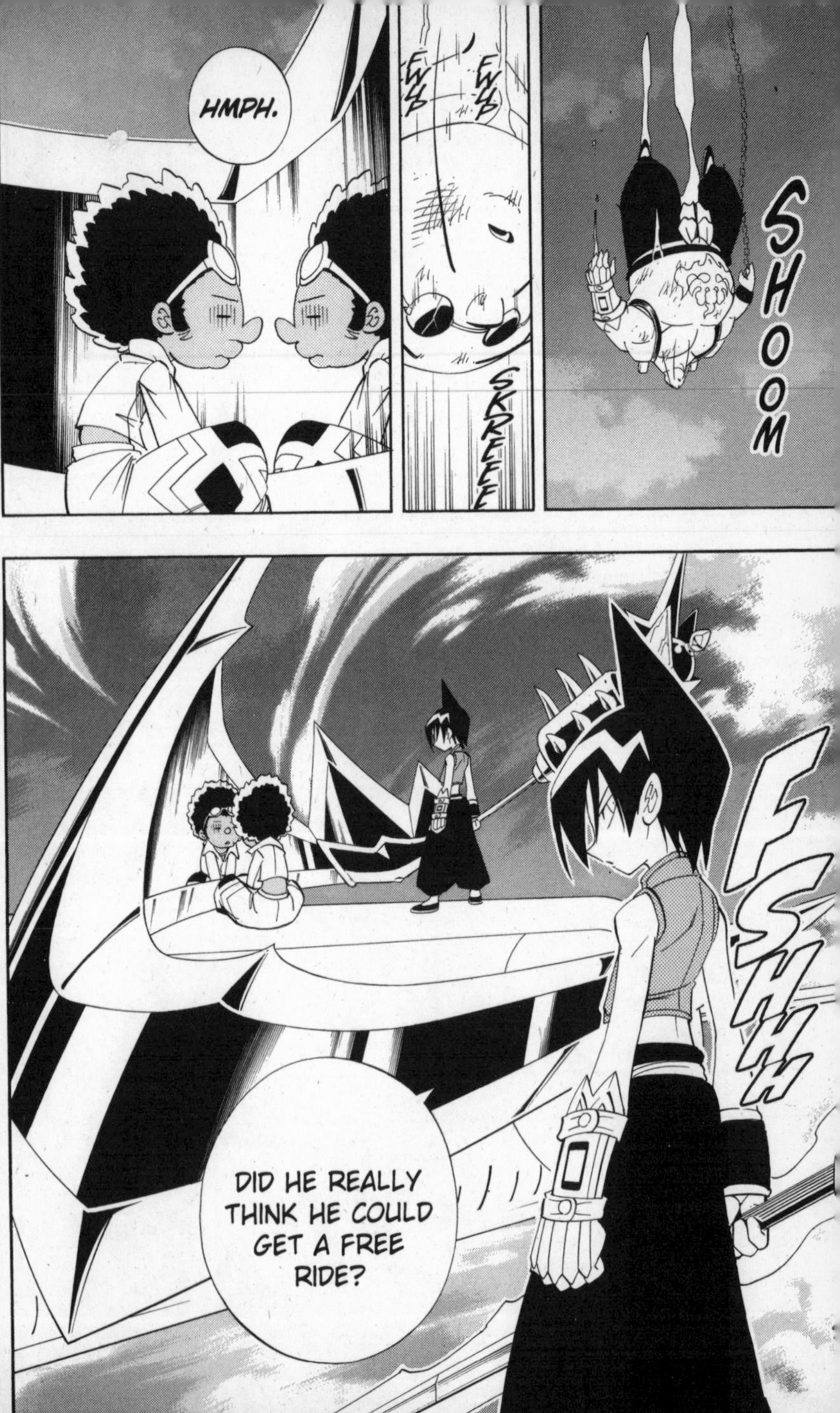
SHOOM
FWUP
FWUP
SKREEEE
HMPH.
FSHHH
DID HE REALLY THINK HE COULD GET A FREE RIDE?

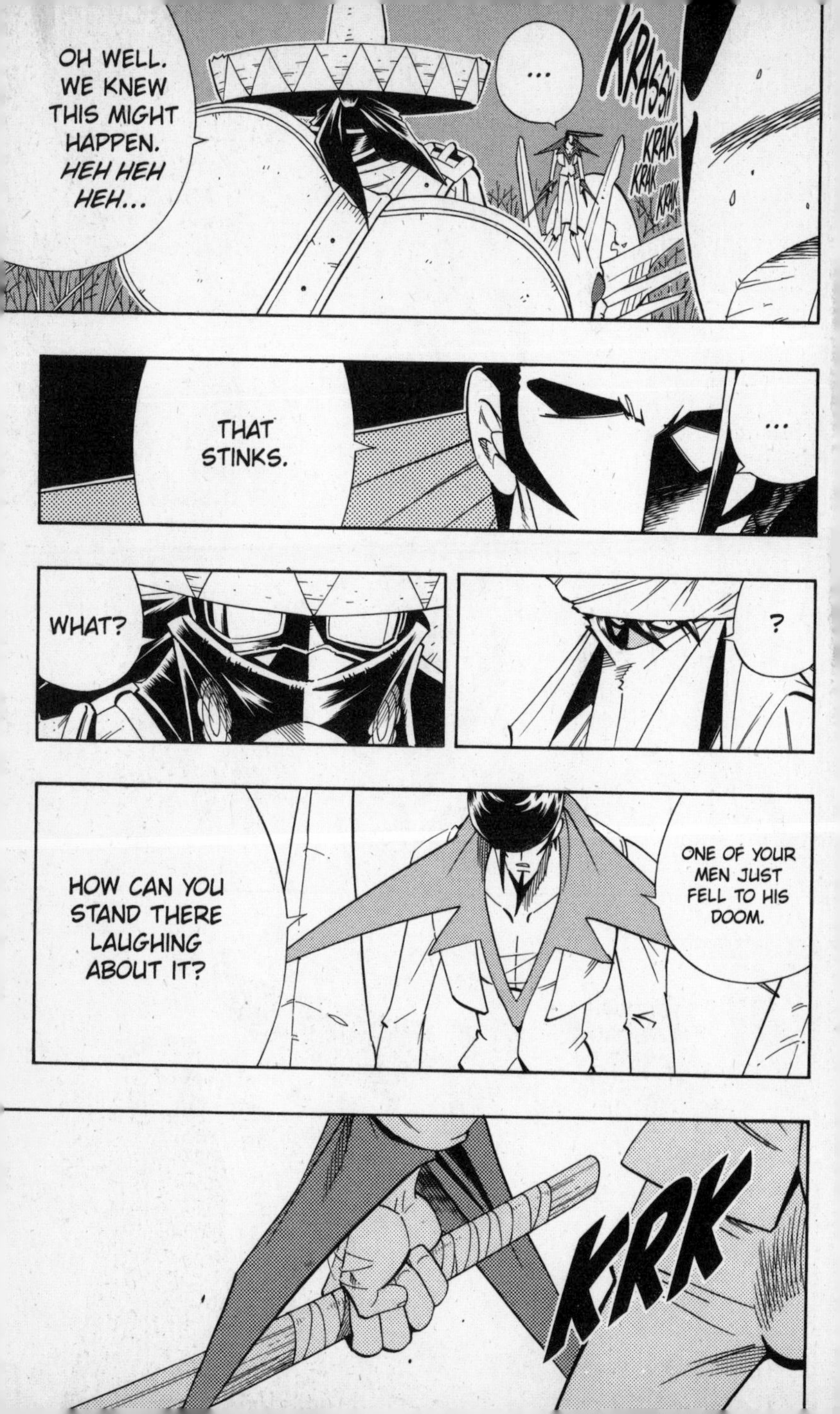
KRASSH
KRAK KRAK KRAK
...
OH WELL. WE KNEW THIS MIGHT HAPPEN. HEH HEH HEH...
...
THAT STINKS.
?
WHAT?
ONE OF YOUR MEN JUST FELL TO HIS DOOM.
HOW CAN YOU STAND THERE LAUGHING ABOUT IT?
KRK

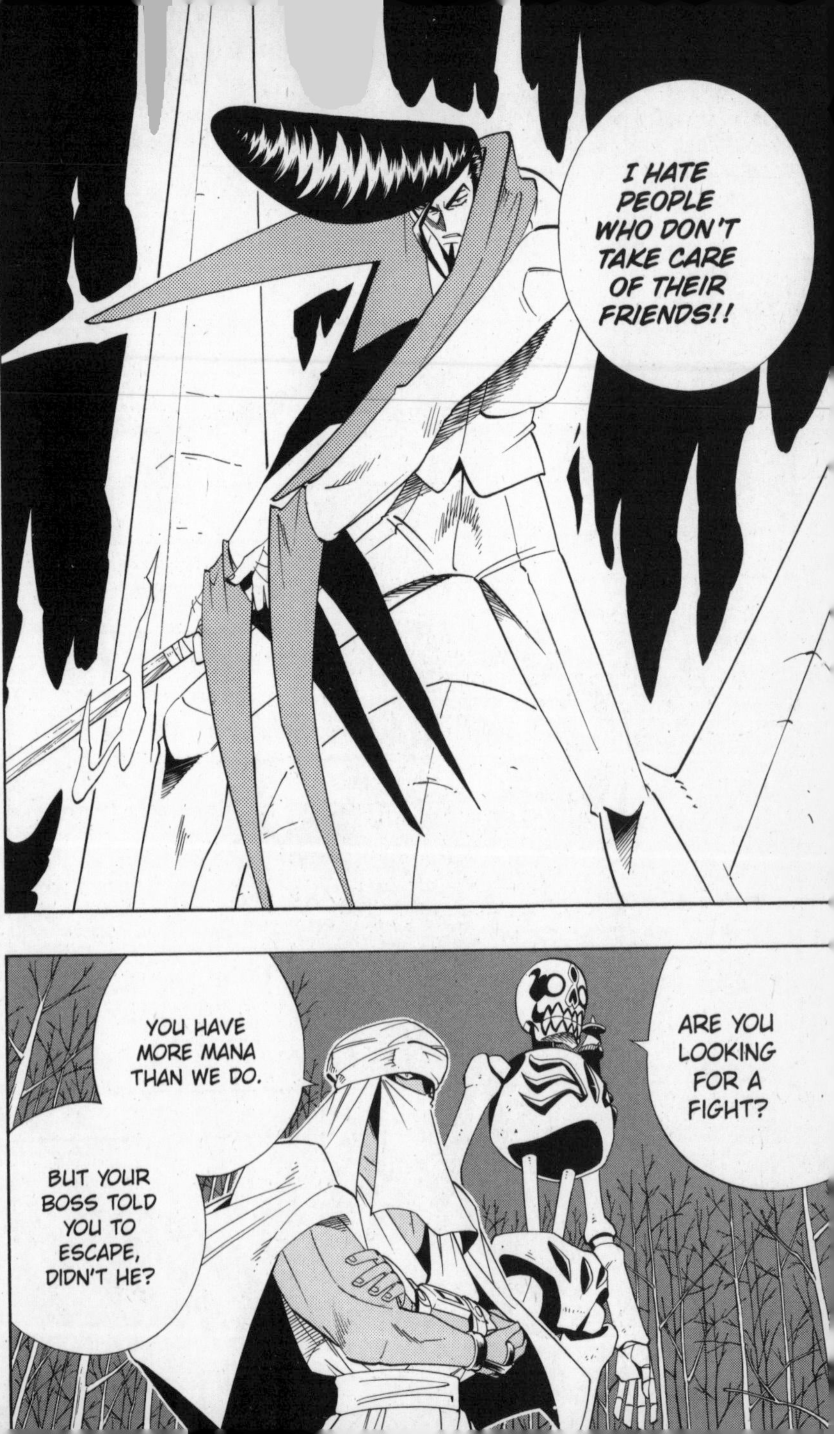
I HATE PEOPLE WHO DON'T TAKE CARE OF THEIR FRIENDS!!
ARE YOU LOOKING FOR A FIGHT?
YOU HAVE MORE MANA THAN WE DO.
BUT YOUR BOSS TOLD YOU TO ESCAPE, DIDN'T HE?

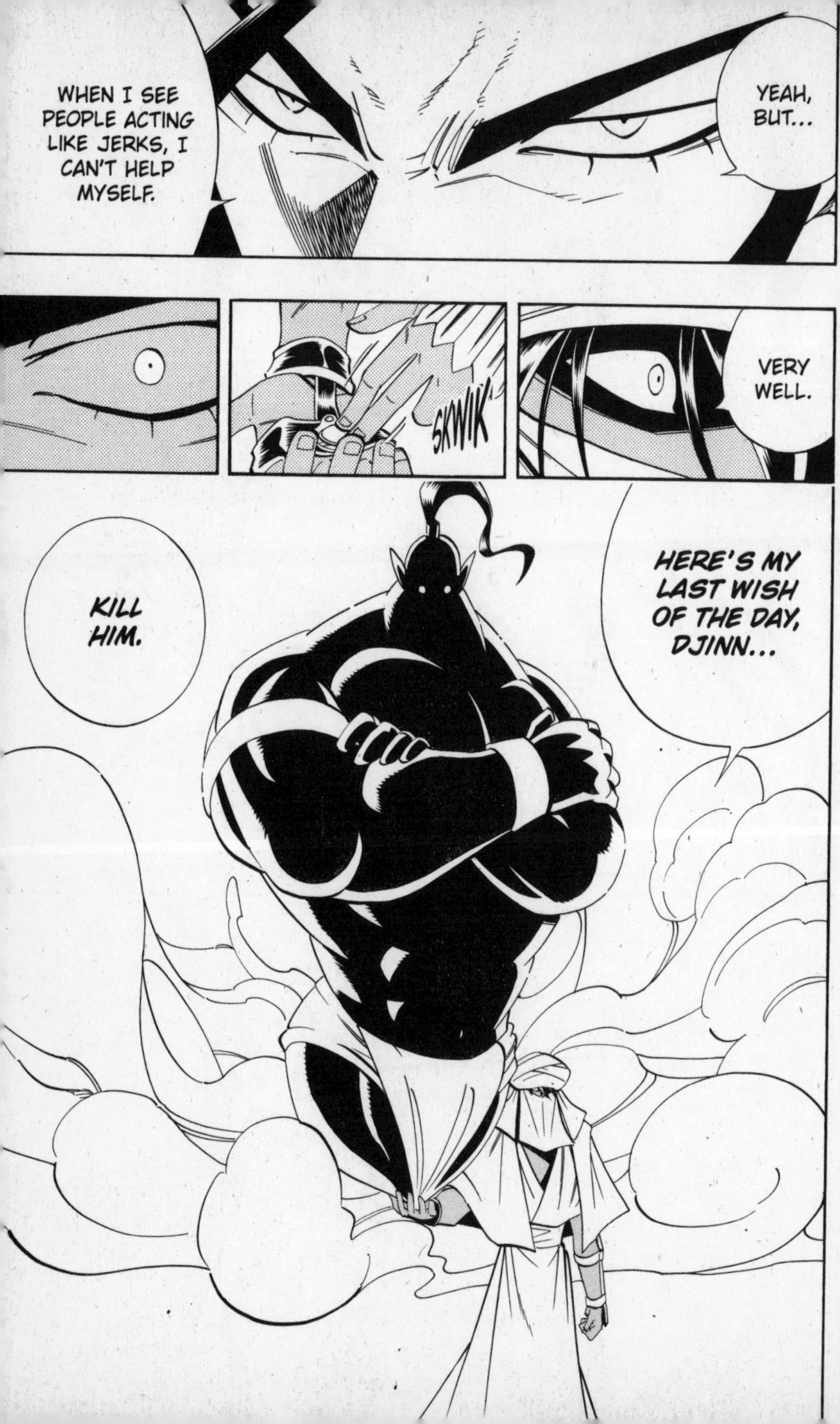
YEAH, BUT...
WHEN I SEE PEOPLE ACTING LIKE JERKS, I CAN'T HELP MYSELF.
VERY WELL.
SKWIK
HERE'S MY LAST WISH OF THE DAY, DJINN...
KILL HIM.

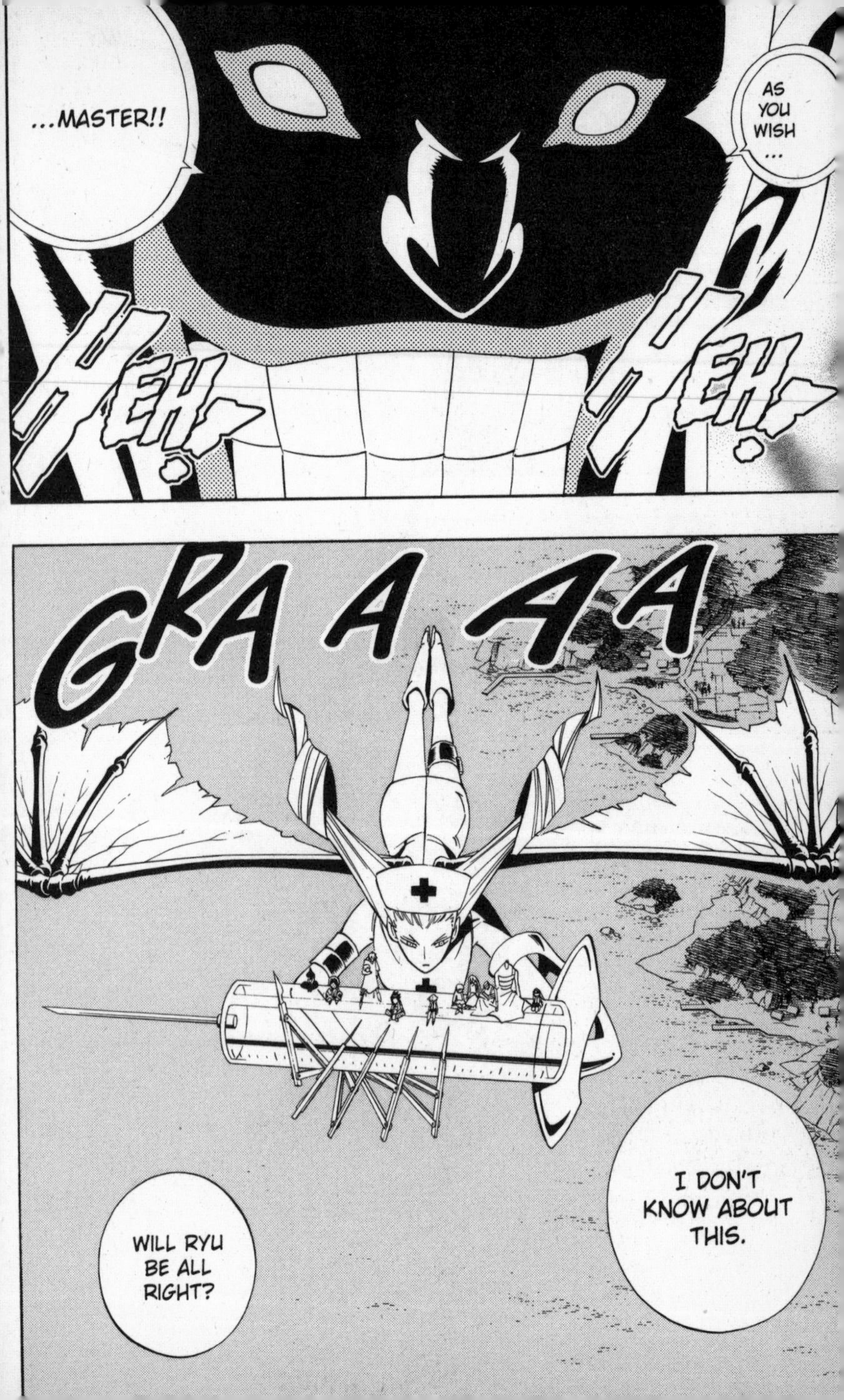
AS YOU WISH...
...MASTER!!
HEH!
HEH!
GRAAAAA
I DON'T KNOW ABOUT THIS.
WILL RYU BE ALL RIGHT?

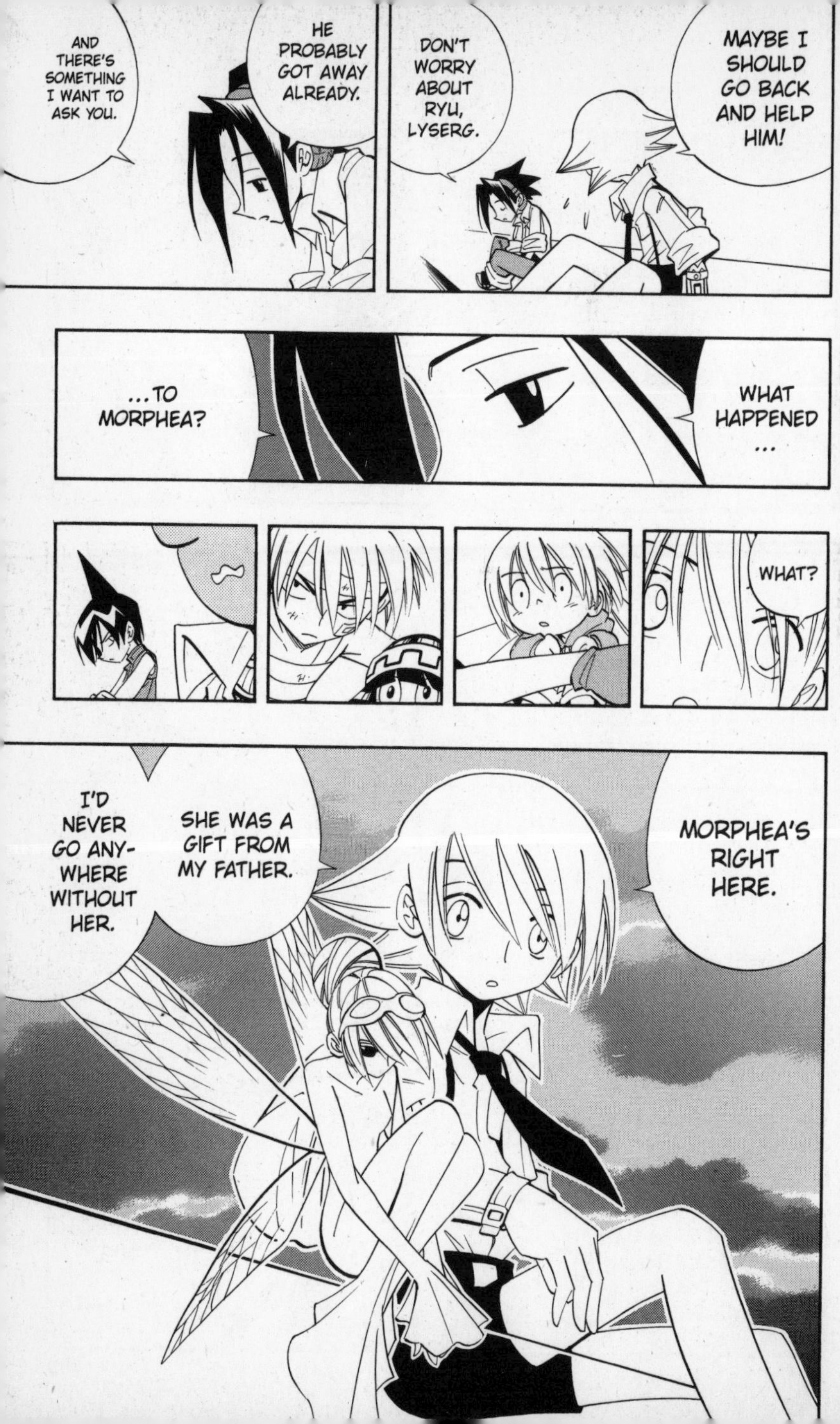
MAYBE I SHOULD GO BACK AND HELP HIM!
DON'T WORRY ABOUT RYU, LYSERG.
HE PROBABLY GOT AWAY ALREADY.
AND THERE'S SOMETHING I WANT TO ASK YOU.
WHAT HAPPENED ...
...TO MORPHEA?
WHAT?
MORPHEA'S RIGHT HERE.
SHE WAS A GIFT FROM MY FATHER.
I'D NEVER GO ANY-WHERE WITHOUT HER.

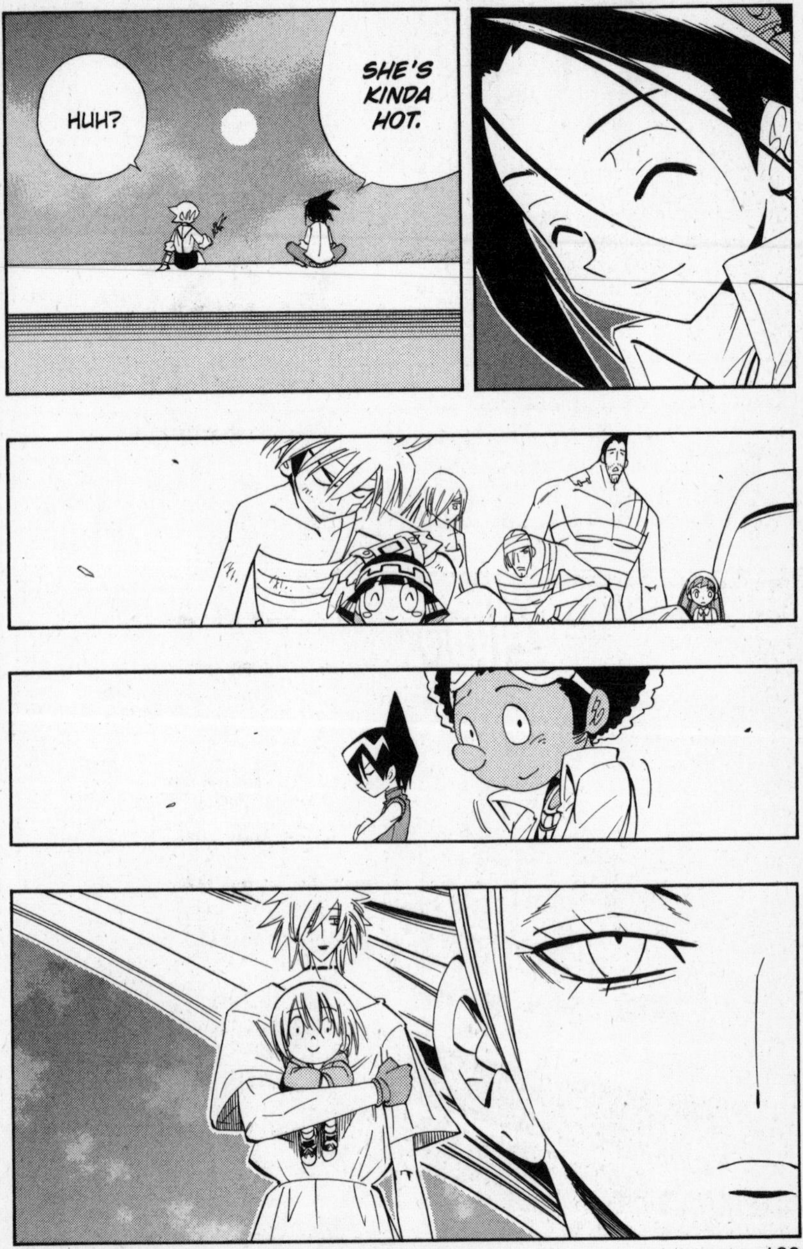
SHE'S KINDA HOT.
HUH?

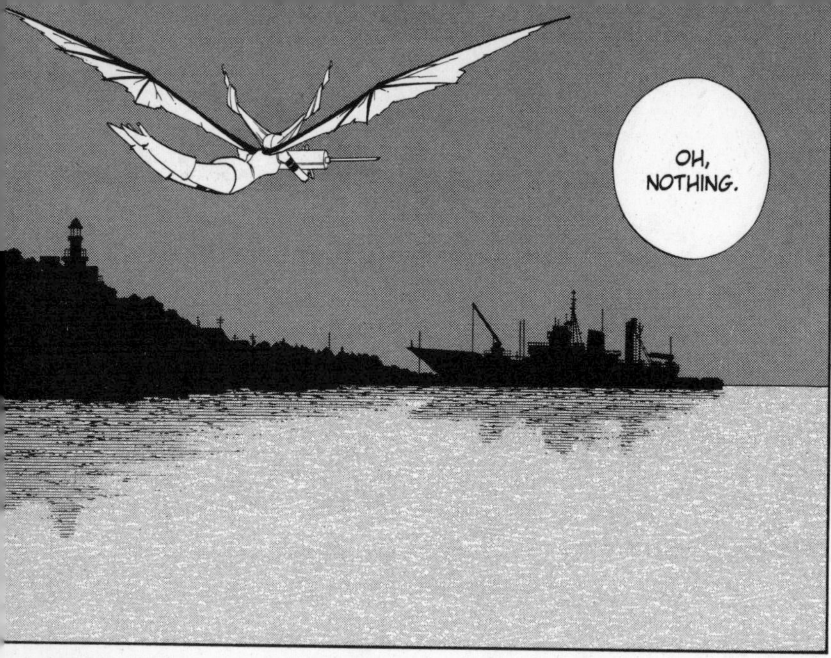
OH, NOTHING.

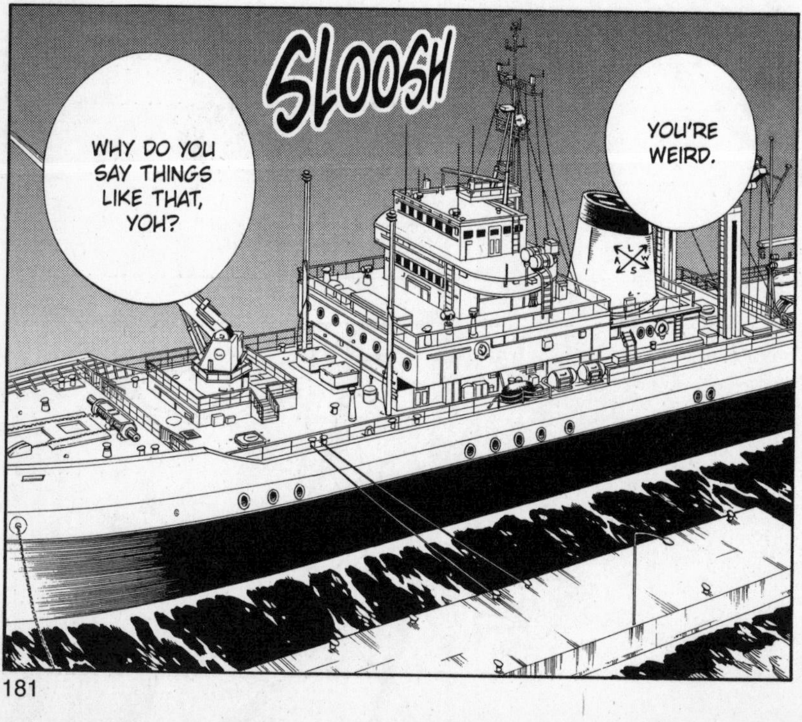
YOU'RE WEIRD.
SLOOSH
WHY DO YOU SAY THINGS LIKE THAT, YOH?

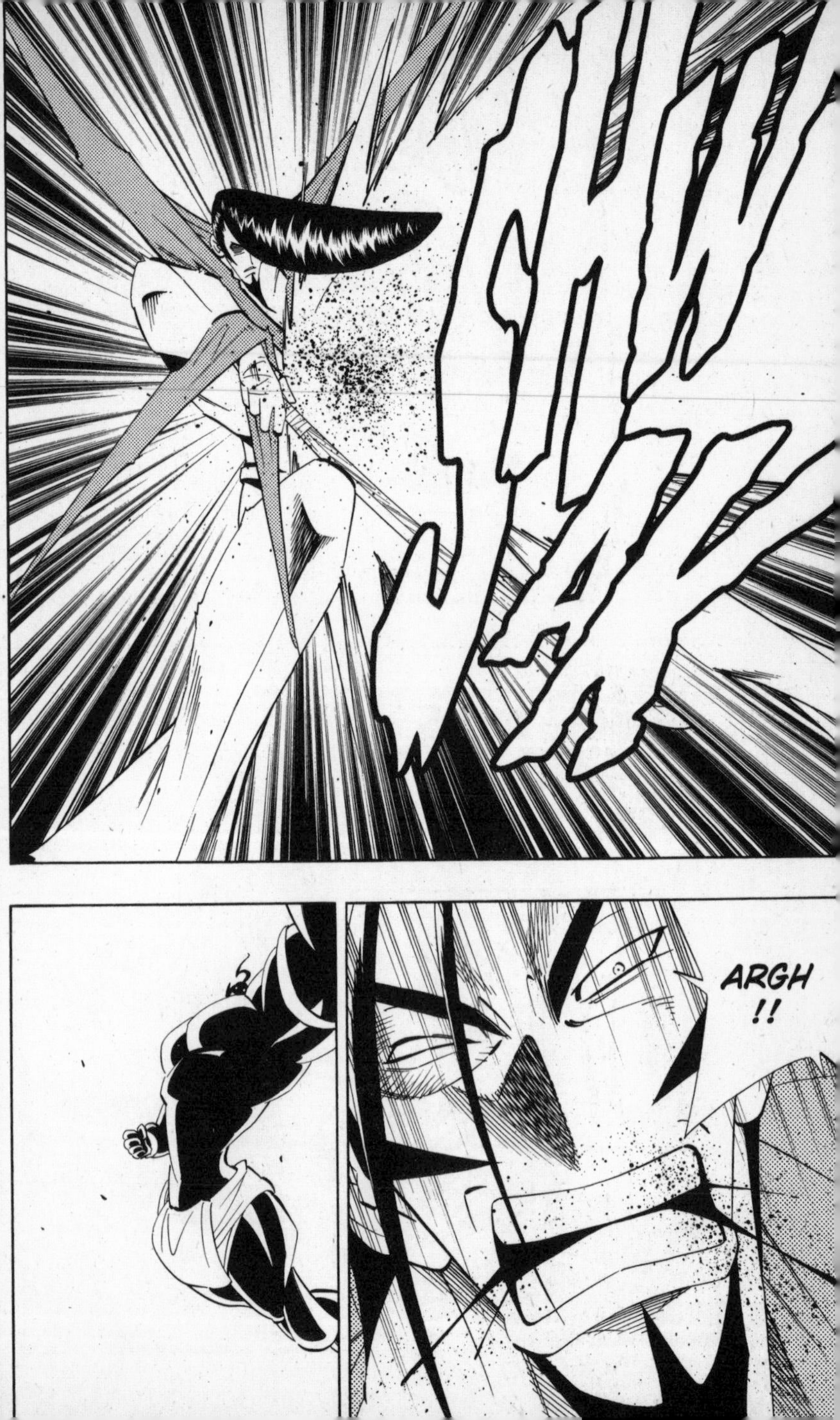
ARGH !!

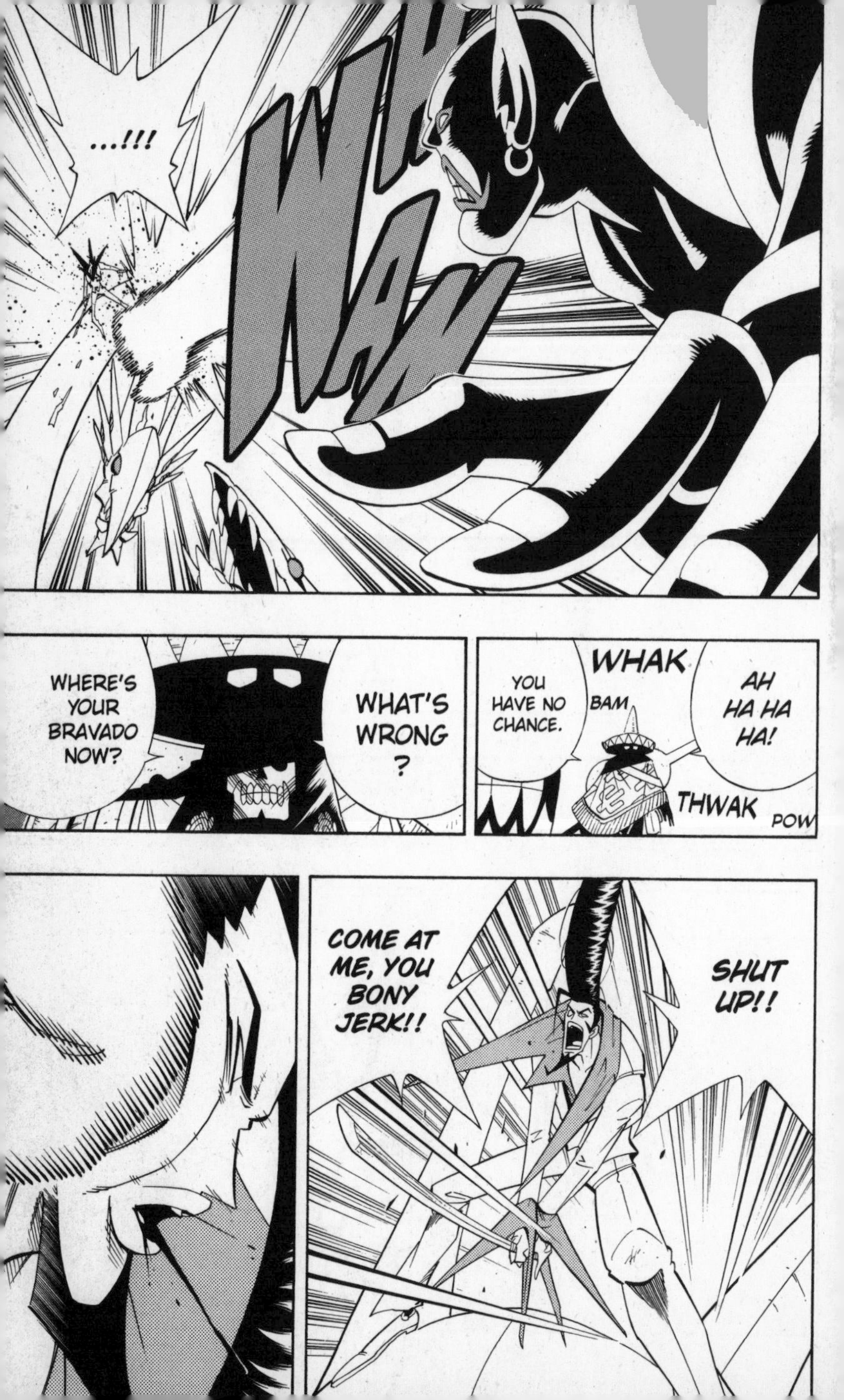
...!!!
AH HA HA HA!
WHAK
YOU HAVE NO CHANCE.
BAM
POW
THWAK
WHAT'S WRONG?
WHERE'S YOUR BRAVADO NOW?
SHUT UP!!
COME AT ME, YOU BONY JERK!!

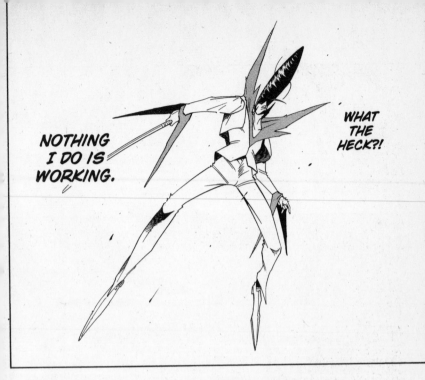

NOTHING I DO IS WORKING.

WHAT THE HECK?!

MAYBE I REALLY BLEW IT THIS TIME.

THIS IS BAD.

READ THIS WAY

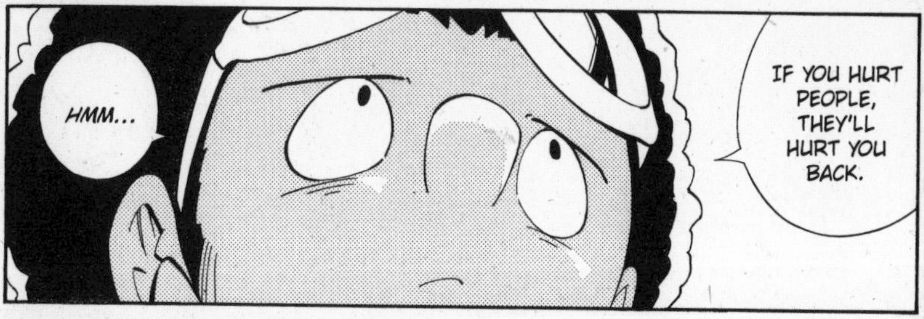
IF YOU HURT PEOPLE, THEY'LL HURT YOU BACK.
HMM...

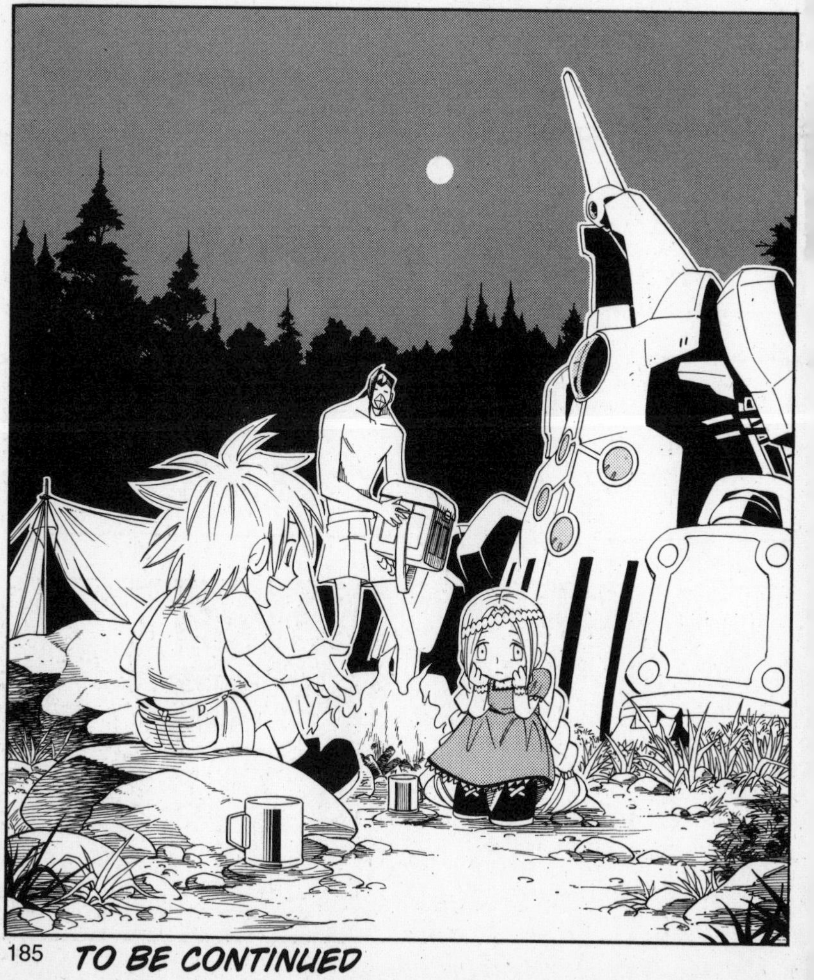

 TO BE CONTINUED

SHAMAN KING ITEM FILE No.54

リゼルグ
デリンジャー

LYSERG'S DERRINGER

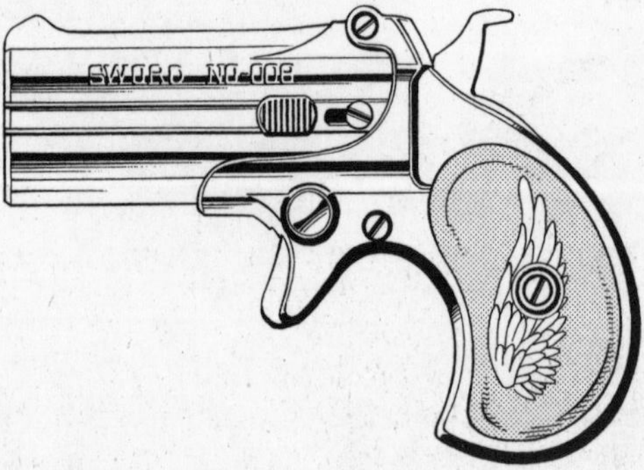
SWORD NO-008

IN THE NEXT VOLUME...

After hearing from Amidamaru, Yoh rushes to Ryu's rescue!
Meanwhile, Joco decides to visit chums from his old gang who
are participating in the Shaman Fight on another team. But he
is in for a nasty surprise...and all the while, Hao's team waits in
the shadows for Yoh and his friends to let down their guard for
just one moment.

AVAILABLE MAY 2009!

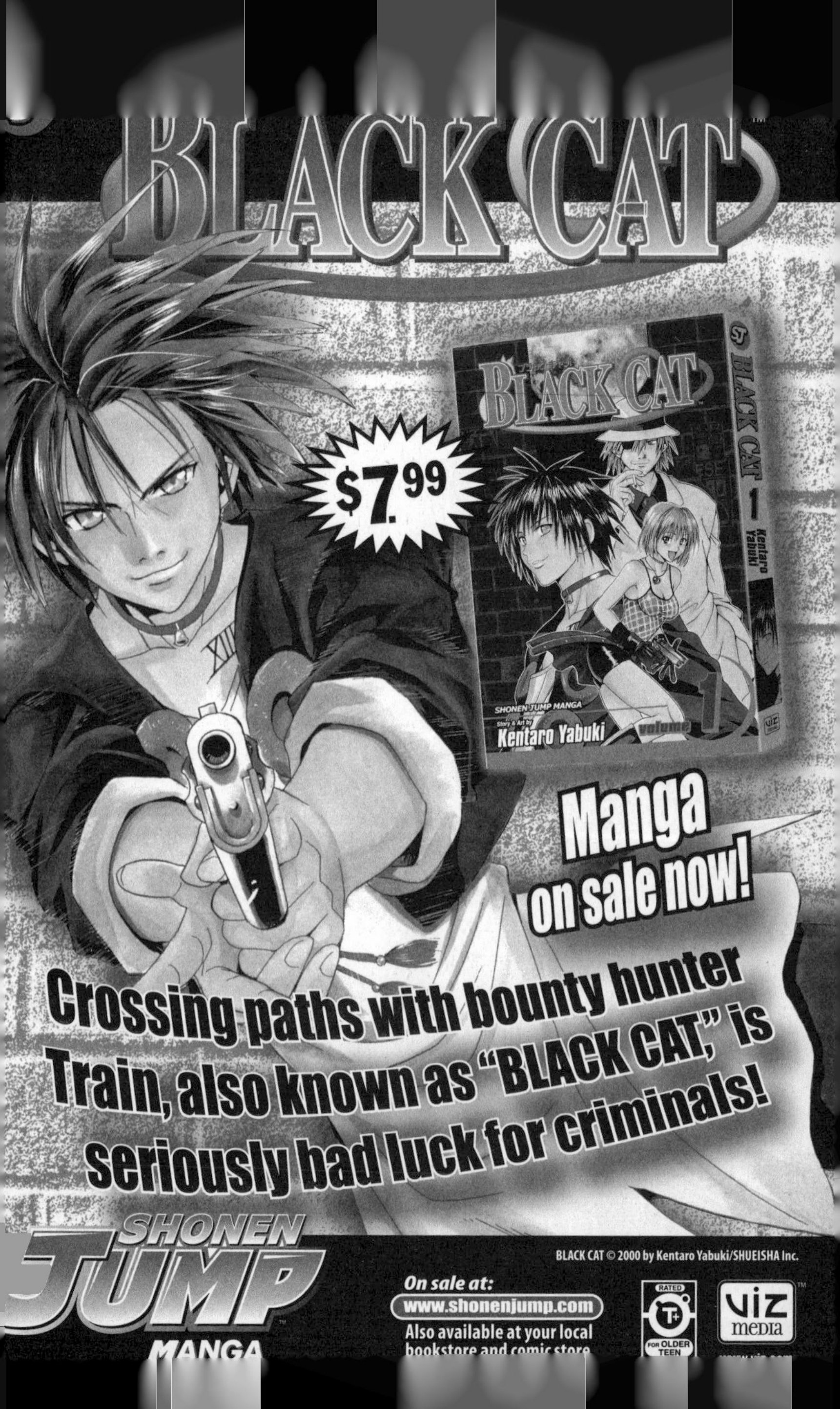

BLACK CAT™
$7.99
BLACK CAT
SHONEN JUMP MANGA
Story & Art by
Kentaro Yabuki
volume 1
Manga on sale now!
Crossing paths with bounty hunter Train, also known as "BLACK CAT," is seriously bad luck for criminals!
SHONEN JUMP MANGA
BLACK CAT © 2000 by Kentaro Yabuki/SHUEISHA Inc.
On sale at:
www.shonenjump.com
Also available at your local bookstore and comic store.
RATED T+ FOR OLDER TEEN
viz media

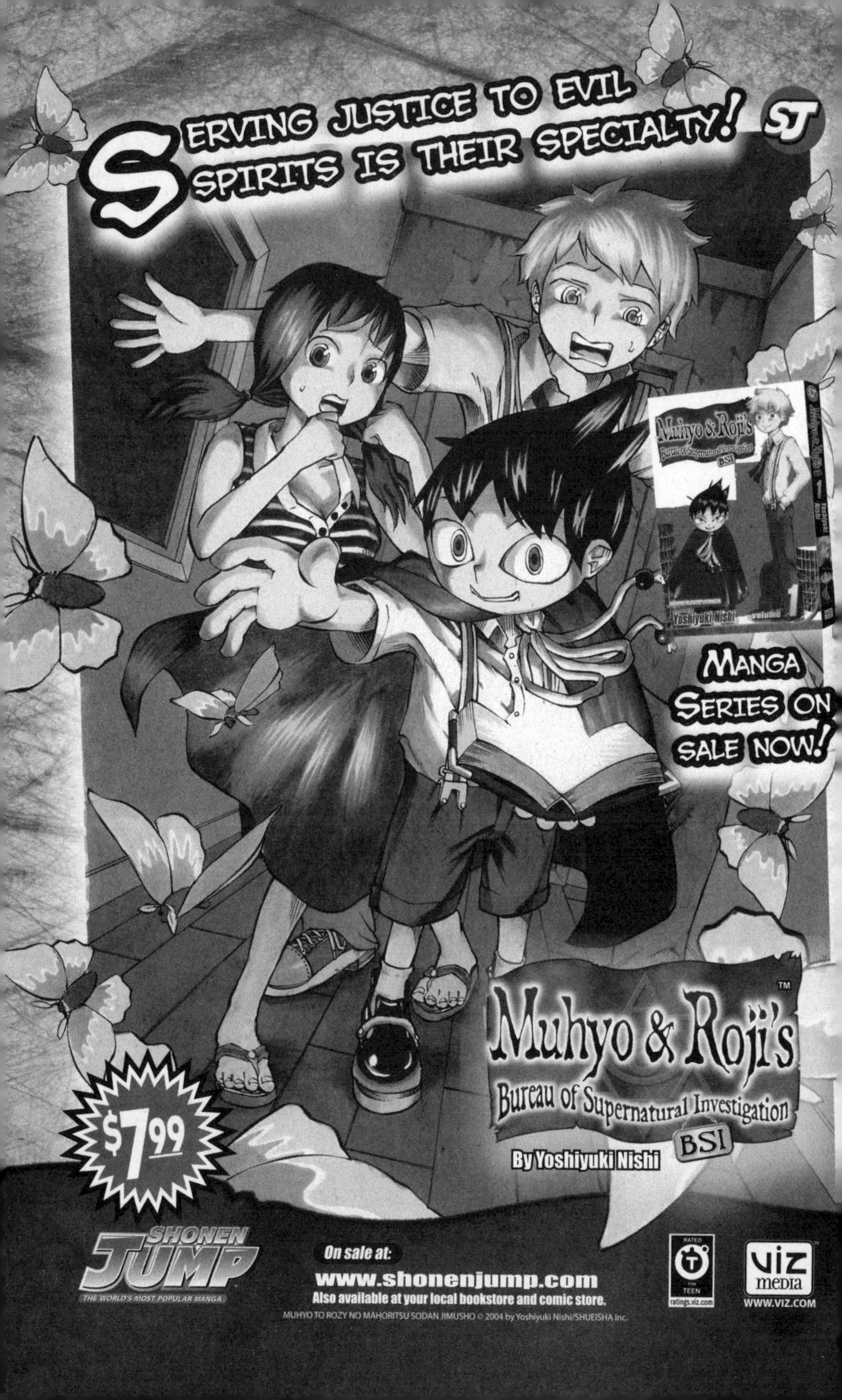

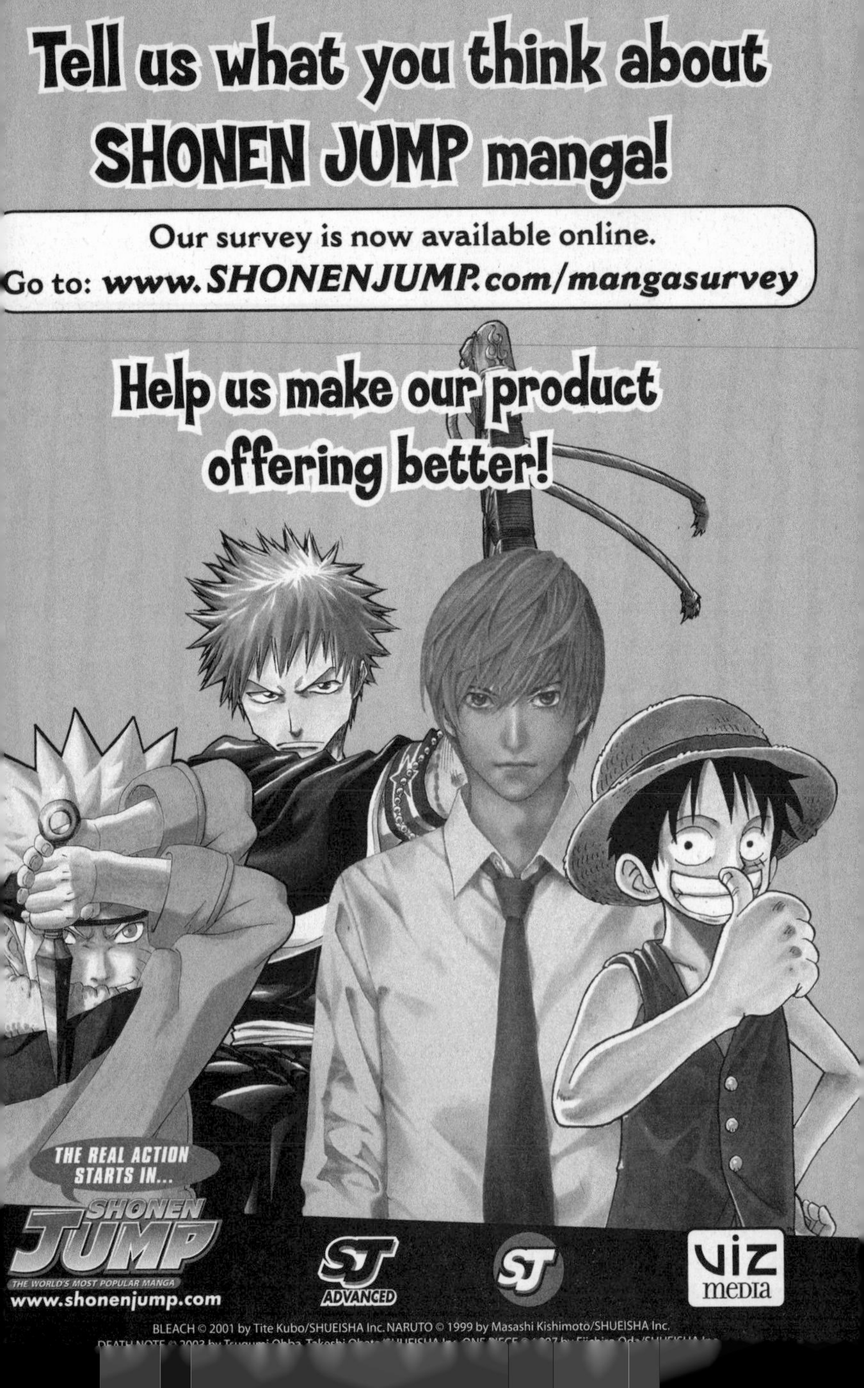
Tell us what you think about SHONEN JUMP manga!
Our survey is now available online.
Go to: www.SHONENJUMP.com/mangasurvey
Help us make our product offering better!
THE REAL ACTION STARTS IN...
SHONEN JUMP
THE WORLD'S MOST POPULAR MANGA
www.shonenjump.com
SJ ADVANCED
SJ
viz media
BLEACH © 2001 by Tite Kubo/SHUEISHA Inc. NARUTO © 1999 by Masashi Kishimoto/SHUEISHA Inc.

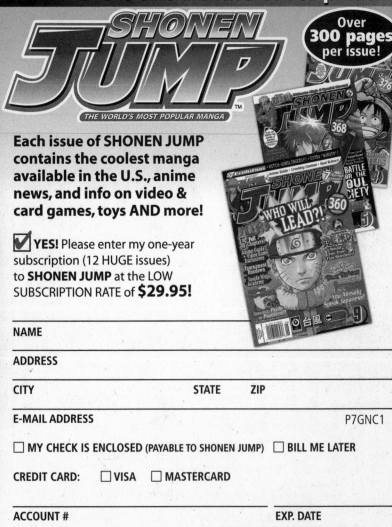